CAROLINE MOOREHEAD is the biographer of Bertrand Russell, Freya Stark, Iris Origo and Martha Gellhorn. Well known for her work in human rights, she has published a history of the Red Cross and a book about refugees, *Human Cargo*. She has been shortlisted for the Costa Biography Award in 2009. She lives in London.

By Caroline Moorehead

Iris Origo: Marchesa of Val d'Orcia
Freya Stark

a&b

Iris Origo:

Marchesa of Val d'Orcia

CAROLINE MOOREHEAD

Allison & Busby Limited
11 Wardour Mews
London W1F 8AN
www.allisonandbusby.com

First published in Great Britain in 2000.
This paperback edition published by Allison & Busby in 2014.

A CIP catalogue record for this book is available from
the British Library.

10 9 8 7 6 5 4 3 2

ISBN 978-0-7490-1656-2

Typeset in 10/15 pt Sabon by
Allison & Busby Ltd.

The paper used for this Allison & Busby publication
has been produced from trees that have been legally sourced
from well-managed and credibly certified forests.

Printed and bound by
CPI Group (UK) Ltd, Croydon, CR0 4YY

For my brother Richard, 1951–1998

CONTENTS

ILLUSTRATIONS

1. Lord Desart, Iris's Anglo-Irish grandfather

2. Lady Desart

3. The Cutting family at Westbrook, May 1909

4. Bayard, Iris's father

5. Sybil, Iris's mother

6. Iris in Switzerland

7. Bernhard Berenson

8. The Villa Medici in Fiesole

9. *La sala degli uccelli* in the Villa Medici

10. Antonio Origo

11. Iris with Gianni

12. La Foce

13. Pinsent's top terrace at La Foce

14. La Foce after water had been brought to the estate

All the illustrations have been provided by the Origo archive at La Foce.

'Perhaps this is the most that a biographer can ever hope to do, to clear, in the icy patch of each man's incomprehension of other men, a little patch, through which a faint, intermittent light can shine. But at best it will only be a very little light, in a great sea of darkness, and it is surely very arrogant to attempt more than this.'

Iris Origo: 'Biography True and False'

CHAPTER ONE

A different child

'All this national feeling makes people so unhappy,' wrote Bayard Cutting in his last letter to his wife Sybil, as he lay dying, about the future of their only child Iris. 'Bring her up somewhere where she does not belong, then she can't have it. I'd rather France or Italy than England, so that she should really be cosmopolitan, from deep down . . . She *must* be English now, just as she'd have been more American if I had lived and not you. That is natural and right. But I'd like her to be a little "foreign" too so that when she grows up she really will be free to love or marry anyone she likes, of any country, without it being difficult.'

Iris was then seven. Sybil respected her husband's wishes, and her only daughter grew up far from both England and America. But this left her uncertain about where she belonged, with a precarious feeling about being a stranger, and with a need for and reliance on close and intimate friends as marked as the uneasiness she often felt in the company of acquaintances. It made her a very good friend, but it also made her restless. In her autobiography *Images and Shadows*, written when she was seventy, she recorded the 'sense of rootlessness and insecurity during my youth' and the way that each 'uprooting was followed by a readjustment of my manners, and, to some extent, of my values'. She became, each time, a different child.

With an American father, an English mother, and ancestors from Holland, France and Scotland, Iris's divided identity began at birth.

Her mother Sybil was the second daughter of an Anglo-Irish peer, Lord Desart, to whom Iris became deeply attached. As Hamilton Cuffe, younger son of an impoverished family, he had had so few apparent prospects that at the age of twelve he had signed on with a wooden frigate, the *Orlando*, bound for Halifax, Nova Scotia. But he was both determined and able, and it was not long before he made his way back to England, went up to Cambridge and then read for the Bar. He was also lucky. In 1898 he inherited an earldom and an estate in Ireland he had never expected to come his way. By then he was married to Margaret, one of the fourth Earl of Harewood's fourteen children, had been appointed Assistant Solicitor to the Treasury by Disraeli and was living in London, in a tall, narrow house 'like a sentry box' in Rutland Gate, to which his bride had brought, as trousseau, twelve of everything, chemises, nightgowns and flannel petticoats of such fine quality that she wore them until she died. Punctual and affectionate, he came home every evening at six to spend an hour with Sybil and her elder sister Joan; he was later to say that these were the happiest days of his life. Not long afterwards he was appointed Queen's Proctor, and became involved in Oscar Wilde's trial. It is said that he tried to delay the warrant for Wilde's arrest in order to give him time to escape to France: Wilde turned down the offer. The Desarts never had much money, but everywhere they went they took the privileges of Victorian England for granted, and

12

Iris soon learnt that her grandfather's mildness, his openness to the views of others, concealed extremely firm and strong moral convictions.

The Cuttings were richer and more orderly. William Bayard Cutting, Iris's father, belonged to a prosperous and philanthropic New York family, whose money came from railroads, shipping, land development and sugar beet. They spent their weekends and holidays in a house called Westbrook on the southern shore of Long Island, where they had turned a spit of sandy, marshy land into a botanical garden and built what looked like an enormous English country cottage, covered in creepers. Here Bayard played lawn tennis and held house parties with his younger brother Bronson and two sisters, Olivia (named after their mother) and Justine. All four later claimed to be 'particularly allergic to the taste of their silver spoons'. In New York, where he owned a brownstone house on the corner of Madison Avenue and 72nd Street, Bayard Cutting's father – also Bayard – was one of a group of men who took a close interest in the arts, architecture and furniture; he was a founding member of the New York Public Library and of the Metropolitan Opera, where he had a box. Edith Wharton, a family friend, whose novel *The Age of Innocence* might have been written about life at Westbrook, later complained that the New York of her youth was like 'an empty vessel into which no new wine would ever again be poured'. She made an exception of Bayard Cutting, Iris's grandfather, and one or two other friends, because as men of 'a cultivated taste with marked social gifts' they stood apart from their contemporaries, who lived in what she called 'dilettantism leisure'. The 'self-appointed aristocracy' of New York, she also said, 'does not often produce eagles'; Cutting, on the other hand, 'stirred the stagnant air of old New York', thereby generating the 'dust of new ideas'. It was with her grandparents at Westbrook that Iris, as a small child, first knew the sensation of being, not alone, but one in a long and dignified line of people, 'the last and smallest acorn on the tree'. One Sunday morning after church, her grandmother told her to climb up onto a chair so that she could read the first page of the family Bible that stood open on a lectern. There, at the very bottom of a long line of names, in fresh ink, was her own.

Bayard Cutting, Iris's father, was a cheerful, gifted and extremely successful schoolboy. At Groton, a private boarding school, he edited the paper, played the violin in the orchestra and was vice-president of the debating society. At Harvard he took a BA degree *summa cum laude* in history, economics and philosophy, and was a pupil of George Santayana, who later remarked on his 'multitudinousness and quickness of ideas'. He played golf and football, rode and shot, and belonged to the most desirable college clubs. In appearance he was slight and dark; he later grew a pointed beard that Iris said gave him the look of a distinguished Frenchman.

In the summer of his junior year, Bayard was asked whether he would like to accompany Joseph Choate, newly appointed Ambassador to London, as his private secretary. He accepted, but though the shooting weekends were fun, he did not entirely enjoy what he was soon calling 'this infernal social act'. To his younger brother Bronson, just off to school, he wrote an affectionate letter about his own schooldays, full of rather revealing advice. 'Sometimes I was a little blue, but there were so few minutes to be blue in that I soon got out of the habit . . . There's no place where half so much as at a school, the good comes out on top . . . So if one finds one is not getting on well at school, one can be absolutely sure it's one's own fault somehow . . .' To a remarkable degree, Bayard was a man who remained in control of his own emotions and fears.

Early in 1900, riding in Hyde Park with Joseph Choate, he met Lord Desart. With him was his daughter Sybil. She was slightly plump and very fair, with china-blue eyes. She was also clever and full of charm, if prone to self absorption. 'Sybil's always ill', her mother remarked on one occasion, 'when she can't get what she wants.'

She was, however, just about to get, as she usually did, precisely what she wanted. The morning ride became a regular event. Bayard and Sybil exchanged books, and discussed the Boer War. In the summer Bayard was invited to Desart Court in Ireland, an Italianate house built at the beginning of the eighteenth century in what was called 'Kilkenny marble', the local grey limestone. The house looked out over parkland and the overgrown remains of a former Italian garden. The weather was fine, and together Bayard and Sybil rode around the estate, meeting people who, as Bayard wrote to a friend, greeted them with the words 'Ah, Lady Sybil, it's a grand/beautiful/ honourable young man you've got.' When they announced they wanted to become engaged, both sets of parents disapproved, on the grounds that they were too young, and their worlds too different. But they were determined, and anxious to waste no time. Bayard wrote to his father that they planned to explore California to see whether the life there suited them, particularly Sybil, who needed 'to live in the country, in one place, without any occasion to exhaust nervous energy'. He should perhaps have been warned, for Sybil was not just prone to get her own way, but deeply immersed in her own health. She now caught a cold, and was irritable. Neither of them enjoyed the strict rules of chaperonage which prevented Bayard from acting as her escort in the evenings, or the etiquette which restricted their meetings to three dinners at Rutland Gate each week. Before very long, their parents capitulated.

On 30 April 1901 Bayard and Sybil were married at All Saints' Church in Ennismore Gardens. The church was decorated with palms and white flowers, and the two pageboys wore Watteauesque costumes of pale blue silk.

After the wedding they sailed to America. They did indeed go to California, but only briefly, before returning to New York, where Bayard enrolled at the Columbia Law School. It was on their return to London the following June, in time for the birth of their first child, that Bayard suddenly had a haemorrhage. Little was made of what was described as a weak spot on one lung, and he was sent to convalesce at a sanatorium in the Cotswolds; the word 'tuberculosis' was carefully avoided. It was in the nearby village of Birdlip, on 15 August 1902, that Iris was born. Bayard wrote to his father that 'Sybil dined with Malcolm Donald, Lady Desart and me, and after dinner sat out till nine in the moonlight looking and feeling as well as possible. At about one the trouble began, and was over at seven, the doctor arriving about 4.30 . . .' He was delighted with his daughter, writing to a friend that she was 'a healthy-looking child, chubby and fair, with a loud voice and an excellent appetite, and not uglier than most of her kind'. He added: 'Of course, I had rather hoped for a boy – but after all, a boy is much harder to bring up, and I feel too inexperienced to do it decently.' Soon after, he started an album, 'Bayard's Accounts of Iris his daughter, 1902–1903', largely made up of copies of letters to his family and friends describing the baby. On 11 September he recorded, 'She is as fat as butter, with a gigantic crop of golden hair'; on 4 October she was 'developing a temper crying herself hoarse if left in bed'; on 7 November her temper was becoming 'daily worse. She cries and bawls whenever she leaves her nurse, and Sybil cannot stand the crying long': she was 'terribly distressed at her baby's minding being with her'.

Neither Sybil nor Bayard wanted Iris to be christened, but their parents felt strongly and a christening of sorts took place on 30 September in the Chintz Bedroom of Desart Court, Sybil being too unwell to leave her bed. The baby was given the middle name Margaret, after her grandmother; 'Iris', protested Bayard's brother and a sister in America, was too botanical – 'Iris Cutting', they felt, 'suggests a gardener's catalogue'. Sybil's sister Joan was asked to be one godmother and a friend, Patience Cockerell, another; William Phillips and Joseph Choate, both Americans, were the godfathers. To Joseph Choate, Bayard later wrote that neither he nor Sybil cared about the religious views of the godparents – 'only about our friendship with them'.

On 7 December Sybil, Bayard and Iris left for Italy. According to a separate album kept by Sybil, Iris had learnt to crawl and imitate the noises of animals by the age of between eight and nine months, and particularly enjoyed being played to on the piano. With Iris's nurse, they moved between various hotels in Portofino and Sestri Levante; for the few remaining years of Bayard's life, they were to keep moving, to different climates, different cures, different doctors, as the weakness in his lungs spread and he suffered repeated haemorrhages. Bayard's diary of Iris's progress charts their route. In December they stopped in a little fishing village south-east of Genoa, 'in a deep bay well-sheltered from the wind, with pine woods behind. The view is lovely, the air all soft . . . our kid is in good health . . . but has a very imperious will.' He had had a worrying 'bilious' attack, which he blamed partly on being at sea level and partly on the local milk, which he thought provided too little nourishment for his bones. There was by now no avoiding the word tuberculosis.

Sybil spent Christmas Day in bed with a sore throat and a weak pulse, while Iris's temper continued uncertain and Bayard longed to go home to America: 'I am tired of being an exile,' he wrote to a friend, adding that what he really needed was a companion to go about with. On 1 February they rented four adjoining rooms with a large terrace in Portofino, in order to have a change of walks and different meals, and spoke of a possible visit to Florence, 'just to have a little fun'. Bayard neither complained, nor railed against his condition. As the months passed and his horizons grew ever smaller, so his ambitions became more modest; he was now talking of returning to Harvard to study economics, perhaps for 'university work and diplomacy', jobs best suited 'to a person who is not strong'. Sybil's health takes up almost as many lines as Iris's temper: on 1 February in Portofino, Sybil was 'pretty feeble and dreadfully thin', having worked too hard at her Italian; on 3 February she was 'very poorly'. But on 12 February the weather improved, Edith Wharton came to visit them, and, he noted, 'It is a pleasure to be alive'. She had always liked Bayard. He had, she wrote many years later, a rare quality of 'a sort of quiet radiance which sent its beam through the dark fog of weakness and pain enveloping the years that ought to have been his happiest . . . We have always needed such men sorely in American public life.'

In the autumn of 1903 they did what they had planned to do when they first married, and set off to explore California. The doctors had advised Bayard to live in a climate which was neither very hot nor very cold, nor muggy, nor windy, and to spend as much time as possible outside, sleeping in a tent or shelter and doing a lot of riding. Eventually they found themselves in a rented house in a place called Nordhoff, up in the hills between Los Angeles and Santa Barbara. The house was rundown and lacking in furniture, supplies were hard to come by, and it was far more isolated than they had expected. However, Christmas was cheerful. Iris played on her own in a way 'quite remarkable for so young a child'. They were all charmed by the number of birds, and Bayard, who looked for work wherever he went, for a while edited the local newspaper, the *Ojai*. Sybil, Bayard wrote to his mother, 'shows great talent for settling'. Iris's temper had improved, but she still greatly preferred people to her toys, though she much enjoyed looking at pictures. The following summer Sybil noted that her daughter's hair was golden in colour and very soft, but that she was backward in talking. Her health was 'perfect', which, in a family so focused on illness, was fortunate. She also had an excellent memory, and 'her mind seems never at rest'.

Joseph Choate asked Bayard to stand as godfather to his own new daughter, and in accepting Bayard wrote: 'I don't know whether you are glad or sorry at having a daughter instead of a son . . . I know that no boy could be half as amusing as Iris has been, or a quarter as full of odd little affections.' He added that he had had to abandon his journalism because he had become 'so thin (and irritable!) . . . I was born to vegetate, apparently'. Soon they were on the move again, this time to the Adirondacks in north-eastern New York state, where there was a sanatorium which provided a radical hew treatment. He wrote again to Joseph Choate: 'I am absolutely sick of being on the sick list, and mean to try what a little "consummate caution" for a year or so is worth. I hope you and your wife never have to think about anything as annoying as health . . .'

In June 1905 Bayard set down on paper, in two columns,

the advantages and disadvantages as between life in the United States or Switzerland. America came out on top, with a better climate, the possibility of setting up a proper home, and seeing his old friends; St Moritz might, he conceded, be better for his health, but there would be no chance of having a house or a dog of their own. Either way, he added, 'I look ahead of me at a lot more travelling . . . but nothing resembling a continuous cure.'

The decision as to where they should go next was taken out of his hands, for the doctors now recommended the high mountains of Switzerland, and in the spring of 1906 they arrived in St Moritz. As always, Bayard's letters were resolutely optimistic: 'We like the place on the whole better than anywhere we have ever been,' he wrote to Joseph Choate. 'Sybil is well too, and I am doing fairly.' By now his health dogged every decision: there was so much he wanted to do, so much he was offered and might have done, but he was constantly obliged to alter their plans in order to rest, in the right climate. 'Of course,' he wrote to his brother Bronson on his fourteenth birthday, 'I may get all right and be good for something, but what a time wasted.' His letters to his friends and family were lively, full of observations about what he had seen and done. He asked constantly that they keep him up to date with world affairs, and particularly politics. He started a political notebook, saying that he had to make himself learn to understand politics better and to have clearer views about them: 'I am still without political affiliation, and, what is more serious, without definite political principles.' Writing to a friend in Japan, he reported that 'Our young daughter Iris . . . has become a speaker of German, and is rapidly ceasing to be a speaker of English.' Iris apparently had no trouble remembering the Greek names in her story books. In April they moved down to Varese, and Iris was soon adding

Italian to her German and English. By her fourth birthday, in August 1906, she was tall for her age, knew a great deal of poetry, and was beginning to count and to read.

Seven letters from Bayard to his daughter survive. They are loving and teasing, covered in crosses for kisses and circles for hugs. On one he has drawn an O with 'small bullet kiss for bullet-headed girl' and 'fat kiss for Fatty'.

And so the Cuttings went on, wandering up to the mountains and down to the lakes, Sybil taking to her bed with aches and fevers, Iris and her nurse learning poems and words in different languages, while Bayard devoted his ever-diminishing energy to making the most of his surroundings – painting in Tuscany, reading about opera, and keeping a close eye on Iris's development. He wrote a paper on international law, and went on dreaming about getting well enough to enter politics. When, soon afterwards, his brother Bronson had a haemorrhage, Bayard wrote to him: 'You are going to see other fellows go ahead of you all along the line, and must learn not to mind.'

Then, in 1908, at a moment of better health, he was suddenly offered a job he felt he could accept, that of American Vice-Consul in Milan. It was at last something real to do. One of his first tasks was to prepare a report on the vitamin deficiency skin disease pellagra, common in Italy, which he did with speed and clarity. To Iris, in London at the time, he wrote telling her that he had bought a car, and that they would make many trips in it together.

He had not been in Milan long when news came of an earthquake in Sicily. Messina was the third largest port in Italy. At five o'clock on the morning of 28 December 1908 its inhabitants woke to the sound of a great subterranean roar. The next second, according to the German Consul, 'one shriek arose from the whole town, piercing, despairing. Then the sudden thunder of a thousand falling walls, and – utter silence. It was all over in about twelve seconds.' The shock was followed by a thirty-foot tidal wave which levelled the ruins, drowned many who had survived the earthquake, and swept thousands of bodies out to sea. It also destroyed a large number of Italian ships that had been anchored in the bay, and caused havoc along the coast of Calabria; in all, some fifty towns and villages were reported destroyed. There were fears that the American Consul in Messina might be among the dead, and Bayard was dispatched to set up a new Consulate, and to represent the American Red Cross. He took funds with him which included a thousand dollars from his father.

The *New York Times* correspondent had reached Messina quickly. In his first article he described sailing into the bay on a fine pink dawn: 'Then, suddenly, as we turned the point – horror and desolation – Messina spread before us, ruin on ruin. Churches, public buildings, homes lay in one great heap of rubbish, save where skeletons of half a dozen homes stood cracked and tottering . . . No one spoke.'

By the time help arrived, 90,000 of the 120,000 inhabitants of Messina were believed to be dead. Many of the living were still trapped underneath the rubble; cries could be heard coming from the ruins. The rescuers – the crews of Russian, British and American ships that had sped to the area, members of various Red Cross societies, survivors frantically searching for their families – dug and dug. The English Chaplain, his wife and three children could be heard calling from the ruins of their house. The Bishop of Malta and a party of British sailors dug desperately, but the cries grew fainter and fainter, and finally stopped. Of the large foreign community in Messina, the

German Consul, the American Vice-Consul and one member of the English Consulate remained alive. The wife of the French Consul, though alive, appeared to have totally lost her senses.

Bayard Cutting reached Messina on 2 January on board the *Nord America*, in company with troops, doctors, nurses and journalists. He pitched a tent from which he flew the US consular flag, and that day he dispatched his first report: 'Behind a thin screen of fairly intact walls . . . the scenes are awful – houses open, with corpses in every room. At present the search is almost exclusively for the living: the officers have orders to pay no attention to dead bodies . . . Officers are lowered in ruins head first, with a rope tied to their feet, and in this way they have rescued many. To get a man out today, Dr Luzzali had to cut off first a leg and then an arm; of course, the man died . . . Up to today all the work has been done by foreigners, the Italians have seemed more or less dazed.' Bayard requested 'lots of sterilised milk – not condensed, but stuff that is ready to drink. It is all you can give to the half starved women and children . . . Tinned meat will also come in useful . . . woollen underclothes, socks and shirts are wanted.' By 3 January there were enough doctors and nurses, but, as he reported, 'the smells are getting bad . . . in view of paying no attention to corpses until all the living are rescued'. At night the scene of devastation was lit up by searchlights from the warships.

In a letter to Sybil on 6 January, Bayard was extremely critical of the way the Italians were handling the earthquake. They were preventing the foreigners from working, he wrote, while they themselves did nothing but talk. What was more, the local mayor was incompetent and corrupt. A field some way away from the city had been designated as a base for the survivors, and no rations were allowed to be distributed in

23

Messina itself, so that the survivors who were still desperately searching the ruins were now also starving. 'I feel that we are doing nothing,' Bayard wrote, 'that our only useful function would be as a registration and investigation bureau' into how foreign helpers could 'give more intelligently' – a view on aid in the wake of disasters that was far ahead of its time. When some of the few remaining able-bodied members of families came searching for food they were quickly 'deported'. 'The brutality and folly', he noted forlornly, 'are simply inconceivable.'

On 10 January he wrote to his father that he had 'accomplished practically nothing', and had decided to explore conditions in Catania, Syracuse and Palermo, in order to find ways of spending his funds more profitably.

Among the searchers in Palermo was the historian and writer Gaetano Salvemini, who years later met Iris in Fiesole. He had come home late on the evening of 27 December and was still awake for the first warning signs of the earthquake, the ringing of bells and the howling of dogs. He just had time to leap out of the window as the walls of his house collapsed inwards like a pack of cards. Though he jumped from the fifth floor, the architrave of one of the windows broke his fall. When he regained consciousness he found that his entire family had been swallowed up – five children, his wife and his sister. Day after day, with his brother Ugo, Salvemini groped among the ruins in search of the bodies. Those of his two youngest were never found, and for months afterwards, whenever he heard about the survival of a little boy of the same age as Ughetto, who was three, he hurried to the place or sent a telegram, only to come back every time disappointed. He went back to his work, but wrote to a friend: 'I go ahead, work, make speeches . . . in short, go on living. I have on my table some letters that my wife, my sister, or the children wrote. They are like their voices. And when I have read one of them, I have to stop, because a great fit of weeping overcomes me, and I should like to die.' After Salvemini's death, many years later, a letter of his was found, written a few months before the earthquake: 'In my family life I am so happy that I am frightened.'

From Palermo Bayard moved to Rome, where he was outraged to find the Romans unwilling to contribute money for the refugees. There he set up a system of small loans to individual projects and enterprises designed to get families back on their feet. But since the American Vice-Consul in Messina had survived, he was no longer needed in Sicily. From Lloyd Griscom, American Ambassador to Italy, came a letter expressing the 'Department's high approval of the discretion, fidelity and ability shown by you', and Bayard joined Sybil and Iris for a holiday in Portofino. Learning that he had been appointed secretary to the American Legation in Tangiers, he left for Washington to be briefed. The earthquake had done no good for his health: one night he got soaked helping to bring in a boat laden with provisions through a storm, and it was many hours before he found dry clothes. He had not been in Washington long when he had another haemorrhage.

Iris always remembered the summer of her seventh birthday, in 1909. They spent it at Camaldoli, in the forests of the Apennines, taking long walks up to the clearings where timber was sawn, looking for wild strawberries. Iris wore long white muslin dresses and floppy muslin hats. As they walked, Bayard gave her what she later realised were her first lessons in geography and history, and insisted that she should learn poetry correctly, without making mistakes, saying that seven was not too young to be able to 'distinguish between knowing something and half knowing it'. By now she was reading in English, Italian and French. Later she used to say that she could not remember a time when she had not been able to read – 'Of all the pleasures of life, this is the only one that, at every age, has never failed me' – though she never forgot her English grandmother saying to her one day, 'If you read so much now, there'll be no books left for you when you grow up.'

It was at Camaldoli that Bayard finally accepted that, like all the other careers he had given up, he would have to abandon the idea of diplomacy, too. Characteristically, he wrote to his cousin Else that he now realised he had never really wanted to be a diplomat at all, and that a 'quite unexpected joy' had taken hold of him. His self-control and selflessness were remarkable, as was the optimism with which he determinedly greeted every new plan, even though it inevitably spelt the end of previous dreams. He had decided to return to Harvard, to become a specialist in colonial administration, and since Sybil's health was also poor – colds, mild fevers, headaches – they would start by spending the winter in as many British dependencies as they could visit, countries like Egypt, Sudan and Malta. 'I wonder how silly and impracticable such an idea (for people in our health) will seem to you . . .' he wrote. 'It is filling us with excitement, I must say.' Before they left the mountains, Bayard and Sybil had a long talk about the future, and money. Among her papers is a note that Bayard had told her he wanted Iris to have money of her own, because he wanted above all for her to feel, not just bound to no one nationality, but free. Sybil was evidently very worried about her own position, but Bayard reassured her that on his death she would get somewhere between five and six thousand dollars a year – 'Papa and Mama would never let my widow be in difficulty. They are *really* rich you know . . .'

26

In December 1909 the Cuttings boarded a private dahabiyah, a present from Bayard's father, and sailed up the Nile, taking with them a close friend, Gordon Gardiner, a Dr Bishop and a nurse, Iris and her governess, Mademoiselle Nigg, and a crew of ten. There was also a singer for the crew, who took opium and only sang when he was in a good mood. Although in theory this was to be the first of their winter explorations of colonial life, no one any longer pretended that Bayard was not seriously ill. By the middle of the month they were moored in a little bay; a day-house was built on the sand out of matting and thatch, tents were pitched for sleeping quarters, and a shelter was made for their cow and her calf, taken along to provide them with the fresh milk consumptives were assumed to need. At night guards were posted to keep away thieves, wolves and jackals, which yelped incessantly throughout the night. In the early mornings, before it got too hot, Sybil rode out on a camel, her long green veil floating behind her from under her sun helmet. Iris rode a white donkey, and when she came back joined Mademoiselle on deck for lessons. Bayard, apparently strengthened by the warm dry desert air, would read Shakespeare's sonnets aloud to Iris, saying that it was not necessary or even very desirable for a child to understand all that is said to it, and that it was important, always, to aim a little too high. At Christmas the whole party put on fancy dress and pulled crackers. Years later, Iris wondered how much Bayard minded not being allowed to take her on his knee or kiss her, as he had done so lovingly before his illness grew worse.

In January they moved on again, in the direction of Aswan, and Sybil wrote to Bayard's father how, from his cabin, Bayard was looking 'out across the great blue river to the green palms . . . with the fresh breeze and the warm air pouring into his cabin . . . He is sitting up, had a steak for lunch and can read and write with far less fatigue.' She evidently felt more optimistic than Dr Bishop, who was worried about the sharp swings between the heat of the day and the cold of the night, and the occasional sudden cold winds. Their new camp looked out across the desert, but also lay nearer to medical help. A renowned London specialist in bacteriology was looking after Sir Ernest Cassel's tubercular daughter, staying on another boat moored not far away, and came over to take blood from Sybil, to check that she was not tubercular. The Cassels sent some of their own supply of milk, since the cow the Cuttings had brought with them was not yielding enough.

Though she was free of tuberculosis, Sybil was not well, her constant pains and suspected heart trouble not helped by the sea-sickness she suffered every time the dahabiyah shifted its moorings. Dr Bishop dosed her with a combination of strychnine and brandy, and her weight fell to just over six stone. Iris saw little of her parents, but on her father's good days she was rowed out to sit with him for an hour, or even just stand at his cabin door. To her grandmother she wrote in French, telling her about her white donkey, and that her father was '*faible*' and she could not read to him as she would have liked. Bayard had begun haemorrhaging again. On 14 January he wrote to his father. His tone was cheerful as ever, but it is clear he realised he was going to have to give up his latest plan and again reduce his expectations: 'I wish and intend to come home this year. Our day dream is to take a little furnished house in or near Cambridge for the autumn . . . I am not sure I shouldn't like to have a tiny villa near Florence . . . You see all this plan abandons for good the idea of colonial work, though it has interested me more than anything I have ever done (and I can't quite get out

28

of the back of my head the hope that somehow and sometime studies of Egypt, Tunis, Algiers and Malta and Cyprus may yet be possible during the late winter months). Now, however, I'm with you in wanting to get settled somewhere near where I belong and providing Iris with a home background.' Even as he wrote, this new dream was already an impossibility. Time was running out.

The Desarts, increasingly alarmed by the reports of both Bayard's and Sybil's health, arrived from England. They were only just in time to see Bayard. The haemorrhages had continued and he was now running a high temperature.

On 10 March 1910, not long after his thirtieth birthday, Bayard died. Next day Sybil wrote to his parents, describing his last hours: 'At 1.30 he woke and talked almost like himself, not quite, for a few moments. "I just want you to be happy," he said, "to be well and happy. I'm not interested in life – I'm too tired." I kissed him; and he passed into unconsciousness and so died. There was no pain, no struggle, no fear.' It was her grandmother Lady Desart who, taking Iris on her knee, told her that her father was dead. A note was sent across from Sybil on the boat to the camp on shore adding that Bayard was now 'where there is no sadness and pain'. Iris was judged too young to go to the funeral, but before leaving Egypt she was taken to see her father's grave, in a bare cemetery on the edge of the desert, near those of some young British officers who had died in the Sudan. More than sixty years later she wrote in her autobiography of her sense of shame that, in the days following her father's death, she was less conscious of his death than of the black sash she wore, and of being, like the heroine of one of her books, *Les malheurs de Sophie*, an orphan: a form of 'self-picturing' which, she added, 'has been one of my great weaknesses all my life'. Gordon Gardiner was desolate. 'Intellectually and morally', he wrote to Bayard's mother, 'I took on a new lease of life when our friendship began. His instincts [were] the kindest and sweetest . . . I shall never have another friend like him.'

Bayard had asked Sybil to burn the letters he had written her, and his diary, after his death. Before doing so, however, she made a copy of his last letter to her.

My dear wife, dearest Sybil,

I have begun several letters to you and not finished them as I'm so tired. They still say I may get better and, if I do, we shall, I promise you, be much happier than we have been lately . . . If I can just live we'll buy a villa in Italy or somewhere beautiful and travel or go home when you are able to . . . and be happy together and see Iris get big and strong. I'd like that – and read and talk . . . I'm not quite happy about my Will. I hope you'll have enough money to buy a house – if not Papa will help you. And later it will be just the same as if I lived. He'll leave my share to you or Iris, I know, he won't let my dying make a difference to my wife and child. And if Iris has the money and not you, she will not touch what I've left her. There *must be* plenty for you both eventually. I just wanted her to be free to marry or love whom she liked after she has grown up – but I hope it will always be with you as long as you want her. But it is easier to be independent. Only I can't bear you to be poor.

It is the fight that has made it so hard – and the family – they don't understand, they didn't mean to, they always meant to be kind, but they couldn't let us alone, couldn't let us, let you decide . . . It made me mad. They always remembered you were English – as if that mattered – and thought that I wanted what I didn't want.

I'd like it to be different for Iris . . . Make a home for her and yourself, all this travelling and homelessness is so bad for you and will be bad for her. And I don't want her to go to school. I hate girls' schools. I think you would both be happiest in Italy, Florence perhaps or, if Florence is too cold, somewhere near Naples. I've been happiest in Italy . . . And later, when you are well, get her to get to know my family and America, they will be so fond of her and you. But she must live with you *always* wherever you choose, be your child. It is all you have now, my dear. And when she is big she will take care of you. I want you to be everything to each other. Only don't think I don't want you to marry again – only not yet, not too soon. But you won't, I know. Some time I'd like you to be happy, *really* happy again . . . But I thought I'd live longer . . . burn all my papers and letters and my diary. I don't want that read, please. Or anything I've written, published, or anything written about me. I haven't done anything, and it is silly. Mind you don't let them. And get well and happy, girl.

Sybil destroyed everything except a copy of this letter, which must have meant too much to her for it to be sacrificed altogether.

Bayard had been right in his observations about the Cuttings: neither of his parents greatly cared for Sybil, though both his mother and his sisters and brother later became very fond of Iris as she grew older and got to know them. Sybil they perceived as too self-indulgent, too self-centred, and the few times they met again were not successful. It was perhaps not surprising if at this stage they felt strongly that Sybil's own minor ailments had played much too big a part in the family's peregrinations from country to country and climate to climate. Seen in this light, Sybil does not come across as a sympathetic figure; but there was more to her than this, to do with enthusiasm and a very real sense of adventure. It was her health, as it had been Bayard's, that was her undoing.

Even for the times, the tributes to Bayard that were now sent to his parents were exceptional. Groton and Harvard spoke of his brilliance, his personality, and the loss of someone with a 'boy's heart, a man's brain, and a gentleman's great soul'. Santayana, his former tutor, called him the sanest young man he had ever met. And Edith Wharton, in an affectionate and sad privately printed memoir, said that she had never known any other 'intelligence in which the play of ideas was so free, yet their reaction so tinged by the elusive thing called "character".' Bayard's sister Olivia Cutting wrote Edith a touching note: 'Your love and friendship were our Bayard's particular treasures. You helped him over many a rough place . . . and your letters cheered him when all else failed. You knew him as few did . . . I sometimes think it will kill his father . . . Iris's little letters are pathetic and sad beyond words.'

Yet it was Iris who, in the years to come, missed him most deeply. As a child she often cried for him; later, she thought of him as the person who would have saved her from making mistakes. He had left her one great gift, however: that of having been a hero to her during the shadowy and secret world of her childhood. Much later, talking to people who had known him and reading through his letters, she concluded that she owed to his influence her strong feelings about the Latin world, her interest in ideas and people, her satisfaction in tackling intellectual problems, and a sharp and sudden impatience; and also, perhaps, the need to write clearly and always to aim too high. But, she wondered, had he lived to become a friend to her, how would her life have been different?

CHAPTER TWO

The Anglo-Florentines

For all her travels, by the age of nine Iris had spent very little time in England, or with her Desart grandparents. With her father dead and her mother's plans uncertain, she was sent now for holidays to County Kilkenny in Ireland, where she quickly became extremely attached to her grandfather, known to all the children as Gabba, and to her aunt Lady Joan Verney's children, Ulick, Gerald and Joy. They played tennis, rode and went for walks. 'All my cousins are very nice,' she wrote to Irene Lawley, her mother's cousin, ten years older than herself, of whom she was very fond, 'but I don't know if I am more thankful to have cousins or not to have brothers. Otherwise family life is wonderfully like my remembrance of it.' Forever afterwards, Iris thought of Desart Court as a place of 'peace and happiness', recalling the drawing room with its many chintzes, smelling of sweet peas, roses and wet dogs, and the large stable yard where the hunters and ponies were kept. Iris and her grandfather shared a birthday in August, which they used to celebrate by taking a picnic to a wooded hill at a place called Ballykeepe. Iris grew increasingly close to her grandfather, in whom she seems to have recognised some of the qualities that had bound her to her father, such as the need to be stoical; and it was from him she derived some of her convictions about responsibility and morality. 'An unfailing, carefully veiled tenderness', she wrote many years later, 'warmed and lit our friendship. 'These were increasingly difficult times for Lord Desart, who agonised over his feelings of close attachment to both England and Ireland, ever hopeful that some compromise might yet be found to solve the growing trouble between the two. Professionally he was by now highly regarded, having been appointed a member of the Privy Council and Treasurer of the Inner Temple in London.

Bayard had left Sybil $25,000, together with furniture, books, silver and jewellery, and $300,000 in trust, a fortune in those days, the income to go to her during her lifetime and later to Iris. The difficulties with his parents over Sybil not being American, to which he alluded in his last letter to her, had obviously contributed to his request that Iris be brought up free of 'national' ties, and relations between the Cuttings and Sybil remained uneasy. She now decided to use Bayard's money to follow his plan of getting a house in Florence. Renting a small villa at Rifredi, she started searching for something to buy in the hills overlooking the city, an area long popular with foreigners, and particularly the English.

One spring day in 1911 Sybil took Iris up a steep winding hill road leading to Fiesole, the walls on either side covered in wisteria and yellow Banksia roses. They turned down a drive lined with ilex trees, emerging onto a large terrace over which lay scattered mauve flowers fallen from two tall paulownias. The terrace and the loggia to one side of the large square house looked out across the domes and palaces of Florence, and across the Arno to the hills beyond. The house was called the Villa Medici, Sybil told Iris, and she proposed to rent it. It had a chapel, five main bedrooms, and a separate small house, known as *Il Villino*; the ground floor had hardly been touched since the fifteenth century. What was important, however, given Sybil's precarious health, was that Fiesole was warmer and got more sun than the hills on the other side of the city. Later Iris learnt some of its history, which she repeated 'like a diligent little parrot', though sometimes adding her own bloodthirsty embellishments, to the many visitors who wanted to be shown over the house. It had been designed by the Florentine architect Michelozzo Michelozzi for Cosimo de' Medici, who on spring and summer nights had held banquets on the loggia, after which there would be dancing and the reciting of poetry. Here Poliziano wrote his poem *Rusticus*, and Lorenzo the Magnificent discussed the nature of verse. Vasari described the Villa Medici as a 'magnificent and noble palace'.

In the eighteenth century the Villa Medici was bought by Horace Walpole's sister-in-law, Lady Orford, who chose the exceptionally beautiful yellow Chinese silk wallpaper that still remained in the drawing rooms, and who was well known to Florentine society for powdering her hair, smoking cigars, and riding, as Sir Horace Mann put it, with a 'vivacity not common at her age'. In the nineteenth century the villa passed to the English painter and collector William Blundell Spence, when it was known as the Villa Spence and became *the* meeting-place for the English in Florence.

And so Sybil rented the Villa Medici, with its wonderful views across Florence and its exotic yellow Chinese wallpaper, and began the long process of furnishing it to her own taste. A third person also moved in with them: Sybil's maid, Kate Leuty, known to all as Doody, described later by Iris as the 'embodiment of stability, kindness and uncompromising British common sense', and who provided some of the down-to-earth affectionate warmth lacking in Sybil. Dressed in a neat and invariably black coat and skirt and all-purpose comfortable shoes, her stocky figure could be seen stumping after Sybil, through Grecian temples or Egyptian bazaars, clutching all that might suddenly be needed, a hot-water bottle, perhaps, a folding stool, some smelling salts. For Sybil belonged to the tradition of the eighteenth century travellers: enterprising, imperious, immune to criticism or ridicule, carrying her own world around with her. After a long ride into the desert on a camel one day, Doody was asked whether she was very tired; 'No, m'lady,' she is said to have replied, 'we are here for pleasure.' Everywhere Sybil, Iris and Doody went, whether to an inn in Austria or to a houseboat on the water, Doody's authority was immediately recognised and her orders obeyed. If they were camping, Sybil would stroll off looking for adventure, taking Iris with her. They would return to find Sybil's tent put up or her room prepared, clean linen sheets and cashmere shawls on the bed, tea prepared, medicine chest opened, and possibly the 'aroma of roast chicken' wafting across from the kitchen tent, while from the bathroom quarters came the unmistakable smell of Condy's Fluid. It was to Doody that Iris now wrote a touching and surprisingly childish note, signing it 'best love and kisses from your baby' and adding a PS:

'I like the villa we are going to live in so much.'

The Florence to which Sybil and Iris came was a city beset by gossip and feuds, split up into cliques, exotic, eccentric, and – to those accustomed to the grey light of the north and the formality and starchiness of northern society – shocking in its heat and brilliance, and gloriously free. The foreign community felt less bound by convention than they might have in London, Paris or New York; it was also a very adult society, since the English in particular preferred to leave their children at school than at home. Theirs was a largely foreign social world. In 1911 the British community in and around Florence numbered about 35,000 and there were sizeable if largely self-contained groups – Iris later called them archipelagos – of French, Germans, Poles, Americans, and Russians. The old Italian families did not choose to entertain the foreigners much and sometime referred to them as the '*anglo-beceri*', '*becero*' meaning 'boor' in the local dialect. Of the many English residents the author Harold Acton, himself born in Florence in 1904, wrote: 'They took root among the vineyards and became a part of the landscape. Their eccentricities flourished in the clear Tuscan light.' The Anglo-Florentines loved hospitality, and admired oddity.

There was, for example, the theosophist Lady Paget, widow of Sir Augustus Paget, former ambassador to Rome and Vienna, who made all her own shoes by hand, exotic but highly impractical creations in velvet and silk, embroidered in fur. Lady Paget stayed on in Florence because the British quarantine laws prevented her taking her dachshunds back to England. Then there was a Marchese Fioravanti, a passionate anglophile who gave parties at which guests danced Scottish reels. More peculiarly, perhaps, he kept a pet crocodile in a pond in the garden, netted over so that it could not escape, and carried down to the cellar on a stretcher by four men when it showed signs of wanting to hibernate. It grew into a large and fierce animal. One spring, however, the Marchese returned home from a trip to find the crocodile dead; he had a proper funeral held in its honour, and forever after suspected his mother of its murder. Crocodiles, indeed, seem to have been something of a feature of Florentine life, for an early visitor, the composer and suffragette Ethel Smyth, has left a curious story of meeting a man in the Piazza Santa Maria Novella who was leading a long line of crocodiles, addressing them as *bimbi*: little children.

By 1911 it was getting on for half a century since Florence had been, briefly, the capital of Italy, and most of the city's best-known foreign residents, Swinburne, Dickens, Trollope, the Brownings, Mark Twain, Henry James and the Goncourt brothers, had long since departed, gone home to write memoirs of their Florentine lives, leaving behind much gossip about their visits. Among the grandest, and still much discussed throughout the city, were the three paid by Queen Victoria in the 1890s. She had brought with her eighty attendants, including her Indian servants, as well as her bed, her desk, and her favourite pictures. The Florentines continued to marvel over her arrival by private train and her demands that the villa in which she was to stay should have a special water supply installed and a telephone connected. Once the red despatch boxes had been dealt with Queen Victoria was apparently keen to see the sights of Florence and in front of the Duomo one day is said to have drawn out a locket with a miniature of Prince Albert and, as she held it up, to have observed that she thought he would be interested to see how the building had been repaired.

As the Goncourt brothers had rightly observed, Florence was indeed a *'ville toute anglaise'*. There was at least one English bank, several English doctors, an English chemist and dentist; there were English shops, where could be found tea, tweeds, mackintoshes, and tennis rackets. Molini's stocked Reeves colours and painting brushes, pens and ink. Doney's and Giacosa, the two most fashionable cafés in the Via Tornabuoni, where the Anglo-Florentines did most of their shopping, served muffins and seedcake. Vieusseux's Circulating Library provided

English books. There were two English-language newspapers, the *Florence Directory* and the *Florence Herald*, both of which listed the social engagements of the residents and noted the arrival of visitors. Shortly before the First World War a Miss Smedly arrived from London to organise the first Women's Club in Italy, to be called the Lyceum, a venture warmly supported by many Florentine ladies who like her wanted to bridge the gap between foreigners and Florentines, and between aristocratic and 'bourgeois' ladies. Social life was taken very seriously, with white tie worn for balls, and dancing classes to teach the tango and the foxtrot. All this was also much enjoyed by the smaller colony of Americans, for whom Europe in the early years of the century seemed to offer a complexity and a sense of history they could not find at home.

Nor did you have to be rich to enjoy Florence. Living was cheap, as were servants, who could soon be taught to produce a mixture of Italian and English food, with all the advantages of vegetables that were not overcooked, and who were strangers to the English plague of 'Sunday evenings out'. Houses, villas, palazzi and even flats could all be rented cheaply, although they seemed disconcertingly under-furnished to people more accustomed to velvet curtains and fringed sofas. Some took long leases for very low rents, in exchange for repairing properties which were often primitive and long neglected by their owners. And since it was possible to find small apartments, Florence in 1911 continued to attract single women, who swapped suburban lodgings in English seaside towns for top-floor flats with marvellous views over the city. The old and crumbling walls and faded decorations sometimes contrasted oddly with the new furniture and the mementoes with which these ladies tried their best to turn their small new flats into cosy English homes.

For the visitors who came for a few months in the late spring, as for the residents who sat out the *tramontana*, the freezing north wind, and the winter fogs, there was a great deal to do. The city with its grand buildings and open boulevards was still comfortably empty, even if Ruskin had declared it already ruined some years before, after he found hackney coaches and omnibuses parked before Giotto's tower. Guidebooks of the time listed 152 churches, 18 merchant halls, and 150 statues, quite apart from the Boboli gardens, the Frangelicos at San Marco, and the Pitti Palace. And days could be spent in Fiesole or strolling along the banks of the Arno, haggling for little gold boxes and miniatures in the antique shops – to buy without bargaining was the equivalent of shooting sitting pheasants. Among the visitors to the antique shops on Via de Fossi and Via Maggio was Edith Wharton, as described later by Percy Lubbock, with 'eyes bright and rapacious' as a robin's darting over the furniture, bargaining with determination and skill.

Georgina Grahame, who in the early years of the twentieth century wrote a book called *In a Tuscan Garden* about her life in Florence, devised a test for the English who came there. It concerned their attitude towards the olive tree: if they lamented 'our beautiful English trees' and spoke of olives as 'colourless grey trees', then she knew they would never see Italy 'with an appreciative eye or understanding brain'. There was a list of things Mrs Grahame considered essential to anyone making an excursion from Florence: it included tea, brandy, English biscuits, a teapot and a spirit lamp, a folding chair, a book box, a pillow, a pair of dark blue calico or linen blinds, a mosquito net, and a hot-water bottle. And it was Mrs Grahame who instructed her servants to treat her pets as they would be treated in England, '*come not altri*', like us human beings.

And of course, for these residents, who for the most part felt decidedly superior to the tourists and a little superior to the Italians whose language they did not often bother to master beyond a few useful commands, there was the extremely serious business of gardening. In the Middle Ages Fiesole and Settignano were the hillsides to which Florentines went to escape the plague, where humanists and wealthy Renaissance merchants built villas, of varying degrees of grandeur, in which to enjoy country living. And to these hillsides and their villas came the foreign visitors, especially the English, gossiping about the inhabitants of other villas, or falling in love with those villas and offering to buy them. At the turn of the twentieth century there were still many villas to be had, some of immense splendour, like the Villa Medici, some small and unremarkable, but nearly all including land and woods and gardens full of ilex, cypress, stone pines, olive trees, oleanders, bougainvillaea, exotic to northern eyes more accustomed to oaks and herbaceous borders. It was exciting yet somehow safe, with so many other British about, and such familiar items in the Florence shops; it made many feel daring, but not so daring as to be alarmed.

The more hardy, whose health was not as uncertain as Sybil's, also took houses across on the other side of Florence, at Bellosguardo orAcetri, where the villas were as fine but the sun set far earlier. Almost every house had a lemon store, where orange and lemon trees, camellias and delicate shrubs were kept in winter. And because it was largely the English who colonized the Florentine hillsides, it was the English who imposed their taste and their fashion on the gardens they took over. Olives and vineyards were replaced with lawns and deciduous shade trees, herbaceous borders were planted with irises, crocuses, peonies and daffodils, woods and scrub were cleared, and steep dry-stone-walled terraces were covered with roses: Banksias, 'Irene Watts' and 'Madame Metral'. These English residents knew and cared about their gardens: they ordered their bulbs from England, and they never went away at planting time. Often, like Georgina Grahame, they wrote books about them. The mists and fogs could be depressing, the sudden frosts terrifying because of the lemon trees, but when the fireflies arrived in May and the acacias flowered, the wild dog roses sprouted on the fringes of bright green cornfields and white and red lilies bloomed, the Judas trees turned deep pink and wisteria scented the air around the house, all under a perfect blue sky, then they knew why they had come to Florence. Mabel Dodge Luhan, who spent months and a great deal of money doing up the Villa Curonia above San Miniato with red damask walls, silk brocades and Flemish tapestries, described the particular scent of Florence's hillside villas: 'A smell of damp, old stone, of damp box and laurel from dark garden corners where the roots are never dry, and of cypress trees soaked in sunshine, cypresses which have known only air and light. And mixed with these, the odour of dust and roses.'

One local resident who knew a great deal about gardening soon befriended Sybil and Iris. Janet Ross, one of the most interesting and constant of the Anglo-Florentines, daughter of the famous Lucie, Lady Duff Gordon, lived in a villa at Settignano, called Poggio Gherardo, a house described by Boccaccio in *The Decameron*. It had walls washed a light stone-grey colour and magnificent views across to Vallombrosa, almost a hundred miles away. From a grassy terrace you could see the domes and towers of Florence. Janet Ross was sixty-nine in 1911, the year Sybil and Iris settled in the Villa Medici. Henry James described her as 'still handsome in a utilitarian kind of way', but Harold Acton was more precise, noting her thick eyebrows and very sharp eyes; according to him she swore like a trooper and dismissed, female suffrage as ludicrous, but he considered that she had done a brilliant job when for a short time she was a correspondent for *The Times* in Egypt.

Her banker husband Henry, who had kept guinea pigs which followed him around the garden and bred almost a thousand varieties of orchid, was dead; she now lived on her own, with dozens of birds in cages and a wolfhound, but she welcomed visitors, mosty of a literary kind, people who came to write their books and who knew a great deal about Tuscany and went for long walks in the surrounding hills. In winter Janet Ross could be seen in a felt hat with feathers, a black leather belt around her waist from which hung a leather notebook and the three keys to the gates of Poggio Gherardo, tramping around her land, overseeing the production of wine, oil and vegetables that brought her a regular and necessary income. In summer she exchanged the felt hat for a white linen one with two layers of embroidered muslin, rather like a child's seaside hat. Most important among her produce was a vermouth made according to a secret recipe that she said had been given to her by the last of the Medici and which she sold to the Army and Navy Stores in London.

Like many of her guests Janet Ross wrote at some speed and on many subjects. By 1911 she had published more than a dozen books and was considered an authority on Tuscan husbandry and food, and the history of Florentine villas and palazzi. She proved a good friend to Sybil, advising her on the most reliable dealers from whom to buy furniture – she had an excellent eye for genuine antiques and paintings – and steering her through the currents of the feuding expatriate world. The English artist William Rothenstein, who visited Florence in these years, felt Mrs Ross could have walked out of the pages of Meredith: 'A proud manner distinguished her, and courage, with a wide experience in the world. And how handsome she still was! And what a splendid villa was hers! . . . and what a garden, and what a table she kept!'

Janet Ross herself had strong feelings about her neighbours. Roughly at the time the Cuttings arrived she was going through a patch of animosity towards another famous Fiesole resident, the writer Vernon Lee, who lived in the Villa Il Palmerino, an unimposing but charming house with a fine umbrella pine by the gate and a delightful walled garden. Vernon Lee was outspoken, trenchant, consumed by causes, many of them unpopular, and could be extremely rude. She had protruding teeth, wore mannish clothes with her hair cropped short, and her eyes gleamed from behind little spectacles. Bernhard Berenson's secretary Nicky Mariano, who in later years used to meet her on the tram coming down from Settignano into Florence, remarked both on the high collar and necktie Vernon Lee wore under her tailor-made clothes, and on 'a face fascinating not only because of its almost baroque ugliness, but through the intelligence of its expression'. Maurice Baring considered her to be the cleverest person he had ever met, and Henry James pronounced hers 'far away the most able mind in Florence'. Janet Ross, who disputed her claim to be the literary queen of Fiesole, complained about her exceptional ugliness, arguing that ugliness should be classed as a sin.

More spectacularly, Janet Ross had fallen foul of Ouida. The novelist's dog had bitten her young son Henry, and she had had the dog punished; but Ouida, who made Florence her home for twenty-three years, was renowned for the way she treated her dogs: they ruled the household at the Villa Fannola, lapped cream out of Capodimonti teacups, ate lobster and *petits fours* from the table and peed wherever they wished to. Ouida believed house-training was cruel. In *Friendship*, a scathing three-volume novel about Florence and its foreign inhabitants, Ouida described Janet Ross, barely disguised as 'Lady Joan Challoner', as an immoral and witch-like woman, 'a faggot of contradictions . . . a bully, but a coward', who was cruel to dogs. *Friendship* split Florence into Ouida-supporters and Ouida-foes. Few of the city's many foreign eccentrics inspired such interest, or so many pen-portraits. Percy Lubbock, another frequent visitor to Florence, spoke of her as 'tall and angular in her stiff collar and her drab coat, fixed in rumination, absorbed and unheeding, her rugged face working in the coil and labour of her burrowing thought'. In a city of oddities, Ouida was queen.

Also in Settignano, a quarter of an hour's walk from Poggio Gherardo, lived a couple who liked and admired Janet Ross, and who by 1911 were among the most prized and courted members of the English-speaking Florentine world, Bernhard and Mary Berenson. They sat at the centre of a small group of intellectuals, writers, historians and philosophers who spent much of their time talking and going off on expeditions to look at works of art. They did not always make themselves popular when visiting collections of paintings owned by English families: sometimes they would claim to have 'discovered' a lost masterpiece, but they were more apt to remark on misattributions. When they had visitors they toured the Florentine countryside on bicycles, and read the Bible out loud to each other, as well as Greek, Latin and English poetry. At night, on these outings, they slept in little inns and talked about poetry.

The Berensons' house, I Tatti, which they had bought in 1907, was not monumental in the style of the Villa Medici but looked more like an overgrown farmhouse, a *casa colonica*, of the fifteenth century, with good proportions, standing on a hill above the church of San Martino. A long avenue of cypresses led to its entrance at the side and it was surrounded by hills covered in vines and olives. The Berensons had rented I Tatti for some years after their marriage in 1900 – they had already been together for ten years of the fifty-five they spent together; not until the death of Mary's first husband Frank Costelloe, an Irish barrister by whom she had two daughters, were they free to marry. In appearance, as in character, they made a somewhat curious pair. Mary was a Philadelphia Quaker of 'majestic proportions' with a wonderful smile who addressed people as 'thee', in the Quaker tradition, and was untidy, somewhat greedy, profligate with money, and easily fired by lunatic schemes; Bernhard was Jewish, slender, delicate, neat, easily bored and careful with money. He loved to walk, she quickly tired; where she was rather slovenly, he fell into terrible rages over negligence and inefficiency; and while she planned endlessly to see and keep in contact with her large family (her sister Alys was married to Bertrand Russell, and her brother was the writer Logan Pearsall Smith) he went to considerable lengths to stay away from his. But they shared a passion for art; she first glimpsed Bernhard at a concert at Harvard, and from the time they met they had talked to each other about art, and also argued about it. 'Bernhard', Mary once wrote approvingly, 'never lets *anything* stand in his way of appreciating a work of art, if it has any qualities whatever.' By 1911 Mary and Bernhard were in their middle forties.

Berenson's standing in Florence was due in large part to the fact that he was a recognised authority on Italian art – his chosen period was the Italian renaissance – the author of four books on the subject, and the leading figure in the sale of Italian renaissance paintings in Europe and America, particularly through his connection with the art dealer Joseph Duveen, who paid him a ten per cent commission on every picture he sold to which Berenson had given an attribution. He did this despite the existence of the Pacca Law, called after Cardinal Pacca, Secretary of State to Pius VII, who early in the nineteenth century had tried to curb the looting of Italian masterpieces for sale in foreign countries. Together the Berensons worked on the endless revision and extension of Berenson's 'lists' of Italian paintings, recording where they were and establishing their attribution.

I Tatti was known, even in a city of foreigners who liked to entertain, for its unending stream of guests, disciples, friends, and what Berenson sometimes called 'enemy-friends'. Both Berensons, wrote Nicky Mariano, who came to work for and live with them after the First World War, seemed to feed on visitors, almost irrespective of how nice or interesting they were. They were happy to talk by the hour about people, their manners and their scandals, 'so long', recorded Percy Lubbock, 'as these throw light upon the chase of human nature, fit quarry for a noble curiosity'. Mary once told Kenneth Clark that no poem in the English language meant more to her than Hood's lines 'Give me new faces, new faces; I've seen all the old ones a thousand times o'er', while even Berenson, who had the most delicate of digestions, 'could swallow the toughest American bore'. The art historian Hermann Keyserling once remarked that Mary marshalled her guests 'like a station master his trains, her chief ambition being not to have a car return empty from Florence'. Like Janet Ross, however, Berenson was not on speaking terms with Vernon Lee, having fallen out with her in 1897 when he accused her of plagiarism: he claimed she had stolen part of an essay written for the *Contemporary Review* from a conversation he had had with her. Their feud lasted twenty years. After her death a large bundle of letters was found with the word 'rows' on it.

Through Janet Ross, or possibly Edith Wharton, who first became acquainted with the Berensons about this time, Mary and B. B., as he was usually known, went to call on Sybil and Iris on 2 December 1911. 'She is interesting and pleasant,' recorded Mary in a letter to her family in England, 'and she has a dear little girl named Iris.' On 11 January Sybil returned the call, and the ladies evidently got on well enough for Mary to remark that it would be good if Berenson found 'someone in Florence whom he really cares to see'. Soon afterwards Iris and her mother drove up 'to the Tuscan wood of aromatic cypress and pine which was that day's meeting place', where a 'trim figure in a pale grey suit' with a red carnation in his buttonhole was waiting impatiently to show them a view before the light went. Berenson, according to Iris many years later, skipped up the hill and stood on the ledge looking out over the valley of the Sieve; she thought that she had seldom 'seen anyone stand so still . . . Of all the facets of that complex personality,' she wrote later, 'this is the one that I remember the best: the way in which he would look at what lay before him.' On another day, looking at some frescos, Berenson told her how the Indian god of the bow and arrow had taught his son to hit a mark: 'He took him into a wood and asked him what he saw. The boy said, "I see a tree." "Look again." "I see a bird." "Look again." "I see its head." "Again." "I see its eye." "Then shoot."' It was just the same, Berenson told her, when looking at a view or a work of art: 'One moment is enough, if the concentration is absolute.'

How to see and how to take in what you are looking at, Iris learnt from Berenson. From her American grandparents and from her grandfather Desart came quite another lesson, one that was to be of great significance to her in the years to come: that of helping those less fortunate than herself. On 12 December 1911 her grandfather Bayard Cutting wrote to tell Iris he would not be sending her a Christmas present that year; instead, in her name, he planned to give a Christmas dinner and a Christmas present to every child in one or perhaps two children's homes in New York. These were children who 'cannot have much fun, and there is no one to see they have a merry Christmas . . . It will be for them the 'Iris Cutting' Christmas . . . I am sure that there is nothing that your dead Daddy would like so much as to know that his little daughter was bringing light into the lives of others . . .' A tough and uncomfortable message for a child of barely nine.

By the summer of 1912, when Sybil set off first to Switzerland and then to America, her friendship with Berenson was such that she wrote him long, somewhat rambling letters (in handwriting almost as illegible as Iris's later became) about books, about the way he had 'opened' her eyes to art – and about her health. 'You see', she wrote to him from the RMS *Baltic* on her way to New York, having left Iris once again with the Desarts, 'I am taking you at your word and writing to you when I feel like talking . . .'

During their first years at I Tatti, while it was still rented, the Berensons had relied on their own ideas for improvements, and on the services of a local workman. The house had, and continued to have, no electricity or telephone, and only one bathroom. In 1907, with the house at last theirs, they decided the moment had come to plan it all rather better, and more comfortably. While they were installing electricity and a second bathroom, Mary argued, why not add an entire new kitchen wing, some more bedrooms and, above all, a proper library to house their growing collection of books and photographs? A local builder named Zanoni was taken on, and he brought with him his foreman, Ammannati.

A few years earlier, looking for suitable young men to accompany her two daughters, Ray and Karin Costelloe, on a motor trip around Tuscany, Mary had written to her sister Alys Russell asking for suggestions. Alys proposed Lytton Strachey, John Maynard Keynes and Geoffrey Scott, nephew of C. R. Scott, editor of the *Manchester Guardian*, who had not long since won the coveted Oxford Newdigate Prize for Poetry. Strachey refused, but Scott duly arrived from Pisa and its 'groggy tower' and Keynes from 'eating omelettes and discussing ethics and sodomy' with Strachey in Genoa.

The excursion was not altogether successful. First it poured with rain; then it snowed. The car broke down. But in the evenings the young people talked about philosophy and art, and when they got back to I Tatti the party went on. Mary wrote to her mother of her delight in finding for her daughters two nice, thoroughly intelligent boys who 'rouse all their intellectual ambitions and do not lead them into any nonsense'. But it was really Mary rather than her daughters who had become attracted, at least to Scott – Karin dismissed him as a 'quivering freak', maintaining that his sexual orientation was unclear and his hands trembled – though at this stage she placed him in her large category of lame ducks. Scott was just twenty-three, a pale, tall, thin young man with lank black hair brushed back from his forehead, and a pince-nez. He had very long legs, and Harold Acton thought he 'never looked quite clean'. Iris found his face ugly and his movements ungainly, but noted that his features were suddenly lit up by 'flashes of intelligence and laughter'. William Rothenstein, who had been invited to Settignano to paint Berenson's portrait, said that Scott looked strikingly like a Botticelli. He was certainly high-spirited, brilliant and very receptive to the culture and hedonism offered by I Tatti and its inhabitants; just how neurotic he was did not become clear until later.

Two of Mary's English friends, Edward and Mary Houghton, fringe members of The Souls, came to lunch soon after this Tuscan excursion, bringing with them a young English architect, Cecil Pinsent, to whom they were showing Italy. Mary remarked that he was good-looking 'in a frail sort of way' and that he seemed nice 'but not very exciting . . . we talked and talked and the boy listened in a kind of daze'. On a visit to London soon afterwards she introduced Pinsent to Scott. On the surface, at least, although they were the same age, the two could hardly have been more different: Scott was passionate about aesthetics, philosophy and literature, while the shy and solitary Pinsent professed to care more about cars and mechanics. Yet Scott, having missed his expected First at Oxford, and therefore any chance of a good Civil Service job, was now training as an architect. To her mother Mary complained that he had turned into a 'milk-coddling sort of person'.

By 1909 it was becoming clear that Zanoni and Ammannati were idle, and that their work at I Tatti was catastrophic. Edward Houghton proposed to the Berensons that they employ

Pinsent, who was now settled in Florence and working for a Harvard art collector friend of Berenson's, Charles Loeser, as well as designing a water parterre for Princess Ghyka at the Villa Gamberaia. Mary, increasingly captivated by Geoffrey Scott, proposed her protege, who had recently won the Chancellor's Prize with an essay on English architecture, as Pinsent's partner. For offices and a flat the young men, both now in their late twenties, rented two floors in the Via delle Terme by the Ponte della Trinita, from which, once one had climbed many flights of stairs, there were marvellous views over the roofs to the Duomo. While waiting for it to be ready, they moved into I Tatti and set to work. Mary called them the Artichokes, writing somewhat wistfully in her diary that the idea of 'love of that sort' with Scott was 'inconceivable . . . Literature has nothing but contempt for an old woman growing fond of boys.'

Their progress with the building was neither rapid nor smooth, however. Scott developed boils, as he often did when he was anxious, as well as lumbago and rheumatism; he preferred talking about his future to overseeing the work at I Tatti. He had excellent taste, but little energy generally and none at all at this time. The Firm, as the Scott–Pinsent partnership had been dubbed by the Anglo-Florentines, was now nicknamed the Infirm. Pinsent was conscientious, hardworking and an excellent draughtsman, but also highly impractical, unsure of his own taste or style, and could not control the workmen. To her family Mary wrote an evocative portrait of their two young employees. Pinsent, she observed, 'has strange periods of purposeless activity, when he will sit up all night to get a new sort of clip fastened onto his old piles of letters . . . These fits overtake him just when his clients' affairs have reached *le moment psychologique* when he can either finish things on time . . . or when, by delaying . . . he gives his clients the idea of disorder and inattention, enrages and despairs them . . . Geoffrey foresees everything that people will feel, he understands the psychological effect that will be produced . . . Cecil is a human eel-monkey and slips out of his grasp and chatters in a tree, so to speak.' Berenson, who was capable of terrifying fury – Mary called his uncontrollable rages at the mishaps of daily life his 'black serpent days' – understandably fumed when doors were discovered to have handles that would not turn, and the bills for the alterations rose to $100,000, more than three times what he had spent buying I Tatti and all its land. One day, according to Mary, he was so outraged by the Artichokes' inefficiency and overspending that hetold her he did not see how he could ever again 'recommend Cecil for any similar job except as a *pis-aller* to a swindling incompetent Italian'. Berenson was also jealous of Mary's undisguised attraction to Scott, even though he was himself in love with Belle de Costa Greene, John Pierpont Morgan's librarian. (Belle once remarked to Berenson that Mary was so large in size 'that she makes me feel uncomfortably like a weasel'.)

Not all exchanges between Berenson and the Artichokes were bitter, however, and there were days when he emerged to admire a newly finished corner of the house or progress on the library on which they all set such store. By 1911 the mood of disenchantment at I Tatti had been replaced by a sort of relieved surprise. The library was pronounced splendid, the new stairway 'graceful', and Scott's talents and classical education had come into their own as he furnished the new rooms, travelling to Milan, Paris and London in search of carpets and chairs. So much indeed had Berenson come to trust Scott's eye that he often encouraged him to say where he thought pictures should hang, and where sculptures would be best placed; for a while, Scott acted as Berenson's secretary. Edith Wharton, who arrived at about this time for the first of many visits to I Tatti, called the new library 'a bookworm's heaven'. The house was now extremely comfortable, with a wing of quiet rooms set a side for those who wished to spend their mornings working. Edith Wharton rapidly became a close friend of both Berensons, Mary remarking that she was 'more *our* sort than most people . . . a tempered New Englandism . . . She *is* heavy handed, but when you like her it becomes rather endearing' – as well as of Scott, with whom she would spend long evenings discussing literature and art, and laughing over gossip and stories.

Life at I Tatti now settled into a routine of steady work, pleasurable afternoon excursions to look at pictures, or to go for walks – the car would drive them into the hills and pick them up later from some designated spot four or five miles away – and a great deal of serious talk in the evenings with the many visitors. Berenson, wrote William Rothenstein, 'with his astonishing intellect, delighted in the play of ideas; he could illuminate regions, however remote; not of art only, but also of literature, philosophy, politics, history, ethics and psychology. And sometimes', he added, 'we gossiped . . .'

Sometimes, too, they played 'conoshing' (from the Italian *conoscere*, to know), a game that involved spreading some of the Berensons' vast collection of photographs of paintings on to a table; then all of a painting except one detail, like a cloak, or a face, would be masked with paper, and the game was to guess the artist. Mabel Dodge Luhan, who finally left Florence shortly before the First World War, remarked that there was always talk of paintings, and schools of art, and of Berenson's theory of 'tactile values' throughout the city: 'Everybody in Florence was like that. The life was built up around the productions of the dead.' Even Rothenstein, who enjoyed his time in Florence, had reservations about its intensity. 'The palatial rooms in which the scholar–aesthetes lived,' he wrote, 'their mauve Italian furniture, their primitives, bronzes, wood carvings and Venetian stuff which one was expected to appraise, wearied me . . . The atmosphere in these vast apartments seemed heavy with past intrigue.'

By now Scott and Pinsent, the main works to the house done, had turned their attentions to the gardens. Fifty acres of land had come with the house, given mainly to olives, vines and meadows. The Artichokes brought to their garden designs, as to their architectural plans, two very different sets of qualities. Pinsent, who had spent his early childhood on the rolling open pampas of Uruguay, and then at his uncle's house in the Midlands with a romantic folly made from the remains of clay pits, was practical and inventive; Scott, the Classical scholar, contributed a love of pure thought and a good grounding in literature. Both were knowledgeable about the recent history of gardening, and its current trends: the formal gardens of Edwardian England, the ornamental work of the Arts and Crafts movement, with its shrubs and old-fashioned flowers and enclosures created by trellises and pergolas, and the new-found love of nature and the rural life. They were agreed on the principle that gardens ought to be designed in close relation to the house, to be indeed an extension of the house itself; essentially this was a return to the ideas of Italian Renaissance gardens, which Scott and Pinsent, steered by Berenson and his friends, were just discovering. It was a time, too, of influential garden writing, such as that of George Sitwell, who in 1909 had written: 'If the world is to make great gardens again, we must both discover and apply in the changed circumstances of modern life the principles which guided the garden makers of the Renaissance . . .' Nearer to home, Berenson's friend Edith Wharton, herself a keen gardener, was extremely dismissive of what she called the 'flower-loveliness' – the herbaceous borders – introduced by so many of the Anglo-Florentines, and eager to educate garden makers in the magic of clipped green and stonework. Like Sitwell, she argued that it was important to adapt a garden to its surroundings, with 'an understanding of the gardener's purpose, and of the uses to which he meant his garden to be put'. One of these cross-currents would come something quite new, not a recreation of original Renaissance forms but, rather, a restoration in a 'historicising' style which combined elements of everything.

Of the two, Pinsent was the better gardener. Scott was said to have difficulty distinguishing between one plant and another. Though the virtually untouched acres surrounding I Tatti were something of a gardener's dream, the land had a problem common to many of Fiesole's gardens: it consisted for the most part of a steep, sloping hillside. It also came with a small enclosed lemon garden, a lemon house, and a number of old cypresses. Pinsent began by incorporating the lemon house into the new garden, carrying the main axis of his overall design through its tall doorways and down the steep hill; he terraced the hillside, building short flights of steps between the levels; on every terrace he planted symmetrical pairs of parterres, the box clipped low; at the bottom he put two lily ponds; he added rectangles of *ciottolato*, patterns made in coloured pebbles. What became known as the Green Garden had no flowers, no herbaceous borders with roses, irises, peonies or dahlias.

Apart from the problem of the steep slope, Pinsent had

the problem of Mary: Mary liked flowers, and she wanted to watch things grow, and blossom. She wished to have wisteria, honeysuckle, clematis and begonias. She loved gardenias, which she picked to put on her guests' breakfast trays. Behind Pinsent's back she consulted Janet Ross's niece's husband, Aubrey Waterfield, who was a painter and gardener. After some initial confusion, the two men agreed to carve out their own areas. Pinsent concentrated on his green garden, while Waterfield planted a meadow with narcissi, fritillaries and anemones and a walkway of wisteria. What role Berenson took in all this is not entirely clear, but his hand is probably to be seen in an avenue of three hundred ilexes leading down to a round pool, and in the line of cypresses that runs from the house to the gate at the bottom of the estate. At first he fumed uncomfortably about his new garden, but towards the end of his life admitted: 'Though I have travelled all over the world and seen many lovely places, I now feel all the beauty I need is my own garden.'

The many guests who came to lunch at I Tatti walked around the new gardens, looked closely at the terraces, the pools, the avenues of trees and the *limonaia*, and liked what they saw. The reputation of Pinsent and Scott as architects and gardeners with a particular style of their own which was nearly but not quite a revival of the Renaissance spread through the rich and design-conscious Anglo-Florentine world, and they were invited to consider other jobs. One of the first was the Villa Medici.

It was Pinsent rather than Scott who first helped Sybil with the Villa Medici, restoring the gardens to their original design and taking heron expeditions to buy furniture in Florence's many antique shops, or to call on the middlemen who acted for indigent Florentine noble families. Here, in the dark vaulted rooms of

Renaissance palazzo could be found rococo mirrors, gold picture frames, monastery tables, brocades, fragments of sculpture: *Americani con soldi* (Americans with money) made most desirable clients. The Villa Medici was soon exquisitely furnished: too much so, some considered, though all admired the *sala degli uccelli*, the 'room of birds', with its exquisite silk eighteenth-century Chinese wallpaper of scarlet parrots, pied finches, chanticleers, pheasants, magnolias, kingfishers and flycatchers against a yellow background of flowers and inter-woven boughs.

But Pinsent was also a keen planner of picnics and excursions – an almost daily activity during the spring and summer months – and Scott was an entertaining provider of local gossip, so the two young men were soon frequent visitors to the Villa Medici. Pinsent in particular, wrote Iris, was becoming one of her 'grown-up friends'. When they first met, she was nine and he in his late twenties. He teased her and drew cartoons about her life. One of them shows the two of them with Sybil, all three very thin and tall, standing shivering by the sea; another is a visual joke about Iris's difficulty with geometry and mathematics.

Florence was where Iris began to discover what Sybil was really like. While her earlier memories were all of a reclining figure in a distant drawing room, the portrait she later drew of her mother in the first years at the Villa Medici is a generous and affectionate one, remarkably little touched by exasperation or bitterness. What she first became aware of, as the two settled down to their new life in Fiesole, was her mother's intense vitality and 'infectious eagerness'. When Sybil was well, which on the whole she was at this time, she would rise purposefully from her bed, dress in brightly-coloured and extremely fashionable clothes, scarlet silk cloaks, heavy pleated silk Fortuny gowns, gossamer chiffon dresses and cashmere shawls, beside which Iris's own pinafores looked very dowdy, and prepare to go out. Wherever she went, she travelled in style: if by train, she took her own silk sheets, claiming that those on trains were invariably damp, and a maid, nearly always Doody, who immediately had the basin washed out with lavender water; if by car, she took a lavish picnic and all possible comforts, and wore a dust-coat. A popular outing was to Chianciano, a small town across the plain well known for its hot springs and waters, with a tall campanile perched on the hill above, and great grey walls. The fields that surrounded it were full of oak trees, and in the autumn the long-snouted, short-legged wiry pigs, looking rather more like greyhounds, were driven along the edge of the woods to rootle for cyclamen, known locally as *panporcini* or pigs' bread. Then there were the hot baths at Rapolano, known to be good for sciatica, and those at Bagni di Casciani above Pisa, with their strong stench of sulphur, for rheumatism. From time to time they drove to San Gimignano, Arezzo or Montepulciano for lunch.

These outings could be excruciatingly embarrassing for Iris. Out driving, if Sybil happened to catch sight of an interesting villa, she would instruct the chauffeur to turn in up the drive so that she could take a closer look, in total disregard of its owners or inhabitants. Iris later described a comic but evidently agonising scene in her autobiography. Setting off by train one day, Sybil suddenly exclaimed, 'Darling, I'm sure I smell a cigar. *Would* you mind explaining to the man – no, not in the next carriage, I think it must be three or four doors off – that I am very delicate . . .' In agonies of embarrassment Iris would find the smoker, who did not always turn out to be very agreeable about the message she bore, then hurry back to her compartment. A few minutes later, her mother would remark plaintively, 'Darling, I don't think you *can* have explained yourself properly. Would you call the conductor?' At such moments, as Iris recalled many years later, 'I wished that I were dead.'

On the other hand, Sybil's outings could also be magical, for she thrived on the exciting and the exotic, and thought nothing of spending hours searching out rare mosaics or crumbling frescos, or driving for miles down a long valley on dusty rutted tracks for the sake of a Roman bridge hidden in the undergrowth at the far end. 'It was at such times', Iris later wrote, 'that I knew . . . I was lucky to be with her.' And as Iris grew older Sybil took her further and further afield, to Sicily, Greece, Algeria and Tunisia, to see the Roman ruins. Invariably, travelling through some exotic place, Sybil would shed her invalidism and her insistence upon comfort, and think nothing of riding all day on a camel in search of some little-known site.

At home, there were also memorable times. Soon after they were settled in Sybil took to reading aloud to Iris in the *sala degli uccelli* in the afternoons after tea, Iris happily settled on the hearth rug. If she later felt she owed her satisfaction in tackling intellectual problems and her interest in ideas and people to her father, it was to her mother that she felt she owed her love of travel and of books.

Sybil was rich, and young, and lived in one of Fiesole's most spectacular villas. The Cuttings were soon caught up in the social round of excursions, At Homes and luncheon parties; not many of the Anglo-Florentines had cars, and it was easier to pay calls, whether by carriage or tram, in the daytime. Sybil decided she would receive at teatime on Sundays, saying privately that this was when she 'got done' her obligations. An efficient and admired hostess, she looked 'incredibly fragile and elegant in a capricious and original way', the precious stones on her rings unusually turned inwards, speaking very quickly in a 'twittering' voice. As Iris wrote later, she had a very slight lisp, a sort of roll on her *r*s and *l*s. The tea party would be split up into congenial groups, and Iris was often detailed to take visitors around the villa. Occasionally Vernon Lee would appear, and Iris found her tailored appearance and clever conversation daunting. Or there might be an old acquaintance of the Cuttings from New York, or perhaps a member of the English Bloomsbury group, on a tour of Tuscany – many of them, as Mabel Dodge Luhan noted, learnt and sophisticated women 'inclined, at the same time, to be emotional'. At this point Bloomsbury was not very admiring of the I Tatti circle; Virginia Woolf declared after a tea party there that it seemed to consist only of 'numbers of weak young men and old ladies arriving in four-wheelers', though she greatly admired the roses in Berenson's garden. Since Sybil was prone to sudden chills and viruses, the Sunday tea party was always an uncertain event, however, and even as a young child Iris was often on the telephone, putting people off or altering arrangements her mother had made. But recovery came quickly, at least in those early days, and Sybil would rise again from her bed, ready for a new excursion to some suspected treasure.

All over the hillsides of Fiesole, Settignano and Bellosguardo the foreigners met and gossiped and jealousies and rivalries simmered, particularly among those who considered themselves art experts. 'An atmosphere of Ouida lingered,' wrote Harold Acton later, 'and the Guelfs and the Ghibellines had been replaced by rival schools of art historians. Between Berenson, Home, Loeser and Perkins one never knew what fresh crisis had arisen. It must have been a difficult time for hostesses.'

On Sunday mornings the English met at the Anglican church

on Via La Marmora. From time to time one or other of the better established Anglo-Florentines, with a villa or a large apartment in a palazzo, would give a party, with charades and amateur theatricals. The *Ballet Russe* and Diaghilev's galas influenced all Europe, and fancy dress balls with tableaux vivants became the fashion. In Florence, in the Villa Schifanoia, a ball was held on the theme of the visit of the Shah of Persia to the Doge of Venice, combining Persian and Venetian costumes; Harold Acton's parents wore costumes designed from Persian miniatures. And when the tango took over Florence, some of the older children like Harold Acton and Iris were allowed to attend the tango-teas to which the English flocked. There were also teas for children, often given by people who had none of their own, like Janet Ross or Mary Berenson. Even Sybil gave a fancy dress party for children every year on May Day, at which snap-dragon featured: this game, usually played at Christmas, involved snatching raisins out of a dish of flaming brandy and eating them while still alight. Iris always remembered a party at I Tatti, when a group of shy and nervous children was hanging back from whatever entertainment had been laid on for them, and Mary stepped forward saying firmly: 'If a child performs the *gestures* of happiness, it becomes happy.' On such occasions one of Iris's most profound wishes was not to be confronted by Berenson, whom she found infinitely more alarming at I Tatti, in his immaculate pale grey suit, than when he was leaping about the rocks on a picnic. When later she learnt that some of the Florentine mothers had felt considerable sympathy for Iris over what they saw as a lonely and constricted childhood, she wrote that they had been wrong. Her childhood, she would say, had not been unhappy, even if it *had* been disconcerting 'in its swift alterations between excitement and tedium, between caviar and bread and milk'.

Not everyone either enjoyed or admired life in Florence in the years before 1914. In the many books about their Florentine villas and gardens, residents have left surprisingly bitter attacks on neighbours and friends, curious mixtures of fascination and revulsion. Mabel Dodge Luhan recalled how hard she had found it not to 'become embroiled in unending, bickering intrigues, take a side, be converted to the opposite side, carry tales, repeat secrets, constantly hear horrors about one's friends . . .' Few spoke out more sharply than an American critic, Harriet Waters Preston, who wrote of the frivolity, irresponsibility and meanness, 'moral and pecuniary', of the foreign colony, of 'its prostrate subservience to rank, and its pest of parasitic toadies and busybodies'.

Pinsent, still working on improvements to the Villa Medici while much caught up in its social life, wrote to Mary Berenson, 'I want nothing better than a compulsory occupation with a fringe of voluntary madness: the wish to get married is as far off, if not farther off than ever, in spite of (perhaps because of) the boiling atmosphere of love-making.' Among the protagonists in this boiling atmosphere was Sybil, whose friendship with Berenson, sometime in 1914, turned into an affair. For the moment, Mary was unperturbed. To a friend she wrote that she welcomed what she called a 'rather romantic friendship', on the grounds that it would finally get rid of Belle Greene. 'Sybil is *such* an improvement on that horrible creature! She is really an awfully nice person who can have nothing but a good influence on anyone who gets to know her.'

CHAPTER THREE

An unpleasant noise off-stage

Bayard had never wanted Iris to go to school, but in the autumn of 1914, Sybil enrolled her briefly at Miss Woolf's school in South Audley Street in London. Here she was discovered to be so advanced that she was put to study with girls three years older than herself; she was happy, and begged her mother to let her stay, but Sybil took her back to Fiesole and a series of French and German governesses. Her days, like those of many other privileged girls before the First World War, were largely spent upstairs at her lessons, or taking healthy walks in the lanes and paths that led up and down from Fiesole's main square. An American visitor to a nearby villa later recalled looking across to the terrace of the Villa Medici, watching a young girl playing and thinking how lonely and unhappy she looked. Apart from her hour's reading with her mother in the *sala degli uccelli* after tea, they also lunched together in the dining room, but meals were no more enjoyable or festive than the dull routine of lessons. Sybil, often ill or on the verge of becoming ill, kept to a plain and monotonous diet, and expected Iris to follow it too, even on the rare occasions when she was asked to one of the foreign colony's children's tea parties, and was forced to watch the other children eating ice cream. To escape the tedium of her mostly rather silent and low-spirited governesses, Iris escaped whenever she could to the wilder corners of the Villa Medici's gardens, where steep terraces of ilex gave way to plots of vegetables clinging to the hillside, and where, like Mabel Dodge Luhan, she would smell the particular odour of an Italian garden, of damp, rotting leaves and dry cypress and box. On wet days, or during breaks in her lessons, she began to try her hand at writing stories and poems. In England at the age of ten she had won 10s. 6d. for an essay submitted to a competition in the children's paper *Little Folks* and experienced a 'moment of as pure and unalloyed pleasure as has ever come to me out of an envelope'. During her years growing up at the Villa Medici Iris produced a translation of Leopardi's poems, and an account of the lives of the Medici children. And despite her grandmother's dire warning about running out of books, she spent many hours every day reading. Later she quoted Rumer Godden's words: 'When you learn to read you will be born again . . . and you will never be quite so alone again.'

Berenson was now a constant figure in their lives. Occasionally Iris would be asked to accompany Sybil and him on one of their many excursions, and it was he who brought about a delightful change in her life. All children, he told Sybil, should be given a proper classical education. He recommended a short, myopic and scholarly man in Florence, and it was with Professor Solone Monti that Iris spent what she later recalled as the 'happiest hours of my childhood – perhaps the happiest I have ever known'. Iris was forever grateful to Berenson: long after she had forgotten the texts themselves, she remembered the pleasure and excitement of the actual process of learning, and what it gave her: 'a love of study and poetry that have never left me'. By nature and upbringing biddable and law-abiding, she needed people to look up to, and, unlike her governesses, Monti was someone for whom she soon felt complete respect. At their first lesson, he did no more than read to her from Pascoli's *Epos*, and Tennyson, on the Trojan wars.

As for Monti, the education of Iris Cutting gave him the chance to experiment with his long-cherished dream of getting away from the straitjacket of conventional schooling by teaching Greek and Latin together as living languages to someone who knew nothing of either, rather along the lines of the Humanist education given to Cecilia Gonzaga and her brother in Mantua by Vittorino de Feltre in the fifteenth century. During their lessons they would read texts aloud and discuss them as Monti seized first one book and then another from his crowded shelves. The grammar Iris was meant to work at on her own, at home or on the slow tram that took her down the hill to Fiesole. Each lesson ended with a 'surprise', a few perfect lines for her to carry back with her in her mind as she went home. Her imagination, Iris later wrote, was completely overtaken by the magical world that Monti conjured up for her with such intensity.

Neither Iris nor her mother, who found them intensely boring, cared for the governesses, and the governesses cared little for Sybil, whose exotic life and clothes they envied while resenting her lack of interest in them or their lives. Iris therefore met with little resistance when, her three afternoons each week with Monti settled, she argued that she no longer needed a full-time governess, particularly as there were teachers in Florence with whom she could have private lessons in other subjects. Sybil agreed, and soon Signora Signorini was coming to the Villa Medici twice a week to give Iris Italian lessons. From time to time, on a Saturday afternoon, the Signora, who was supporting two daughters much the same age as Iris, as well as an acutely depressed husband, brought her daughters to the villa with her. The girls' modesty and natural good manners, and their mother's 'deep family affection and sense of duty' and her 'dignity of self-effacement', made a deep impression on Iris, who in retrospect saw herself as confused by the life around her, 'a child living in a world too sophisticated for it, too varied, too rich'. Sometimes, she wrote later, the memory of Signora Signorini and her daughters 'made the life of luxury a little thin'.

In the early summer of 1914 Sybil and Iris were in London, where they went to see Nijinsky dance at Covent Garden and took seats for *The Merchant of Venice* at the Royal Victoria Hall, the 'Old Vic'. For the first time, Iris wrote, 'beauty and delight reached me through my eyes and not through a book'. Despite the advice of friends, Sybil and Iris sailed for America on 2 August, to visit the Cuttings at Westbrook. On 4 August all the passengers were summoned to the main saloon, where the Captain announced that England was at war. They docked in New York, and Sybil booked passages on the next boat back to Europe, despite the entreaties of the Cuttings. As it turned out, theirs was the last to carry civilians.

They returned to Florence after Christmas 1914 to find a mood of extreme uncertainty: people were divided not only over whether Italy should enter the war at all, but also as to which side she should support if she did. Businessmen and financiers grown rich through German backing – most of the capital in the Banca Commerciale Italiana which owned much of Italy's steel industry, for example, was Austrian and German – tended to hold that Italy should remain neutral, though their sympathies clearly lay with the Germans. The early years of the twentieth century in Italy had been marked by increasing German and

Austrian influence in philosophy, literature and the sciences. The Socialists opposed war in any circumstances, as did the former prime minister Giolitti, who still had a strong voice in Italian life. The Vatican favoured Catholic Austria and opposed Orthodox Russia. More importantly, perhaps, the Italian political world was disorganised, lacking coherent policies, and corrupt, while the country as a whole was lawless – and brigandage still common in the south.

For a while the daily routine of the Anglo-Florentines continued almost unchanged. Pinsent was hard at work building the Villa LeBaize for the American art critic Charles Strong, whose father had made a fortune with a large Boston department store and whose wife had died in 1906, leaving him with a nine-year-old daughter, Margaret. Le Baize stood just across the road from the Villa Medici, and its construction was an extraordinary feat of engineering. The land Strong had bought consisted of an almost sheer hillside, so that terracing and supporting walls entailing about 1200 tonnes of new earth had to be constructed before work on the villa itself could begin. Freed from Berenson's occasional terrifying tantrums and Mary's obsession with brightly coloured flowers, Pinsent now had his first real opportunity to explore fully his ideas about houses and gardens and their relationship to one another, and he made the most of the narrow strip of land, creating shadows and distant prospects around seven formal gardens. He also designed a secret garden, and a grotto with the busts of Aristotle, Socrates, Demosthenes, Zeus and, in a pedimented niche, Venus. Scott meanwhile was deep in writing a book he hoped would make its readers question the ways in which they had previously perceived architectural design.

As the months passed, so the Italians came to feel that it

was wrong and undignified not to intervene in the conflict, and that their continuing neutrality looked more like cowardice. On 24 May 1915 Italy declared war on Austria, prompted in part by the radicals and the republicans and in the wake of a secret treaty with Britain and her allies which embodied generous promises of Austrian territory and a zone of influence in Asia Minor. The first Italian soldiers were put onto a war footing. In August Italy declared war on Germany. Though there was now considerable anxiety among the two thousand or so Germans living in or around Florence, the life of the British community was still barely upset. Extra locks were put on doors and gates, and some families dithered about whether they should stay or go, and what to take with them if they went; but for the most part the foreigners simply became more closely entwined, sharing their supplies of jam, going to each other's houses, and doing their best to counter the panicky tone of the Italian newspapers, with their tendency to report every frightening war rumour as fact. In November Sybil organised a 'Dramatic & Musical Entertainment' at the Villa Medici in aid of the British Red Cross. Iris wrote a play for it called *The Princess's Supper*, in which she played the princess and Maria Louise Bourbon del Monte the cobbler's boy. This was followed by a one-act drama, *The Kings Messenger*, with Cecil Pinsent in the title role. The performance ended with a rousing 'God Save the King.' Now that no more money could be sent from England, Scott and Pinsent, who had to juggle the funding of their various architectural commitments, went on working at I Tatti, the Villa Medici and the Villa Le Baize. They searched the city for bridge and poker players, and rented a piano for their flat in Via delle Terme so that Nesta de Robeck, who played Bach with 'great energy and enjoyment', could come and give musical soirees.

Nesta, an Anglo-Irish woman with remarkable lavender blue eyes, had been settled in Florence for many years. She was teaching Iris the piano and had become, after Pinsent, her other 'close grown-up friend' – having got over feeling intimidated by Sybil's own soirees at the Villa Medici at which she was 'magnificent in white' and her guests ate off Venetian glass. Janet Ross, who stayed on in Florence throughout the war, often asked Sybil and Iris to Poggio Gherardo, and occasionally they would look in through the gates of the Villa Gamberaia on their way there, Iris hoping to catch a glimpse of the fabled Princess Ghyka who, her beauty gone, had become a recluse inside her magnificent villa.

In these early wartime summers Sybil continued to rent villas by the sea, to which she invited the Berensons, Pinsent and Scott, Nesta de Robeck and any other congenial friend who had not fled the city. Mornings were spent swimming and lying on the rocks, afternoons sleeping. In the evenings they all took a hand at bezique, while Nesta played Bach. Among Iris's papers is a scrapbook, the first entries dated 15 August 1916, her fourteenth birthday, at Marina di Massa; most likely the album was a birthday present. Iris must have asked her mother's guests to contribute to it, for Scott has sketched a man sitting on a beach with a pipe, his head in his hands, desperate for ideas, while a stern young girl with long straight hair and a quill and pot of ink in her hand stands over him, above a rueful poem about inspiration. Pinsent has drawn several pages of cartoons, one showing Iris reading aloud from a book to Sybil who is lying prone on a sofa, another with her coming adrift in a canoe as a result of trying too hard to calculate the mathematical properties of the waves. But the most revealing and somewhat cruel entry is Berenson's. 'What a nuisance!' he has written simply, with a large scrawling flourish, signing it 'B. B.'

Before travel across Europe closed down completely, the Cuttings received a visit from Irene Lawley and her mother, Aunt 'Concon', Lady Desart's elder sister. Evidently a wise woman, and much admired, Lady Wenlock was growing increasingly deaf, and had taken to carrying around with her an ear trumpet, trimmed with lace to match the colour of her dresses. Despite the difference in their ages Irene was obviously very fond of her young cousin and in the years to come they kept up a steady and intimate correspondence. Her visits to Fiesole changed Iris's life: energetic and good-humoured, she planned moonlight picnics and invited young men to the villa. There is something decidedly wistful in a letter of Sybil's to Lady Wenlock about the fact that Irene had not yet found a husband: 'It seems as if she had not met her fate yet. It seems odd to me, for I find it so hard not to be in love and her difficulty is all the other way . . .'

It was to Irene that Iris wrote in October 1916 about the six boy scouts she had just taken charge of, and how she was getting their uniforms together, and asking her to send out a 'decent girl's paper, with competitions . . . I don't care how silly the stories and articles are, if there are only some decent literary articles.' A few months later she reported that she had a founded a 'Cosmopolitan, Literary, Artistic and Dramatic Society, whose members are called clads . . .' Seven girls aged between ten and sixteen met once a fortnight, bringing with them contributions for a magazine which was to appear three times a year. The girls staged charades and plays, and held musical evenings at which Nesta played the piano. Lively and unselfconscious, these letters to Irene suggest that Iris's life had become somewhat less lonely. Iris, wrote Sybil to Lady Wenlock, 'to whom typing, motor driving and such like come as a matter of course', now generally took possession of her typewriter.

Even before the outbreak of war Lord Desart had been in the habit of writing regularly to Iris with news of her English family, evidently determined not to lose touch with her. Remarkably, the letters continued to arrive all through the war, and though many were subsequently lost, those that remain are extremely affectionate, almost like diary entries, written more as to a friend than a child. Photographs must occasionally have been posted to him, for in November 1916 Lord Desart wrote, 'Oh my dear Iris, why are you getting so tall? I don't know what I shall make of a giant Iris.' Always he was concerned that she should fully understand the importance of the times she was living through, times he considered exceptional for the 'magnitude of the struggle between the forces of right and wrong'.

The winter of 1916 to 1917 also delivered Iris a terrible blow: influenza, which was just reaching Florence and would soon overrun many parts of the world, taking more lives than the war itself, carried off Professor Monti, leaving her bereft not only of the lessons in the Classics on which she had come to rely but also of a man she greatly admired. Though Sybil in due course found her a replacement, it was not the same: only Monti had seen how captivating it was to read and learn the poetry first, and master the grammar later, and his loss left Iris wondering forever afterwards whether, had he lived, she might have become a classical scholar, or perhaps an archaeologist. She described Monti later as 'the best teacher and the most charming companion I have ever known'.

As the months passed, and the war went on, many of the English residents began to leave Florence. Vernon Lee, who had become a pacifist, went back to England. Those who stayed behind organised fundraising events for the Red Cross: one which somehow incorporated Dionysus and the Muses was described by Harold Acton as a 'blend of cosmopolitan parochialism and unselfconscious elegance peculiarly Florentine'. The few long-term residents who remained continued with their outings to see pictures or sites, much enjoying the absence of tourists, while the art historians pursued their researches in libraries and archives wonderfully empty of people. For them, Iris wrote later, 'the war was only a distant rumble, an inconvenient and unpleasant noise offstage'. 'Only the I Tatti party left of our friends here,' she wrote to Irene. 'And that's not much use to me!' Indeed, the war had further elevated the social tone of the city, bringing as it did a number of royal refugees, such as Prince Paul of Serbia and various members of the Greek royal family.

Scott's book, *The Architecture of Humanism*, published in 1914, had been greeted by critics as the single most important work on architecture since Ruskin's *The Stones of Venice*, for the clarity with which it laid down architectural principles, and because it introduced Continental ideas about architecture to English circles largely ignorant about them; for some of its readers, the Baroque suddenly became fashionable. At the Villa Medici Sybil started work on an anthology about the sea, originally planned in the course of one of those long summers by the beach with the Berensons, Scott and Pinsent, and intended as a tribute to the seamen of the merchant navy. Iris did much of the copying out; she also contributed some entries of her own, in French and Italian, and enjoyed the extra hours it gave her with her mother, working in the *sala degli uccelli*. The anthology was published by the Oxford Clarendon Press in 1918 with a rousing foreword by Lord Desart, who praised the heroism of those 'hardy watchmen of the sea'. It was not Sybil's only contribution to literature: she subsequently wrote a lively autobiography, *The Crystal in the Glass*, a travel book about

Egypt, Palestine and Syria, and a collection of fairy tales heard in her childhood, dedicated to Iris; but few people remember them now.

After the Gallipoli campaign of 1915 to 1916 Sybil wrote to the Red Cross offering to take in convalescent officers: there was some competition between expatriate families to put them up. Wounded and recovering young Britons, New Zealanders and Australians arriving in batches of twenty or twenty-five were divided between the Villa Medici, the Villa Le Baize, I Tatti and the Actons' house, La Pietra. Iris, who had looked forward to their arrival, found them in low spirits, suffering from dysentery and gastritis, and quickly bored. Few were interested in the Villa Medici's high-minded talk, and those who could were apt to escape by tram down into Florence, in search of Italian girls who were not too closely chaperoned. Iris, describing their officer guests to Irene as 'varied: mixed seeds but none of them chilling', was very stern about the way none of them seemed to want to go sight-seeing.

At this point Sybil was receiving a visit from Berenson every afternoon, and she dined with him twice a week. Ill in bed one day with colitis, she wrote to Lady Wenlock: 'I find that since my illness I don't think much of the wounded in the thousands of hospitals all over the world with the least the same vividness and constancy that I did before . . . It seems as if one's mind was antiseptic in a way . . . The whole thing is on too vast a scale now . . .' Whether she was really quite as self-absorbed as she sounds is hard to say. Mary Berenson, who had taken a number of convalescent officers into her *villinu*, a small house attached to I Tatti and sometimes used for guests, complained that they were drinking a great deal of Berenson's whisky. She was becoming increasingly irritated by Sybil, and had been staying in Paris with Edith Wharton, who evidently shared her feelings. As she wrote to Scott, 'We feel exactly the same about her, though I try harder than she does to like her, and I know that her illness isn't hysterical exhibitionism, which is Edith's view.' Life at I Tatti had become somewhat like a scene from *Les Liaisons Dangereuses*, with Berenson constantly away and embarking on new amorous attachments, Mary coming and going to ensure the safety of the house, and Scott falling in love with one person after another and longing to find a wife, each meanwhile writing to the others of their adventures and their feelings. For a middle-aged woman whose life had in many ways become ghastly – what with her crumbling looks and increasing weight, her painful cystitis and urinary infections, and having to live in the shadow of an unfaithful, vain and self-obsessed man everywhere revered for his brilliance and expertise – Mary displayed courage, and a certain bravura. She was now desperate that Scott should marry someone she liked, and urged him to think of Nicky Mariano, daughter of a Neapolitan intellectual and a Balkan aristocrat, who had been brought up to I Tatti one day and shown round by Scott, but was now trapped in the Baltic states by the war. Pinsent, meanwhile, had joined a Red Cross unit in Verona, travelling around with an ambulance and X-ray equipment, and Scott had found himself a job with the British Embassy in Rome, as honorary attache and later press secretary to the ambassador, Sir James Rennell Rodd.

By the autumn of 1917 all the male servants in the villas had long since been called up, and those landowners who, like Janet Ross, depended on their farms for their income had to rely on old men, young boys, and women. Florentine restaurants were illegally serving cat, and one proprietor discovered to be fattening seventeen likely specimens in his cellar was fined. The weather was terrible. It rained, and it went on raining until January 1918, when the rain turned to snow; all fuel supplies were severely rationed, and the cold was intense. Flour, butter and sugar were already scarce and expensive, but food generally became scarcer when refugees from a series of earthquakes in the north began to reach Tuscany, and scarcer still after the Italian defeat by the Austrians reinforced by the Germans at Caporetto at the end of October 1917, which forced their withdrawal to a new line on the river Piave. In November there were about 9,000 refugees in and around Florence; by December there were 20,000, most of them hungry and without winter clothes. Janet Ross, who early on had sacrificed her golden pheasants for food and let the orchids die in greenhouses she could no longer keep warm, set up a refugee committee and appealed for money in a letter to *The Times*. Iris, who could still just remember collecting clothes for the Messina earthquake in the winter of 1908, was pleased to find that at last there was something she could do to help. Taking the car and chauffeur, she made the rounds of the villas belonging to foreign residents asking for donations of clothes and blankets, which she delivered to her natural history teacher, Professor Vaccari, himself from the Veneto, who was much involved with the refugees. Vaccari took Iris with him when he went to meet the refugee trains arriving at Florence station, and they handed out the clothes. Iris also persuaded Sybil to let a refugee family move into the top floor of the gardener's house in the grounds of the Villa Medici.

There remained considerable uncertainty, among both educated Florentines and the young Italian recruits whose songs and stamping feet Iris sometimes awoke to at the Villa Medici in the early hours, about why Italy had entered the war at all. 'The feeling against the Signori is acute all over

Italy,' Janet Ross wrote to Mary Berenson as she set about organising a series of lectures on various aspects of Allied policy, and helping to form a 'British-Italian Relations in Tuscany' society and an Anglo-Italian society, with a library. As they had donated clothes for refugees, so the foreigners ransacked their villa libraries for suitable English books.

Mary Berenson, having spent the autumn of 1917 in London, returned to find Geoffrey Scott on the point of becoming engaged to Sybil, despite having told her not so very long before, as she remembered all too clearly, that Sybil reminded him of a cicada, 'no body or inside but all voice'. Trying to appear pleased, she remarked that Sybil was 'so definite in her standards that he will be immediately braced up'. Her equanimity did not last. '*Dentro di me* (Inside me),' she wrote to Berenson in December, 'I feel a natural movement of disgust that *both* my men should have been snatched away by that chatterbox.' By January she was miserable. 'I confess that having got rid of Sybil is a great help to me – and I dare say thee will say the same about my getting my Penguin, Geoffrey, off my feet – although I do not think thee loathed him as I always have Sybil.' To Scott she now sent letter after letter in which she rehearsed Sybil's defects of hypochondria and self-obsession, adding uncharitably that a masseuse they shared once said 'Wait until you see her naked'. Not all her letters were malicious, however; some are most forlorn. 'I know no active and effective way of dealing with what seems to turn life into a desert where nothing matters particularly,' she wrote to him on 19 January 1918. Edith Wharton wrote to Berenson that she 'shrank to an inarticulate squeak – so overwhelmed was I by Geoffrey's news'. Having 'practised liking it for twenty-four hours', she felt 'obliged [to say] that the results aren't promising'. The more she went on thinking about it, the less she liked it. She had long objected to Sybil's voice and the way it rose higher and higher until it became 'just like the whizzing of an electric fan', while she admired Scott's *The Archicture of Humanism* greatly. To Berenson she now wrote: 'I hardly ever saw Geoffrey, but some subtle link of understanding on most subjects bound us together with hooks of steel, and never again to see him except encircled by that well meaning waste of intelligence; oh, dear – *enfin "C'est la guerre".*'

How much of all this irritation and disapproval was known to Sybil is not clear, but she seems to have dealt quite calmly with the hostility blowing across the valley from I Tatti. Nicky Mariano said later of her that, contrary to what nearly everyone supposed, Sybil had a strong, even manly side to her character, 'and whoever had had the chance of getting to know that side of her would never forget it'. To Berenson, soon afterwards, Sybil herself wrote: '. . . now you know, and we can have our friendship, a little changed, of course, but so very dear and vital still.'

In that vast and presumably very cold villa, now that there was no fuel for heating, Sybil must have been lonely and preoccupied about the future. She was nearly forty and often unwell; Iris, almost sixteen, would not be at home for much longer. During a long and ill-judged meeting she hoped would regain her Mary's friendship but at which she only maddened Mary by talking incessantly about herself, Sybil commented that at least Scott was not, as Bayard had been, 'subject to depression'. Mary was quick to contradict her. Years later, in her autobiography, Iris commented on her mother's marriage with exemplary restraint. 'I watched her become so much younger

79

and so much more vulnerable . . .' she wrote, but 'My instinct told me the choice was not wise . . .' – not least because Scott's moods him so hard to live with. About her mother's moods, and her increasing ill-health, she said nothing. In fact Iris was fond of Scott, even if his excellent mimicry of the Anglican canon who prepared her for confirmation had done nothing to help her find the faith and enlightenment the example of her devout churchgoing grandmother had caused her to long for. With the engagement announced, Scott now visited the Villa Medici every weekend from his job in Rome, and Iris soon felt herself very much the 'unwelcome third' on their picnics and excursions. She felt not jealous but lonely, and longed for a life of her own.

Such was the weight of antagonism towards the marriage that Scott himself now fell ill, with a recurrence of the boils that plagued him in times of anxiety. Yet he and Sybil did marry, at the end of April 1918; because they were both so unwell, they took their short honeymoon in the Villa Medici, before Scott returned to his job in Rome. Observing her newlywed mother, Iris reflected that her childhood was over but that she was not yet a grown-up either.

CHAPTER FOUR

Launched

Iris and Sybil were on Capri when the mayor emerged in his tricolour sash, the bells rang out from all the churches, and the Armistice was proclaimed. It was 4 November 1918, a week before the announcement was made in England. Rejoicing was muted, as Capri was one of the places hardest hit by the Spanish 'flu which swept through Italy that autumn, closing schools and cinemas and killing thousands. In Capri, with its little white houses built one close upon another, there was hardly a family untouched by the virus; Iris watched it 'spread like the plague in the Middle Ages' and observed with admiration the way Dr Axel Munthe, a Swedish physician who had retired to the island, and later wrote *The Story of San Michele*, went tirelessly from house to house doing what little he could. Never one to escape a possible indisposition, Sybil took to her bed; but what was at first diagnosed as typhoid turned out to be a mild case of the 'flu everyone else had.

Iris was nearly seventeen: with the war over and Sybil married to Scott, the time had come to launch her in society. For Sybil this posed few problems, beyond summoning the energy to hold a coming-out ball at the Villa Medici. For Iris, shy and entirely unsure about where she belonged, the prospect was terrifying, not least because her English and American grandmothers had decided she must also 'come out' in London and New York as well as Florence. It might all have been expressly designed to emphasise her sense of statelessness. What made everything worse was that she convinced herself, with the help of her mirror, that she was spotty, with a too-large mouth, unattractively mouse-coloured hair, and a decidedly plump figure. About some of this she was, in fact, right: she was indeed on the plump side, and it was some years before she grew thinner and discovered her own style, elegant and perfectly turned-out. Perhaps because of the attitude towards beauty fostered at I Tatti, she had been conscious as she grew up of a feeling of revulsion towards ugliness, rather like Janet Ross's, and a corresponding appreciation of people who were beautiful. All through her adolescence she made careful notes of the physical types she thought most attractive and appealing among the young girls she met and played with. There were three Russian sisters, as she wrote later, 'lissom and slim as ballet dancers with large almond shaped eyes, [and] long pigtails of glossy chestnut coloured hair', who seemed to her the very models of beauty. Now she was on the brink of being launched into competition with the best-looking and most marriageable girls in not one but three countries; briefly she wondered whether she might at the very least be considered *jolte-laide*, but concluded sadly that she was simply plain. 'At thirty', she unfortunately overheard Scott say to Sybil, 'she may be quite attractive.'

It had been decided to open the social round in Florence, where Iris at least knew some of the other young girls, with names like Frescobaldi and Ricasoli, and whose families lived in palaces with frescos by Ghirlandaio or Filippino Lippi and owned vast estates in Chianti. As Mary Berenson observed, 'You could see all the palaces – the Strozzi, Pandolfini, Ridolfi, Guicciardini, Rucellai, Torrigiani, Corsini, etc., suddenly taken on human shape, as it were, and appear in a solemn quadrille.' But while these girls had been every bit as dumpy, giggly and appallingly dressed as herself at the wartime tea parties, Iris now discovered them to have undergone some sudden and miraculous transformation, not only of their dress – hers remained, she felt, somehow not quite right, for all Sybil's rather casual attempts to make her elegant – but of their manner, so that while she stumbled gawkily before the elderly matriarchs who sat on their little gilt chairs observing the coming-out dances, they seemed to know as if by instinct how to behave in a graceful and becoming way. The only ball she actually enjoyed was her own. It was June, and the Villa Medici, under a full moon, was lit by Japanese lanterns cleverly concealed by Pinsent in the trees. There were fireflies, and the jasmine and roses were out. She even felt properly dressed, a stylish couturier having made her ball-dress, and her mouse-coloured hair had been put up in a way even she found becoming. Between balls she read Browning aloud with Sybil, played Bach with Nesta, and observed in a letter to Irene that marriages between the young in Florence were spoken of 'as an alliance between cities rather than a marriage of individuals'. Though there was no question on her side of a romantic attachment, one young Englishman, Gordon Waterfield, whose mother Lina was Janet Ross's niece and who knew Iris from childhood tea parties at the Villa Medici, was much taken by her.

It had been decided to make the second season the English one. Lord Desart, who had been longing to see her again, wrote of his fear that she would no longer find him 'the amiable elderly relation' of earlier times: 'I shall have lost the child I loved so well, but perhaps find the young woman I shall love even better . . . It is the intolerance of the young and the want of sympathy of the old that produces much unnecessary unhappiness in family life, and I trust we may avoid it.' Desart was gloomy, 'almost despairing', about Ireland, sure now that any chance of reconciliation between the English and the Irish was over, and the 'complete apathy in England adds to one's despair'. About Iris he need not have feared: their meeting after the long years of separation was very warm, and they grew ever closer in the coming years, with Desart providing at least some of the affection she longed for and felt she had lost with her father, while he evidently recognised in her certain qualities that mattered to him. In a perceptive letter early in 1921 he wrote to her from Rutland Gate: 'I do not want to pay compliments, but I think you have got from some hereditary source balance and practical common sense which will help you through difficulties, and the sympathy which will enable you to understand and to see the views of others, even though you may not always be able to accept them.'

Soon Iris found herself at a hunt ball in Dorset – the daughter of the house had once visited the Villa Medici. It was the first of many miserable social events at which she invariably felt her clothes to be wrong and her conversation inappropriate. Because her aunt, Lady Joan Verney, was now a Lady-in-Waiting to the Queen, Iris's season was conducted in great style. Only occasionally did she allow herself to reflect on how truly bored she felt, and how the England she had dreamt of – the England of her grandfather's letters and of her books – was not the England she now encountered. 'I must admit', she wrote to Irene, the confidante of her three seasons, 'that the average Englishman struck me as *much* duller, though doubtless more estimable, than the equivalent Italian, besides dancing rather badly . . . I liked the freaks I met and what Aunt Joan calls 'middle class society', while *hating* the suitable friends' introduced to her by the family. Her best times were those spend with her cousins, particularly Ulick, whom she described as irresponsible and light-hearted, with a winning smile, and with whom, despite the fact that they had nothing in common, she used to 'rag ceaselessly'. Ulick always remained a friend, as did another cousin, Charlie Meade, met at about this time, whose wife Aileen would become the closest and most intimate of all her English friends. Aileen was the person to whom she confided her secrets, with whom she laughed most freely and played Mozart duets on the piano, saying to each other, usually while giggling loudly, *'rendezvous au bas de la page'*. Aileen much enjoyed spending her mornings in bed, gossiping and laughing, surrounded by novels, dogs, a telephone, and visitors who came to talk to her.

In the autumn of 1920 she faced her third coming-out ordeal. Iris had visited her grandmother at Westbrook briefly in 1919, when she was barely seventeen, crossing the Atlantic alone with a maid, and was then very conscious of the rift between Sybil and the Cuttings. Her social debut in New York was conducted with great panache – it started with visits to various dressmakers, for her grandmother, after a quick inspection of her wardrobe, decided Iris must be outfitted from scratch – but Iris knew no one among the American young. The days in New York were crammed and exhausting: a debutante's 'girlish' lunch, a matinee, a dinner party and two or three balls every night. Popular girls were constantly on their feet, as swains cut in; the unsought-after remained 'mercilessly linked' to their partners, 'like two figures in Dante's inferno'. It was a world of 'chocolate boxes and rosebuds and sweet young girls and chivalrous young Americans', she wrote to Irene. 'But oh! I hunger for Italy, and leisure, and inefficiency, and un-stodginess and some "goats" mixed up among the "sheep".' Already she was acquiring a delight in words, and an unmistakable talent for the quick pen portrait; one young man to whom she was introduced, Chester Aldwick, looked like a 'very friendly intelligent squirrel', while another, Edgar Wells, was 'like a romantic pugilist – he has the brow of a poet and the chin of a boxer . . .' Describing a dinner party she wrote: 'The animals went in twenty by twenty – Good gracious said Noah, that's plenty, that's plenty. At how many New York dinner parties have I not felt like that!'

Iris's happiest moments were spent in her grandmother's box at the Metropolitan Opera, or at Westbrook on Long Island, where she had grown fond of her aunt Justine, who taught Gregorian chant at Catholic schools, and her uncle Bronson, now a Republican Senator for New Mexico, with whom she played Handel and Bach duets on the piano. Justine and Bronson shared something that appealed to her enormously, a delight in the ridiculous, and this even though the Cuttings had been beset by ill-health. Both Bronson and Olivia, Iris's other aunt, had contracted but shaken off tuberculosis, while her grandfather had not long survived the misery of Bayard's death, carried off within two years by heart disease and gout. Like the Villa Medici, Westbrook, with its butler and footmen, its exquisite china and glass, was ruled by a constant preoccupation with health, only here, rather than Sybil's Spartan diet, rich food and creamy milk were the nature of the regime, with morning walks and long afternoon rests. For someone like Iris, regretting her interrupted education, Justine provided a comforting ear: very musical, she had suffered acutely from her parents' unquestioning assumption that 'having a child that was musical was like having an epileptic in the family or a hunchback'.

America provided at least one other enjoyable interlude. One evening, at a dinner party in New York, Iris sat next to a young diplomat on his first posting called Arthur Yencken. He impressed her by telling her of the MC he had won in the war, though he would not tell her what for, claiming that it had been awarded as much for his comrades as for himself. She confided to him what a lonely time she was having among the debutantes, and he gave a dinner for her with some friends when she visited Washington. In a letter written in 1986, not long before she died, Iris described her meetings with Yencken to his son David. 'It was driving back from it [the dinner party] on a beautiful moonlit night, that I suddenly realised that I was falling in love, and asked your father not to drive me straight back to my aunt's house but to drive down first to the lake. At this point I think he thought (great mistake) that I wanted him to make love to me, but when he saw how surprised and alarmed I was by his first attempt to kiss me, said briskly: "Time to go home now".' Next day they went on a picnic, 'a very happy, completely innocent day', talking about Australia – where he had grown up – and Italy. They met again several times in New York, before she sailed home to Europe.

Years later, looking back on her three seasons, Iris felt they had brought out sides to her character that she did not like, such as a striving for prizes she did not really want to win; and that vanity and a lack of self-confidence had deflected her from what should have been her natural course – a degree at Oxford. More immediately, she felt enormous relief on reaching Florence again. 'The sky is blue,' she wrote to Irene, 'the garden full of snowdrops, violets and daffodils, the hill-side covered with fruit blossoms, the *sala degli uccelli* still has its painted birds and lacquer furniture; books, *real* books, are still read and talked about; the houses are made of stone or stucco instead of wood or steel; God has taken some trouble over the shape of the hills, and man over that of the gardens . . .'

It was said that of the five million men the Italians claimed to have had under arms in 1915, nearly a seventh, 700,000, were dead by the end of the war. If the negotiations at Versailles did yield Italy the promised territorial gains of a frontier on the Alps, Trieste, and a few colonial outposts, they also generated profound discontent. The war was estimated to have cost Italy 148 billion lire, twice the entire government expenditure for all the years between 1861 and 1913; and once the Allies stopped providing food, the country was reduced to a state of complete economic collapse. Italian politicians appeared to be helpless in the face of the widespread mood of exhaustion and bankruptcy. The lira was devalued, inflation went out of control, and with demobilisation came high unemployment, banditry, and mounting debts. Florence alone was reported to owe 20 million lire and to have run out of sugar, maize and rice. Rival groups roamed the streets, looting from shops and rioting in protest against the cost of living – prices in 1919 were six times those of 1915. In Fiesole and Settignano marauding gangs commandeered food from ill-defended villas: about fifty men descended on Poggio Gherardo and took wine, oil, maize, and a cart in which to carry them away. Whisky and wine were looted from the cellars of I Tatti. Strikes were called, of hospital workers, railway employees, postmen, even gardeners, and several factories were shut. In January 1921 a two-day strike closed down Florence completely, and the subsequent rioting left several dead and wounded.

It was clear that peace had failed to bring with it the prosperity people had been counting on, or to diminish, as many had imagined it would, the vast disparity in wealth between the social classes. To some extent all political parties now began to play on the rising popular discontent. In the industrial cities of the north, such as Genoa and Milan, the Socialists did well; their membership had quadrupled in the war years, but they lacked good leadership and were unwilling to compromise, to forge links with other parties or to devise workable policies. Among the Catholics, on the other side, were Don Sturzo and the Christian Democrats, who condemned imperialism and favoured votes for women and the break-up of the big estates; however, *i populari* were not sufficiently united to influence politics. In opposition to both these groups, and to the liberals, was a man both able and unscrupulous enough to exploit them all: Benito Mussolini, son of a blacksmith from the Romagna, former Socialist and editor of *Avanti*, then founder of *Il Popolo d'Italia*, a man by nature violent and rebellious against all authority. When in March 1919 a hotchpotch of discontented men met in Milan's Piazza San Sepolcro, condemning censorship and militarism and calling for the confiscation of Church property, the Fascist Party – from *fascio*, the bundle borne by Roman lictors – was launched, with Mussolini as its leader.

Mussolini had gone into the First World War a neutralist, believing that Italy should never fight alongside Germany and Austria in a Triple Alliance; when it began to look as if Germany was losing, he became equally fervent as an interventionist on the Allied side. In 1918 *Il Popolo d'Italia* came out against class war and ridiculed the idea of the rule of the proletariat; in the

Piazza San Sepolcro there was talk of 'land for peasants' of the nationalisation of the arms industry, and of votes for women, ideals later quietly shelved by the Fascists.

Though the new party fared disastrously in the elections of November 1919, Fascism was soon attracting support among both the wealthier peasants and landowners frightened by moves to breakup large estates and distribute land to the returning soldiers. As the government announced plans to increase income tax and bring fuel and power under state ownership, the landowners went on the offensive, setting up a General Confederation of Industry and arming bands of unemployed men and demobilised soldiers. These Fascist *squadri* roamed the countryside, provoking clashes which the government, intent upon playing off one side against the other, did nothing to prevent; under the pretext of saving Italy from total lawlessness, they began to foster the very conditions of anarchy most likely to make people call for strong authoritarian rule. Among the nervous Anglo-Florentines, as across the country as a whole, a movement that might prove strong enough to give Italy a stable government had its appeal, particularly after the chaos of a general strike in August 1920. After a riot in Florence in March 1921 which left more than four hundred people wounded, and a Fascist *festa* at Settignano, with placards reading 'Viva l'Italia, Viva il Fascio', Janet Ross wrote to Mary Berenson: 'Luckily the Fascisti came to the rescue and the cursed socialists and communists are thoroughly frightened, so many of them have been well beaten with big sticks . . . Bombs seem to be as common as gooseberries now.' Janet Ross was not alone in finding it impossible to imagine that revolution could come from anywhere but the left, and that what was now needed was a well organised and, above all, law-abiding party. Mussolini put Fascism forward as the only force capable of checking the Bolshevik advance; he was duly elected a deputy for Milan in May 1921, in which the Fascists won a very respectable 35 seats. In October 1922, after the threatened 'march on Rome', Mussolini became, at the age of thirty-nine, the youngest prime minister in the history of Italy.

Janet Ross was now seventy-nine but still intent on putting Poggi Gherardo back in working order, despite a further minor disaster: one day, taking milk down into Florence, her horse and cart got stuck in the tram lines – the horse was killed and the cart totally destroyed by the oncoming tram. Mary Berenson noted somewhat unkindly that it was no longer any use expecting 'real conversation' from Janet Ross: 'She had hardened into fixed opinions, and narrowed her interests to local events.' All she could talk about now, complained Mary, was being poor, and how the lack of rain was ruining her garden. Nicky Mariano, who had returned from her wartime exile and was now effectively running both the library and the household at I Tatti, stated that Mary for her part had become extremely manipulative, with a 'wild' sense of power, and had turned into a schemer incapable of real friendship. Even war, it seemed, had done little to dull the appetite for bickering among the Anglo-Florentines.

Those foreigners who had left Florence in the course of the war were now beginning to drift back. The hotels were full of Italians who discovered living in them to be cheaper than opening up their own villas and trying to heat them. Berenson had embarked on an affair with an art collector in Paris called Baroness Gabrielle la Caze, reducing Mary to such anguish that she had tried to throw herself out of a window. After a stay in England arranged by her daughter Ray she returned to Florence, where her health grew increasingly poor and her figure extremely stout. Kenneth Clark, who met her at I Tatti soon after her return, noted that she had a 'very large face and a pleasant Chaucerian common sense', but that of her reputed former beauty he 'could see no trace'.

On this first visit to I Tatti Clark was not greatly taken with Berenson, who seemed to him to speak in the language of pre-war Paris, and to laugh heartily at all his own stories; but like all visitors to the house he was captivated by Nicky Mariano. She seemed to be able to diffuse some of the irritation and temper Mary provoked in Berenson, and her presence had a soothing effect.

Up the road, at Il Palmerino, Vernon Lee was now back, worrying gloomily about the direction Italian politics was taking and remarking to Mary that the older she got the more bored she became both with others and herself. She and Berenson, after twenty years of not speaking, had decided to put aside their feud. 'Miss Paget came to lunch,' noted Mary in her diary, 'and she and BB outdid themselves in glittering lies of a general nature.' The only serious change in the membership of the foreign colony involved the Russians, who had been ruined by the Revolution of 1917, and were now selling their villas and art collections. But there was a new note in the air, and the foreigners were not made to feel as welcome as once they had been. Though the wealthier among them went on adding to their art collections, they lowered their voices when discussing politics, and looked the other way when troops of blackshirts appeared on the streets of Florence. Aldous Huxley, visiting the city in June 1921, remarked on the outrageous behaviour of the Fascists, already 'usurping powers that should belong to the state, sometimes resorting to incredible acts of violence and brutality. People look on with a sort of resignation . . .' Mussolini was referred to as Mr Smith, or Mr Brown – or, by Mary Berenson, as Teddy.

There were newcomers too, to the foreign community, particularly writers, though they tended to have much less money to spend than the wealthy Anglo-Florentines in the hills and no desire at all to visit them, though they bumped into them occasionally in Orioli's bookshop. Soon after the war Norman Douglas came to Florence, as did D. H. Lawrence, Scott Moncrieff, George Santayana, and Ronald Firbank, who wanted to have nothing to do with the foreign residents, but thrived on the rich diet of gossip. Not all of them cared much for Florence, either the city or its inhabitants. 'The English colony', wrote Aldous Huxley, 'is a queer collection; a sort of decayed provincial intelligentsia . . . the spectacle of that second rate town with its repulsive Gothic architecture and its acres of Christmas card primitives makes me almost sick . . . The Florentine country is, of course, as good as anything in the world; but the town . . . pooh.' Vanessa Bell, Maynard Keynes and Duncan Grant all passed through the city in 1920, but Bloomsbury too avoided the residents, though their company would probably have entertained Sybil and Scott. It was all a different world.

A number of Americans were drawn to Italy by the sun and the Mediterranean life. They rented the empty villas on the hillsides, and they gave many parties, or descended into Florence in the evenings to attend one of the newly opened nightclubs. Up in Bellosguardo, in 1925, Mrs Keppel, mistress of the late King Edward VII, bought the Villa L'Ombrellino with money left her by the King. From every room you could look out over the Duomo, the Ponte Vecchio, and the Pitti Palace; her daughter

Violet remarked that it made her feel as if she were on the deck of 'some great ship about to sail'. The terrace of L'Ombrellino became the meeting-place for the Anglo-Florentines and European aristocracy, as the Villa Medici was when the Spences lived there in the eighteenth century. From London Mrs Keppel had brought with her Chinese pagodas given to her by the King, Chinese porcelain, tapestries, and Chippendale chairs. Lunches at L'Ombrellino were said to last for at least three hours, and Colonel Keppel, who had a fine military moustache, was pronounced to be excessively boring. Mrs Keppel never learnt Italian. Iris overhead her one day saying, loudly and slowly, as she prodded the gardener with her parasol, gesturing imperiously towards the herbaceous borders: 'Bisogna begonia! Bisogna begonia!' The next time they called at L'Ombrellino, Iris wrote, 'the begonias were there as luxuriant and trim as in the beds at Sandringham.'

Across on the other side of Florence, in Fiesole, Sybil's marriage to Geoffrey Scott was not going well. Feeding one another's anxieties about health, they took constantly to their beds. Iris, returning from her debutante seasons in London and New York, worried continually about her mother and yet longed to get away. One afternoon during a short holiday in Portofino, Sybil and Scott set out for a walk; hours passed, it began to grow dark, and then it rained heavily. Describing the 'adventure' to a friend later, Iris wrote '. . . and so a wonderful search party was organised – contadini, lanterns, brandy, smelling salts, etc.' The two were soon discovered, struggling along the road, soaked. 'I then experienced', continued Iris, 'all the sensations of annoyance of the mother whose careless child has just *not* been run over by the train!' To fill the hours and distract herself, she had started work on a 'little monograph on Fiesole, Settignano and S. Domenico, approached rather differently from the ways they've been treated till now. A terribly dull little book it will be . . .' Already she was beginning to envisage a different kind of history, the telling of the past through the details of people's lives. It was hard, however, to remain altogether detached from the growing unhappiness of the Villa Medici, where the atmosphere had become 'intolerable'. Iris clung to 'the sense of possible life ahead, of future freedom . . .' Writing many years later, she recalled that watching Scott and her mother taught her, far too early, to be 'tactful and blind'.

In February 1922 came terrible news from Ireland, where civil war was raging: a raiding party from Tipperary had burnt Desart Court to the ground. Lord Desart was in London at the time and reached Kilkenny to find just a small pile of things rescued by a housemaid. Everything else – pictures, furniture, the family's whole history – had been destroyed. 'The main house is a shell,' Desart wrote in reply to a letter of sympathy from Mrs Cutting, 'and the contents mere ashes.' He never went back to Ireland. 'The wound is so deep,' he wrote to Iris, 'and there is no cure for it . . . I sometimes feel I can hardly bear it – and at my age, how can one plan out a new life?'

One happier interlude in the Scott marriage was dreamt up during a wet and dismal afternoon at Ouchy in Switzerland, where they had all gone for one of Sybil's cures. Scott, frantic with boredom, caught the tram into town in search of a new book, returning with a biography of Madame de Charriere, the witty, unhappy eighteenth-century novelist Zelide, Boswell's Belle de Zuylen, later in love with the young Benjamin Constant. That evening he read passages aloud to Sybil and next day they searched Lausanne for copies of Zelide's novels. Within three days the idea for Scott's *Portrait of Zelide* had been born, and as they worked on it together, they laughed. In the evenings Iris listened as they read each new chapter aloud, and though she felt some relief at their closeness, she later wondered whether such a vivid picture of a clever but miserable woman who dealt with her profound unhappiness by being intensely rational was suitable for a girl as naive as she then was, or one so anxious not to let it show. The moral that cynicism was all that could really be expected of life was not an altogether helpful lesson.

When not in bed, lying on a sofa, or taking a cure, Sybil was extremely social. It was not long before she made peace of a kind with Mary Berenson, who invited the Scotts to dinner and found Sybil 'simply buzzing with energy' and very much nicer now that she had stopped telling everyone her symptoms – though just as self-obsessed. Mary was less forgiving towards Scott, commenting smugly that he had become 'very pale and thin, trembling as he used to when he was twenty, and more miserably unhappy'. Iris, who occasionally accompanied her mother and Scott to I Tatti, noted after one dinner, with a certain chilly clarity: 'We were all very intellectual. Half the party would naturally have spoken Italian, the other half English; consequently we all spoke indifferent, carefully modulated French, and discussed the single-mindedness of the Middle Ages as revealed by XII-century manuscripts . . . All quite amusing at the time – and really rather tiresome.' On one of his visits to Fiesole, Sybil took her father over to dinner at I Tatti; given a camomile *tisane*, which he had never encountered before, he later remarked anxiously that he hoped it would do him no harm. (Lord Desart did not altogether enjoy his Florentine visits. 'I like a *little* Italian art,' he was heard to say, 'not too much and not every day.') Of her return social call at the Villa Medici not long after their conciliatory dinner, Mary noted, with the mixture of malice, sympathy and acuity that marks her excellent letters and diaries: 'Lady Sybil fainted at our approach, so that we had a pleasant time with Geoffrey and Iris and the Strongs.' Janet Ross, who could also be exceedingly sharp, remarked that Sybil's petticoats 'were shorter than ever' and that Scott was growing 'very fat and very important'. Fiesole, like Florence, had lost none of its asperity in the war.

With the arrival of spring each year came what Iris called the 'avalanche' of foreign visitors. Some, like Sybil's cousin Irene Lawley and her mother Lady Wenlock, were welcome; others, total strangers who arrived at the Villa Medici or at I Tatti with introductions from American or English friends or relations, were less so. Nicky Mariano compared I Tatti to a great rumbling bus: some passengers stayed on board for one stop – Berenson could be merciless with the shy and tongue-tied – others for longer. 'Any guests who *enjoy* themselves are fun to have,' was Iris's verdict. 'It is the ones who neither derive pleasure from Florence themselves, nor let us derive pleasure from them, whom I resent a little. Mummy and I agreed that the [Villa Medici] from having been a tea shop, is now become a pension.' Life became particularly social around Easter, when Iris arranged a children's party 'for my small Fiesole girls' with an Easter-egg hunt, an occasion she enjoyed far more than the regular Sunday At Homes. We've had some *awful* afternoons,' she told a friend, 'and I am daily becoming more savage . . . Why are elderly Americans like apes?' That Sunday it had rained hard, trapping the twenty guests – numbers sometimes rose to double that – inside the house. What she called 'Villa Medicitis', the particular diet of culture and high-minded talk, she was beginning to find increasingly depressing. Aldous Huxley, who spoke of Sybil during his visit to Florence as one of the 'brightest spots' among the city's deeply boring provincial intelligentsia, later and rather more unkindly used her as the model for Mrs Aldwinkle in *Those Barren Leaves*, the Englishwoman with the enormous villa who, in buying her palazzo, felt she had bought Italy itself – 'everything it contained [was] her property and her secret. She had bought its arts, its music, its melodious language, its literature, its wine and cooking, the beauty of its women and the virility of its Fascists . . . She had acquired Italian passion: cuore, amore and dolore were hers.'

These last were about to break over Sybil, but not in relation to her Italian life. In October 1923 the writer and diplomat Harold Nicolson and his wife Vita Sackville-West, whose long entanglement with Violet Trefusis was now over, went to stay at the Villa Medici: Scott had known Vita in Florence before the war. They were there for about a week. In the mornings Nicolson, who had been in Greece doing research for his book on Byron, worked in the loggia; in the afternoons they went on expeditions, to see Sir George Sitwell at the Villa Montegufoni, or to call on Janet Ross, now in her mid eighties but still moving the heavy lemon pots around her terrace herself and still, as Nicolson put it, 'a fierce old thing'. A love affair was brewing: Scott decided that he was falling in love with Vita and, whatever the reason, whether it was the intense beauty of Florence during those bright October days, or their companionable talks about literature, she responded. It was to be her one and only affair with a man. They discussed and criticised each other's books – he was just coming to the end of *Zelide*, and recognised that in his own relationship with Mary Berenson there was more than a little of that between Zelide and Benjamin Constant, while she was just beginning *The Land*. At the end of the week Vita returned to England and wrote to Scott: 'My love and tenderness is a bank on which you can draw unlimited cheques' – though, as it turned out, the limit on them was in fact rather small. Scott, suffering from one of his periodic bouts of extremely low spirits, admitted to Mary that his life at the moment was 'like swimming on and on with no knowledge of where the shore lies'. To escape their bewilderment and uncertainty about the future, and because Princess Mary had asked whether she and Viscount Lascelles might spend their honeymoon at the Villa Medici (causing Sybil to fret about Fiesole's erratic water supply), the Scotts went off to Palermo and Tunis, leaving behind British detectives, Italian *carabinieri*, and photographers climbing over the garden walls to take pictures of the house.

It was not long before Harold Nicolson and Sybil realised what was happening, but while Nicolson rightly sensed that the affair would have none of Violet's 'hypnotic influence', Sybil was devastated. Given her propensity to fainting fits and anxieties about what she could and could not tolerate, however, she took it surprisingly well, and did not retire to her bed; she even gave Scott what she called an 'unwedding ring', though there was no talk, for the present, of a separation. Scott meanwhile helped her to cope with the bureaucratic intricacies of buying the Villa Medici, which hitherto she had merely rented. Writing to Vita, Sybil observed sadly that 'You are in love with each other, and he is not in love with me', a remark made all the sadder by the fact it was not so very long since she had confessed to Berenson that, having been very lonely, longing to be wanted and needed, she was at last becoming happy with Scott.

Scott himself was somewhat adrift. *A Box of Paints*, a collection of poems and his first book since *The Architecture of Humanism* nearly a decade earlier, was finally out. It looked handsome, and the reviewers were generous. J. C. Squire, one of the most highly respected literary critics of the day, noted in the *Observer* Scott's 'real gift for rich, compact description'. But he remained completely blocked on what was to be a 'history of taste'. In the evenings at the Villa Medici there was much discussion with Sybil and Iris about what such a book should contain; but as Iris recalled in her memoirs, one day many years later she came across a large piece of foolscap paper on which were written, in Scott's neat and elegant hand, the words 'A History of Taste, Volume I, Chapter 1', and underneath a single fragment of a sentence: 'It is very difficult . . .' It could stand as a caricature of every stillborn book. Scott never got beyond those words, it seems. Nor did his partnership with Pinsent, a working relationship as indivisible as that of 'Chatto and Windus', as Harold Acton once remarked, survive the war or his marriage to Sybil. The Firm – Pinsent technical and empirical and good on sewers, Scott artistic and aesthetic – had done valuable work, but it was Pinsent who went on to develop that special contribution to Florentine gardens they had first explored at I Tatti and Le Baize.

Pinsent is an interesting and largely forgotten figure. Returning from his wartime ambulance service to a Florence anxious to put the war behind it and enjoy the magnificent villas and gardens, he began to find himself much in demand. Foreign villa owners now felt they needed an architect-cum-garden designer who was interested in historical accuracy and Renaissance and Tuscan ideas, yet capable of adapting them to particular plots of land. They knew about and had seen the gardens at I Tatti and Le Baize, which during the war years had had time to grow and find their place in the landscape. The lethargy Mary Berenson had observed at I Tatti, what Pinsent called his 'blankets of inertia', descended on him again, but only briefly, and by the summer of 1920 he was writing excitedly to Irene Lawley that 'once more, work seemed to me the only really worthwhile thing, and all else faded away before the brightness of this my kindest mistress'. Comissions flowed in throughout the Twenties. Charles Strong welcomed him back to Le Baize to create a baroque garden stairway with sponge-stone sculptures and mosaics; Mrs Keppel asked him to make her a garden with beds in the shape of a Union Jack. The Anglo-Florentines liked Pinsent; they found his shyness appealing, his manners courteous, and he was fun to be with. They felt comfortable with his designs.

The war years had sharpened Pinsent's sense of what he wanted to do: to 'restore' the landscape, looking both to the Italian Renaissance and to Victorian and contemporary gardens in England, and in doing so to create spaces more intimate in scale than the open vistas of the traditional Renaissance villa, designed to convey man's supremacy over nature, but based on the same principle, that of the garden as an extension of the house. Pinsent was intrigued by mystery, and by the thought of planning gardens in such a way that walls and terraces and steps felt pleasant all the year round; and he was still far more interested in fountains and running water and in statues than in brightly coloured flowers. The finished gardens were hybrids, certainly: his pebble mosaic paths, for example, ultimately had more in common with the Arts and Crafts movement in England than with the Italian Renaissance, but there were always geometric designs, often in box, reminiscent of the pavements and gardens of the late Renaissance. Though he was now working entirely on his own, Pinsent continued to be strongly influenced by Scott's dictum, expounded in *The Architecture of Humanism*, that man 'may construct, within the world as it is, a pattern of the world as he would have it. This is the way to humanism, in philosophy, in life and in the arts.' He wrote almost nothing down about his own ideas, but a rare note records his belief that the gardens nearest to a house should be planted 'so that to step from the house to the terrace, or from the terrace to the various parts of the garden, should only seem like going from one room to another'. Harold Acton called his work the epitome of 'Anglo-Fiorentino', and thought the 'proportions, and even the meticulous precision of the details . . . more English than Florentine'. Over the next few years, moving from garden to garden, making box-hedged 'rooms' and parterres and sunken pools, creating secret gardens closed off from the sweeping and sometimes overpowering views of Florence and the valley of the Arno, working intuitively, interpreting the spirit if not the letter of the Renaissance garden, Pinsent single-handedly partly redesigned Florence's hill-sides, particularly Fiesole and Arcetri. Sir Geoffrey Jellicoe, one of the great scholars of historical gardens, called him 'a maestro in placing buildings in landscape'. And if the Italians did not greatly care for his designs, his Anglo-Florentine patrons, many of them rich and eccentric intellectuals, loved them; though they never attracted imitators, they constituted a 'school' of their own, distinguishable to this day by their somewhat wider than usual box borders, often in the shape of high hedges pruned into architectural shapes, their parterres, often of grass, and their many vases, fountains and pieces of statuary. Pinsent remained close to Scott, as a friend, and spent a great deal of time at the Villa Medici, tinkering with alterations to the house and gardens, helping with difficult guests, and taking part in the many picnics and excursions. Like

Sybil and Scott he was a keen motoring enthusiast; motorcars were everywhere replacing the carriages used before the war by all but the richest, and increased the scope for outings and excursions, which became ever more adventurous. He was filled with plans; he collected mandolins, organ-clocks and lutes; and he was determined not to fall in love, for it took him 'not like a tonic, but like a disease', as he told Irene Lawley. Iris was teaching him to play the piano, and it seems that at about this time she fell in love with him – though infatuation probably better describes her feelings – while he still thought of her as the daughter he had never had. It was Iris who would soon provide him with the opportunity of creating his most successful garden.

Iris may have felt herself to be ungainly, but she had several admirers. It was becoming ever clearer that she had a real need for close friends, born of the wandering years with her dying father and the solitariness of the Villa Medici schoolroom, a deep desire to know how others were feeling, a genuine sympathy for their misfortunes, and with all this a gift for intimacy. She liked to be close to people, but could be gauche with strangers; and because she was so obviously clever and well read, she could be intimidating to young people her own age. Her grandfather had remarked on her warmth and the pleasure it gave him, as it did Pinsent, who wrote to her that she had been 'one of the bright spots' in his life. Gordon Waterfield, Janet Ross's great-nephew, continued to be in love with her, regretful of his youth – he was a year younger – and of the fact that as a university student he had nothing to offer. Arthur Yencken, the diplomat from Australia, wanted her to marry him, and though she wrote a long letter to him in America explaining that she was not in love with him, he never received it, but went on believing that they might soon become engaged.

And then, some time in 1922, a far more important figure entered her life. He was called Colin MacKenzie, and was currently working for a Scottish firm in Milan; he was twenty-four, and had lost a leg during the last months of the war, having abandoned his degree in economics at Cambridge to join the army at the age of nineteen. He was gregarious but moody, wore enormous cloaks, and liked fancy dress parties. Maynard Keynes had thought highly of him as an undergraduate. He had completed his degree at King's and was now working for the Paisley thread company J & P. Coats, but his interests were more literary and musical: he wrote poetry and, like Iris, had read and continued to read widely in Greek, Latin, French, English, Italian and German. A love of words, a certain inherent seriousness of mind, what they called a 'private and slightly malicious understanding', and a maturity far beyond their years – hers the result of too much time spent in the sole company of literate adults, his of a war that had seen the death of his two closest friends – brought them together. It was to Colin that Iris now confided, in letters that became more frequent and intimate as the months passed, her feelings about Fiesole and her mother, her hopes for the future, and the details, many of them amusingly presented, of her daily life. Most of the letters were serious, a few exuberant. There was much literary criticism, many recommendations of books, a great deal of quotation (in all the languages they read), and some gossip about their lives; of the two, Colin comes across as the more rounded, tolerant and wry, Iris the more socially acute, but also on occasion a little prim. It is apparent from the very beginning of their correspondence that Colin was the more emotionally involved of the two. On 1 January 1923 he told her he had been trying to work, 'but far from attaining to a scientific calm I began to feel physically ill with the desire to see you again . . .' Iris's reply was cautious: 'I should like you to realise to yourself how large a part in our sudden friendship was owing, not to any qualities in me (oh Colin, I am such a poor object for hero-worship, as you will only too soon discover!) but just by the fact that you had been a good many months . . . without seeing any "real human being". . .'

After this they settled down to an exchange of letters that is awesome in its erudition and touching in the growing attachment it reveals. They quoted Donne to one another, St Augustine, Ezra Pound, Nietzsche, Poliziano, Chapman, Plutarch, and Dionysius; and she confessed to him that Hardy's *Jude the Obscure* depressed her unutterably. Such was her apparent worldliness and scholarship that it is often hard to remember that she was not yet twenty-one. They dissected literary texts and discussed scansion and metre, but devoted no space to politics or current affairs. He introduced her to Marlowe; she told him there were aspects of American life that made her feel quite sick – 'it is all very vital, very energetic, very creative, no doubt . . . But I find it overwhelming, chaotic, shapeless – a many-headed monster . . .' – and praised Lucca as the 'most signorile and perhaps one of the loveliest of the Italian towns . . .' Just occasionally she could sound snooty – 'it is peculiar, isn't it, how some people seem to be deprived of the faculty of looking at things' – but contrition followed swiftly: 'Don't let me become superior and sniffy, Colin, it's a horrible characteristic.' He told her of his travels in Scotland, where he had fallen in love with the Black Isle and Ben Wyris, 'a solitary sentinel who will not fail'. She told him about the ball she had been to, dressed as a Restoration lady complete with 'curls, white fichu, red rose and all. But I *do* detest the period!' They discussed virtues, Iris writing to Colin, in a letter which says much about both her preoccupation with self-knowledge, and how little she still knew about herself: 'I wonder if I agree with you about courage as the crowning virtue; I know so many charming people without it, but possibly I am really only biased by my consciousness of *not* possessing it . . . honesty to oneself or to others I have got, but that is not so much courage as the dislike of living in a fog, but when it comes down to the only real thing which courage is needed for, physical pain . . . then I am the most hopeless, shameful coward – utterly despicable . . .'

She told him, repeatedly, of her feelings of alienation, how she never knew quite where she belonged: 'It's a complicated starting point to belong to three countries at once,' she wrote one day, 'with the desire for the charms and attitudes of at least two of them . . .' And on another: 'It sounds ridiculous, but if I marry a foreigner, one of the things I most hate to think of is that I shall never have a son at Eton.' And on another: 'I am 3/8 Scotch, 1/8 French (which may account for a good deal), 1/4 Irish and 1/4 English – the complete mongrel.'

They shared a dislike of formal life, and palazzi full of furniture, 'the muddle . . . of several generations of maiden aunts . . .' as Iris described it; Colin replied: 'I'm all in favour of butterflies – but spiritual butterflies, per amor di Dio – these people are spiritual earthworms.' He called her suitors 'door posts'; and she signed herself Basketta, for they had agreed that they had become the wastepaper baskets for each other's thoughts. In one youthful letter she said she very much doubted 'whether any experience gained in the course of life really compensates for the freshness of the first bite', and also told him that she had been 'troubled and hurt enough and more than enough'.

Yet for all their intimacy there is something mysterious

about these letters, something that rings a little false. It is as if there was an invisible wall somewhere between them. They seemed, on the surface, so suited to one another; but the letters are curiously guarded. In March 1923 the reason became clear: Iris was going to marry someone else.

In 1920, when Iris at eighteen was in the middle of her various debutante seasons, she was introduced to an Italian ten years older than herself, Antonio Origo. He was the illegitimate son of a cavalry officer and painter and sculptor, Marchese Clemente Origo, a close friend of the poet and political adventurer Gabriele d'Annunzio. Clemente had caused a great scandal by running off with Rosa Tarsis, Russian-born wife of Duke Pompeo Litta. When she joined Origo, having already given birth to Antonio in 1892, she left behind two small daughters, Antonella and Giulia. Clemente and Rosa were able to marry only in 1899, and Antonio, repudiated by Litta in 1895 and, '*figlio di ignoti*' (father unknown), given the surname of Pelagi by the courts, was recognised as the natural son of Clemente only in 1921. Rosa had abandoned him for a month when he was seven weeks old. His childhood was spent largely hidden away, when he was not at boarding school in Switzerland, from where he wrote rather forlorn letters home. He then worked in a bank in Brussels and for the champagne firm of Mumm in Rheims, before serving in the Italian cavalry in the First World War. 'I grew up in the laundry with the servants,' he used to tell people, 'I was only shown to intimate friends.' Letters reveal that as a small boy he was allowed home from his school at either Christmas or Easter – not both – and that his father in particular was very strict with him. When Antonio did badly at his studies, Clemente wrote: 'We have placed you in a good, *very expensive*, college, not to play but to study.' Because of the scandal surrounding them his parents felt unable to live in either Rome or Milan, so had settled in Florence, where Clemente sculpted.

When Iris and Antonio first met, at a reception in Florence, Iris was both grateful and disbelieving that such a charming and elegant older man, who loved Wagner and football, seemed to want to talk to her. Tall and smiling, and much liked in Florentine circles, Antonio not only had charm but was widely considered to be very good-looking, with his high forehead and rather round head. He was affectionately teasing in manner, and perceptive and honest, though he was reluctant to spend much time on his inner thoughts. Two years after they first met, when his father was dying of cancer in Florence and Antonio was spending the nights at his bedside, he would go up to Fiesole in the early mornings and meet Iris to walk in the hills. These romantic encounters became the subject of gossip among the Anglo-Florentines after Berthe Michel, an elderly French teacher who had once given Iris lessons, claimed that she had acted as go-between, carrying messages between them. In the autumn of 1922, in Venice, Antonio asked Iris to marry him. Sybil protested strongly: he was Italian, he was a Catholic, and he was much too grown-up and good-looking. A deal was struck: they would have no contact with each other, not even by letter, for six months, and if they still felt the same way, they could become engaged. 'I had one romantic evening,' Iris wrote to Irene. 'It's going to be a beastly winter, but almost better than dragging on in that sort of footling way.' Pinsent, who happened to run into Antonio during this period of separation, reported to Iris that the long wait was making him very miserable, though it seems possible that Iris plotted and achieved a brief encounter in Pisa. 'And you are sailing off,' wrote Pinsent, 'with your great capacity for managing people; sure of success; probably stimulated by the difficulties; your love returned, and in the way you want.' Pinsent knew Iris very well, and had perceived a fundamental trait in her character: it was not so much that she was tough and determined to get her own way; rather, she had a tendency to try to manipulate life around her so as to make it safe and manageable, and bring about the ends she had convinced herself were best for everyone concerned. It was a trait she displayed all her life, and it grew stronger with the years. When the six months of separation were up a letter arrived from Antonio repeating his proposal; Sybil reluctantly agreed to the marriage, but insisted on a long engagement, with no formal announcement made until after Iris's twenty-first birthday.

Sybil was not the only person who was less than pleased. Arthur Yencken – her letter explaining that she did not love him having gone astray, and having made little of her somewhat vague references to Antonio – arrived to settle, as he thought, details of his marriage to Iris. Appalled by the news of her engagement, he declared the break between them to be final: they never met or spoke again. Finding herself in Paris many years later, at a time when he was *en poste* there as a diplomat, Iris tried to contact him, but he did not reply; during the Second World War he was killed in a plane crash.

The Desarts were also appalled. Lady Desart wrote that, though they loved Iris deeply and nothing could change that, they were extremely sad about the gulf religion and nationality would put between them in such a marriage, and they hoped Iris and Antonio were '*quite* certain that you love each other well enough to bear the strain'. Lord Desart repeated what he had once asked Sybil: was Iris really sure she wanted to change her nationality? Bayard Cutting, however, whose feelings about the ill effects of nationalism were so strong, would have been pleased that Iris had grown up free of its clutches, though what it would do to the rest of her life and her sense of never quite belonging was not yet clear.

Colin, who had been aware all along of the existence of a shadowy figure in Iris's life, though he knew nothing about him – not even, interestingly, his name – was resigned, though he cannot have been altogether reassured about her prospective happiness when she wrote: 'I did *not* mean to marry him, though I was in love with him, for all the reasons and prejudices which you know and share.' She was firm and utterly clear about any future relationship between Colin and herself, in a long letter remarkable, when one remembers her youth, for its powerful analysis: 'If it is true that, in human relationships, one must always go back or forward, but can't stay in the same place – then it is backward we must go.'

According to visitors to the Villa Medici at the time when Iris's engagement was still unofficial, there was in Florence a distinct and persistent air of disapproval regarding Antonio, despite his general popularity a barely concealed suspicion that all he was after was her fortune. Sybil, 'permanently horizontal' in her bed or on a *chaise-longue* in the Chinese drawing room, had continued to make plain her reservations about the marriage, but Iris went on with her life, running her Fiesole girl guide troop, and taking pains to ensure that visitors had a good time even during Sybil's many indispositions. She struck newcomers as not particularly good-looking, a girl who paid very little attention to her appearance, but who had nice manners and great charm. Scott supported her from the wings; he considered that though Iris was indeed very young, a youthful marriage was inevitable for someone with her 'romantic cum serious temperament', and personally found Antonio 'quite one of the most charming men I have known in this country and very suited to Iris in character'. But of course, Scott too was in love.

Iris was now dispatched on a round of visits to her grandparents, to announce her intentions in person and introduce Antonio to them. She went on ahead of him to New York, to 'let the bomb burst', as she told Doody, adding, 'It's odd I don't feel more nervous – perhaps it is because at bottom I am so *sure* and so happy', though to Colin she wrote that she somewhat dreaded what was likely to be a 'summer of confession, and possibly, conflict'. As on all her visits to the United States, she felt a great ambivalence towards the country. New York continued to strike her as a city in which, compared to Paris, Rome and London, 'the women's pearls are perhaps a little larger, their dresses a little more elaborately simple, their men a little inferior, and their sweep into the room more royal', while the inhabitants of New England were shrewd, reliable and kindly; it was 'a world completely without glamour, but also without pretence and self-consciousness'. Wherever she went, Cutting relations told her how very like her Aunt Olivia she had become: Olivia was a reticent, generous woman, somewhat manly in appearance, who had returned to live at Westbrook with her mother after the failure of her marriage.

Iris recalled later her feeling of love for Westbrook as she waited for Antonio to arrive. It was full of dragonflies, 'masses of them glittering and darting over the reeds and water lilies, like blue flames'; local people called them 'darning needles'. She was reading Katherine Mansfield's *Journal* and, revealing the sense of respect for the secret lives of other people that she was

111

beginning to be aware of, she wrote to Colin: 'It makes me feel rather like the old lady who took out the Brownings' letters from a circulating library, but brought it back next day, saying "I was going to read this, but I see it is private".'

Antonio, somewhat to her surprise, was a great success with Mrs Cutting, an impression confirmed by Edith Wharton, who wrote to congratulate her and to pass on such pleasant remarks as this, which, 'communicated to a third person, carry added conviction'. To Irene, Iris now wrote that she was '*deeply* happy about myself . . . I have come to a confidence and hope for the future which I did not think I should ever obtain. I am very much in love, of course; but besides and beyond that there is a feeling of certainty, of complete satisfaction.' To Colin, who had cautiously voiced his fears about her marrying an Italian, her tone was rather more revealing, and slightly defensive: 'First of all then I must tell you, Colin, that I am deeply happy – with a completeness and serenity of happiness for which I had never dared hope. It has grown very slowly, and you know the doubts and hesitations from which it has sprung. At first, in March, I was hardly conscious of more than the relief which the killing of that nightmare goddess, indecision, gives one, and of that temporary exaltation which is part of the divine madness! but is not necessarily anything like happiness . . . Origo *is* a masterful man but his attitude in this respect is not the Latin one . . . Our relationship is starting on a basis of equality and independence . . . or shall we say *equal* lack of independence . . .' The somewhat awkward question of finances had been settled so that Sybil could remain at the Villa Medici – there had apparently been some question of it passing to Iris – and while Iris now had 'complete independence', she was not in the 'intolerable position of heiress – indeed Origo and I will be on an almost exactly equal financial footing'. Iris felt what she had felt on every visit to the United States: 'It leaves me with a yet greater horror of large fortunes, and of all that they bring with them.'

On their way home Iris and Antonio stopped in London, where Antonio, expecting a stern inquisition from Lord Desart, found him exceptionally courteous; Desart in fact said little, beyond observing that Iris was very extravagant when it came to stockings. Later he reported to his granddaughter that 'nothing could be happier than our first meeting with him'. While they were in London, Colin introduced them to Frances Marshall, not yet married to Ralph Patridge, who remembers how strange and ill-judged the marriage seemed to her, with Iris 'so slight, like a flame, very delicate, almost like a Botticelli, with a very quick voice and a mind as quick, running from one thing to another, and alarming because so clever', while Antonio struck her as 'a large heavy man, with not very good English'.

Iris was now twenty-one, and in theory there was no longer any obstacle to her marriage. Sybil began to prevaricate, however, taking to her bed ever more frequently as Iris's impending departure and Scott's affair with Vita made her realise that she might soon be alone. Somerset Maugham later published a cruel and barely disguised portrait of the ailing and manipulative Sybil in a short story called 'Louise'. Louise, frail and delicate, with a supposedly weak heart, was married twice, to Tom, who died of pneumonia, and to George, who was killed in the war. When her daughter – Maugham quite blatantly named her Iris – wished to marry, Louise went to devious lengths to get the marriage postponed – and then died on her daughter's wedding day.

Iris herself went down with 'flu and colitis. The Villa Medici was engulfed in what Scott described to Vita as an 'invalidy' atmosphere. Talking of Sybil, he went on: 'I see no sense in it, this rigidity, this making of mountains out of molehills, this perpetual claim, on others, this treating of human things like business contexts . . .' He protested at what he called 'Sybil's blind torturing tenacity'; but he felt sorry for her. Early in October, to Sybil's great reluctance, the engagement was formally announced; Iris's remark that 'a marriage has been arranged' was a very odd choice of words, given how hard everyone had tried to prevent it. 'Sybil blew in', Mary Berenson noted in her diary, 'in a tornado of chatter about her daughter's engagement.' Early in 1924, Mary wrote to her sister Alys: 'BB went to see Sybil, partly to tell her to let Iris choose to keep her American nationality, as women can on marriage. For there is a sort of feeling abroad that she cannot be long happy with that anti-intellectual young man.'

Over the years, in company with the Berensons and Pinsent and the many guests to the Villa Medici, Iris had covered much of Tuscany in search of unknown frescos or paintings and good picnic spots. Chianciano and Montalcino were two hill towns they had visited, and it was near here that in the autumn of 1923 she and Antonio began to look for an estate to buy. They were both certain that they wanted to leave Florence and its social intrigues: Antonio because he had no taste for the world of business or diplomacy for which he had trained, and had long dreamt of farming, Iris because she wanted to do something useful with her life. She was now spending three mornings a week at the First Aid Dispensary of San Domenico, 'learning to treat all the minor and more disgusting ailments of the Poor. I cannot tell you how much I dislike it, or how bad I am at it . . .' For all her distaste, however, she sounded excited, buoyant. A possible estate at Castelfiorentino had to be abandoned because it was too expensive. But on 28 October 1923 she reported to Colin that they had been to see 'a huge property just south of Pienza called "La Foce", looking one side over the whole of the Val D'Orcia, and on the other most of Umbria . . . It is quite the most beautiful – and the wildest bit of country I have ever seen . . . and the whole quality of the beauty is one of loveliness and desolation.' They spent three days with the agent-manager, the *fattore*, riding around the estate and visiting the farms. A few days later she wrote again to tell Colin that La Foce was theirs: 'the soil I believe to be that of the Promised Land, but it has been terribly neglected, so there will be a great deal for Antonio to do – and I shall "visit the poor", run the school, play the piano, I hope write – not a bad life, Colin!' To Irene she wrote: 'I long to *see* you, instead of writing nonsense to you . . . I want to talk about a hundred things – I want to show you my Tuscan land, and Antonio and all my happiness.'

Sybil's prevarications continued until a day came when the local doctor, Giglioli, told Iris that she would do better to get on with her marriage, as her mother would never be able to envisage a day on which she might feel well enough to go through with it. Iris and Antonio had hoped to marry and have a mass said in the fine old church of San Francesco, but in the event, after many discussions and interventions from well-placed people, the local authorities, like Sybil, fell into equivocation, and Iris settled instead for the extremely ugly chapel at the Villa Medici itself, which contained the tomb of one of the Villa's previous owners, 'povera Mrs Spence, buon'anima'. Before this there would be a civil ceremony in the Salone dei Matrimoni in Fiesole.

They planned a party for about three hundred guests, most of whom, Iris wrote scornfully, 'will belong to that section of the British colony which looks as if it had been buried and dug up again for the occasion'. Various prominent Florentine families, as well as the British Consul, gave *thés dansants* for the bride. On Tuesday 4 March 1924, in the presence of Aunt Justine from America, Aunt Joan from London, and a number of Antonio's relations (neither set able to communicate with the other), Antonio and Iris were married. Sybil was not present; she was in her bed. It was Doody who wound a wreath of jasmine round Iris's mirror as she dressed that morning, saying that was how a bride should see her face on her wedding morning, and Doody who was there to see her off. The sight of her 'short, motionless figure, standing in the loggia' was Iris's last picture of home as she drove away for her honeymoon.

CHAPTER FIVE

La Foce

Iris and Antonio knew precisely what they were looking for when they set out early in the autumn of 1923 to find somewhere to live in Tuscany. They wanted a 'place with enough work to fill our lifetime', but it also had to be beautiful. Iris had dreamt of one of those Tuscan villas to be seen on the hilltops, a fourteenth- or fifteenth-century house reached by a long, narrow drive of cypresses, perhaps with a loggia and high vaulted rooms. La Foce had none of these things. It was a sixteenth-century brick house of 'quite pleasant proportions', with a stone staircase leading straight to a dark central room, lit by red and blue Victorian glass panels in the doors. The rooms were small. There was no electricity, no telephone, and no bathroom. The general air was one of decay and mustiness. The house, which had not been lived in for many years, stood in 3,500 acres of the poorest farming land of the southern corner of the province of Siena, five miles from the developing spa town of Chianciano.

To reach La Foce Iris and Antonio drove slowly up a steep, stony, winding road through an overgrown and dark wood of scrub oak and pine, doing the last bit on foot. As they emerged at the top, they expected to come out onto a plateau with a magnificent view of the Val d'Orcia, with Monte Amiata beyond; instead, they found themselves on a 'bare, windswept upland' among long ridges of whitened '*crete senesi*', the distinctive low, bare clay hillsides which run down into the valley of the river Orcia, cutting the landscape into a series of steep, dry, watersheds. The eroded land was grey as 'elephant backs, as treeless as the mountains of the moon'. There were a few trees, and scrub, and far below in the stony bed of the Orcia could just be seen a trickle of water. It was, Iris wrote later, on that still autumn evening of 1923 a 'lunar landscape, pale and inhuman', with all the bleakness of a desert. Once the wheat had ripened in summer and the alfalfa was cut, the last traces of green disappeared from the valley, leaving a great dusty plain as far as the eye could see, the soil packed hard, and only the sound of the cicadas in the air. In the winter came the *tramontana*, the icy wind from the north.

But there was something more to La Foce than the bleakness of the desert: it had beauty, and fascination. If you stood on the crumbling loggia you could just see, towards the south, the great medieval tower of Radicofani, standing high above oaks and chestnut trees; to the west, the long-extinct volcano of Monte Amiata which 'dominated and dwarfed the whole landscape', and whose thick forests were said to have supplied the timber for the Second Punic War. On almost every hilltop could be seen the ruins of a castle, a fortress, a battlement or a Romanesque church, while just out of sight to the north lay Pienza, the perfect Renaissance city, built by the Piccolomini Pope, Pius II, who in summertime would convene his cardinals in the Monte Amiata chestnut woods, 'under one tree or another, by the sweet murmur of the stream'.

Much of La Foce's land consisted of scrub oak, with a dense

undergrowth of thorn bushes, juniper, myrtle and ilex, once home to bears and wolves. The one small fertile and cultivated corner produced meagre crops of vines, olives and wheat, for they always suffered from too little water. The estate consisted of twenty-five farms, *case coloniche*, all in a state of almost total disrepair, some inaccessible by road; their roofs leaked and their windows were stuffed with old rags to keep the draughts out, making the rooms dark and airless. The farming families were extremely poor, illiterate and suspicious, and very few of their children had ever been to school. Most of the region's landowners remained, even in the 1920s, almost completely indifferent to the conditions in which their labourers lived. It was an extraordinary, daunting challenge for the Origos to take on – all the more so as there were other, gentler properties to be bought, where they might have found leisure and prosperity.

Between Antonio and Iris there was, however, no disagreement: they had fallen in love with this vast, lonely, uncompromising landscape, and they wanted nothing more than to live in the shadow of the ever-changing Monte Amiata, 'to arrest the erosion of those steep ridges, to turn this bare clay into wheat fields, to rebuild these farms and see prosperity return . . . to restore the greenness of these mutilated woods . . .' Their friends thought they were mad.

Neither Antonio nor Iris had any experience of country work, certainly not of hardship. All their joint capital had gone into buying the estate, and they were now faced with the task of turning it into a working concern for some two hundred people on the $5,000 a year of Iris's American inheritance, a large sum for the times but not unduly so. While they were away on their honeymoon the invaluable Pinsent began to tackle the dinginess of the house. He put a skylight into the gloomy central hall, built bookshelves, distempered the walls, installed travertine fireplaces, and made a first bathroom. He was known to the family as the Passionate Plumber. The garden posed greater problems. La Foce was almost totally without water, and what there was went straight to the crops in the valley. Near to the house stood a few decrepit palms, and the remains of a once agreeable '*giardino inglese*'. In time, Pinsent would turn it into his finest and best-loved garden.

It was not only that the Origos now had to learn a whole new set of skills: they had also to accustom themselves to an entirely new world, one which revolved naturally around the seasons, the weather and the state of the crops, and had nothing at all to do with society, fashion or amusement. All the reaping was still done by hand: from the front of the house, in high summer, the reapers could be seen making their way evenly across the fields in a long, straight line, from before dawn to sunset. Ploughing was done with the help of the colossal pale-grey Maremma oxen. As soon as the property was theirs Antonio threw himself enthusiastically into the work, learning its rhythms and seasons. Immediately he drew up a list of essential initial tasks: ditching, draining and building dykes, rebuilding and modernising the farms, making roads, increasing the herds, raising money for a tractor, a bulldozer, a combine harvester. Working alongside the *fattore* he was introduced to the peasant farmers and taught the intricate layout of the *fattoria* and its outbuildings – storerooms, crushing presses, wood sheds, blacksmith's quarters. Gratifyingly soon he won the respect of the twenty-five families who now found him working alongside them, often for longer hours than they did. However daunting the project, it was in many ways a good time to invest in land.

In 1921 Mussolini had declared private property to be a 'right and a due', thus endearing himself to landowners unnerved by earlier talk of a fairer distribution of the land. Once in power Mussolini had restored order, repressed Communist attacks and banned strikes, and increased the powers of the police – all measures designed initially to reassure Italians following the chaos and confrontations of the immediate post-war years.

As throughout much of Tuscany, La Foce was run on the *mezzadria* system by which the landlord kept the houses in repair and provided half of everything needed to cultivate and improve the land, while the peasant farmers paid for their share in half of all that was produced. By 1924 this system, which in one form or another had been in operation since the days of the Roman Republic, perhaps most notably in Tuscany, after the strong hill castles of the robber barons were razed and the feudal system broken up, was in some state of flux, particularly on estates to which the men had returned from the Great War better educated, and better able to question the way things were done. For all Mussolini had achieved, country life was not yet altogether peaceful; there was great poverty throughout Italy now that the Allies had withdrawn their aid, and far too little of the promised work had been made available. Once or twice every month a dozen or so brigands would turn up in the *fattoria* courtyard to demand five lire each and a good meal.

But La Foce was remote from much of the turmoil that beset the rest of the country, and steadily began to achieve what Antonio had longed and worked for: it gradually became entirely self-sufficient, with every kind of milk product, ham, fruit, jams – even soap, made from the residue of kitchen fats, potato peelings and soda.

Iris found adjusting to life at La Foce somewhat harder.

Though as eager as Antonio to make friends with the peasant families, she neither looked nor sounded quite the part, nor was she quick to learn the rituals or master the dialect. Tall, elegant and foreign, with an unfamiliar rolling *r*, still only twenty-two and rather shy, she found herself gauche and uneasy when making the required visits to the peasant women. She had trouble distinguishing one kind of chicken from another and felt it impertinent to taste the cheeses and pronounce on which was the finest, while her first attempt to give an injection, to an old woman with asthma, ended with her breaking the syringe. They smiled at this strange figure willingly but, certain that they would never be able to understand a word she uttered, merely looked on encouragingly. She was embarrassed by the women who walked for many hours from distant farmhouses to bring her the hens, cheese and eggs traditionally due to a new *padrona* and, though intrigued by the strange rites and observances that governed their lives, felt awkward when she was taken to a spring oozing water and forming stalactites in the shape of udders in order to make prayers of intercession for sterile cows, and wives. Some days she found it hard not to feel depressed as she looked out over the dry, barren land, all of it the colour of dust, particularly when she remembered the 'gentle, trim, Florentine landscape'. Her plans to write a book about the poet Leopardi and finish her pamphlet on Fiesole and Settignano were of necessity abandoned in the course of exhausting days that, beginning at dawn and ending with dinner, never left her a moment even to take stock of what she was doing.

It was La Foce's children who finally caused her to be accepted. From her youngest days in Florence, she had always been happiest when teaching her small packs of guides and scouts or providing festive occasions for Fiesole's children. One of the things she and Antonio had discussed at length during the long months of their engagement was the idea that they should do more than simply farm their land, that they should engage in a somewhat revolutionary social experiment and turn the estate into an entirely self-sufficient community, bringing schooling and rudimentary medicine to one of the most backward parts of Tuscany. At La Foce she had everything she needed: about fifty children of different ages and degrees of literacy, outbuildings which could be converted at relatively little cost into a school, and the total backing of Antonio who, though he had no time in which to help her, shared her passion for what they owed to their new home and its inhabitants.

Eighty per cent of the local population could neither read nor write. In the early post-war years some efforts were made in the Roman countryside to give country children the rudiments of education, and it was on those small schools that Iris modelled her own. The outbuildings, which stood across the road from La Foce's main gates, were cleaned, patched up and painted; Iris brought over the beginnings of a library (*Uncle Tom's Cabin* and *Robinson Crusoe*), benches, little tables, a gramophone, records, a clock, a crucifix, a globe, scissors, and the obligatory pictures of the King and Mussolini. A teacher was employed, and given a bicycle. At the opening ceremony, in September 1924, both Iris and Antonio made speeches, and the local priest blessed the school.

Every morning the children from the outlying farms were collected – by horse and cart, or by oxen if the road was very bad; in winter they were covered in blankets – and their voices could be heard drawing nearer as they approached slowly along the rough track. At 12.30 they were given a proper lunch, followed by a short rest on camp beds that Iris had ordered, and before leaving for home at four they were given a second meal of bread, butter, cheese, ham and jam, sent over in large wicker baskets from the *fattoria*. Within weeks, pinched-looking children had begun to fill out. Iris, who later wrote in *Allegra*, her account of the short life of Byron's small daughter, that order and stability meant a great deal to children, allocated a plot of land behind the school for the pupils' own use, to grow fruit and vegetables, and sent over flowers in pots to decorate the schoolroom. She started to spend more and more time among the children, and as they thrived, so their mothers warmed to their alien *padrona*. It became a joke, many years later, that what she was really interested in was teaching her pupils about biology.

In the summer were marvellous days when La Foce seemed to becoming together in ways neither Iris nor Antonio had imagined possible. After the reaping was over at dusk supper would be laid under the trees, fireflies just beginning to be visible against the blue and purple light and the unmistakable sound of nightingales in the woods. When it rained, the earth turned a deep Sienese red. On their first wedding anniversary Iris presented Antonio with a pair of young Maremma oxen, their horns painted gold for the occasion and their flanks decorated with silver stars.

Iris had her piano and her carpets, and a new car, a Lancia Lambda; in the evenings, when she was not too tired, she listened to music on her new gramophone. She was reading Russian history for the first time, lives of Peter the Great and Ivan the Terrible; but, as she wrote to Colin in one of a series of high-spirited, almost jocular letters, 'I don't really like these formidable, gigantesque barbarians.' When she took to her bed with a cold she read the Brontë sisters, admitting to Colin that she preferred Charlotte to Emily's 'touch of the inhuman and super-human'. Colin preferred Emily – 'But that's the old difference between us,' Iris wrote back. 'I do like humanity, and you don't. I agree my taste is the more boring of the two – but I'm blest if it doesn't lead to more happiness! However, there we are at the old question – happiness versus intensity – warm water every day, or a kettle lid jammed down over boiling water . . .' She planned a library for herself, putting onto its shelves her first books, observing that it would probably be the last time in her life that she would actually have enough space for all the books she wanted. In her letters to friends in England, she sounded happy. '*Everything* you said to me about the complete and utter happiness of being "married" is true,' she wrote to Irene, 'and it only seems to get better and better.'

In the evenings, when Iris and Antonio returned to the house from the fields and the school, they talked over the small successes and failures of the day, the start of a new road, the progress some of the children were making now that they had enough to eat. They did not discuss politics, not the recent spate of arrests Mussolini had ordered, or the way Italian intellectuals were being rounded up and sent off to the *confine*, exile in primitive villages high in the mountains, on remote islands, or the brutality of the blackshirts, even though Italy's growing political uncertainty and Mussolini's excesses were becoming more marked all the time. With a note of – apology? embarrassment? defiance? – Iris explained in a letter to a friend that they felt the daily world news was something to be listened to on the wireless, not talked about over dinner. Nor, it seems, did they talk about books, despite the parcels of new biographies, histories and poetry the post brought most days from friends in England. What did they talk about? Why did they not discuss the politics of the day? Or did they, and we know nothing of it? There are no papers by, about or from Antonio in the archives at La Foce, and barely a photograph of him among the many hundreds in Iris's drawers; though he was obviously a man of great charm and warmth, intelligent and fond of his friends, it is often hard to get any real sense of him.

Life was not without its pleasures. There were excursions to Florence in the new car, a journey of about three and a half hours, while Pinsent pressed on with improvements. They stayed in the Villino in the grounds of the Villa Medici, which had been made over to them by Sybil not long after their marriage. The word *Villino*, little villa, is something of a misnomer, for by most standards it was generous in size, and elegant, with exceptional views over the city. Pinsent had been at work there, too: the room in which Iris once trained her boy scouts became the dining room, and a kitchen was built next door to it. Today the Villino, long since in other hands, is remarkably unchanged, particularly its bright marble and tile bathrooms, perhaps some of the least pleasing of all Pinsent's designs. Until the outbreak of the Second World War, there was not a time when Pinsent was not involved, in one way or another, with a building project for either Iris or Sybil.

Florence was livelier than ever, full of English and Americans who had hurried back after the war and seemed determined to pay as little attention as possible to either the past or the future. Surrounded by their pets, adding to their magnificent collections of paintings and books, and giving sumptuous dinners, their intention was to have fun. The wealthier families arranged concerts, staged operas, and spent a great deal of time planning fancy dress balls and amateur theatricals. Tea parties were held for the new debutantes. The foxtrot was danced.

One figure who had survived the war and was now back on the terrace of the Villa Medici – and on many other terraces – was Reggie Temple, a friend of Oscar Wilde's, who earned his living painting little boxes with pictures of eighteenth-century French scenes, lacquered and relacquered until they looked antique; he was so expert a copyist that he was also commissioned to reproduce panels in the sometimes dilapidated furniture bought and restored by the Anglo-Florentines. He was said to have been the model for the diminutive Maltby in Max Beerbohm's *Seven Men*, who lived on buttered toast and nightmares. As Mabel Dodge Luhan described him, he was a 'soft, round little thing, so blond and so neat, always showing lavender and mauve in his exquisite handkerchiefs as they edged his pale grey shirts.' He had been to many of the receptions of Iris's childhood, and was a great favourite at tea parties. His very presence, his appearance virtually unchanged, his conversation as acerbic and witty as ever, was a reflection of how little the foreign community in Florence seemed inclined to change.

In the summer the smart social set moved to the seaside, at Fortedei Marmi; in winter, as before the war, up to St Moritz or Gstaad. Among the Italian patrician families everyone spoke excellent English, and appeared delighted when their daughters had the good fortune to make a foreign catch. Iris and Antonio, with their expensive foreign clothes and their ease with languages, were warmly welcomed whenever they visited Florence. People found it exotic to imagine their remote and hard-working lives. Antonio had cousins and friends in the city and they were overwhelmed with invitations, though Iris never really took to Antonio's relations who, once La Foce was ready, descended to inspect what they had done, and spent hours gossiping while she was longing to get on with her work. To a friend, Iris wrote that she shared with Antonio 'a desire for gaiety – a reaction fortunately of equal violence in both of us'.

Not everyone ventured often into society: the reclusive Princess Ghyka still clearly preferred her water fountains to the cafés on the Via Tornabuoni, while Mrs Keppel, over at Bellosguardo, devoted more and more time to bridge parties. And not everyone was displeased with the way Italian politics seemed to be going. The increasingly heavy hand of Mussolini's blackshirts brought feelings of relief and security to those who could envisage only mayhem in any alliance of socialists and centrists. The American residents, in particular, favoured Fascism, which received a further boost in Florence among the foreigners when the British Institute, founded by Janet Ross's niece Lina Waterfield during the war, was taken over by Harold Goad, who was very openly a Fascist sympathiser. Iris, in one of her rare observations on politics, reported to Irene that 'we've had an exciting and amusing autumn with the Fascisti. It has been interesting watching an *opera bouffe* revolution being transformed into a serious government, and Mussolini is a very remarkable man to have been able to do it – and more remarkable still if he can make it last.' She was intensely annoyed by the way the British Embassy in Rome was so solidly anti-Fascist. 'You may have noticed that it is one of the subjects on which I get prickly,' she wrote to Colin. 'But all forms of sweeping contempt irritate me dreadfully . . . the stupidity of the intelligent is always maddening.' It is difficult to know how to interpret these comments: was she merely vexed by the air of lazy diplomatic contempt displayed for the preening blackshirts, or genuinely interested in what Mussolini had to offer? The very little she ever wrote on the governance of Italy – a line or two only in all her letters during the Fascist years – suggests that perhaps this highly intelligent and perceptive woman had resolved to distance herself from the implications of Fascism, as the only way to survive.

At I Tatti those implications were not so readily glossed over. Berenson and his guests felt extremely strongly about Mussolini, and I Tatti had become a sort of foreign club for anti-Fascist talk. Mary had never properly recovered from her various illnesses during the war. Harold Acton described her at this time as 'monumental', and she still enjoyed gargantuan meals and local gossip, and tottered along Pinsent's paths leaning on the small, frail Berenson. As Acton's father remarked, 'Those goat-like little men are made of steel'.

Mussolini's considerable success as a popular and rousing journalist had left him with the pleasant feeling that he had it in his power to solve seemingly intractable problems. Italians and Anglo-Florentines alike were lulled into a mood of security by his reassuring and apparently rational speeches, never analysing them deeply enough to see just how vacillating and confused they were. By 1924, with the biggest majority in Parliament since Cavour, Mussolini was powerful enough to suppress his adversaries and enemies more openly. Opposition deputies were isolated, assaulted, and sometimes tortured. In June 1924 Giacomo Matteotti, a brilliant economist, an eloquent speaker in Parliament, and one of the few men with the courage to confront Mussolini openly, was kidnapped on the embankment of the Tiber, where he had gone to buy cigarettes: the following day he was to have given a speech in Parliament revealing fresh evidence of Fascist brutality. His body was found near the Via Flaminia on 16 August; it showed clear signs of torture. For the rest of that year Romans made a shrine at the spot where he had been kidnapped, and prayed there. While Mussolini appears not to have been directly involved in Matteotti's murder, such was the uproar resulting from it that he nearly fell from power. Italy was again on the brink of financial chaos, however, with the cost of living rising steadily and the stock exchange uncertain, and Mussolini alone seemed to promise normality and calm: the Senate gave him a vote of confidence. Subsequently the liberal journalists on one of the best Italian newspapers, the *Corriere della Sera*, were sacked and replaced by more biddable ones, and Mussolini extended what amounted to his censorship by prescribing precisely the terms in which he should be portrayed in the newspapers: the impression given was to be one of serious-mindedness and youthfulness. No mention was ever to be made of the fact that he was a grandfather. He was not to be shown smiling or dancing. References to his prowess on the ski slopes, or to him fencing, playing tennis and boxing, on the other hand, were warmly encouraged. 'It is a horrid country to live in,' wrote Mary to her sister Alys Russell, 'a country of bullies and cowards.' Iris's regular letters to Colin at this time are full of Emily Dickinson, Zola, the Paglio, Venice, lines in Italian from Leopardi; there is no mention of Matteotti.

At I Tatti Iris found Italians, Americans and British, journalists like Victor Cunard of *The Times*, opposition politicians like Giovanni Amendola and Gaetano Salvemini, the Sicilian historian who had lost his children in the Palermo earthquake. Salvemini and Berenson were somewhat alike, both bald, with broad heads and short beards, but whereas Berenson was exquisitely neat and elegant, Salvemini had the rumpled look of a stocky and vigorous campaigner. Evenings in their company were fun, as both men were impetuous and quick to laugh. Count Umberto Morra was also often there, another historian and essayist; he was lame from polio, had inherited a house near Cortona from his mother, and later translated Virginia Woolf into Italian; he also contributed to the magazine *Rivoluzione Liberale*, the most outspoken voice of the dissidents. Morra's commonsense liberalism, Nicky Mariano noted later, 'made one forget the confusion and fanaticism of the world outside'.

These men came to lunch and tea and brought their friends, and the talk went on urgently all through the day about the misery and chaos being brought to Italy by Mussolini's brutality and irresoluteness. Ever more violent measures were taken against the slightest signs of opposition. One day Giovanni Amendola's car was stopped by a gang of Fascist youths; he was so badly beaten up that he died of his injuries. Salvemini had founded a circle devoted to the development of political thought, and refused to sign the oath of allegiance to the regime that soon became obligatory; he escaped arrest and fled to Paris and London, and then to America. Other opposition intellectuals were left in peace only after falling totally silent. All this, and much more, was discussed round the table at I Tatti, while formerly quarrelsome neighbours, like Vernon Lee, now also a violent opponent of Fascism, were welcomed back into the fold. Around Florence there was enjoyable gossip about Berenson being a spy, though spy-mania, which started as something of a joke, was now spreading uneasily among the more nervous. The mystery is why Iris, in her frequent and long letters to friends, made virtually no reference, ever, to the growing pattern of brutality, though an explanation of sorts does emerge very much later in her life.

Italy's post-war generation and her dozing foreign residents were slow and reluctant to take in the illiberality of the Fascists, but by 1924 it was no longer easy to fool oneself about the growing brutishness of the arrogant young men in black who strutted around the streets pushing people they did not like the look of into the gutter. Over the next years, month by month, Italy became steadily and more absolutely authoritarian. Mussolini replaced the mayor of every town and village with his own *podestà*, or administrative head. He declared his own person to be inviolable. When it amused him to do so, he would announce that all members of Parliament were to shout slogans and wear Fascist uniform; on such days the few Socialists left in Parliament tended to absent themselves. He talked about the 'putrefying corpse of liberty' and the need for an 'authoritarian centralized democracy'. 'Believe, obey and fight' he shouted when addressing crowds; but it was far from clear, to many of them, just exactly what he meant.

Sybil was now in her mid-forties, still good-looking, in an endearingly frail way, still ready to set out on an impromptu excursion to see a little-known Roman ruin or unspoilt church, provided she felt well enough. Increasingly, she did not. The most vivid memory Iris retained of her mother as she grew older was of Sybil lying in her sea-blue bedroom at the Villa Medici, surrounded by flowers, the heat turned up as high as it would go. Having spent her childhood at the whim of her mother's health, Iris felt both irritated and anxious whenever she was called back to the villa from La Foce to deal with some domestic crisis her mother did not feel strong enough to handle.

Sybil's marriage to Scott was drawing to an end. When he could, he fled to London to be with Vita, who welcomed his passionate admiration less and less but for a while pretended nothing had changed and took him down to Long Barn for weekends with Harold. People began to refer to him as a bounder, but few have been less like bounders than this sad, obsessed man, to whose long letters desperately reaffirming their love and begging for reassurance Vita replied in ever cooler terms. When Iris was told that Sybil planned to divorce Scott, she wrote to Colin that she felt her mother was entirely right to do so: 'But I hate the sheer human spectacle of it all – the staring eyes and the pointing fingers – not what people, who know nothing about it, may say and think – but the ugliness of their voices.' Sybil's father, Lord Desart, was extremely upset. In 1927 she and Scott were formally divorced.

Although Aldous Huxley rather unkindly said of *Zelide* that it was 'full of that kind of exquisitely good writing that is, one feels instinctively, only another kind of bad writing', the book had won the James Tait Black Memorial Prize on its publication in 1925, and Scott's clear and sympathetic profile of Boswell prompted an invitation to write a life of Boswell for the 'English Men of Letters' series. He was on the point of accepting when he was approached by Colonel R. H. Isham, an American who had recently acquired an important collection of Boswell's letters in Ireland, and wanted Scott to edit them. In October 1927 he sailed for New York to begin work on the letters in Isham's house: like Berenson so many years before, Isham was to be his patron.

Scott did not take to America. He felt a prisoner in Isham's grand house, and when he could he escaped the endless smart parties and went downtown. He liked the feeling of energy in Manhattan, and had an affair with the interior decorator Muriel Draper. His skin turned rather sallow and his teeth rather yellow; and to those who now met him for the first time, he often seemed scruffy and unkempt. To the disgust of his secretary, he referred to Americans as 'the barbarians'.

Nevertheless, he was exhilarated by editing Boswell. A holiday in London in 1929 coincided with a visit to England by Iris, who found 'so little trace in his strong, erect figure and smiling face of the worn unquiet being I had parted from three years earlier that at first I hardly recognised him'. Iris was always fond of Scott, who as her stepfather had done his best to weaken Sybil's hold over her. In London they went to picture galleries together, and Iris noted these hours as the 'happiest I ever had with him. He had found his work and himself. The old irony, old mockery and subtlety were there but tempered by a confident hope in the future.'

At the end of July Scott sailed for New York on the SS *Adriatic*, taking Pinsent with him. They checked into the Hotel Shelton, where Scott soon complained of feeling unwell. At first they thought it was 'flu, but his condition worsened and he was taken into the Rockefeller Institute Hospital, where the doctors diagnosed pneumonia. On the morning of 14 August 1929, Geoffrey Scott died; he was forty-six. Iris's grandmother, Mrs Cutting, paid for the funeral. To a friend Iris wrote sadly that she had always felt him to be a tragic figure, bringing unhappiness to himself and often to his friends. 'Life is ugly, ugly . . . I feel frightened and alone.'

Pinsent carried the ashes back to England, where they were interred in the cloisters of his old Oxford college, New College; the plate bears the words 'Scott: Humanist and Boswellian Scholar'. His last years and his book *The Architecture of Humanism* indicate how much more there was to him than the idle, somewhat precious dilettante who had so irritated Berenson at I Tatti so many years before. *The Architecture of Humanism* was a highly original and scholarly book, a work of pure theory rare in its field, which caused those who read and understood it to re-examine many of their views on architecture and aesthetics. In his obituary *The Times* referred to him as the 'finished product of a high civilisation'.

Edith Wharton had been very fond of him, and though she once accused him jokingly of being like an 'over-fed squirrel who only cared to crack every nut once and then threw them away', she subsequently admitted that he had become 'the master of a perfect prose and of a delicate lyrical gift'.

In the autumn of 1924 snow came early to the Val d'Orcia. From the terrace of La Foce you could see the great medieval tower of Radicofani gleaming white against the green mountains. Iris both liked and felt easy with children, and throughout her life delighted in celebrations and anniversaries: she was determined to make a proper Christmas for the seventy-five tenant farmers' children of La Foce. The tireless Pinsent was already at work building a nativity out of clay in the granary, having 'stolen, or borrowed', as Iris put it, 'some lovely settocento figures' carved in wood which he found in the attics. Iris was charmed by it, and in the very few notes Pinsent left about his work, this nativity is highlighted as one of the things he most valued doing. Iris had decided to give each child a woollen garment and some toys, so was busy knitting sweaters with 'sleeves of curiously varying length'. On 21 December the children arrived through the snow on the ox-carts, wrapped up in layers of blankets. It was the kind of occasion that Iris, practical, energetic, and with a strong sense of duty inherited from both the Cuttings and her English grandfather, most enjoyed.

Antonio had been low and feeling ill for some time and was becoming increasingly anxious about what might be wrong with him; in January he was found to have the beginnings of an abscess on one lung, possibly left over from the war. The Origos went to London, where Antonio was admitted to a hospital in Putney and Iris stayed with the Desarts in Rutland Gardens. Her grandmother was suffering from one of her recurring bouts of heart trouble, so she acted as hostess for a dinner Lord Desart gave at the Inner Temple, where he was Treasurer. In the daytime she wandered around the shops looking for carpets for La Foce. On her way home to Italy she stopped in Paris to search the stalls along the banks of the Seine for prints for her room, and was delighted to find that Pinsent had a present waiting for her of five prints of Japanese fish. She was pleased to be home. The daffodils were out, and she wrote to a friend that never had she felt such a sense of gaiety and warmth. To curious visitors who came to discover what had drawn the Origos into their absurd adventure she pointed out the 'miles and miles of empty land, with great scudding white clouds, and rocks', and the beauty of the cultivated fields. She was at last finding time to begin the research for her planned life of Leopardi, whose story and personality intrigued her more and more. To Colin, she wrote that 'It is positively ridiculous how much happier I am since I have a definite job again.' Then another occupation, for the time being far more engrossing, relegated the Leopardi book to the sidelines once more: she discovered that she was pregnant. To Colin, she wrote: 'I am going to have a baby . . . I don't suppose it seems an epoch making event to anyone else . . . I wonder whether one will be able to give it a good start – and if it makes any difference in the end. Wish it luck, Colin.' Writing to other friends of her excitement she speculated at length on whether a 'man-child' might be more suitable for La Foce; but 'little girls are so much more intelligent! And demonstrative!' Colin sent her the complete works of Aristophanes to fill the hours of waiting.

The baby was due towards the end of June. The spring of 1925 was cold and stormy, and at La Foce mice ate the carpets and damp got into the piano. Iris kept busy planning the nursery and preparing the garden for the summer, chafing at the long delay involved in turning 'a dust heap' into fertile ground. It snowed hard at the end of April and she worried about her tulips and daffodils; then came the magical Italian spring weather. In May Iris moved back to the Villa Medici; in Florence she had her hair cut short, fearing it would be very hot in bed in July. She filled her days by going to operas and concerts, and contemplated joining a class to learn Arabic and Persian with a tutor brought back to Florence by a friend who had just returned from Cairo. 'I *am* excited – happy – anxious – all at once,' she confided to Colin.

The birth began at four o'clock in the morning of 24 June, just as bells began to ring out and fireworks were set off for the feast of St John the Baptist; by ten past nine Iris had a small son, weighing just over seven pounds. On 3 July he was christened Gian Clemente (after Antonio's father) Bayard in her bedroom at the Villa Medici by the Franciscan missionary, Padre Girolamo Golubovich, who had married them. 'Gianni' avoided what Iris considered the 'slight priggishness of Clemente'. Two of the godparents were Ottavia Sanseverino and Dino Franceschi, old friends of Antonio's; America was represented by her aunt Olivia James and Gordon Gardiner, her father's friend. Though she complained that childbirth felt like being torn to pieces, she much enjoyed feeding Gianni like a 'good cow.' 'And now I'm getting well very quickly,' she wrote to a friend, 'and enjoying a quality of happiness and peacefulness entirely different from anything I have ever known, and quite indestructible.' She lay in bed at the Villa Medici listening to the fountains in the gardens while

Antonio read to her from D'Annunzio, or Aksakov's *Russian Gentleman*. The baby was considered rather ugly, with a red face and a long head. After ten days, Nanny Lawrence took him on.

On 23 July the Origos returned to La Foce, setting off from Florence at five in the morning to avoid the heat, and arrived home to find a great banquet in preparation for the end of the threshing; Gian Clemente was shown off and praised. Iris felt, she told a friend, 'the utter contentment and passivity of the Italian summer stealing over me'. Like her parents when she was a baby, she began an album registering Gianni's progress, with dates and photographs. At five and a half months, by which time he was judged rather prettier, with long eyelashes and very fair hair, he went on his first train journey to Florence; at seven months 'he is very happy and good tempered, and adores being played with'. At eight-and-a-half months he crawled backwards and said his first words. On 30 September she weaned him. The following summer, when he was one, the Meades came to stay and they all went to the sea at Castiglioncello, near Livorno; Gianni learnt to walk. That autumn, when Nancy Lawrence took a holiday and was briefly replaced by Nanny Halliday, Iris noted that 'he first began to show a marked preference for my company'. He was, she reported to her American grandmother, an observant and 'completely companionable' child, 'full of character and humour'. On hot days she would sit with him for hours under the pergola of vines while he lay asleep in his pram. So restless and uncertain in other ways, Iris was captivated by her small son. These were perhaps the happiest months of her life.

CHAPTER SIX

No past and no future

Iris's life over the next few years settled down to one of hard work at La Foce, and a great deal of travelling; it was a time when women in her position thought little of leaving their small children in the care of a succession of trained nannies. Once again she was forced to abandon all plans for writing about Leopardi. Intimate and cosy weeks spent with Gianni and his nanny at La Foce, planting bulbs in the new garden made possible by a present from Mrs Cutting of a pipe to carry water up from the valley to the house, were interspersed with travel – to Egypt, the Middle East, Sicily, Capri – with Antonio, and sometimes with Pinsent. Like the short diaries she kept of their travels, Iris's letters are lively and energetic and give a good idea of the pace at which the party moved, and of her eye for what mattered and stood out. Apart from Nanny, Iris wrote to Mrs Cutting, Gianni was at his happiest with her and with a small spaniel called Cosimo. When Nanny fell ill and Iris and Antonio were left to look after the baby, 'I washed, dressed, fed and exercised him and really got a lot of fun out of it.' Gianni was never cross, she reported to Mrs Cutting, though he had strong likes and dislikes; and he looked very sweet in the sweater his great-grandmother had knitted him, with its matching pink and blue knickers. He hated the touch of fur. He was developing 'a most infectious smile'.

In the summer of 1925 and in the midst of a sudden domestic crisis caused by the unexpected departure of La Foce's footman and cook, Mrs Cutting arrived from Westbrook. She brought with her a butler and maid, and Iris felt obliged to give them the best guest rooms. Iris's uncle Bronson, her father's younger brother, was of the party. At first Iris had found him grossly fat, imperturbably silent and sometimes very rude, but she grew fond of him once she realised how much of his silence was the result of his mother's relentless chatter. When Sybil joined them from the Villa Medici Iris spent a wretched time acting as a buffer between her mother and grandmother, for relations between them had if anything grown more tense over the years since Bayard's death . . . 'and how they dislike each other!' And although Iris was very fond of Mrs Cutting, she did not find her particularly easy, either. 'Why do some people drive one to this unfortunate combination of irrepressible irritation and remorse?' she asked a friend. In the autumn, after a week in Florence, Iris returned to La Foce to plant bulbs and roses sent as presents from Colin, and to prepare La Foce's Christmas party for the farm children, now risen in number to a hundred. While she was knitting Christmas presents she could hear the children rehearsing carols in the schoolroom across the road. If not precisely bored, she was growing restless, and began to long for new books and people, even a few new clothes. 'You are, however much as you may deny it,' Colin mocked her in a letter, 'an extremely social animal.'

For a while, at least, some of the restlessness was assuaged by a trip with Antonio to Egypt, Palestine and Syria. The journal she kept was more self-conscious in tone than her letters, and at times even somewhat over-written, in sharp contrast to the taut and highly controlled style of her later years. Rather like the introduction to a school essay, the preface stated her goal very precisely: to tell 'only of personal experience and the appearance of things. It is a record of facts and impressions.' The early Egyptian tombs at Sakhara she found 'sensual if you like – but sunnily and not darkly so'. In Luxor she 'saw beauty as if I were born again'; in Palestine she decided she preferred the waywardness of the Arab world 'away from Jewry old or new, to the world of Arabian romance'. On moonlit nights 'we went out muffled in furs'. They rode donkeys and walked, sailed on the Nile, and decided that they found Egyptology 'tedious: the names are too similar, and there are too many of them . . . all too hieratic and remote . . .'

With Iris and Antonio on their trip went Walsh, Iris and Sybil's maid, another figure in the mould of Doody, who took charge in the desert when their party became bogged down in confusion and inefficiency. She engaged a caravan of twelve camels, onto which were loaded three iron bedsteads, and they set off on a gruelling twelve-day trip across the desert riding donkeys or camels. Iris loved it all, but was not sorry to sleep in a real bed again – 'For we *are* civilised, and that was not a civilised life. But what a holiday, what a blessed, beautiful holiday it had been.' She felt a certain distaste for the 'locust-like hordes of Clark's tourists . . . descended from America', but another comment is perhaps more revealing. In Tripoli, to her considerable surprise, she found the dining room of the hotel full of French officers 'with smartly dressed wives and pale-faced children, all mingling socially and with no apparent sense of incongruity with the coal-black Singalese [Senegalese?] . . . for the Singalese are, after all, *very* far removed from our civilisation . . .' In the diary are complaints about the cold and the inefficiency, and about not feeling very well, but also repeated accounts of the immense pleasure provided by everything she had seen. This was the kind of journey she dreamt about, one that would provide her with thoughts and ideas for months to come. When they finally returned to La Foce they had been away for more than two months.

Christmas itself was celebrated, as was customary, at the Villa Medici, with Pinsent, Reggie Temple, Percy Lubbock, and an old family friend, Maud Trelawney, who took to her bed with 'flu. Iris saw her first film in Florence, and was so captivated that she went back to the cinema every day. On her way home to La Foce after Christmas she made a detour to Milan to go to the opera; Gianni had been sent on ahead. When she got back, the mimosa and violets were out and Gianni was waiting impatiently for her in the drive. Soon she was on her way again, this time with Sybil to Sicily, from where she wrote to Colin: 'It's so beautiful! – a landscape to soothe and console!' In Messina, the almond blossom was out. Iris and Antonio were planning to make their way from Sicily to Barcelona, as the first step in an exploration of Spain. With Colin, in the course of their usual exchange of discursive letters, she speculated about which were the most moving passages in literature: she chose Plato's death of Socrates, and Prince Andre's death in *War and Peace*, but then confessed that she could not think of a satisfactory third. Gianni, almost overwhelmingly loved, totally wanted, spent most of his time with his nanny.

Plans for Spain were abruptly postponed when Antonio developed appendicitis and the Desarts then announced that they would like to spend Easter in Italy. Iris hurried back to La Foce, where spring was just beginning. Antonio and Pinsent, their urge to travel unassuaged, were now discussing plans to camp and climb in theAbruzzi mountains south of Rome.

Iris had been coughing for some months, and there was growing unease about her health. Her father Bayard, uncle Bronson and aunt Justine had all developed tuberculosis between twenty-three and twenty-five: Iris was now twenty-four. 'It's all nonsense,' she wrote crossly to a friend, 'but I shall take their advice and go up to Switzerland this winter . . . for I love life much too much to take any foolish risks.'

To Colin at about this time, Iris tried to explain why her letters never touched on politics. 'I like to ignore strikes and such things in letters. What are the papers for? Correspondence should have a more intimate flavour.' It was much the same as her explanation of why she and Antonio never discussed Fascism. Iris's health had now improved enough for her to make, with Antonio, the 'best motor trip I have ever been on', to see the shepherds in the Abruzzi mountains migrating with their flocks to the high pastures. The only drawback, she noted, was the large crowd that gathered each morning to watch the strangers dress.

However, her cough grew no better. An X-ray in Florence showed, not the lesion they feared, but still a 'patch altogether prepared for tuberculosis'. The Origos had vaguely been thinking of a winter in New York; instead it was now decided that they should settle for a while in Switzerland. They made a quick visit to London, to see more doctors, for Antonio was suffering from liver trouble. While he was in hospital Iris went to stay first with the Meades, the attraction being, she wrote, their mixture of 'warmth and casualness', then to Yorkshire to see her much-loved and now totally deaf great-aunt, Lady Wenlock, a 'figure carved in finest ivory' for whom, despite her deafness, conversation was the great joy of her life; 'but the charm still clings to her, like the folds of her velvet gown'. Antonio joined her in Yorkshire, and before leaving bought some pigs for La Foce.

In September 1926 Iris arrived back at La Foce, having seen little of Gianni more than in passing for many months. The house and gardens, the farms, everything was doing better than she had feared: 'No cows have died recently – the rats are not in the piano, nor phylloxera in the vines . . .' The autumn rains had just arrived and the valley was fast losing its desolate, parched look, but it was still extremely hot in the middle of the day. Iris was enchanted afresh by her small son, now over two and 'most affectionate, and very sensitive to any form of beauty, music, pretty stuffs, etc.' In the cool of the evening she and Antonio sat out on the terrace and read stories to him. Nanny took off on her holidays, and Iris found that Gianni still had all the pretty baby ways, and yet was discovering all the 'companionableness' of a little boy. His hair was still very fair, and he had dark eyelashes. Photographs show a sturdy, winning toddler, in absurdly fashionable clothes. Mrs Cutting had sent him a hundred dollars to open a savings account.

The family party travelled to St Moritz by way of Paris, for some shopping. They then had to change trains three times before reaching St Moritz, and for much of the time Gianni howled. But when they reached Suvretta House and found they had a suite with a beautiful view of the mountains, high up above the skating rink, their spirits rose. Iris, told to rest, spent most of her days swathed in furs on a *chaise-longue* on the terrace, reading, writing letters and watching the skaters. She sent her American grandmother frequent bulletins about Gianni and what he could do; he and Nanny were roaming cheerfully around St Moritz. Unable to conceive of Christmas without a festivity for children, Iris gave a party for some small cousins staying in a nearby hotel. Pinsent joined them for Christmas 'in his usual dust-covered, moth-eaten, town suit'. On New Year's

Eve she was allowed to attend the grand dinner, for which she had bought a dress of gold lame and a fan-shaped headdress.

Reflecting on marriage during the many hours she passed on her sunny terrace, Iris wrote to Colin, who was increasingly eager to find a wife, that in her view marriage without children was somewhat pointless, but that 'unless you start into [it] with a quite unlimited desire to make the other (not yourself) happy, and a practically unlimited intention of tolerance (I say intention because of course it breaks down, but still it's the only thing that keeps one going), in order to achieve that end – you'd much better not marry anyone.' Stern words for a young woman of barely twenty-four; but there had been something almost ageless about Iris since her childhood days in Fiesole, and she changed remarkably little over the years.

Iris now caught influenza, and was instructed by the Davos doctor to lead a complete invalid's life – sleep late in the morning, skate for one hour a day, spend the rest of the time on her balcony. 'What a place!' she noted forlornly. 'What a life! My thoughts turn longingly to the gardens of Luxor – to the temples of Sicily – to everywhere that is not white and cold.' In the evenings she played patience while Antonio read the *Corriere della Sera*. As a young girl she had realised how much she wanted to travel; it had now become a restless longing, a source of daydreams and half-impossible projects, encouraged by Antonio, who felt much as she did. 'I think I like even ugly new places,' she wrote to a friend, 'provided they are really new – something rich and strange.' A year spent, like the last, between La Foce, Florence, London and Switzerland (conveniently forgetting Milan, Paris, Sicily and the Abruzzi) struck her as time largely wasted and completely stationary.

By the middle of March 1927 they were back in Italy,

enchanted by the early spring blossom and, as Iris put it, finding the people 'incredibly good looking and intelligent' compared to the Swiss. They also had a trip planned that had every prospect of success: another visit to Sicily, to see the Greek temples, staying in a magnificent nineteenth-century seafront hotel, the Villa Igeia in Palermo, set in a grove of orange and lemon trees. She was amazed by the stories she heard about the Mafia and admired the new Fascist prefect of Palermo, who seemed to be winning what amounted to a civil war against them by rounding up not only the immediate families of Mafia suspects but all their relations and even their friends. The prefect was, she remarked, a man of great personal courage and complete ruthlessness. Struck wherever she went by Sicily's flowers and plants, Iris was even more delighted when they got back to La Foce to find the new roses in full bloom and Pinsent's fountain with its dolphin spouting. They were just in time, too, to catch the first days of the haymaking. Plans for the garden became all the more exciting when they found that twice as much water as had been expected came up Mrs Cutting's pipe from the valley. Iris instantly began to plan where to put jonquils and daffodils, the highly scented red roses she loved, and wisteria. Later she used to say that she had never looked at a garden until she had her own. Iris, reported her aunt Olivia, who had been staying at La Foce while they were away, still looked a bit thin and tired, but distinctly better: 'In fact the thinness is most becoming. That, combined with her happiness, makes her look quite beautiful.' Gianni, who had flourished in Switzerland, was 'the picture of health – sturdy and strong'. To Irene, who was as close a confidante as Colin, and in some matters closer, Iris wrote: 'I *do* mean to have another, some day, as I want a daughter – but I still look back on it as an indescribable nightmare.' Later she added: 'Could you please get for me, and bring out, whatever you on the whole think the *safest* method of not presenting Jan [Gianni] with a sister just yet! Dutch caps?'

The journeys for 1927 were far from over. There was England for a hot July, and Iris revelled in a visit to her ever-closer friends the Meades, in Wales, reading stories aloud to an assortment of differently-aged children in the garden. Then London for the Russian Ballet – 'even when bad it is so much better than almost any other entertainment' – and a very 'curiously conceived' luncheon party given by Sibyl Colefax, with Lytton Strachey, E. V. Lucas, Francis Birrell, Geoffrey Scott and Vita Sackville-West, as well as an unfortunate American visitor, 'presumably a relic of Lady Colefax's tour', who 'like others of her breed was curiously unassimilable'. Iris talked to Vita about her recently published *The Land*, for which she had just won the Hawthornden Prize, then went off to see an exhibition of paintings by Sickert, two of which she longed to possess. There was something about all these clever, highly educated and sharp-tongued people in London that was beginning to draw Iris, particularly as her shyness was now receding. Antonio lasted through five days of 'family parties', then gave up and fled to La Foce.

In Castiglioncello, where they took a villa once again for the swimming, what was to prove a defining moment in Iris's life occurred. Castellani, an outstanding Tuscan specialist in whom they all had great faith, decided that she had been wrongly diagnosed: her trouble was really a bronchial fungus, not TB, and she needed regular courses of injections – in London.

1926 was the year that Sybil decided to marry again. She had never cared for being alone, and the Villa Medici, empty of all but staff apart from the occasional visit of old friends like Pinsent, was echoing and immense. Her new husband was an unexpected choice and, like Geoffrey Scott, did not go down well with the Anglo-Florentines. Once again, he was a man much loved by a clique that was quick to reject outsiders. Yet it was on the whole a happy marriage and the man she settled for, known if anything for his indifference to women, proved kind and loving.

Percy Lubbock was forty-nine when he married Sybil; she was forty-eight. One of five brothers, he had never married, perhaps not least because he belonged to Edith Wharton's 'Inner Circle', as it was known, a small, lethally mocking band of friends of which she was the conductor from 1904 until her death in 1937, and Henry James the presiding genius. As a group, scattered across Italy, America and England – Walter Berry, head of the American Chamber of Commerce in Paris, Gaillard Lapsley, medieval historian at Cambridge, the author Howard Sturgis, as well as Wharton and James – they seldom met in more than twos or threes, but wherever and whenever it was, they clearly had a lot of fun. They regarded themselves as exiles, members of a tribe doomed to rapid extinction by the Philistine invaders for whom Europe offered a sense of civilisation that America lacked. Edith Wharton in particular spoke of her love of a landscape 'where the face of nature seems moulded by the passions and imaginings of men'. Sybil did not belong among these sharp, witty people, any more than she had really belonged at I Tatti, where Mary Berenson now observed that a marriage between Sybil and Lubbock would be a disaster: 'they could not be happy, for she can't adapt herself and Percy has a dangerous temper'. Nor were the Desarts much taken with Sybil's third husband, although Iris, who was not overly taken with him herself, did her best to praise him to them.

Lubbock was a relative latecomer to the Inner Circle, sometimes also called the 'happy few'. Almost as much interested in friendship as in the arts, the group had no fixed topics, beyond the celebration of friendship and the pleasure they took in their literary friends, people like H. G. Wells, Joseph Conrad, Proust and Virginia Woolf. After Edith Wharton's first visit to Berenson she went to I Tatti every year, to work in the library and talk about art with her host; Lubbock once said of her that her mind was that of a 'hungry young hawk . . . [which had] . . . somehow to be fed'. Geoffrey Scott, after his marriage to Sybil and exile from I Tatti, spoke of the Inner Circle dismissively as 'Edith Wharton's invertebrate friends'. Henry James, who acknowledged Edith Wharton's supremacy of the group, said that he always had warning of an impeding visit from her because it was heralded by what he called 'urgent and terrible signals'; he also once said of Edith – they all talked and wrote incessantly to and about each other – that there was 'nothing stupid in her and nothing small'. She would talk by the hour about people, their manners and customs, '. . . so long as they throw light upon the chase of human nature, fit quarry for a noble curiosity'. Of herself, with surprising and slightly melancholy diffidence, Edith Wharton once wrote that she felt her mind was 'A country where the lights are low/And where the roads are hard to find.'

Lubbock had met the Inner Circle in 1906, when he first went to Italy and fell in love with it. As a writer who produced books in a sometimes whimsical, old-fashioned tone that aped Henry James he is no longer fashionable, but Graham Greene described his by now long-forgotten *The Craft of Fiction* as 'an admirable primer', and *Earlham*, which takes the form almost

149

of a travel book, is a charming evocation of the Norfolk house in which he spent his holidays as the child of banking Quaker parents and grandparents. His grandparents were obviously kind and affectionate, and Earlham smelt of clean wood, fresh linen and roses; there were prayers every morning, games with his rumbustious uncles, and a wonderful sense of order and safety. He was at his best with literary biography, and in 1906 he was editing a book based on the letters of Elizabeth Browning and was about to be made Librarian of the Pepys Library at Magdalene College, Cambridge. Friends described him as a 'dark, long man'. Berenson once said that while for him friendships were only like 'flying sunlight on a bright morning', for Lubbock they were a series of 'deep thrills, exaltations and agonies'. Lubbock was moody and introspective, his own faith in himself 'small'; his inner self, he would say, was not for exposure, and his image of himself was that of a 'silent young man'.

Sybil deceived herself in the same way. In *The Child in the Crystal*, her own book of reminiscences, she spoke of herself as a child 'only desirous of escaping notice', and it is hard not to sense something ingenuous in her words. By the time they met, Lubbock was known for his fine voice and for his propensity to recite anecdotes at the breakfast table.

Unlike the I Tatti coterie, in which everyone analysed their own feelings and everyone else's, the 'happy few' were careful to keep their personal concerns private even from other members of the group – which may account for its peaceful survival over so many years: there was in fact no open disagreement of any kind until the day when Lubbock announced to Edith Wharton that he intended to marry Sybil. Mrs Wharton, who particularly loathed chattering women and had come to despise Sybil, now wrote crossly to another of the Inner Circle: 'This is the third of my friends she has annexed, and I see you and Robert going next, and then BB, and then finally even Walter – kicking and screaming!!! Isn't it queer? . . . Apparently, with Percy, the fainting did it.. He is still much impressed, early Victorianism probably never come his way before.' Edith Wharton found Sybil's knack of fainting dead away when crossed extremely tiresome. Her immediate reaction was to belittle Lubbock's abilities; hurt, he responded by accusing her of insularity.

Lubbock seems to have entertained no doubts about his bride. Many years later, after Sybil's death, he wrote a soliloquy on their marriage, as sentimental as it is adoring. 'For our minds,' he wrote, 'hers and mine, march together – I don't say with an equal sonority of tramp and tread, much less with an equal alacrity or swing and spring, but as best they may follow one road in the same direction, the high road of reason; and otherwise a more complete contrast of composition, hers and mine, I never knew . . .' The vain, spoilt and self-obsessed Sybil is hard to recognise in Lubbock's memoir (it was never published); but charming Sybil clearly was, with a sense of sudden fun and, when she had the energy for it, the ability to give great pleasure to others.

Together she and Lubbock now embarked on what were to be nearly twenty years of close companionship – much of it dominated by a real or imaginary virus she believed she had caught somewhere on her foreign travels. More and more of her life was spent in the twilight of her rooms, while more and more of Lubbock's was spent in the twilight of daily life, for he was gradually going blind. But they were kind to each other, even if it was Lubbock who did most of the looking-after. The Inner Circle and I Tatti set were somewhat disconcerted by all this happiness.

In his writing Lubbock was capable of passages that were both leisurely and contrived, interspersed with sharp and perceptive insights about people; and he was remarkably generous of spirit. In 1947, ten years after her death, he wrote a portrait of Edith Wharton, the restless intellectual who had come to Europe in her youth 'for talk – for more talk, with more people, and with people as fearless of talk, as familiar with it, as dependent on it as herself . . .' It is nowhere as unkind as her memoirs of him.

The late 1920s turned out to be a time of deaths as well as alliances, leaving a poorer world for Iris. Geoffrey Scott died of pneumonia in America. Janet Ross, the most enduring and plucky of the Anglo-Florentines, died in Florence in 1927, having written not long before: 'The story of my life is finished. A happy one on the whole, save that I am rather solitary and feel the void left by the death of old friends.' Then there was Iris's English grandmother, who had suffered from heart trouble for many years, and now died in 1927, the year of her golden wedding anniversary. Lord Desart, devastated, scribbled a desolate note in pencil to Iris: 'We knew in our hearts that we loved each other in 1871, recognised it in 1872, were separated by order from 1873 to Christmas 1875. It really began when I put her skates on in 1870 when she was seventeen – no one had paid her such an attention before. I feel I often failed her in many things, but not in love, which was the same when she was seventeen, and when she was seventy-four. I believe that love in marriage is better than anything in life – ambition, success are not in the running with it. My real life has always been in my home – wife, children and grandchildren. It is a happy record, but without it life is very strange and difficult.' Desart now came to rely more than ever on Iris's affection, and wrote to her constantly, with great tenderness. Seeing her off at the station the first time she left him alone after his wife's death, he went back five times to say goodbye to her. In the following years he made regular trips to Italy, and she went whenever she could to stay with him at Rudand Gate. So often Iris had felt that his approval and interest had done something to replace the loss of her father; now she was anguished by his sadness. Often, too, around this time, as she told a friend, she dreamt again of her own father. Lord Desart did not have long to live; he quickly grew increasingly frail, and died in 1934.

And almost as painful as any of the deaths was that of Doody, the maid who had loved Iris and done so much for her as a child. Doody was in London with Sybil when she was run over by a bus. Iris was in Venice: she caught the next train to London, but arrived too late to see Doody alive.

There was nowhere in the world that Iris preferred to Charlie and Aileen Meade's house, Pen-y-lan, in Wales. It was in empty, mountainous country, with great sloping fields covered in sheep. There she felt safe: she helped Aileen with the garden, she read aloud to the four Meade children, and she gossiped, lying for hours at the foot of Aileen's bed, among the dogs and the books. People rarely associate Iris Origo with fits of intimate laughter and cosy, leisurely jokes, yet the Meades' three surviving children, Pin, Flavia and Simon, all vividly recall the giggles and merriment coming from their mother's bedroom for what seemed to them like mornings on end. The twelve-year difference in age between Aileen and Iris seemed never to matter at all.

Her health still somewhat uncertain, Iris came frequently to London for courses of injections from the noted Dr Castellani, who treated all the members of the Cutting, Desart and Origo families. She stayed with her grandfather, whose mourning for his wife seemed barely to lift and whose loving attitude continued to remind her of her father. She went to the theatre with friends; she dined at the Savoy. There was something about England that never failed to captivate her and, as she had written to Colin, so she occasionally regretted aloud to friends the fact that Antonio would never allow her to send Gianni to Eton. The endless literary talk far into the night, refreshingly less inward-looking than the precious exchanges at I Tatti or among the Inner Circle, suited her. She liked gossip of a comic and wry kind, but did not greatly care for the often vicious tone heard in Florence. She loved intimacy and thrived on close friends like Aileen and Irene, but at twenty-five she was still rather shy, and could seem haughty when she was ill at ease.

It was just over five years since she had begun exchanging letters, sometimes as many as two or three a week each, with Colin MacKenzie, the young man from Glasgow wounded in the war who was in love with her when she married Antonio. Often they were more like diaries than letters, containing not just the small dramas of everyday life, but views on everything from philosophy to architecture and, most importantly, music, for Colin was very musical. For him and to a greater extent for Iris, their correspondence was a mutual and unending education, as they wrote, and quoted, in Latin, French, German, Italian and English. Early in their exchanges they made what seems a surprising decision – to keep all their letters to each other, and to have them typed up. Are the letters complete, or were passages removed in the typing? Did they intend, one day, to publish them? The letters exist to this day, in leather-bound volumes. In its completeness and apparent total frankness and honesty about themselves and the people in their lives, it is a remarkable correspondence.

Early in October 1927 Iris went to London, leaving Antonio and Gianni at La Foce. She had planned a weekend with the Meades, and discovered that Colin was also to be at Pen-y-lan. The Meade children had taken to Colin; Pin, then aged five, told him seriously that she hoped his wooden leg would get better very quickly. From Wales they travelled back together to London, where Colin had business. It is clear from the letters they wrote one another when Iris left three days later that something between them had profoundly altered: the long literary correspondence had become a love affair. Five days, they seem to have agreed upon, with no past and no future: but the future proved hard to control.

'You have entered into the very heart of my life,' wrote Colin, even before they had parted. 'I only pray that I haven't done you more harm than good, my darling . . . What I said to you this morning is true – I shall never feel beauty again without being close to you . . .' A few days later he wrote again: 'I want words beyond all the vocabulary of lovers – how otherwise can I express my love for you? . . . Iris Darling, I still cannot get over the wonder of it – after these years of silence and restraint . . . these last days have been pure magic – your words, my beautiful Iris.'

Iris's first replies were written as in a daze. 'I feel as if today I could say nothing but your name . . . Colin, my dear, where are you? Can I really have lost you? Colin, Colin.' Next day she wrote again: 'What shall I do, my dear, when I wake up and you are not there? Every inch of my body is calling out for you and I can still feel your kisses, my lips are bruised by your lips, I am trembling. Oh Colin, Colin, I should not write to you like this. It is the last time.' Even she did not believe what she was saying. For years they had said nothing; now it all came out, with an urgency that seemed irrepressible. It is clear that they had at least discussed the possibility of going away together but had rejected it, for the moment at least. Iris, now in bed with 'flu, began to reflect on what she had done, and while she was agonising over the possible consequences received a letter from La Foce: Gianni had set off up the road towards Chianciano and, when found and brought back, said that he had been going to the station to meet his mother. 'Can you imagine what I felt, reading it? I am ashamed my dear, ashamed.'

Later she wrote again, obviously feeling a need to explain to him something of her relationship with Antonio. 'I agree with you, Colin, in despising remorse. You must not think that I regret one hour, one minute of our days together . . . But somehow, by some metamorphosis of the brain, some purification, I must turn my feeling for you into a thing apart . . . I can take nothing from him to give to you. There is a part of me – some mental, spiritual understanding – that has never been his. There we can meet, so close, so close . . . But I must be able to think of you and look him in the face. I must not betray his secrets to you . . . We *can* keep it beautiful. I know that you will help me.' It was not easy. At Folkestone, as she was returning to Italy, she found a telegram: 'Your going becomes almost intolerable.' She answered: 'I too can hardly bear it. God bless you always.'

They did their best. They were discreet. For a long time they did not confide even in their closest friends. They were extremely careful about their letters. For a while Pinsent was Iris's *poste-restante*, until a resourceful Florentine postman thought he noticed that her mail was going astray, and rerouted Colin's letters to the Villa Medici. If letters did not come when she expected them, Iris agonised. In Glasgow, Colin had them typed up, checked them with Iris, then locked them away. In their letters they dwell very little on guilt. It says much for Iris's character, about her stoicism and determination that, throughout the course of their affair, each time she returned from a few days with Colin – clearly, from her letters, in an agony of missing him, and uncertainty – she forced herself quickly back into the life of La Foce and the daily routine of its children. There was something in her nature that was tough – on herself and on others – and absolutely without self-pity. She felt closer to Gianni than ever, and played rousing tunes for him on her piano so that he could march up and down like a soldier. She planted a new peach orchard. The formalities of daily life at La Foce went on as usual: even when they were alone, she and Antonio changed for dinner, and sat in the library afterwards.

Most surprising, perhaps, is that their own love affair did not prevent Iris and Colin from confiding in one another, as they always had, about other involvements. On Iris's part there was just one other flirtation, but it was most surprising. When she was seventeen, she told Colin, she had fallen in love with Pinsent, only to have her love firmly rejected. Now, some eight years later, both somewhat drunk one evening, they had fallen into each other's arms. 'I told you', she now wrote to Colin, 'that I was never physically in love with Antonio', whereas with Pinsent there was 'a very strong physical attraction. Well – nothing happened. We are not technically lovers . . .'

Now, missing Colin, in a strange and confused state, she felt very drawn to Pinsent again – and she wanted Colin's forgiveness. Many years later someone asked her whether she and Pinsent had ever been in love with each other. 'Yes,' she replied, 'I was and he was. But not at the same time.'

For his part, Colin not only found many women attractive, but at twenty-nine he was keen to get married and have children. Warm, sympathetic, highly educated, he appealed to dozens of marriageable girls, and occasionally believed himself to be infatuated with one or another of them – but only in moments of despair, when he became convinced that Iris didn't really love him. Then from Glasgow came long letters begging for understanding, advice. Iris was surprisingly generous and accommodating – except, perhaps, when he decided he was falling in love with Frances Marshall, herself in love with Ralph Partridge, who was then still living in a *ménage à trois* with Lytton Strachey and Dora Carrington. At first, Colin wrote, he merely found her 'immensely attractive . . . but I do agree with you that marriage isn't worthwhile unless there is some flame of fire about it – to warm one's hands, if not to carry one up to heaven . . .' Later he had become so caught up with Frances that Iris was obliged to talk him through the 'shock' of her decision to be with Ralph, though he was still married. Frances, for her part, was very clear that she was not about to become embroiled in more confusion: 'I feel that our relationship, yours and mine,' she wrote to Colin, 'is now something with an existence and solidarity of its own. One has grown an apple tree, and now there is nothing to do but pick the apples.' Through it all Iris remained poised, dignified and calm, apparently possessed of a wisdom and understanding well beyond her years.

Perhaps the greatest importance of these letters for the biographer is that because there were so many of them, because they were so often written like a diary, it is possible to follow most of Iris's life throughout the 1920s – though not Antonio's, which features surprisingly little. We know, for example, that Charlie Meade and Antonio climbed together, that Antonio loved duck-shooting in the Pontine marshes, that Nesta de Robeck was often at La Foce, where she and Iris played duets together on the piano, that Desart was very fond of piquet. Iris profoundly mourned the lack of 'easy-going civilised society' in Florence, and often felt extremely lonely at La Foce; she once wrote to Colin that it was only the thought of him that kept her alive. 'It seems disloyal to admit it, even to myself – but I can't not. I made the mistake, early in our marriage, of suppressing the whole of that side of me, so as to make him happier . . . but for suppression one always pays, sooner or later. You called me back to freedom again . . . and now it is bubbling out all over . . .'

The Christmas of 1927 was not an enormous success. As usual the family gathered at the Villa Medici, but Sybil took to her bed feeling faint, Desart was still painfully sad about his wife, Antonio was aching to get back to his ducks in the Pontine marshes, and only Pinsent made any effort to be cheerful. Antonio, noted Iris somewhat bitterly, seldom listened to any woman's conversation, and certainly never to that of plain ones. His very real family feeling was increasingly offset by his contempt for Americans, and his growing dislike of British post-war politics.

After Christmas, however, everyone was once again on the move, a state of affairs that Iris longed for. Colin was off to Colombia in South America, where he was setting up a new works for his business. The Origos were taking Gianni with them to New York to see Mrs Cutting, and then planned a trip round Mexico. 'I am a little afraid of this New Year,' Iris wrote to Colin. 'Let us not lose each other in it, like children groping in the dark. Let us hold firmly to that [which], however incomplete, the Gods *have* given us . . . My dear, my dear . . .'

They had been apart four months, and once again their correspondence was returning to exchanges about literature and philosophy, interspersed with passages about their love for each other. On the *Roma*, a fast ship from Naples to New York, Iris read Bertrand Russell's *Outline of Philosophy* with considerable pleasure, and wrote to tell Colin how much she had enjoyed it; unlike him, she did not care for moral philosophy, but was 'fascinated by the elusive pursuit of abstract truth'. However, she was hating Wagner: 'I am oppressed by the monstrous, the all-pervading bad taste.'

At sea, the *Roma* tossed in gales and snowstorms, 'all the horrors of St Moritz with sickness added', the other first-class passengers appeared to Iris 'equally repulsive', Nanny got sea-sick and took to her bunk: but nothing ever prevented Iris's enjoyment of a journey. It was four years since she had been in New York, and as the ship docked she was awed afresh by the 'sheer, brute abundance of humanity and wealthy vitality, that has to be lodged, and multiplied, and piled to the sky'. At first, as always, she was overcome by New York. 'It is all so monstrous,' she wrote to Colin, 'terrifying if you like – yet on so large a scale I cannot but feel some strange barbaric force that will come through triumphant over us all.' The Origos were given a most enthusiastic welcome. They were lent a flat on the top floor of a skyscraper, with a French maid, a car and a chauffeur. Chaliapin was singing in *Boris Godunov* at the Metropolitan, and Mrs Cutting asked Segovia to play at a private luncheon party. Antonio, charming and courteous as ever, but as ever longing to get away to the countryside, was making plans to visit California and its fruit orchards. They went to Washington, where at a dance one evening at the Italian Embassy, Iris was sure she spied a woman she believed had once had an affair with Antonio.

In the middle of February, when the weather on the East Coast was at its worst, they set off for the west by train. Chicago, their first stop, was hidden under snow, but what she could see of it looked to Iris poor and depressed. 'Oh the ugliness,' she wrote, 'the universal ugliness.' In New Mexico they were met by friends of her Uncle Bronson, who as well as being a New Mexico Senator also owned and edited a newspaper, having settled in this sunny, dry place in the hope of a reprieve from tuberculosis. New Mexico was bright and very blue, and Iris loved it, riding each morning in the dawn mist, 'deeply moved by beauty'.

Back in New York Gianni was waiting for her impatiently. 'The kind of happiness he gives me', she wrote to Colin, 'is quite impossible to describe.' Before leaving for Europe Iris went to Long Island to see the Boswell manuscripts Geoffrey Scott was editing, and came back pleased with the prospect of translating some of the Italian letters relating to his Corsican travels. Already she and Colin were planning a brief meeting in London in May, and once again, as the encounter drew nearer, the tone of her letters changed, from that of often brisk *reportage* to anguish and longing. During her sea voyages to and from America Iris often reflected on the nature of her life. This time she had just finished reading Gertrude Bell's letters, which had filled her with envy. 'Oh my dear, what vitality! . . . The whole book filled me with discontent – divine or otherwise. So much of one's life frittered away – nothing done with it, nothing seen . . . When I look back on these last five years, and think that in them I have written nothing, learnt nothing . . . furnished a house, rather indifferently – produced one child – it isn't much, is it?' Her failure to get down to her own writing irritated her continually, and she was now far too caught up in trying to make sense of 'real life'; but as for 'decisions – I hope not. More and more I believe that the really important things in one's life just happen – and are not decided.' In Glasgow, Colin was also brooding about the future: 'Five years ago I was a young man with possibilities – now I am a mediocre man of business.' Fears about themselves, their futures, their lack of accomplishment or success, lay always near the surface for both of them: one of the things that made them so alike, just as a constant analysis of their own characters and motivations was another. After one long bout of self-examination, Iris noted that the people Colin had to fear in their future would never be the Pinsents, but Antonio and Gianni. 'When I *married* Antonio I meant to give everything to him, to merge myself in his whole. And it is the memory of that absolute surrender, that complete giving, that makes the marriage worth going on with to me now.'

By the middle of April the Origos were back at the Villa Medici for a brief social whirl. Iris's friend Ruth Draper, the American *diseuse*, came to tea, as did Violet Trefusis and the Keppels; the cuckoos were calling and the wild cyclamen were just coming out; even Berenson seemed to go out of his way to be nice to Iris, and for the first time she felt that she perceived and understood somethingof his reputed charm.

Having not seen one another for seven months, Colin and Iris were becoming extremely anxious about their next encounter. 'When at last that meeting does come,' Iris wrote to him, 'don't you think we might have a few happy days together before facing final problems? We need not discuss that now – but I personally would never throw away a few days of happiness – even if later they have to be paid for with pain.' They met in London for dinner, and found they had been right to be uneasy. Colin, edgy and truculent, confessed to other affairs, declaring that if he could not have her, he at least needed *someone*. He woke up next morning at the Travellers' Club transfixed with fear. 'My dear, it is not that my love is less but that hope has gone. I'm frightened. Please, please don't leave me.' Iris, staying at Rutland Gate, was calm, as she nearly always was at moments of crisis. 'I only want to give you a few days of real happiness – of something complete enough that we shall be able to look back and say: "This, at least, life has given me, this I have known."' They decided to spend a weekend together at the Bell Hotel in Gloucester. It was peaceful, if not very happy; both seem to have thought that the end had come, and that they were enjoying the last days of happiness together they would ever have. Upon parting they decided not to be in touch for two months, but neither could resist a final letter. 'I shall not be really unhappy for now we know that it was – no, not "good enough" – but the best,' wrote Iris. 'All that I love most in thought will always now be inextricably mixed with you . . . oh all the time, my dear, my love, I remember you – you walking beside me and touching my arm, you sitting by the fire and reading to me . . . your eyes looking at me – dearest, dearest, your body trembling in my arms.'

They kept their word; but then the letters started again, almost as if nothing had happened: they talked about literature, and philosophy – and then, cautiously, about themselves. Colin was agitated, Iris calm but firm, with a distant air that made him more anxious than ever. That summer the Origos went their separate ways, Antonio taking Charlie Meade to shoot duck in the Pontine marshes while Aileen and the Meade children went with Iris and Gianni to Castiglioncello. Iris complained that it was the 'only completely ugly place in Italy', but the Meades remained for her the 'nicest family in the world'.

In September Mrs Cutting, Iris' American grandmother and benefactor of the water for La Foce, arrived on a visit. She had rheumatism and shingles, which combined with her customary scattiness to make her more prone than usual to change her mind. Iris had planned to fit in a meeting with Colin somewhere along Mrs Cutting's itinerary, but was forced to revise their plans by telegram every day. Mrs Cutting travelled with twenty-nine pieces of luggage, 'fussed and agitated by this machinery of comfort that she herself has put in motion', but was, Iris thought, 'fundamentally terribly lonely.' She was also a ferocious shopper. Even Iris's calm was tested: 'Oh my dear – let us have two days of forgetfulness . . . let us not be troubled by the past or the future but just know that we are together.'

Though brief and constantly interrupted, their meeting was a surprising success. Iris, who did not believe in disguising her real feelings when with friends, wrote after Colin left: 'While your need for me is stronger than your other needs – the door remains open, which I had thought was finally shut.' Like everyone in love, she felt herself to be a nicer, more generous person, and on her return to La Foce went to great pains to be friendly to Antonio. Despite Mrs Cutting's water-pipe the garden had been scorched to the colour of dust by the intense summer heat and weeks with no rain, and the gardener had carefully planted a row of orange marigolds alongside one of mauve petunias; but she had brought Gianni a mechanical frog to play with in the fountain. Only Pinsent, still spending a lot of time on the structure of the garden, was irritable, telling her that her agitated movements were exacdy like those of an ape; she was always starting things and never finishing them, leaving doors half-open and envelopes half-sealed. In her absence he had again 'built up' his feelings for her, and she was forced to have an 'interview' about it which ended with her 'hurting him a good deal' and feeling guilty because of all his work and help. The weather was very hot. In the afternoons, when it grew cooler, they walked down the valley to watch the harvest. Once again they had taken the Villa Carter at Castiglioncello, and set off by car; a lorry, principally containing Gianni's equipment, following behind.

Whenever the Meades came to stay, Iris's mood lightened. In September 1929 the entire family arrived at La Foce and settled into their usual routine of making blackberry jam, playing duets on the piano and reading aloud. Sybil considered the Meades to be *her* friends and, much irritated by her discovery of Iris's intimacy with them, made jealous scenes, further distracting Iris, in whom suspicions that Antonio was having a serious affair with someone had been aroused by his chilly welcome on her return. To Colin, Iris wrote despondently: 'Antonio really has no use whatever for any woman's society, unless he happens to be in love with her . . . Oh my dear, I should not write you this I know – but always I feel that the fault *must* somehow lie in me and feel so humiliated and ashamed.' One evening, after the children had gone to bed, the adults had a discussion about the 'relative importance for happiness of places, people and climate. Aileen maintained that places came first, then climate and people last of all, and Charlie agreed with her – but then they have never known what it is like to lack people – real people, with whom you can talk and laugh. I should put places and people bracketed together first – and climate a long way further on.' In October a friend's child fell very ill and Iris, who was far more involved with and closer to Gianni than her letters to Colin seem to suggest, wrote agitatedly: 'There are some forms of suffering so unbearable that one does not face them even in one's imagination – I know there is a shut door somewhere in my mind behind which the terror of something happening to Gianni lurks.' Later she added, 'More and more I come to feel that there are only two major virtues, courage and kindness . . .' The Christmas party at La Foce was held early that year. Iris had managed to get hold of a projector and four films: two about agriculture, one about Abyssinia, and a Charlie Chaplin. They were the first films the children had ever seen, arriving in their school ox-carts 'like fowls peeping out of a crate'. Iris loved Christmas, as she loved all celebrations and festivities, and said that it brought out the simplest and most childlike in her. The children's party was very carefully thought out, with dressing-up, singing, the nativity scene carried in to the piping of six small, real shepherds, then the handing out of presents, chocolate, plum biscuits and buns.

Few of Colin and Iris's encounters now had the ease and cosiness of the early years. Occasionally their correspondence was momentarily set alight by a sudden terror, a doubt, a memory, but they kept for the most part surprisingly constant and calm. Their next meeting, in London later in the autumn, once again got off to an unhappy start. Colin had 'flu, and was plaintive; Iris was uncharacteristically sharp, pointing out that it was always she who made the advances and 'I'm not going to do so again. On the other hand, if we're merely going to enjoy a pleasant week of "*amitié amoureuse*" – you might be a little more entertaining.' Colin pulled himself together, abandoned his sickbed, and once again they were talking, with 'forgetfulness and happiness'. Iris found London intoxicating. She had installed Gianni and his nanny at Claridges, and went out with friends to the theatre, dinner, dances and nightclubs. She shopped. Antonio was safely shooting duck. She had totally forgotten, she told Colin, how much fun she could have, 'after the monkey-like performances of my adopted country'. Contrite, she begged him to reassure her that she was not 'really a nasty foreigner in spite of it all'.

Surprisingly, perhaps, the brief moments together snatched from her crammed social visit to London turned out to be some of the happiest times Iris and Colin had ever spent together. When they parted, both wrote of the day when they would never have to do so again – of things becoming so difficult with Antonio that Iris would have no alternative but to leave. They spoke, too, of 'one other eventuality', which must have been a possibility that she was pregnant; Colin felt it 'might almost be taken as a sign'. Mournfully Iris wrote from the Paris-Lyon train of 'a future which, however impossible, however remote, refuses to let itself be excluded from my dreams'. Yet when she was back in Florence and Pinsent, perhaps in contrition for his previous irritability, pressed her to have the courage to go off with Colin, she wrote: 'I can't give up the effort so easily. Even if Gianni – the absolutely final argument – were not involved, I'd still feel this.'

New Year's Eve was one of the most tedious of many tedious celebrations at the Villa Medici. Iris reached Florence to find that Sybil was resentful because the maid Iris had found for her was unsuitable; Percy was struggling heroically and not very successfully to look after Sybil; Antonio was furious because he suspected that Percy wanted Iris to take over as her mother's nurse; Percy was aggravating; Antonio was rude, and once again did not appear very pleased to see Iris. He hung about for one resentful day, then returned to the Pontine marshes and his duck. Whenever she could, Iris escaped down into Florence, which had just acquired a new orchestra of its own.

Sybil's *malaise* had now become an almost permanent state. She was refusing to eat, and the local doctor was being called to her bedside at all hours. Finally, goaded past bearing, he took Iris aside and told her firmly that unless they stopped indulging Sybil she would become a permanent invalid, and Percy would have a nervous breakdown. In his opinion, Sybil's ills were nothing other than '*una forma di vampirismo*' (Somerset Maugham's story 'Louise' was somewhat too near the truth.) Luckily Pinsent was in a 'serene and competent frame of mind', and doing all he could to help. As often as possible, he and Iris escaped the sickbed to walk for miles above Fiesole, exploring parts of the countryside neither knew. Both felt close to the country, part of it – and yet profoundly alien from its inhabitants.

At moments like these, Iris always turned to Colin. 'Without you,' she wrote, 'I could not manage at all . . . the knowledge that you are there, and that you love me makes the whole of life seem full. . . .' To cheer herself up, she accepted an invitation to dine at I Tatti, and reflected afterwards that though she had had a good time, this was not always the case: 'more often one feels that one had either been ridiculous or stupid – and I feel that this is a reflection on their hospitality, as well as one's own stupidity.' More and more she was becoming acutely aware of the people around her, and not always in the most charitable way. Come the *Befana*, Epiphany, she and Nesta de Robeck went around the children's wards of a nearby hospital, delivering stockings full of presents.

Consumed by questions of morality, Iris sometimes sounded in her letters like a tortured character from a play by Corneille: 'How is one to deal with the constant struggle between one's intelligence, which is free, and traditions by which one is bound fast. I can't regret our love. Only, just because there are feelings that we share, and that will recur again, I *must* do all that is humanly possible – and after that, still try again – to make a success of what I have undertaken.' She dined once again at I Tatti, where she at last felt that she had become an adult guest in her own right, and came back weighed down with German books – she intended to practise her German – and exhilarated by a conversation about the paths taken by Byzantine influence through Russia, Germany and Sweden. 'That's one thing about I Tatti – I don't think I have been there without returning with a fresh sense of the vividness and excitement to be found in adventures of the mind – and Heaven knows that Florence doesn't provide any other kind!' Once again, however, she found herself longing for the company of women friends, of the kind she had made in London. And now, just in case something changed, she decided to put Gianni's name down for Eton.

Then her mood sank. She began to reflect on her relationship with Colin, how the years were passing while he remained tied to her, how he had told her he wanted children. Frances Marshall was urging him to press Iris to leave Antonio, on the grounds that it was vital to take risks in life. Iris wrote to him sadly, telling him that he should consider himself free. In the end, she never sent it. Later, however, she referred to its contents. 'We are not children . . . When conditions become unbearable, one stops bearing them – and when freedom is possible to you, you will take it – and God knows that I shall be glad, my dear, if happiness comes to you with it . . . I can only feel that I want you near me. I want to hear your voice say: "Don't worry, my darling, it's all right". It wouldn't be true – but I want to hear you say it.' It was now clear that she was not pregnant: 'I cannot believe', she noted somewhat balefully, 'in any happiness that would begin like that.' For days her mood was low. 'It's no use pretending that I'm not depressed. I resent, too, this constant preoccupation with human relationships – we're all caught in it – you, I, Irene, Mother, Cecil – and the world is so full of exciting things, nice hard things, like nuts to crack and countries to see and books to read – and we muddle along in our own little sloppy ponds of sentiment . . .'

It was now January 1929, and their affair had been going on since October 1927, a see-saw of passion and despair out of which neither could see a way. Colin, to judge by his letters, had changed little in these months; Iris had found a whole new world – England – that she could hardly bear not to explore.

Iris and Gianni spent the first weeks of the New Year at the Villa Medici. There was not much for Iris to explore in Florence, but she was now frequendy asked to dine at I Tatti, where one night she met the charming and highly educated anti-Fascist Umberto Morra. Briefly she thought of inviting him to La Foce, then realised that he and Antonio would never get on; Antonio, moreover, was already angry about all the time she was spending at I Tatti. She was reading Kipling's 'The Cat that Walked by Himself', aloud to Gianni: 'I feel very unlike him! I have never been very good at walking quite by myself – and now – Colin dear, I want you by my side.' Seldom in their relationship had they needed each other more, but Colin was leaving on a business trip to America; he wrote to tell Iris he was putting their letters, typed, in a black deed-box and depositing them with his bank. Before he left Iris wrote: 'My dear, my dear, whatever may come, we have been happy – few people can say as much.' Next day she wrote again: 'I can't destroy the belief that somehow, someday, we shall be happy together.' Colin's reply was poetical: 'I have loved you when you have shone among others and my love and pride in you became one. I have loved you when you have been most happy . . . I have loved you in the moments when you have most loved me. I have loved you when you have played the child – the pouting dissatisfied little child . . . But I believe that I loved you best – with a love more nearly worthy of you – one night when I suddenly saw you leaning against the doorway – your head against your arm, crying – barefooted – like a child.'

In the middle of February the whole of Europe was gripped by freezing cold. The Arno iced over, and for forty-eight hours the Villa Medici was completely cut off; Iris walked down into Florence from Fiesole through heavy snow, and the weather postponed a ten-day trip to Berlin and Paris she had planned to make with Antonio; though so much less sociable, he was just as restless. Their trip was further delayed by the news that the snow was so heavy in Berlin that the city was running out of water, light and coal. But nothing could have kept Iris from the trip. Though she considered Berlin and its inhabitants ugly, she loved the galleries, dances and theatres. She and Antonio were on friendly terms again, planning a great ball at the Villa Medici for the spring. Iris talked excitedly of stopping at Worth in Paris, on the way home, to get them to copy one of their 'creations', but her moods and spirits fluctuated, as they did throughout her life: enchanted by the idea when she went to sleep, she woke wondering whether she really wanted to give a dance for a large number of people 'whom one does not really like'. Just the same, they returned to Florence and another social event: the exiled Queen of Greece came to tea. ('They are unbearable, these unemployed queens,' said Antonio, and took the train to La Foce). Iris found her so boring as to have difficulty believing her intelligent enough to have been 'wicked' in the war, and was herself soon very bored 'with the usual British colony fossils'.

Even Pinsent, who from the letters seems to have been as much in love with her as ever, failed to raise her spirits. In search of some distraction, as she could not be with Colin, Iris was constantly on the move over the next months: first to Greece and Yugoslavia, writing to Colin that any travel was 'enough to make me quite ridiculously, illogically happy' for she liked being alone, and free. 'Why does one ever stop travelling? This is the perfection of happiness.' Aileen, stuck at home with her four children, wrote enviously: 'Sometimes we seemed to fly along in a fairy sledge tinkling bells – but more often lately – it has been an old cab.' Towards the end of November, Iris made a quick trip into Florence to buy woolly jerseys and corduroy trousers for the farm children for Christmas: she came back with 114 garments. No member of the household seemed happy. Antonio was dreading the prospect of the usual family Christmas, Percy was frantic with worry about Sybil, and even Pinsent was wondering whether he would not do better to spend the holiday in Albania. Colin and Iris had now reverted to writing literary letters, a mixture of Greek, Latin, philosophy and mysticism, quoting long passages. They were both reading Hemingway, and agreed that though 'second-rate' he was capable of being 'sincere' and writing 'vital passages'.

The early spring months passed, and their relationship fell into its usual see-saw. As Iris grew emotionally stronger, writing almost clinically about the value of what they had created between them: ('We've got something inside our imaginations, that no one can ever take away'), so Colin, sensing her restraint, again grew more passionate and pressing. He was conscious of growing older, and wanting someone of his own. Was he free, or not free? Just the same, they were planning a whole week together on Skye, but towards the end of April Iris wrote

Colin one of her cooler notes: 'I have a curiously intense feeling . . . that this is the last time that we shall have just that kind of happiness.' Colin replied instantly: 'I want to be with you again, more than anything else in the world . . . most of all perhaps because when I see you life seems to make sense – the rest of the time I see it most indubitably as a tale told by an idiot.'

This time, they managed not only a whole week together, on Skye, but a perfect week. From Chamonix, where she went afterwards to join the Meades, Iris wrote letters so happy that they are almost painful to read. A particularly glowing one describes a day spent on the glacier, with Gianni 'nearly dying of excitement and pride', and bilberries and wild strawberries in the woods below. 'Dear Heart,' she wrote, 'I do believe this time that you love me – more than I have dared to believe it before.' A letter from Colin which crossed with hers conjured up a last day, spent with the Meades not long before. 'Soon we shall leave them, and go upstairs – the fire will be flickering in my room, and soon, soon, my lover, you will come to me.' Iris, overcome by love and a sudden optimism, told Aileen that, short of Colin marrying someone else, she had no intention of ever giving him up. She now saw Colin in everything, remarking that what she loved in the valley at La Foce was what she loved in Skye: 'the same emptiness and sense of space, the same absence of towns and walls and man made things – and a similar, if a different, sadness.'

Iris was twenty-eight on 15 August 1930. She was woken at La Foce by Gianni, bringing her some flowers; Antonio gave her a ring, and Mrs Cutting a diamond hair-clip; telegrams arrived from Sybil and Pinsent. The festive atmosphere was destroyed by an anonymous telegram informing Antonio that his chauffeur Carlo had been spreading a rumour that while the Marchese was always working hard with his farm, the Marchesa was enjoying herself with the engineer. Since 'the engineer' could refer to no one but Pinsent, there was general embarrassment, and Antonio made it plain that he should stay away from La Foce, despite all the work he had in hand there. Colin and Iris were planning to meet later in the year in London. As she watched Gianni leaping about in the fountain and enjoyed her sweet peas and roses, Iris was looking forward with pleasure to another stay in England. 'It's not only the longing for you,' she wrote, 'but for the whole manner of living – a sanity of values – a certainty of standards – kindliness – tolerance – harmony.' Another trip, this time to Corfu, Athens, Chios, Smyrna and Samos, distracted her for a bit. From the Orient Express Iris wrote that the moments of closeness and love she shared with Colin made her feel invulnerable: 'Surely these moments are as near as any of us can hope to get to immortality . . .'

Both Colin and Iris were capable of writing letters of exceptional frankness: the love letter had become their style, their way of talking to each other, their belief in some kind of future. Given their young age, both in their twenties, and the times, soon after the First World War, and their backgrounds, they had taken to a passionate love affair with surprising ease and openness. More perhaps than any of her other writing, which was marked rather by coolness and control, Iris's letters to Colin, written before she was thirty, bring to life her exuberance, her eagerness to be happy, her intense awareness of feelings and the meaning of words, and her sense of duty. The feeling of energy they give off is very attractive; as is her ability to love with such intensity, and the ease with which she put it into words, without shame. Colin once said of her that she gave people the 'enthusiasm, the light to see that there was a joy to be got out of living'.

For all their passion, however, both Colin and Iris had a very clear sense of propriety. Though they would talk about the future as if everything were possible, there were in fact some things they would not do. On one occasion, when they were planning a quick meeting in Paris, Antonio's sister fell ill: neither questioned that Iris would stay with Antonio. Colin did not reproach her. 'As long as we stick to our present lives we must make the best of them . . . We have chosen to stay on the bank – and when the choice seems hardest, we must not complain.'

And now, just when they were feeling particularly loving and hopeful, the end came suddenly. It was all over in a single day. On 14 October Colin received a telegram: 'Don't write this week writing explanation Iris'. It might have been something of very little importance, but the letter she now wrote to him was the last of this kind they ever exchanged.

Dated 15 October 1930 from the Villa Medici, 'My dearest', it began: 'The worst thing of all has happened. Antonio has read some of your recent letters and has offered me the choice between a legal separation, or a complete break with you . . . But it's no use, Colin, I must stay where I am and stick it out somehow. I can't leave Gianni . . . You will feel perhaps that it is only that I have not got the courage to make the break – but it is something more fundamental than that. If I came away, the first few years would be difficult enough – but with divorce unrecognised in Italy . . . I should always feel that our whole marriage was based on something fundamentally wrong – on destruction and unhappiness . . .

'Forgive me, my darling, forgive me . . . Nothing can ever

175

make me regret that we have loved each other. It has been the most wonderful thing in my life – and having had it, I shall always be richer than most people . . . Goodbye my dearest. . . . I shut my eyes and I can hear your voice and feel your kiss. Oh Colin, Colin I shall never forget.'

And there the letters end; there is no reply from Colin. But Browning's 'A death in the desert' has been typed out and put at the end of the last file:

. . . And, having gained truth, keep truth; and that is all.

Iris and Colin had met, as lovers rather than friends, seven times in a little more than nine years, and even then seldom for more than a few days at a time. During that period they had written to each other nearly two thousand letters. In them, they had discussed everything that is possible for two human beings to discuss – except politics and world affairs, about which they had said virtually nothing. Given the times they were living in, this is sometimes hard to understand. Were some letters destroyed?

Iris was twenty when their friendship began, Colin twenty-four. In some ways this remarkable correspondence was not only a journal of nearly ten years of their lives, and the lives of those close to them, but a mutual education, chiefly in music, pictures and books. There is virtually no letter which does not have a reference to a writer, a composer, an opera. For over nine years they had confided in each other all their fears, hopes, and memories, and they had made each other laugh, with their teasing, and their mockery – which could sometimes be of a curiously similar and not always kind variety. They were critical, but not spiteful. Few private correspondences can ever have led to such intimacy from two such normally reticent people.

Most remarkably, perhaps, their relationship had constantly survived the confession of other loves. But Iris, when talking about the possible risks to their own affair, had been entirely right when she said to Colin that no major threat would ever come to them from an outsider: on her part, she said, disaster could only come from Antonio and Gianni.

What can they have felt when they finally fell totally silent? How did they decide what to do with the letters? For all their hesitations and misgivings, they must often have believed that one day they would be together. One can only imagine the sense of loss and pain. On Iris's part guilt, loneliness and abnegation; on Colin's, perhaps, final rejection. Would they have been happy together? Did Antonio really have no idea before? One can only guess.

After the letter of 15 October 1930, no single word seems to have been exchanged between Iris and Colin for some years – by which time they were very different people.

CHAPTER SEVEN

Water

What saved Iris in those first terrible days when she knew that her affair with Colin was irrevocably over were Gianni and La Foce, with their many demands on her. Later, an escape from unhappiness of every kind would also come to her from writing.

Gianni was now five and a half, a slight, good-looking boy with fair hair. People who lived and worked at La Foce in the 1930s remember today his affectionate nature and his ease with everyone on the estate. He was indulged, certainly, but had not been spoilt by the attention; and he seemed to delight in all the things most guaranteed to endear him to Iris. He loved stories and being read to; he had a good ear for languages; he was basically shy but tried hard to overcome it; and he made her laugh. Photographs taken when he was a page at the wedding of his cousin Joy Verney to Tony Hamilton-Russell in London show a most beguiling and serious child, dressed in a Guards uniform of 1815, complete with busby and sword. By the age of five he had already travelled a great deal – to England, America, Switzerland and France – but La Foce remained his home, with his miniature donkey Cariad, a present from his American great-grandmother, his dog, his wind-up frog, and his new canary, which he called Pin.

La Foce had been almost entirely transformed by six years of extremely hard labour; it would no longer have been recognisable to the casual driver coming up the slow dirt track from Chianciano. Antonio's immediate goal in 1924 had been to build roads to connect outlying and isolated farms, to preserve what arable land was spared by the regular flooding, and to turn the twenty-five crumbling farmhouses into proper homes, with water and electricity. A mercury mine on the Monte Amiata had lately been closed down, and about two hundred of the men put out of work were recruited to help with the new projects. Achievements were impressive: in the space of no tmuch more than five years, 102 kilometres of new road were made, thirty new farmhouses were built, wells were sunk, bridges and dykes constructed, and vines, orchards, olives and grain planted. Erosion was the first problem to be tackled, and twenty-five tonnes of earth and stone were put into the river and the creeks to control the flow of the Orcia and divert water where it was needed. With the help of water-diviners, artesian wells were sunk. Two nurseries of young trees were established, and 545 acres were planted with seedling oak and cypress. Threshing was now carried out by steam-driven machinery, and a tractor, a reaper-binder, a combine harvester and a bulldozer were all bought. Some funding came from the government, but none was available for electricity, telephones, or the clearing of forests, and into these projects the Origos put the money that came to Iris from America, as well as the generous cheque Mrs Cutting sent her every Christmas.

Much of the violence of the early 1920s in Italy had died away by the time the Origos settled at La Foce, since the Fascists had won almost all the votes in and around Chianciano in the election of 1924 – mainly those of shopkeepers and farm labourers – and there was little need any longer for the repressive measures that had brought them to power.

What was more important for La Foce, perhaps, was that the director of the Istituto Agrario e Forestale in Florence was a dedicated and inspired agriculturalist called Professore Serpieri. Serpieri was a great deal more interested in land than in Fascism. In 1923 he had been made Under-Secretary of State for Agriculture; and in 1929 Under-Secretary responsible for the Bonifica Integrale, the salvage and reclamation of derelict land. Serpieri was absolutely committed to the aims of the Bonifica, and a great admirer of the experiments taking place at La Foce, where he was a frequent visitor. In its early days, the idea behind the Bonifica had been to do primarily with agriculture and water, such as the draining of the Pontine marshes, where Antonio went to shoot his duck. There, two towns, Littoria and Sabaudia, rose on what had once been malarial marshland. One of the earliest Fascist campaigns was the 'battle for corn', by which Mussolini hoped to make Italy self-sufficient in grain and impressive in the eyes of Europe. Under the guidance and impetus of landowners like Antonio, the plans for the Bonifica were widened to include all that made the lives of local people better – such as housing and roads.

On 20 June 1926 local landowners, including Antonio, were summoned to a meeting at Montepulciano. Here they were addressed by an agricultural expert from Siena called Giorgio Garavini, who urged them to carry out a study of the potential local applications of the Bonifica, and to think of setting up their own *consorzio* – a consortium of local landowners sharing the same ideals. They did so, and Antonio was named Vice President and, in 1931, President, an office he held for forty years. The *consorzio*, which covered almost the whole of the Val d'Orcia, taking in the estates of landowners like the Piccolomini, the Simonelli and the Cervini, consisted of 34,000 hectares and ran the length of the d'Orcia valley from Pienza to San Quirico. It was soon flourishing. La Foce itself had become a place of study for those interested in the Bonifica, and local newsletters of the times list lunches given there in honour of inspectors, foresters and local dignitaries. Serpieri, watching with admiration the land turn from a dry dust-bowl into green fields and orchards, sent a telegram to the 'successful farmers of the Val d'Orcia who will hand down to their sons the now fertile but once desolate chalk ridges' of the area. In November 1932 Antonio was singled out for special praise during a meeting of the Council of Delegates in Rome.

What the Origos were doing at La Foce fitted in extremely well with Mussolini's agricultural plans. Of all the Duce did, the Bonifica was one of his genuinely successful contributions to ameliorating Italy's rural poverty, and by providing government contributions enabled the richer landowners to bring prosperity to their areas. The Bonifica, it was widely said, had set out on its great journey 'guided by the enormous will of the Duce'. From the very few papers or letters concerning Antonio that remain at La Foce, it seems highly unlikely that he himself was much interested in national politics, beyond the occasional outburst when he felt that Italy's sovereignty was at stake; but he did have a very true love of the land. Flavia della Gherardesca, who married Antonio's oldest friend Ugolino, says of Antonio that she had never met a man less interested in politics. 'I am not a technician,' he told the Academy in Florence, before which he had been invited to speak. 'And I am not an academic. I am simply a passionate and amateur farmer, who at a certain moment in my life, perhaps the most romantic since it coincided with my marriage, experienced the eternal fascination that comes from the earth, and who wished to make of this, and of those people eking out their lives from the earth, the object of my life's work.' He was in the process of buying the Castelluccio Bifolchi, which stood on the site of an Etruscan settlement, and which had once been part of the La Foce estate. It included some 2,150 acres and the parish church of San Bernardino da Siena. By the middle of the 1930s, most of the major building works at La Foce had been completed, greatly helped by the sudden death of a misanthropic American cousin of Iris's who had spent the last years of his life determinedly repelling visitors to his yacht on the Isle of Wight, but who just the same had left his cousins a great deal of money. Useful as this was, the Origos agreed between themselves that it had been no bad thing that their adventure had started at La Foce with so little money, since it had saved them from many mistakes and given 'a certain basic reality to our efforts'.

To make the improvements Antonio wanted to make he was prepared, it seems, to ignore what was happening elsewhere in the country, or what other activities Mussolini and the Fascists were engaged in. He wished neither to discuss them nor to hear about them. Yet he was prepared, in the interests of his land, as photographs show, to wear a black shirt when Fascist dignitaries came to La Foce, despite a fierce denial that he had ever done so in a letter that Iris wrote to a friend after word had reached England that Antonio occasionally wore Fascist dress. Part of his antipathy towards I Tatti was undoubtedly to do with the marked anti-Fascism of Berenson and his visitors, and the endless anti-Fascist talk which he would not have been able to avoid. Unfairly or not, Antonio's silence about Mussolini and Fascism, his refusal to engage with its darker aspects, has left a distinct taint of Fascist complicity; and Antonio was never, for the rest of his life, entirely able to escape it. Even as late as the 1990s, many of those who remember nothing of his work for the land, nothing of his charm and good nature, recollect his involvement with the Fascists. To many people whose record against the Fascists was one of constant opposition, his very silence became suspect.

It was, of course, all rather more complicated than that. In the 1920s there were very few big landowners or Italian aristocrats who did not, at least up to a point, admire what Mussolini was doing for Italy, not least because it was they, together with the industrialists and bankers, rather than, as they had been promised, the peasants and workers, who most benefited from these Fascist reforms. They really did feel that he had saved the country from anarchy and their own properties from expropriation, and that by using government grants, as well as their own money, they would be able to improve the vast tracts of land that had long been unusable. It would bring more profit for them, and a better life for the farmers. In the early 1920s, fifteen aristocratic Italian families still held between them over one million acres of land. Like Antonio, many found it best simply to ignore Mussolini's ideas, such as they were. At the very end of the 1920s, Janet Ross's niece Lina Waterfield, writing for the *Observer*, visited Benedetto Croce in Naples to ask him his views on Fascist policies. Looking at her with an amused expression, Croce replied: 'But there is nothing in Fascism, nothing, nothing at all. As yet they have not written a single page. I can see nothing constructive in Fascism.' Ignazio Silone called it a 'kind of mental and political margarine'. Having come in without a programme, Mussolini repeated the formula 'our programme is deeds', and soon this took on the tone of a moral force. What people wanted, in the economic collapse of the 1920s, was not democracy but prosperity: it was Mussolini's strength that he gave them the feeling that he could deliver it. Furthermore, in the countryside Fascism was often so little apparent that its brutalities could be ignored, particularly by a post-war generation either slow or reluctant to understand how profoundly illiberal it really was. What is more, the dissidents were few and made little impression, and in any case were speedily removed, either sent to the 'confine' in total isolation, or exiled abroad. Opposition was in fact so weak that, when in 1931 professors were requested to swear an oath of loyalty to Fascism, only eleven – among them de Sanctis the historian and Edoardo Ruffini the Vatican lawyer – refused to do so. As Harold Acton wrote at the beginning of the 1930s, it was still perfectly possible for foreigners at least to remain absolutely aloof from politics, while admiring the new roads and the comforting manner in which the trains now at last ran on time. Antonio was not, of course, a foreigner, but he spent much of his life with foreigners, and it was easy for him, like the vast majority of big landowners, to have little to do with active Fascists, particularly as Mussolini made no effort to oppose them provided they did nothing to provoke him. What Antonio did not do, until the German occupation, was take a stand against Fascism.

It was both harder and easier for Iris. As a woman in Italy she was not expected to have views, and her silence during these years is seldom held against her. In her two volumes of autobiography she scarcely ventures to examine her own feelings until the end of the 1930s, by which time there was really no avoiding it. Yet even her silence on the subject of Fascism is taken today not so much for complicity as for a certain detachment over the affairs of the world; in her remarkable *Images and Shadows* she repeatedly insists on the right of people to remain private. She neither mentions nor condemns matters in which she feels she played no part, simply reporting what she has seen. Yet for someone as clear-sighted as Iris, these must often have been profoundly difficult times. On visits to I Tatti, there was, as Antonio had perceived, no avoiding the subject, particularly after Berenson's close friend Gaetano Salvemini was forced to flee to America for fear of arrest. Every meal at I Tatti now included diatribes against the Fascists. These were, Kenneth Clark the art historian would later write, 'laudable, but monotonous', and he did not really listen all the time. What he did always remember, however, was the day when Hitler attained real power, and Berenson observed: 'This will turn into something that will make Mussolini look like a fairy tale.'

Far closer to hand, at Montepulciano, less than ten kilometres from La Foce, lived Iris's only real friends in the area, the Bracci; and their opposition to the Fascists was so strong that it had driven them into voluntary exile from Rome to Tuscany, where their house was constantly full of those who opposed Mussolini. What Iris really felt about it all, at this stage at least, is impossible to say. Her stated position after 1939 and the work she did for the tracing service of the Italian Red Cross in Rome and later at La Foce, cleared up all doubts about her sympathies but it is hard, sometimes, not to wonder whether she did not protest too much later, as a way of making up for the silence of the past.

In order to meet the ministers and agricultural experts concerned with the Bonifica, Antonio was often in Rome or Florence. Since the Origos were known for the excellent work they were doing in Tuscany, they were regularly invited to official dinners given in Mussolini's honour. Iris attended at least two of these in the early 1930s, at which both her admiration for some of the things Il Duce was doing and her apprehension about the future were clearly visible. In May 1930 Mussolini made a tour of Tuscany. Watching the excessive preparations in Florence, brocades and tapestries flung from every window, a pathway of sand laid down in the middle of the street so that Mussolini's horse would not slip, it looked, she wrote to a friend, as if 'all might turn into a comic opera entertainment. Well – it didn't and what prevented it from doing so was Mussolini himself. My dear, he is a very great man – whatever one may feel about the nature of his various achievements, there can be no doubt about that – and the curious thing is that the impression he produced isn't caused by the infection of the popular enthusiasm, but rather in spite of it.' Her first sight of Mussolini was at a gala performance of *L'Italiana in Algeri* ('of course'), at which the whole of Florence in their best jewellery and the local Fascist notables in their black shirts shouted themselves hoarse. 'The whole performance held up for Giovinezza as the Duce came in – and then for a minute, as he stood motionless in the front of the box, complete breathless silence, more impressive than any applause, before the shouting and clapping began.' From where she and Antonio were sitting, just below him, 'it was possible to see his face in repose, with all the histrionics removed. Something very fine remained – a firmness and a *reality* which I had somehow not expected – and a sense of complete remoteness and loneliness . . . I know you would have felt it too, that here was someone on a larger scale than most people, something that made all the histrionics and the noise, which he himself utilises, seem quite irrelevant and unimportant.' She was not, however, impressed by the '*pezzigrossi*', the luminaries of Fascism who accompanied him.

Later that evening there was a ball in the Palazzo Veneto – Iris had been asked to be a patroness – which had been filled for the occasion with some of Florence's most important works of art. She enjoyed the evening 'enormously' and found many old friends among the guests. Next morning came a military review on the Cascine, and though Iris found the sight very fine, she could not help, later, 'feeling rather frightened. All these loud words *may* be pure bluff, but surely it is playing with dynamite, and even if the dynamite is still pretty damp – it is nonetheless expensive, and may blow up when it is not meant to.' The review went on for so long that she scarcely listened to Mussolini's words about the gravity of Italy's economic situation. A letter from Lina Waterfield to her editor on the *Observer* in London described it all rather more forcefully. Wondering whether the wild delirium of Mussolini's followers was simple madness and not sincere at all, she described his ride through Florence: 'Mussolini at the head of the regular troops, contingents of the navy and of thousands of the National Fascist Militia, riding through Florence, in the swagger uniform of the Militia, his white plume very stiff and erect in his astrakhan cap, acted the part of circus manager very ably, for he just escaped being ridiculous.' She too attended the reception given for him, and noted that he looked tired. 'I watched the members of the Italian aristocracy closely. They were all keen to see the Duce, some mounted the steps to the mediaeval windows, but not one of them made an effort to go up and speak to him. He seemed as though belonging to another world, far removed from that of the old nobility. . . . It is true that many Italians continue to say what a wonderful man Mussolini is and to separate him from the undesirable elements in his party. . . . at the back of their minds perhaps they feel he is leading them into the unknown and they are nervous.' Italy was a deeply class-conscious society: he was not 'one of them', and they were not all sure of the nature of the animal they were dealing with.

Later, at a time when Iris was immersed in new plans for La Foce's tenants and their children, she and Antonio attended a party given by Mussolini for some departing diplomats. Both had long private talks with him. She wrote to Irene: 'He sticks to the middle of the room after dinner, and has people taken up to him, like royalty. . . . I was *very* much impressed by him – he gives one a real feeling of greatness, as well as of tragic isolation. A. had a long farming talk with him, and I tackled him about my district nurse scheme, with the result that he said that if ever I have any difficulty over it, I am to go straight to him.' Both Antonio and Iris chose to see in Mussolini a patron for the schemes they believed in, preferring to ignore the rest. But it would be wrong not to recall certain details. By this time, the early 1930s, Mussolini had the power to issue decrees which carried the force of law; his person had been declared 'inviolable', and the death penalty was automatic for anyone who even spoke of his death; strikes had been outlawed; no one could get a job without a worker's pass which included political as well as personal details; after 1933, compulsory uniforms were introduced even for civil servants; members of the Italian Academy – set up to co-ordinate work in the arts and sciences – wore plumed hats and swords and were addressed as *Eccellenza*; and some three or four hundred thousand Italians were still living in hovels or caves. Pirandello, who tacidy supported Mussolini, produced risky plays that caricatured Italian life: his characters felt that life was a joke, useless and full of vanity, and that only private illusions kept one sane.

It must also be recalled that, well into the 1930s, such figures as Chamberlain, Churchill and Lloyd George were full of praise for Mussolini's transformation of Italy through the building of roads, bridges, hospitals and schools, his drainage of the marshes, and his archaeological excavations in Italy and Libya. 'Italy', Mussolini once told a journalist, 'wants to be treated as one of the great nations of the world, as a sister, not as a chambermaid': few European statesmen of the day found much fault with this aspiration, and foreign journalists and businessmen were also on the whole flattering. Lord Rothermere compared him to Napoleon; Otto Kahn called him a 'genius'. It was not only the Italians who failed to see the direction he was heading in.

Iris was absolutely clear that she had a role to play at La Foce – but it had nothing to do with the politics of the day, even if some of the more absurd Fascist decrees touched on what she was doing. If anything, Mussolini's laws regarding education were, like the Bonifica, helpful, at least in the early days. He appointed the Sicilian philosopher Giovanni Gentile as Minister of Education, and Gentile held strong views about education, blaming the corruption and mediocrity of Italian government since the Risorgimento as well as the military defeat at Caporetto in 1917 on the Italian education system. His plan was to grant teachers far more freedom in what they taught, while increasing the importance of philosophy in the school curriculum. Though Gentile was not altogether popular with the Fascists, who thought his plans 'un-Italian' and too reliant on German influence, he was warmly backed by Mussolini, who announced that the new educational policies were the most 'Fascist of Fascist reforms'. Though he once described the Fascist State as the 'most democratic. . . . par excellence', Gentile later became one of Mussolini's strongest opponents.

An act of 1923 allowed considerable freedom to private schools, and further laws in 1925, 'L'Opera Materna e Infantile' (maternal and infant), called for the improvement of 'physical and moral conditions.' In particular, there was to be a great increase in the provision of nursery schools for children aged between three and six, and proposals for their establishment were to be overseen by local 'patrons and patronesses' of 'utmost probity'; since there were no suitable *fasci femminili* in the Val d'Orcia, no Fascist women, Iris was asked to be a 'patroness'. In this role she was able to involve herself in other schools, further afield than La Foce, and papers in the archives show the extent to which she became caught up in the kind of small local issues that most interested her. There are papers about the contribution from central government towards hot lunches for nursery school pupils, especially those coming from far away; there is the question of money for a child needing an operation, or for a mother needing to see a specialist. Where no money was forthcoming, Iris provided it herself. An article in the local bulletin speaks of her ever-increasing role in school affairs, to which the Marchesa was giving '*tutto il suo passionato senso di squisita finezza*' (her whole passionate sense of exquisite refinement).

In the early 1930s the school at La Foce had seventy-five pupils, their everyday regime reflecting Iris's views on education and those of an enlightened school inspector named Marcucci. They were agreed that the pupils should be kept as much as possible outdoors in the fresh air and, given that they were likely to spend their lives on farms, that the emphasis should be on country matters: growing plants, looking after bees, the difference between various items of farm machinery. La Foce's teacher was instructed to read to her pupils aloud as often as she could, and never to shout at them. When Marcucci returned on a surprise visit to inspect the school, he was 'left speechless' by what Iris had achieved. The Fascist agricultural planners who came to La Foce and looked at the school in passing described Iris, in the highly emotional language that had become the trademark of Fascist expression, as a 'model example of a woman rooted in her work and in her family'.

An essential aspect of Fascist education which Iris all but ignored was the organisation of children into military-style units.

At four a boy became a 'son of the she-wolf' and was given his first black shirt; at eight, he progressed to a Balilla (called after a Genoese boy said to have started a rebellion against the Austrians in 1746); at fourteen he became an *Avanguardista*. Iris noted that only the Balilla were really at all interested in their rank, and that when there were military games to be played, it wasn't always easy to get the boys back to their desks. In keeping with her determination that they should know about the countryside, the children were offered their own small plots, and she discussed with them what they might like to grow. Zinnias perhaps? Dahlias? 'They only wake up to responsiveness', she reported crossly to a friend, 'when we start writing Duce in white pebbles.' In Florence there were special shops selling the various uniforms, badges and insignia; when Mussolini visited Turin in 1933, schoolchildren in full Fascist regalia put on a display of gymnastics before marching through the city in military formation.

Though it was not much in evidence at La Foce, pupils were supposed to be trained in marching, both to and without music, and in military language. New reading books were specially written, with a military slant. 'A child who, even while not refusing to obey, asks "Why?" is like a bayonet made of milk' ran one phrase; 'You must obey because you must' was another. An order was issued that they were to be taught *la cultura fascista* so that they could impart it in the evenings to their families on the distant farms, who knew nothing of such things. Since the contents of the schoolbooks were constantly changing as history was endlessly rewritten and recast in line with current thinking, 'Fascist culture' made little headway in the more remote farmhouses.

Every day that Iris was at La Foce, she spent part of it in the school. Fannina Fe, who even as a small child helped in the school and whose parents and brothers worked for the Origos, remembers: 'La Marchesa came and saw us all the time. She listened to the teacher and even tasted our food, to see if it was good.' When a child was ill and did not come to school, Fannina and the teacher would visit on bicycles to see what was wrong. When Gianni was six he joined the school's first class. After school, he and Fannina roamed around the gardens and the farm, playing with the dogs or winding up the frog to swim round and round the fountain. Iris kept a constant eye on what the school needed. One day, for example, she dropped in at rest time and found the smallest children sleeping at their desks, so she bought them some camp beds. After nearly ten years at La Foce she still felt somewhat shy with the local families, and always conscious of how different she was. It was through the children, now as in her early days, that she could best reach the parents.

Iris was always busy. When she was not at the school or sorting out problems for the farm women she was in the garden, which was fast becoming the great consuming interest in her life. She had come to love 'this bare, parched, austere country', and if she missed Colin intensely, no one was going to be made aware of it; no one except, perhaps, Gianni, who asked her where all 'Tolin's' letters had gone.

By the early 1930s the garden at La Foce was magnificent. It is still today one of the most loved of all Pinsent's projects, with its terraces and inner gardens, roses and wisteria, fountains and pergolas leading down, garden by garden, to a final last, hidden terrace with a balustrade, looking out across to the Monte Amiata; the whole of it covered with climbers and creepers, with a profusion of colours and smells, and an occasional majestic tree to remind Iris of English parkland. It charmed visitors with its sense of space, its contrast with the wild countryside beyond, and the surprise of its being there at all in such a dry desert. Iris admired Pinsent's work greatly; for her, his designs had 'all the dignity and serenity of the best types of Tuscan home' combined with a 'sincerity and brightness of scale that seems to me the work of a very real artist'.

By the time he came to tackle La Foce's garden in the mid 1920s, Pinsent had perfected this form of Anglo-Italian hybrid garden design: that is to say, he was responsible for the layout and the elaborate plans for all the terracing, balustrading, pergolas, the 'hard landscaping', that went with it; he knew and cared little for flowers. Iris knew little about design, but had come to love the flowers planted by Sybil at the Villa Medici. Together they made an excellent team, learning as they gardened; and they had a lot of fun.

The site chosen for the garden posed real problems. It was in itself extraordinary, lying as it did on the rim of a broad valley, with the famous *crete senesi* running down the mountainsides. 'Treeless and shrubless but for some tufts of broom,' Iris wrote many years later, 'these corrugated ridges formed a lunar landscape, pale and inhuman.' At the top of the hill it was dry, windy, and extremely cold in winter. Until Mrs Cutting paid for the water pipes which alone made a garden possible at all, Pinsent could only keep working on the house itself, dreaming of the day when it could be given a suitable setting.

In 1927 the pipes which brought water to the garden from a spring six miles away in a beech wood enabled Pinsent to create his first small garden: a lawn, flowerbeds edged in box and a stone fountain standing on two dolphins, in which Gianni played with his wind-up frog. Since Pinsent was designing a new wing for the house at the same time, he connected the two with a pergola of roses and wisteria. In one corner of the lawn a stone seat and a table were set into a recessed arbour of laurel. The major planting phase was carried out in 1929 and 1930, a larger walled garden and box hedges around a second, less formal flower garden with lemon trees in terracotta pots. Iris became engrossed in the suitability of different plants for different places and effects. She edged the grass with spring flowers and irises and covered the walls in climbing roses, honey suckle and jasmine, with some tree peonies and pomegranates in front. While Pinsent designed, she ordered and planted – tulips, forget-me-nots, hyacinths, marigolds, zinnias and chrysanthemums – getting many of her seeds sent out from Suttons in England, and a garden sofa from Fortnum & Mason. Her degree of planning was as precise in this as in all parts of her life. The wooden labels for the plants were ordered from Paglienti & Figli in Pistoia, dahlias from Lyons, seeds from Suttons, shrubs and trees from Gaundett and Co. in Surrey, roses from Murcell in Shepperton, irises from Orpington in Kent, and peonies from Millet et Fils in France. Her gardening book lists precise measurements: 'Bed by laurels: m. 10.50 long, planted by rows of thirty-two irises each – 30 cm. between each iris, 1st row: Her Majesty; 2nd row: Queen of May; 3rd row: Caprice; 4th row: Alcazar.' Sweet peas were grown in abundance, for picking for the house; in pots decorating the terrace were morning glory and geraniums. The woods immediately above the house were scattered with daffodils and narcissi.

Of all her flowers, Iris best loved the scented red roses. Her garden book for 1930 lists ten kinds of standard rose for her new rose bed, irises and roses for an orange and yellow border, chrysanthemums, dahlias and peonies. In pencil, down the side, she has made brief notes about how well the flowers were doing in the Tuscan earth and despite the winds that swept across the valley from Monte Amiata. Tulips and irises were thriving, not yet plagued, as they were later, by porcupines which came to root up the bulbs and tubers. To Mrs Cutting, who had made it all possible, Iris announced that she was 'entirely absorbed by the complete loveliness of my flowers'. Later she told a friend that what she had wanted, and got, from her garden was a peaceful place in which to walk and think, and that was why there were so many arcades and alleys. Friends found her more relaxed and content at La Foce than anywhere else, spending hours in the garden, with Gianni playing near her.

Visitors found it marvellous, in this dry desert landscape, to come across such a lush and luxuriant garden, and would stroll about in amazement while Iris explained what she was doing; later, when they had left, she would walk under the wisteria, planning for the day when she might write a book. It was not until after the Second World War that eating and drinking outside in the garden or on a terrace became fashionable, so Iris's visitors wandered, admired and went back indoors. Most meals were in the dining room, drinks were served in the sitting room or library. Only many years later, when Iris had become frail, did she agree to be wheeled out, in a wicker *chaise-longue*, to sit under the pergola to read and write.

After the garden immediately around the house was planted, Iris and Pinsent turned their energies to the higher reaches, where they put a long pergola of wisteria which framed the rose garden and led out into open wild woodland of scrub oak and pine trees. From a carefully placed stone seat, a pleasing joke shared by herself and Pinsent, could be seen a farmhouse on top of a distant hill, reached by a winding road up the hillside which was planted with cypresses to remind them of the landscapes of fourteenth-century Tuscan painters. 'I like the slowness of the process [of gardening],' wrote Iris, 'and its continuity, and its cruelty, and its hopefulness.' One December weekend, having left the bulb-planting rather late, she spent three entire days putting 2,500 into the garden. She was thinking of founding a garden club for amateur gardeners, with its own journal; it would, she wrote to Irene, be a 'dull little monthly bulletin if possible. . . . Such things abound of course, in England, but are unknown here.' The first issue was planned for January 1931, and it was to be kept very cheap so as to reach 'all the corners of small "villini", station masters etc.' Later she was hoping to arrange flower shows.

Now that there was enough water, a kitchen garden was started, with vegetables and raspberry canes; during the war, it supplied La Foce and the many people who lived there with all the fruit and vegetables needed. Iris had been introduced to Mary Senni, a renowned plantswoman. Iris noted that she was 'very fat, middle aged. . . . but her enthusiasm for gardening is most delightful and infectious'. Under Mary Senni's guidance she went to Rome and spoke to about eighty people at a flower show ('it is a much nicer place than Florence – though perhaps that is not saying much'); she also became a frequent visitor to the Sennis' house where she made 'exciting lists of new tulips and irises': irises were Mary Senni's passion. She helped Iris with the gardening magazine, *Il Giardino Fiorito*, which ran to fifteen issues, went out to 120 subscribers, and was full of serious and informative pieces about gardens.

What architects and gardeners particularly admire about La Foce is the way the buildings and garden have been adapted to follow the contours of the land. There is a cypress-lined alley leading down to steps to a rose garden, and the hillside is planted with flowering quinces, forsythia, shrub roses, and herbs such as rosemary and lavender. All the time Iris was learning: that delphiniums, lupins and phlox would not grow in the heavy clay soil, nor would bluebells, but that roses flourished. One day lightning hit the school and garage and wind blew down telephone and electricity wires; Iris would have met these disasters with more equanimity had the spring seedlings not also been ruined, the gardener – the 'king of apes' as she described him crossly – having forgotten to put them into the glass frames. But as ever, she set about reintroducing order with great efficiency. Many of her English visitors, like Constance Wenlock, were themselves enthusiastic gardeners, and could be seen in the early morning dead-heading flowers or feeding them with liquid manure. When he came to La Foce, which was often during the first couple of years after his wife's death, Lord Desart worked alongside Iris in the garden. He usually brought with him his prim, elderly and very English butler, who had to be housed in great comfort. Desart was finally beginning to recover, noted Iris with relief, 'much helped by a renewed interest in public affairs – which he thought, as a matter really outside oneself, more helpful than aesthetic pleasures'.

It was not only her garden that Iris loved. She was growing ever more involved with La Foce itself, the cycles and details of farming life, the planting and harvesting of crops. She had come to love the countryside, and the slow familiar drive to Florence, and the *festa* of the threshing in which all her neighbours joined while the women spread white tableclothes under the trees for a supper of stuffed goose. Almost imperceptibly, she was drawn in, to talk to the truant-officers trying to round up children on the distant farms, to arrange evening classes for adults, to listen to the local priest's reports of hardship in the area, to furnish two empty bedrooms, to discuss a new irrigation project with Antonio. That summer the rains arrived early in August, and toads emerged in the garden to sit in the water. Then there were toys and woolly clothes to buy for La Foce's children, worry about whether the new footman had diphtheria, Antonio's pigs (newly arrived from Yorkshire) to inspect. The farm women were also beginning to come to her with their ailments. Minor domestic dramas, activity in all its forms, invariably made her feel more cheerful. Her new plans included the funding of a district nurse – the plan she had discussed with Mussolini – with a small house and dispensary, and a 'well-cared-for-baby' competition. To Irene she wrote: 'I am sure that there must be something wrong with one's own organisation of life so that time has no *leisure* in it – one runs about like a rabbit.'

At this stage Pinsent was working almost full time for the Origos, for when he was not at La Foce he was at the Villa Medici, busy with the Villino there, which was to be Iris and Antonio's Florence house. Once again Iris was charmed and considered the Villino 'one of the most enchanting small houses I have ever seen'. She felt, she told a friend, that it was hers, in a way that, at La Foce, only the garden was really hers.

In 1929, after years of living as an invalid at the Villa Medici, years of 'heart attacks' and a succession of unidentifiable viruses, and with Antonio and Percy always at odds on the rare occasions they met, Sybil made a decision about their lives. They would find and convert, or build, a house by the sea. The Riviera was a possibility, but Percy feared, as he wrote to Constance Wenlock, that it might be a 'hot bed of influenza' with 'raging dengue fever'. Sybil's tantrums and jealousies only increased with the years, affecting the whole household. Young visitors dreaded her intense questioning about their lives. 'She believed that the young were all unhappy,' remembers Pin Meade, 'and she wanted to hear all about it. She sometimes reminded me of an older, less elegant Iris, with a breathy voice.' Pin remembers a visit to the Villa Medici when she was about fifteen, and a typical expedition to the mountains: Sybil fainted in the car but, feeling herself being laid out gently on a grassy bank, said quickly, eyes still shut, 'No, that might be dirty.' She was all the more quarrelsome when depressed, and became envious of Iris's friends, her clothes, even her furniture. Iris's first reaction was irritation; later she felt ashamed, and sorry for her mother's loneliness.

After a number of expeditions along the Italian and French coasts, often accompanied by Pinsent, Sybil and Percy came across an isolated promontory just outside Lerice which seemed to have everything they wanted. Jutting out into the sea, with a small rocky island, it had fine cypresses and olives and pine trees, a large garden suitable for vines and roses to be planted along the steep narrow terraces, a perfect site for a house, and total privacy. The rocks just off the shore were full of caves and grottoes. All three were charmed, and set about planning how a loggia would look, and which was to be the sitting room, and whether it should have eighteenth-century patterns of flowers, with dark green lacquer furniture. It is all but impossible, now that so much of the Italian coast consists of a long straggle of modern houses, to imagine its beauty and peacefulness before the Second World War. Iris went to look at the property and was enchanted, describing it to Irene as 'a divine site, surrounded by olives and ilexes. . . . I think there will be a lot of poetry reading on the rocks what with Shelley and Byron so near. . . . and an increasing disapproval of frivolous pursuits.' The land was bought, Pinsent began drawing and building, and the property was named Gli Scafari. Once again, as at La Foce, Pinsent designed bathrooms in marble brought from Carrara, and the gardens were planted with wisteria and more roses. Later he added a small enclosed garden, away from the salty sea air and strong winds, with a fountain, a lawn and a herbaceous border. Even those who had reservations about Pinsent's domestic architecture, finding it too given to marble and rather harshlines, were invariably captivated by his gardens, where wilderness and formality were artfully contrived side by side. Visitors entered through double iron gates, both piers covered thickly in wisteria, and drove down to a courtyard with lemon trees in pots. In time Gli Scafari became an annual summer retreat for the whole family, but in the early days, however splendid it looked, Iris found it oppressive. 'It is the old feeling of *unreality* about this place – a gilded cage,' she wrote to a friend. 'I think it is partly the absolute silence, total deathly silence, like in a church. . . . And here Percy sits, month after month; I *do* wonder that he is still (even if only partly) alive.' A little later she wrote again, noting how Sybil did not come down until six in the afternoon, when she breakfasted: 'this place is divinely lovely – indeed almost the loveliest place I have ever been in – and yet somehow, already now, it is not a *happy* home – already Percy's anxiety and Mummy's constant talks about health, have touched it.'

More than once Iris noted to friends that Antonio was not really very interested in personal relations, nor very conscious of feelings, but that he still, occasionally, 'put into words some sort of need' for her. They could, and did, have fun together, if not all or even much of the time. They shared a horror of stuffy family weddings, which made them laugh, and he was sympathetic when she felt obliged to take part in three performances of *tableaux vivants* given in Florence for associated royalty assembled from all over Italy. The *tableaux* were of ladies of different periods; Iris began in an Empire frock and went on to the 'Bustle scene'.

One pleasure Iris and Antonio continued to share was travel. Both loved that moment of getting away, of setting out for the unfamiliar and the unknown, and neither had a desire for undue comfort or luxury. Journeys provided some of their happiest moments. In 1929, packing tents, camp beds and provisions into a small Fiat lorry, they set out for the Abruzzi mountains, south of Rome. They saw Aquila and Sulmona and travelled the remote and largely uninhabited mountainsides, where there were still bears and wolves. They saw pilgrims with crucifixes, funeral processions, fairs, black buffaloes, and near a cemetery came across a mother carrying a dead baby in her arms. Touched by the woman's loneliness, Iris wrote an epitaph: 'No bearers did she have, nor torches, but laid him here alone; and around him the cistus blooms and the wild oleander.' Sometimes Antonio cooked scrambled eggs; the car broke down; Iris got hay fever; it rained hard, and was also very cold: the diary Iris wrote records nothing but pleasure. She kept careful notes about hotels and restaurants ('friendly', 'unpretentious', 'unprepossessing'). After a fortnight they returned to La Foce. Gianni had stayed behind with his nanny; in Florence he had started lessons in French and Italian, and was learning the piano with Nesta. Discussing where it would be nicest to live, Iris wrote somewhat bleakly: 'the main point of life has always seemed to me unsatisfactory, in that we know that we ourselves, and most of our friends, have spent most of our lives *reacting* from the atmosphere we were brought up in.'

The following year, 1930, Iris and Antonio sailed via Corfu to Athens, where they stayed at the Grande Bretagne and found the Sitwells and Mussolini's daughter Edda, and then on to the Greek islands, Samos, Patmos, Kos and Rhodes. One day they drove to Sunium, where the cliffs were covered with thyme and wild peas. It was August. Iris bathed, and wrote with delight about the hot sun, the prickly pears and the cactuses. The boat home was an Italian ship full of goats, sheep, pigs, cows, mules and turkeys; the sheep were tethered just outside their first-class cabins, and the goats scaled the ship's sides like chamois. Antonio had a row with the crew about the filthy state of the decks, addressing the ship's officers as 'swine, pigs, rascals' and declaring that he was ashamed to be Italian. Iris caught a bad cold, but nothing could lessen her enchantment as she watched the islands and coastline of Greece from her porthole every day. This was travel of a now long-lost kind: no tourists, few hotels, deserted places. Iris was never to become a travel writer: her style is too spare, and her diary entries are more informative than entertaining, but something of her delight fills every line.

Later they went to Venice and stayed at the Grand Hotel. From her bed Iris could hear the water lapping the sides of the canal. They went out to the Lido to swim, but there were tourists there, and Iris noted sharply that she found the 'German-American zoo repulsive'. A contented traveller perhaps; but a highly critical one when it came to people.

Though Antonio certainly enjoyed social life less than Iris, he was still prepared to accept occasional invitations in Rome or Florence. On one particularly successful trip to Rome they went to see some of the classical sites they had not visited before, then to a new nightclub, the *Quiencenetto*, where Iris met David Osborne, a counsellor at the British Embassy, who turned out to be both charming and an excellent dancer. Invited to tea by friends, she sat next to Lytton Strachey and Lord Berners. Axel Munthe was there, whom she had first met more than ten years before during the 'flu epidemic on Capri; though he was by now old and blind, Iris found him as remarkable as ever – 'A sense of latent force that he gives out is quite terrific.' She was always at her best describing people, her portraits short, memorable, and sometimes painfully acute. 'It is no use pretending that we are not less unhappy when we are with other people of our own kind', she wrote to a friend. Letters to Mrs Cutting in the United States reveal Iris's more social side, her increasing sense of confidence and the pleasure she took in an energetic life which left her little time for thought. In May 1930 she was asked to take part in a Revue, the costumes copied from Velasquez portraits. 'I am dancing the Lancers in a bustle! with three great friends and four most good looking young men.' There are visits to England, to Chamonix, to Castiglioncello, often with the Meades. In June she andAntonio planned what she called a 'spree together'. There are many references to Gianni's progress: at school, in the garden, at the seaside. Though she was never very fond of Antonio's family, and had been heard to mutter that not one of them had ever seen a book, let alone read one, she none the less dutifully gave house parties for them at La Foce.

One autumn they were invited to Naples to celebrate the marriage of a southern aristocrat. Iris was feeling unwell and not much looking forward to it, and Antonio generously volunteered to go to Florence to collect her dress, and the family jewels from the bank. The guests travelled from all over Italy by special train and were put up at the Grand Hotel, where red carpets had been laid and flags hung from the balconies. Next morning they watched the fleet coming in escorting the King of Naples, all guns booming in salute. A grand ball was held in the Palazzo Reale; troops in full-dress uniform lined the streets, the ballroom was hung with *fleurs-de-lis* in red and gold on blue and gold brocade. Some twenty or so royal or former royal families were represented and stood together in a line, and as they arrived guests curtsied or bowed as they passed. Then came the wedding itself. Iris remarked that this great turnout of royalty looked wonderfully like the background to a Veronese or a Rubens. She herself wore an 'oyster-grey satin dress with mauve lights and a huge amethyst at the waist, a long train and the family 17th century diamond rose', part of the Italian crown jewels, given to Antonio's grandmother when she was the Prince's mistress.

Two days later Iris was happily back at La Foce, working on a new peach orchard.

Gianni celebrated his seventh birthday in Florence, at the Grand Hotel. When his parents were away, he now wrote them simple letters in Italian or English, sometimes dictated to his nanny, sometimes in the looped writing of Italian children. In spite of his trustfulness and lovingness, Iris noted that he had built up a little wall of reserve around the things he minded about most; he was undemonstrative, and 'although so loving, hated being kissed'. He had been going to dancing classes, and Iris tried to teach him to kiss a lady's hand when saying goodbye. He was still taking piano lessons from Nesta de Robeck, and Italian lessons with a Signora Morozzi, but Iris now decided to school him herself, in

Italian as well as English, on alternate days. She was finding it harder and harder to leave him, and did not look forward to her travels quite as much as she once had. Gianni was given his own garden by the woods at La Foce, which he planted with bluebells: this was before Iris and Pinsent discovered how badly they did in that heavy soil. Like all seven-year-old Italian boys, he had his own black Balilla shirt. His hair, which when he was a baby had been very fair, had turned slightly darker and was cut in a pudding basin shape.

Towards the end of February 1933, the Origos went skiing with the Meades at Bonneval. Gianni, for whom the Meades were really most like his English family, spent his days in a state of constant excitement. On the last evening he told Iris his mouth was sore, and when she looked she noticed some little ulcers. He cried in the night, and she gave him aspirin. Two days after they got back to Florence, she put him to bed.

The first child specialist to be called diagnosed gastric influenza; Giglioli, the family doctor, suspected paratyphoid fever. Iris read to Gianni continually as he lay in his bed and watched his canary. More specialists came; they, too, talked of paratyphoid. An astrologer in Harrow, whose name was given them by Reggie Davies, 'looked up the Boy's map', but did 'not like the look of things at all. . . . Candidly I think his chances are slim, but it is not a hopeless case and he may pull through.' The Origos cancelled an invitation to dine at the British Embassy in Rome, where they were to meet Mussolini. Pin Meade, then seventeen and staying with them at the Villino, was sent to Rome for a few days.

During the last week in March Gianni seemed to improve. His temperature dropped, but Iris wrote to Irene that he still looked 'like a small, ruffled sparrow'. It was the height of the Florence

Season, and the Origos were inundated with the usual round of visitors and parties. Then Gianni seemed to get weaker. It now seemed possible that he had appendicitis, and X-rays were taken. They showed that the pleura had been touched, filling Iris with despair that she might, while feeding him briefly after he was born, have transmitted the tuberculosis that had affected so many of the Cuttings. On 1 April, she wrote to Irene: Gianni was unable to eat or drink, 'he just lay, cried and cried and coughed'. They started to give him oxygen every two hours; he rallied, ate, slept, and woke up hungry again. 'I do feel that we have now got something to fight *with* . . . now that he has begun to eat again, I do believe that it will be all right.' Later, after tea, she noted: 'Antonio and I walked in the garden, overwhelmed by relief. The whole world seemed bathed in light.'

On 16 April she wrote once more to Irene; Gianni's condition had worsened again – he was nervous, anxious, tearful; his head ached, and he could not sleep. 'But at last, in these last two days, I really *can* say that he is *better* . . . Of course, one's thoughts flew to meningitis, but now since yesterday, his head too is much better . . . It has been, after all, the happiest of Easters.' Three days later came a sudden collapse; Gianni started to feel so cold that nothing could warm him. He was given injections to stimulate his heart, and was very sleepy.

Nothing Iris ever wrote is more touching than her next letter to Irene. The tone is, at times, almost dispassionate; it is as if by writing the details to a friend she had known and loved all her life she could keep the final horror at bay, as if hope and optimism might somehow work the miracle she could see was not happening. 'On Saturday morning, when Castellani came, there could be no doubt. He could not sit up in bed or draw his legs in fully. One side of his face was slightly paralysed and he had great difficulty speaking. Temperature up to 104 and then down again . . . Our one hope is that he does go on asking for food, eats it all (almost mechanically, with his eyes shut) and appears to digest it perfectly. I absolutely refuse to give up hope, I am *sure* that we shall pull through. But oh Rene, it is dreadful to see him like this. He has gone back to being a tiny baby – lies all day playing with my amber beads or clutching at my fingers. Sometimes one can't make out what he says – Today I'm not sure that he recognises me . . . If only he is spared acute pain, anything is bearable.' The pain, for her, was almost unendurable. Years before she had written to Colin of a 'shut door' in her mind 'behind which the terror of something happening to Gianni' lurked: now her worst nightmare had come true.

By 22 April there was no further doubt: it was meningitis. Gianni could no longer sit up, he had trouble speaking, and in some indefinable way his expression had changed. Every day, he grew a little weaker. On 27 April he could no longer swallow. At seven o'clock on the morning of 30 April 1933, after fifty-eight days of illness, Gianni died. He was the age that Iris had been when her father died.

They dressed him in the white suit he had worn for his confirmation, and Iris picked white tulips and azaleas from the garden. During the next day, as he lay in his open coffin, the tenant farmers and their families from La Foce came to see him. Pinsent noticed that 'his hands, which were thinned somewhat, were exactly like Iris's'. Iris sat with him all day, until they came to take him away. The funeral was held in Fiesole, in the chapel of the Blue Sisters at San Girolamo, which Pinsent and Aubrey Waterfield filled with gardenias, lilies, white irises and roses. The coffin, carried by Antonio, Pinsent and two others, was covered by a cross made of lily-of-the-valley and gardenias. Pinsent described the ceremony to Irene: 'Sybil had been ill, but she got up and came to the funeral service. The procession then went to Fiesole cemetery . . . Antonio had arranged for some of the farmers and their children to come, for he preferred their presence to that of all the fashionable people of Florence who were there in great numbers. There were children also from a deaf mute asylum and an orphanage that Iris partly supports.' To Irene, Iris herself wrote: 'I can't pretend that it seems anything but an utterly empty world – but I am trying to struggle back, beyond the weeks of unbearable pain, to the time when Gianni was such a happy little boy . . .' He had died before seeing his bluebells come up. 'Everything is so lovely here now – and the loveliness is almost unbearable. It is in the simplest things – the wind in one's face, the smell of the pinks in the garden – that it seems most intolerable, most *against* nature, that he should never feel again. But that he is at peace I do believe and sometimes (not always) the bond between us, something made by our love for each other, still goes on.'

Iris had no clear religious faith. But she did believe passionately in the need for people to behave well towards each other, and to show courage. As they carried the coffin away, perhaps she thought of her long affair with Colin, and wondered whether this was not a punishment for her happiness.

1. Lord Desart, Iris's Anglo-Irish grandfather

2. Lady Desart

3. The Cutting family at Westbrook, May 1909.
Back row: Bronson and Bayard; *middle*: Iris's
grandparents and Olivia; *seated on the ground*: Justine

4. Bayard, Iris's much-loved father, who
died when she was seven

5. Sybil, Iris's mother, a lifelong hypochondriac
but possessed of considerable charm

6. Iris in Switzerland where Bayard went to convalesce from TB

7. Bernhard Berenson who conducted Florence's most
celebrated salon

8. The Villa Medici in Fiesole built by Michelozzo for Cosimo de Medici. Iris spent most of her childhood here

9. *La sala degli uccelli* in the Villa Medici showing the Chinese silk wallpaper after which it was named

10. Antonio Origo around the time of his engagement to Iris

11. Iris with Gianni, born in June 1925

12. La Foce, the estate bought by the Origos in 1924: 'treeless and shrubless but for some tufts of broom, these corrugated ridges formed a lunar landscape, pale and inhuman . . .'

13. Cecil Pinsent's top terrace at La Foce in its earliest stage

14. La Foce after water had been brought to the estate

15. Pinsent's bottom terrace at the beginning of the 1930s

16. Gianni at a smart London wedding

17. Local Fascist dignitaries visiting La Foce to admire its transformation into a model estate

18. Iris at La Foce in the 1930s

19. Children of the La Foce estate for whom Iris
started a school

20. Antonio, Iris and their two daughters
Donata and Benedetta

21. Elsa Dallolio, Iris's closest friend for twenty years

22. Benedetta and Donata at La Foce

23. Iris at La Foce in the early 1980s

24. Pinsent's chapel, built just below La Foce, where Antonio, Iris, Gianni and Elsa Dallolio lie buried

CHAPTER EIGHT

A long green feather in her hat

Then the letters and telegrams started arriving. They came from relations in England and America, from friends in Italy, from acquaintances everywhere who had heard of the Origos' tragedy and felt with them the unbearable loss of an only child. Iris's godmother Patience Cockerell wrote hoping that she 'would not keep either in the house or in your heart any closed rooms that you dare not go into . . . But neither you, nor life, can ever be the same – indeed – I wonder what you will become – so different to the one I knew.' Harry Verney, her aunt Joan's husband, private secretary to HM The Queen, wrote to say 'how warmly her Majesty sympathises with you and how much you [are] in her thoughts at this moment'. 'I mourn with you, my poor child,' wrote Edith Wharton, 'as only those can who have loved life in all its beauty, and have lived long enough to measure its inexorableness.' She, like many others, used the word 'radiant' to describe Gianni, a word Iris soon picked up and which seemed to give her comfort. There were dozens, perhaps hundreds, of these letters, and today they are still filed away in the desk in the room in which Iris used to write, looking out over the gardens and the fountain in which Gianni had played with his wind-up frog.

Some who lived not too far away, like Berenson, wrote short notes and then came to see her. She was evidently much touched by his visit: 'It made us feel very close to you in our unhappiness . . . It seems an empty world now – but the closeness and affection of one's friends does help.' The longest and perhaps the most profound letter came from George Santayana, her father's friend and tutor, who had come to know Sybil and Iris when he visited I Tatti shortly after the First World War. 'We have no claim on our possessions,' he now wrote to Iris.

We have no claim to exist; and, as we have to die in the end, so we must resign ourselves to die piecemeal, which really happens when we lose somebody or something that was closely intertwined with our existence. It is like a physical wound; we may survive, but maimed and broken in that direction; dead there . . .

Not that we can, or ever do at heart, renounce our affections. Never that. We cannot exercise our full nature all at once in every direction; but the parts that are relatively in abeyance, their centre lying perhaps in the past or the future, belong to us inalienably. We should not be ourselves if we cancelled them . . . All our affections, when clear and pure and not claims to possession, transport us to another world; and the loss of contact, here or there, with those eternal beings is merely like closing a book which we keep at hand for another occasion.

Later Iris used to repeat to friends Santayana's words, 'Who would wish to be consoled?'

Characteristically, Iris now forced herself into the painful business of answering these letters. She kept busy all the time, living behind a wall of hard work and efficiency. As Patience Cockerell had predicted, however, she did indeed become different, more private, less enthusiastic, less exuberant, less able to commit herself: all opposites of the qualities Colin had once told her were what he most loved and admired in her. But as she had when she broke with him in 1930, she showed considerable fortitude, the courage she had once said to Colin was the most important single virtue, and after the first agonised months returned to her old life. For the next few years she scarcely ever spoke about Gianni, except to very close friends; but as she grew older, so she talked about him more and more, and towards the end of her life was apt to describe his short life and death to virtual strangers. With Pinsent she began to discuss plans for the future and things that needed doing at La Foce. 'I know from Aileen', Pinsent wrote to Irene, 'that Iris wants to have people in the house because she is afraid of its emptiness.' Aileen hurried at once to La Foce, and together she and Iris gardened. Antonio was no better at expressing his misery over the loss of his son than he was at talking about any other feelings. He mourned on his own.

Iris's grief eventually found expression in two projects, both of which, connected as they were to the little boy, seemed to bring her some solace. Not long after he died, she began to put together a book about Gianni, an essay of almost unbearable self-control, detailing every little step of his development from the moment he was born, and full of photographs of him and his letters to her and Antonio. She had it privately printed, beautifully bound in white, with a large photograph of Gianni in his coffin, his face peaceful, his thin, delicate hands folded. Each picture is separated by sheets of white tissue. Of the many poignant sentences it contains none perhaps is more so than the following: 'I think,' she wrote, 'he felt safer, more completely reassured, in Nanny's atmosphere of unfailing peace and kindness, than anywhere else.' Did she have haunting regrets about the many trips she had made without him? Nesta helped her send copies to her close friends. It is almost too painful to read.

The other plan concerned Gianni's burial. Not wanting to leave him permanently in the cemetery at Fiesole, the Origos asked Pinsent to design a very simple temple on the edge of the woods at La Foce, some ten minutes' walk through the trees from the house. The grounds were to be large enough to provide burial space for the Origos, and for the people who lived and worked at La Foce. Pinsent worked on the temple, made in the local grey travertine, all summer.

On 20 November, a 'day of utter beauty, cloudless, no leaf stirring', Gianni's coffin was taken from Fiesole and brought home. For the last kilometre of the journey – the cemetery stands on a dirt track through the property – it was accompanied by the children of the estate, carrying flowers. The coffin was then laid in its grave, which had been lined with boughs of cypress and lavender. 'It is more lovely than I can tell,' Iris wrote to Irene, 'exactly what I had hoped for and *completely* right in the landscape.' Watching her son come home, Iris was somewhat soothed. 'It was almost unbearably moving, but now that it is all over, I *have*, although I could not explain why, a greater sense of peace.'

The following year, on the anniversary of Gianni's death, a service was held at the chapel with the farmers and their children. 'Worst of all', Iris noted, '[is] the return of all the spring loveliness of life that he is not sharing.'

All through the mid 1920s Iris had thought about writing, particularly a biography, but seldom found the time to do anything about it. Now, suddenly, she had endless time, too much time, and turned back to an idea that she had long been considering. This was a biography of Giacomo Leopardi, the early nineteenth-century Italian poet from Recanati in the Marches, about whom there were several decent Italian studies, but nothing in English. Iris was absolutely clear in her mind that she was not interested in literary criticism; rather, she wanted to examine the life and character of this lonely man who died at the age of thirty-nine. He was, she wrote, a 'querulous, tortured invalid, mistrustful of his fellow men, with a mind sometimes scornful and cantankerous, and a heart intolerably sad and lonely'; but as a poet, who had written poetry she loved, he had a capacity for feeling 'so intense that his only real contact with reality came from his imagination'. Early on she had encountered one particular difficulty that can afflict the biographer: she did not really like her subject. 'One more chapter on him', she had written to Colin in the summer of 1928, 'but such stodge as it is and such a nasty complaining little hunchback he is really, for all his dreams and cleverness.' Just the same, she had struggled on in spare moments, on her transatlantic crossings, for example, and had made several trips to Recanati.

It was not only Leopardi who interested her, but the whole nature of biography. Many years later, in a book written in the 1970s called *A Need to Testify*, she included an essay on biography; but she had already been writing and lecturing on the subject for many years. Biography, she would say, has one really essential ingredient: that of veracity, the telling of the truth. Close behind comes enthusiasm – a need, a passion, for telling that truth. At the same time, biographers must beware, she warned, of three insidious temptations: that of suppressing material, that of sitting in judgement on a subject, and that of invention – in any shape or form. Like Lytton Strachey, it pleased her to think of biography as the 'most delicate and humane of all branches in the art of writing'. Believer in accurate research that she was, she added that an historian's skills were essential, and that it was a biographer's prime duty to know a great deal more about his subject and his times than he ever put down on paper, so that 'in writing there should be a rich background of unstated knowledge of literature, a tapestry which is never unrolled'. Few biographers would disagree with her, but these views were delivered in a tone of authority unusual in a young woman not yet thirty who had never written a book, and whose entire education came from an inspired classical scholar, Signor Monti, a clever friend, Colin, and a great deal of solitary reading. On occasion she was very poetic about the art she intended to practise: 'I do not think of truth as being made of granite,' she wrote, 'but rather as a note in music – a note which we instantly recognise as the right one, as soon as it is struck.' Humility, listening to one's subject without prejudice and interruption, were absolutely necessary to enable the aspiring biographer to see – 'as suddenly as, at the turn of a passage, one comes upon one's image in a mirror – a living face . . . In that fleeting moment, he may perhaps reach a faint apprehension – as near to the truth as we are ever likely to get – of what another man was like.' Here, perhaps, she hesitated: intrusion bothered her, as we know – and where did the line between knowing a man and intruding in his life really fall?

As with many things that profoundly mattered to Iris, she spoke little about her proposed book, beyond occasional complaints to Colin that she never had any time; there are no references to it in her surviving letters to Aileen, Irene or Pinsent. However, sometime in the months after Gianni's death she finished the book, and sent it to Hamish Hamilton, who with little fuss or noise published it shortly before Christmas 1935.

Perhaps to their surprise, it attracted very good reviews. The *New Republic* called it 'excellent'. The *Observer* remarked with pleasure on its 'tone' – 'less personal than is usual in biography today . . . Her book is a monument to scholarship – the literary and historical background is painted with consummate skill, and a pattern of good taste.' Just what she had striven for, perhaps: a good historical understanding and not too much unseemly intrusion into private matters. She must have been especially pleased by a letter from Frances Partridge: 'I don't know if you can possibly realise what a blessed relief it is – what tremendous gratitude one feels at being given a book not only frightfully well written but with the perfect attitude towards facts and reality – it suddenly made me realise what I'd missed in 9 out of 10 of all biographies that have been written since for instance *Eminent Victorians* cast such a blight on the writers of them – which is really ironical for no one had a higher understanding than Lytton had, and I found myself constantly thinking as I read Leopardi how tremendously he would have appreciated it, and approved of your attitude to reality.'

At the end of 1933 Iris went to Westbrook to see her grandmother. During the Atlantic crossing a blizzard covered the ship in ice, and when she landed she found New York the coldest it had been in fourteen years. She had not meant to stay for long, but Mrs Cutting went down with pneumonia, and she was not very well herself. On Castellani's orders she went for a two-week 'cure' to New Orleans. She loved the French Quarter with its latticed windows and wrought-iron balconies, but was most drawn to the 'strange desolate greyforests, where only great bare leafless trunks and branches are left under the choking tendrils of Spanish moss, miles and miles of swamps, with alligators, and opossums and rattlesnakes'. Barren landscapes always drew her. However miserable she may have been, Iris's innate sense of adventure had not altogether deserted her. 'Through my octoon stenographer', she wrote to Gordon Waterfield, 'I made the acquaintance of darkie-land at night – I frequented a dance-hall known as Eddie Taylor's Bear Garden, where I danced with a charming dusky barman called, simply, Earl, and made friends with an enchanting young creature (3/4 Negro, 1/4 Indian) named Flossie Bell! . . .' This was a side to Iris, independent, adventurous, free, that very few people apart from the Meades ever saw. It was like a sudden explosive escape from the formality of her everyday life, and perhaps explains her restless need to travel and her pleasure and involvement in dramas.

At some point about this time Gordon Waterfield, who had loved Iris from before she married, made some sort of approach to her. She was wary: Gordon was married to Kitty, a woman she liked; and she was not really looking for complications. It seems that they must have had a short affair, however, for a letter from Iris exists in which she writes: 'It has been such a happy time – and it is only the beginning, I know, of a relationship which is going to give us both a great deal more. I liked you to say that you felt 'completed' with me. That is the gift, of all others, that I would like to give you . . . Already I find myself looking back with happiness to many things . . . Such enchanting memories, Gordon. And there will be more . . .' But there were not. Iris seems to have backed off, having decided that the friendship they had long shared was far more appropriate to them. She wrote him a series of friendly, firm letters, before falling silent. Gordon was trying to find a flat in Rome: 'But my dear,' she wrote, 'you mustn't try to time your plans to fit in with mine. You mustn't write letters quite like the last one. I am sorry to write a letter entirely in the categorical imperative – but after all it is what we agreed on! I don't want to be horrid – and I certainly don't want to lose your friendship – but I think you know that I am right.'

Their friends blamed the Origos' love affairs – for Antonio too had had romantic attachments, and was to do so again – on the difference in temperament between them, exacerbated now by Gianni's death. From the moment his coffin was taken away Iris turned his room into a shrine, and would allow nothing to be touched. Antonio was appalled. He thought the only way forward, not for himself alone, but for both of them, was to put the lost child out of their minds, as far as they were able to, and never refer to it again. It was hardly surprising that they should have quarrelled bitterly, and in time turned to other people. Iris's very sense of rootlessness, willed to her by her father, was perhaps the reason why she had fallen for Antonio in the first place, for he was indeed a curious choice; it may explain too why she kept so much of her warmer and more humorous side hidden from all but a very few people.

Antonio's closest friends in the 1930s were Flavia and Ugolino della Gherardesca, who owned a villa built in the walls of the village of Bolgheri, famous for its five-kilometre-long avenue of cypresses, not far from Livorno. When Iris took off for New York and later London in the 1930s, the della Gherardescas invited him to stay, and together they went on a long trip to Canada and the Rocky Mountains. At this stage Antonio was still a keen hunter, happy to join in one of the della Gherardescas' favourite sports: climbing high up into a tree with a tame pigeon decoy to attract wild migrating pigeons and shoot them when they flew in low to investigate. Clearly Antonio was very lonely at La Foce on his own, particularly at first. He once told Flavia that what he missed and had loved about his wife were 'her white arms, the whiteness of her skin, because she never went into the sun'.

In Flavia's mind, there is no doubt that he was still much in love with Iris, and only later began to have affairs. Antonio was, Flavia says, 'an extremely charming, likeable and good-looking man, who laughed a great deal. One trouble was that Iris was a great deal too intellectual for him, too ladylike and seemingly upright.' Did he perhaps never see the side of her that came out with the charming barman Earl? For the time being at least, Iris and Antonio would spend much of their time apart.

What, once again, few but her closest friends knew, was that she was already in the process of finishing a second biography. In Italy, as the wife of a large landowner, the idea of her pursuing a separate career writing books would have been met with incredulity. Predictably it was many years before there was any talk of an Italian edition of her books. She found it easier to say nothing of what she was up to, but would merely disappear into her study looking out over the gardens whenever she could, to read the research materials she had accumulated, and to write.

The second book, perhaps far closer to her heart than anything else she ever wrote, was a short life of Byron's daughter Allegra, who died of typhus in a convent when she was five. The task of writing about this endearing and lonely child, neglected by Byron and prevented from ever seeing her mother, must have touched her profoundly, for nowhere in her other books does such obvious sympathy shine through. Iris wrote, of the days after Allegra's death, when her mother Claire was told what had happened: 'The nature of that letter, written in the first moment of horror and despair, can easily be imagined. After writing it, Claire probably sank into the state of comparative calm which comes at first after an overwhelming blow. That which had been too terrible to be fully faced, even in imagination, had happened

234

in reality. Now nothing more could come; by being utterly bereft, she was secure.' Was she writing about herself? Was this how she had felt? If her later books, elegantly written and conscientiously researched, were on the whole cooler and more restrained; *Allegro*, has a softer, sadder feel to it. What was becoming very apparent was Iris's growing talent for evoking a background, a period of history; and for leaving the reader convinced of an immense amount of knowledge fully digested but never actually used, while the main characters were never lost sight of.

Iris was a writer who constantly went over each manuscript, writing and rewriting. Preliminary drafts of all her work, filed away in the drawers of her desk at La Foce, show endless crossings-out, rewritings, corrections – and, often, total rejection in favour of a new draft, something that later tested her publishers severely. In her autobiography Iris describes the day when she commented on Percy Lubbock's neat and 'decorative' manuscript pages. 'I think' her stepfather replied grandly, '*before* I write.' It was Percy, however, who now read *Allegra* in manuscript and offered to send it to Leonard Woolf at the Hogarth Press. Describing it to Woolf as a 'small work', Percy added that Iris had taken, 'as you will see, a great deal of trouble in ransacking all possible sources – including, I believe, more than one hitherto untouched – and has used it to make what seems to me an attractive sketch.'

Leonard Woolf enjoyed the book but was worried about its brevity – printed, it would make barely more than a hundred pages. Eventually he offered a royalty of ten per cent on the first thousand copies sold, rising thereafter to fifteen per cent; various publishers in the United States turned it down, saying that it was too 'slender and insubstantial'. A growing and what was to prove a lifelong concern of Iris's with every aspect of a book's production – jacket, size, price, print, binding – was now emerging. She asked Leonard for a bright, clear blue binding: they settled on yellow linen, the sort of compromise she would accept less readily in the years to come. In the first six months *Allegra* sold a disappointing 644 copies; but again reviewers were wholehearted in their admiration.

It was *Allegra* that first brought Iris into Virginia Woolf's life, and ultimately into a London world she had long dreamt of. In Florence she had pined for the company of intelligent women friends; in London there was everything that attracted and amused her, particularly people who talked her language and read the same books. Iris called at the Hogarth Press offices to see if Leonard Woolf had accepted *Allegra*; as she was leaving, she heard Virginia's voice from upstairs, shouting to Leonard to bring Iris up to see her. Iris found this first encounter extremely disconcerting. 'What does it feel like,' Virginia immediately asked, 'to wake up in the morning in a Tuscan farmhouse?' Iris was too confused to answer, not knowing that this was the sort of question Virginia put to everyone. (She was reputed to have asked a seller of apples: 'What do you feel, in the dark, in fog, selling apples?') All Iris was able to say was: 'Come and see'. At the time, as Iris wrote many years later, 'Virginia was writing an essay on Highbrows and Lowbrows, saying "Look what a mess the Highbrows make of their lives; when I sit in a bus I always sit next to the conductor. I try to find out what it is like to be a prostitute, a working class woman with seven children . . . All the things, in short, that I am not able to do for myself."' Iris came away impressed by what she considered to be Virginia Woolf's 'intense desire to enter into the minds of others, but often as if looking down a microscope, through glass'. She noted with pleasure that Virginia, like herself, believed the collection of many facts, even when they were not used, to be necessary for a biography: 'a donkey's work, thankless, heavy'.

With people much younger than herself – there were twenty years between them – whom she did not consider her equals, Virginia could be exceptionally kind. Iris had expressed a wish to meet Ethel Smyth, the musician whom Virginia described more than once as a 'game old cock' and who, at seventy-two, seemed to have fallen in love with her. (As she put it, 'It is like being caught by a giant crab'.) Virginia now wrote to Ethel: 'A gifted, sincere and I think rather charming young woman . . . wants more than anything to meet you.' A tea party was arranged, with the Woolfs, Elizabeth Bowen, T. S. Eliot, Ethel Smyth and Iris Origo. The poet and novelist William Plomer, who dropped in, later wrote: 'Eliot was there. His gravity seemed decidedly male in comparison with those exceptionally quick-witted women with their shining eyes and brilliant, rapid utterance (in Iris Origo's case extremely rapid) outpaced by the quickness of their brains and senses.'

One habitué of these London literary circles was the writer Leo Myers, a friend of Charlie Meade and the son of Frederick W. H. Myers, a founder member of the Society for Psychical Research and well known medium who conducted seances in Cambridge. Leo, named after Prince Leopold, whom his father had tutored, had been a successful athlete as a boy at Eton, but later had taken against what he called the school's 'hierarchical distinctions'. Frederick Myers had arranged a seance in the United States at which he proposed to try to contact the relations of a number of American spiritualists when he died suddenly, in 1901. His widow had decided to go in his stead and carry out the seance herself, in the hope of meeting her husband again. It did not work; but she had taken Leo with her, and in

Chicago he met Elsie, the rich daughter of a railway tycoon, General William Palmers. They wanted to marry, but since Leo was twenty-three and Elsie thirty-two, they were persuaded to wait, for seven years; at the end of that time they married, and came back to live in England. Frances Partridge, who had also been pursued by Leo at one point (like Iris, she was courted by both Colin MacKenzie and Leo Myers), describes Elsie as a once-pretty woman who by the time she settled in England had aged badly and was now a 'fat, plain lady, very deaf, with huge spectacles, and treated by Leo as a piece of furniture'. The Myerses had two daughters, who as young women rather disliked their father; he was tyrannical at home and endlessly self-obsessed, as well as 'secretive and aloof'. Frances Partridge remembers Leo as 'tall and slight, dapper, like a gentleman doll'; in his journals, Arnold Bennett described him as a 'thin, dark man, *silencieux*, *un peu precieux*, but apparently of a benevolent mind. Certainly a high brow.'

In 1922 Leo had published a much-praised novel called *The Orissers*, and when Iris arrived in England in the 1930s was just bringing out a second, *The Root and the Flower*. It was hailed as 'superb' by the critics, *Time and Tide* going so far as to say of it that it was not 'the Book of the Month, or the Book of the Year – it is literature'. Leo, now largely forgotten as a novelist, was planning a series 'about the spirit of man, the land in a rich and spacious province of Anywhere'. With the success of his novels, his social circle had expanded. His friends included the Woolfs, the David Cecils, Desmond MacCarthy, L. P. Hartley and Lady Ottoline Morrell. Myers was an odd man, vain and hypochondriacal, having had TB as a boy. He was also a womaniser. But he was not easily awed, and friends admired the individuality of his ideas. His wider family did not care for him much, however; they disliked the way he treated Elsie, and considered him spoilt from having been an adored elder son.

Leo might, had he wished, have entered the heart of the literary world of Bloomsbury but he preferred to drift around its edges, rejecting its private language and esoteric jokes; he would say that he considered private aesthetic contemplation 'distasteful', and loathed 'intellectual gymnastics'. Plain, fat, deaf Elsie, who had grown old quickly, stayed at home.

Sometime in the mid 1930s Iris was introduced, probably by the Meades, to Leo. Lonely, uncertain about her writing future and incapable of forgetting Gianni, she seems to have taken to him immediately; Leo clearly felt the same, though he wrote somewhat apprehensively to Frances Partridge: 'I expect you guessed that I. was largely the cause of my depression. There is a streak of hardness in her, in spite of many great powers of deliberately given kindness and sympathy.' In her diary Frances Partridge noted that it was a 'very grand passion indeed' and that she had never seen Leo so 'carried away and reckless'. He was good-looking (he parted his hair in the middle and brushed the curly bits sideways), attentive, and the sort of literary companion Iris longed for; she does not seem to have minded the vanity and the hypochondria. Leo was not a scholar, but he had read widely, was interested in science, philosophy and the Eastern world – all subjects of which Iris knew practically nothing – and intrigued by Freud and Jung. The fact that he dined at Boulestin's in exquisitely tailored suits while earnestly professing himself to be a socialist annoyed some of his friends, but not Iris, who had perhaps spent too much time in Italy and the United States to be unduly upset by such contradictions. That autumn, when she was back in Italy, planning surreptitious ways of corresponding with him, Leo wrote a long and detailed account of their relationship and posted it to her; Iris was to read it, and return it to him at the Travellers' Club by registered post, the whole episode somewhat reminiscent of the letters between Iris and Colin that once sped backwards and forwards and were then typed up and filed away. On this occasion the envelope arrived at the Travellers' Club empty – it had come unglued, or been opened, and the letter had fallen out; Leo spent several frantic day schivvying the post office, and it eventually turned up.

Soon afterwards, when Iris was again in London – she went backwards and forwards between England and Italy repeatedly during the 1930s – Leo wrote optimistically to Frances Partridge: 'Our meeting has been unbelievably good – and all my furies and despairs have dropped from me . . . I am urging her of course to marry me – but with a very real sense that the considerations that stand in the way are as serious as they could very well be.' 'Another love affair of this summer,' wrote Frances Partridge in her diary. 'It is a very grand passion indeed.' By December Leo was describing their relationship as 'perfect'.

In her diaries Virginia Woolf gives a good account of the early days of their affair. On Friday 28 June 1935 she dined at the Cecils':

Origo was there, whom I like. She is young, tremulous, nervous – very – stammers a little . . . but honest eyed; very blue eyed . . . she's clean and picks her feet up . . . Origo (her name is Iris) sat down on purpose I think by me, and oh dear was it for this I got so free and easy? – she has read my books, and was of course full of stumbling enthusiasm, so I made a rush, and talked about writing, spilling out ideas, of a kind. And we talked about biography and fiction . . . Then the door opened and in came Leo Myers, like a du Maurier drawing; such a perfect white waistcoat and his grizzled distinguished head. But he still looks like a sleepy viper . . . Well then we talked about novels . . . Fear. He is always afraid . . . In the street David [Cecil] said that LM is in love with Iris. That's why he had come. The sleepy viper in his white waistcoat.

Iris and Leo now partly set up house together, in a flat in Pall Mall and later in a rented house, called Hurn Farm, at Ringwood in Hampshire; Leo, who had inherited comfortable amounts of money from a rich homosexual cousin, was rich in his own right. They did their best to be discreet, and indeed remarkably few people ever knew about the affair, though Antonio, in Italy, said crossly to Flavia, 'What is she doing there, reading poetry with that man?' Iris's letters suggest a great fondness for Leo, but little or none of the craving and passion that characterised her love for Colin. She and Leo gave small dinner parties, the food delivered by Fortnum and Mason – Charlie and Aileen Meade, the Cecils, T. S. Eliot, the publisher Francis Meynell. Frances Partridge remembers an occasion when they all read and discussed Bertrand Russell. 'It was impossible not to be excited by Iris . . . She was technically on fire. You felt bored into. She went for people she took to.' One evening, Iris and Leo dined alone with the Woolfs. 'At first', recorded Virginia, 'I thought this too is going to be a wash out. But, chiefly owing to L's charm (Leonard), and making myself a little drunk, we all chattered . . . A genuine woman, I think, honest, intelligent, and, to my pleasure, well dressed; also, being a snob, I like her Bird of Paradise flight through the gay world. A long green feather in her hat suggests the image.'

Iris loved Hurn Farm, as she wrote to Irene: This seems a very quiet little haven, too good to be real. The house is quite full of hyacinths and freesias – which we planted in September, planning for now, and which at one time I thought I should certainly not see.' Whenever she went away, she was happy to get back to Hurn Farm, where swallows nested in the roof, moor hens swam in the pond, and the garden was full of flowers. Think of me as very, very happy at Hurn, and come here.'

During 1935 Leo was at work on a novel, *Strange Glory*, not part of his Indian series, which he referred to as 'my naive and sentimental tale'. Full of Jungian mysticism, like most of his books it is not easy to read today; it is, however, the most romantic, and he used to say there was something of Iris in Paulina, the rich young heroine torn between the world of society and that of 'enduring things', ever searching for 'integration and stability of purpose'.

Their relationship was, however, somewhat strange. Not only was Leo still married to Elsie, but he was extremely fond of her. At weekends he often went to see her, and if Iris was away, he would stay at the house at Wych Cross, in Sussex, where Elsie lived in some grandeur, with a butler, sixteen servants, a Rolls-Royce, and a wonderful walled garden in which she delighted. Leo was said to have no interest in the countryside. Each daughter had her own nanny. In the early days of their marriage they had entertained a great deal, especially such painters as David Jones, Frank Dobson and Ivor Hitchens. Leo's letters to Elsie are extremely affectionate – he always addresses her as 'my angel', assuring her that he loves her and he will never leave her – but at the same time full of ingenuous remarks about Iris and how sad he is that Elsie minds about his affair with her, while giving Elsie a running commentary on Iris's arrivals and departures. 'It makes me sad that you "can't feel gay" about Iris's coming,' he wrote one day. 'She does not come between you and me in any way; I am naturally rather a depressed person, and if I get from her some comfort and stimulus, surely you are glad of *that*? Indeed my feeling for her does not, and never has, changed my unalterable feeling for you. I am looking forward to seeing you, and feeling *rather* better, but I have been through a very low, devitalised time.' What can Elsie have thought? And what would have happened had Iris been free? It is difficult to understand what either woman can have seen in this apparently selfish and neurasthenic man.

Iris herself was eventually brought into this peculiar correspondence with Elsie. 'Iris of course was deeply touched', Leo wrote to Elsie, 'by your thought that you might write to her. She would value that sign from you beyond all measure. Especially as she has been and is suffering from a sense of *worthlessness*, if you know what I mean. A sense of being a person who inflicts *hurt* upon others – this naturally in connection with Antonio – for all that is being even worse than she imagined. It is an absolutely shattering time.'

Fond as they were of each other, this was hardly a relationship designed to last. With Iris constantly travelling between Italy and England and the United States, and Leo regularly visiting a wife he had no intention of leaving, it surprised no one when between them they made the decision to bring it to an end. Not long afterwards, Iris wrote to tell Irene she had had a 'wonderful' letter from Leo: 'And so I feel in some strange way *nothing* is lost (though some things are of course *left behind*) – and that what will be left to us in the future is something very lovely and quite secure and which will do no harm to anyone.' In a postscript she added, 'this would not be possible if we had not been through all that we have, and perhaps if Leo were younger' – (he was twenty-one years her senior). Later, Leo wrote Elsie one of his more self-obsessed and ostensibly loving letters: 'You above all else I have loved. My brief years of passion for Iris were a strange addition, and I would not belittle the feelings I had for her. But you have been the *centre* and the *core* of my life . . .'

Iris had not wasted the 1930s, though she was constantly on the move, returning to Italy a couple of times a year to see how her projects at La Foce were getting on and how her mother and Percy Lubbock were faring at Gli Scafari. Sybil had fallen out still further with Antonio, who maintained that she had been selfish and unhelpful over Gianni's death. (This was not entirely fair. There exists, among Iris's papers, a rather touching note from Sybil, written in pencil not long after Gianni's death, asking whether there was anything at all she could do to help: 'I wish – I pray – I may be like you if I am called on to bear what you are bearing'.) Gli Scafari, perched not far above the sea, with its wide loggia looking out across the water, its garden of terraces and umbrella pines, daffodils, anemones, grape hyacinths and tulips, was a delightful place. It was remote, and private, and anything large, like the piano, had to be brought by sea. After two years of work by Pinsent the house had been decorated entirely by the fashionable Sibyl Colefax, in lime yellows and pale greens, with a red lacquer chinoiserie cabinet in the drawing room. As ever, the flowers in the garden were not Pinsent's idea: Percy had asked for drifts of agapanthus and hundreds of different kinds of iris, ordered from Sicily. One visitor remarked somewhat unkindly that it looked 'as if it had escaped from Chelsea'. You could swim almost from the terrace, and on days when Sybil could not walk she was carried to the water's edge by two servants in a sedan-chair.

Sybil was still constantly unwell. At one point her weight dropped to 5 st 8 oz. Often, she could eat nothing but a little jelly. Iris would arrive from London to find one or other of them – and sometimes both – ill and in bed, Sybil declaring that she was about to die and Percy terrified that she might be right. Within a couple of hours, Sybil would be feeling much better, while Percy was a wreck. 'I wish I knew what to do,' he wrote to Iris. 'Life here, as it is now, is not worth living.' Iris was sympathetic but, however hard she tried, never greatly cared for Percy.

Iris wrote continually, wherever she was, with very little fuss, seldom saying anything to anyone – a skill that later proved useful when she started keeping a diary during the worst of the war. Trains, boats, doctors' waiting rooms, stations, anywhere and everywhere she tried out draughts or made notes. Her next idea, now that *Leopardi* and *Allegra* were out, was to tackle a book she provisionally titled 'Prelude to Living', explaining to Irene that it was 'to be about little girls and young women in all ages and centuries. Almost *too* large a subject – but fun to do. Have just been reading a most revolting diary of a little Austrian girl between the ages of eleven and twelve, during which she apparently never thought about anything but menstruation.' She enjoyed the research enormously – she was a natural and happy historical researcher – and, at the time she wrote to Irene, was deep in accounts of medieval nunneries. 'Prelude to Living' seems to have been finished – its chapters, typed, then corrected and re-corrected, are among Iris's papers at La Foce – but it has never been published, although there is nothing to say why: no publisher's letter, no friend's criticism, no note of her own.

The chapters of 'Prelude to Living', suggesting many hard months of research, having been put to one side, she turned to a biography. Cola di Rienzo, popularly known as Rienzi, was a

Roman innkeeper's son who on 15 August 1347, after leading a successful uprising, was crowned Tribune, hence the title she gave her book, *The Tribune of Rome*. His glory was short-lived: three months later, having dared, publicly, to compare his own accession to power to that of the Ascension of Christ, he was deposed and fled to the Abruzzi, then to Prague; his plan being to convince the Emperor Charles IV that he would be able to restore the unity of the Holy Roman Empire and the supremacy of Rome. Rienzi was arrested and handed over to the Pope at Avignon; pardoned and released by the next pope, he was encouraged to return to Rome, where he rose again to some power, only to be finally undone by his own grandiose and tyrannical behaviour. He was clearly a man for whom Iris felt a certain sympathy. *The Tribune of Rome* was published at the end of October 1938 by the Hogarth Press; they offered the same royalties as for *Allegra*, plus an advance this time of £25. On 13 November Iris wrote to thank Berenson for his help with the illustrations, and chose the occasion to thank him again for what he had done for her when she was a child. 'I think going back to those days when it was your advice that first persuaded my mother to give me a classical education – I admit that it is largely owing to you that I have ever come to write at all. It is a very real and large debt of gratitude that comes to you, dear BB, and I wish I could tell you better how much I feel it – and not least at the moment, when so much of what is valuable in the world is being destroyed.'

Though in America Harcourt Brace turned down *The Tribune of Rome*, and Leonard Woolf advised her that he had only been able to sell three hundred copies in the first month, the critics were, once again, admiring. The *New Statesman* called the story exciting and Iris's style of writing 'distinguished'. The *Sketch* called it a book for both scholars and the general reader: 'Marchesa

Origo wears her learning with lightness and grace. It is apparent not only in her analysis of Cola's baffling personality . . . but also in her brilliant visual reconstruction of the world in which Cola lived.' Sales remained small, but Iris was now attracting only favourable reviews, by people who would review her books faithfully one after the other as they came out. They not only gave her good and respectful reviews – in her whole writing career of some fifty years she scarcely got anything else – but they seemed to understand what she was trying to do. They admired her social history, her enthusiasm, her obvious truthfulness, and her humility, all the things she stressed as important in her essays on biography. At a time when literary biography enjoyed little of the popularity it has today, Iris was carving out a niche very much her own; and readers liked it.

A change was taking place in Iris during these years that she at first appeared little aware of. For so long so curiously uninterested in politics and so reluctant to consider what her position was on the questions of the moment, her thoughts more concentrated on La Foce and her affair with Colin, then on Gianni's death, she now found politics becoming increasingly hard to avoid. With the Italian invasion of Abyssinia in 1935, Mussolini's role in Europe was no longer something that could simply be ignored. Characteristically, once her interest was drawn to it, once she knew that, whatever her differences with Antonio, she personally could no longer duck her responsibilities, she turned her attention energetically to the subject.

She found extremely odd, as she explained almost apologetically in her unpublished diary of 1939, the degree to which she had isolated herself from what was going on in Italy. She had noticed, and instinctively taken against, the truculent manners and boastful speech, the cult of violence, rhetoric and personality encouraged by the Fascists and Mussolini, who was rapidly becoming an idol, his photograph everywhere. With no real political convictions of her own, beyond the sense of responsibility and duty and the conservatism instilled in her by her grandparents, and feeling herself ever a foreigner in Italy, she had taken refuge, she wrote in her diary, in 'the blank vagueness' of a young woman not interested in public affairs. She had, for instance, taken very little heed when the Fascists suppressed all newspapers critical of the regime and began to banish opponents to the *confine*: in all, 10,000 Italians spent at least some time on remote islands or in villages in the high mountains. What really began to bring about a change in her was the fact that some of her friends had sufficiently strong pro-Communist feelings to send them to Spain after 1936 to fight Franco, while in London Max Plowman the well-known pacifist was preaching to huge crowds. Iris was not herself convinced by his arguments, but nonetheless began at last to think through the implications of the various forces at odds with one another throughout Europe. What made it all slightly easier was that Antonio, though a passionate monarchist, was far from admiring when it came to talking about the ruling Fascists. One of the most difficult questions that faced her now, one she had instinctively shied away from hitherto, was that of her real nationality: English and American parents, an Italian husband: was she Italian, or Anglo-Saxon?

In October 1935 the League of Nations reacted to Mussolini's attack on Abyssinia by imposing sanctions against Italy. To raise funds, the Fascists appealed to the patriotism of Italian women, suggesting that they sacrifice their gold wedding rings, replacing them with steel. Ceremonies were held at all the war memorials throughout Italy, at which women threw their wedding rings into cauldrons.

On 10 December the Queen herself led a special ceremony, during which she threw her own ring into the bucket. On a single day in Rome, a quarter of a million Italian women gave up their wedding rings. Not long after this, Iris went to tea with the Woolfs. 'Origo rather contorted', noted Virginia in her diary: 'says Italy is blind red devoted patriotic: has thrown her wedding ring into the cauldron too.' Would Iris have done so a few years earlier? On the face of it, it was a strange and unexpected thing for her to do. She had come increasingly to love England and all the friends there with whom she shared her ideas: having discovered this life, how was she able to abandon it? That she did so gives some idea, perhaps, of the strength of her commitment – to her father's views on nationalism? to La Foce? To Gianni's memory? – that she now decided to return to Italy – and to Antonio, as she later told her daughter, Benedetta. But Benedetta speculates that though duty was important, as well as Iris's inescapable sense of responsibility for the estate she had helped to create, there was more to it than simple commitment. Iris needed Antonio in some profound way, and their very differences were perhaps one of the main causes for the fascination each felt for the other. Antonio very seldom discussed his feelings about integrity and loyalty, but Iris knew them to be an essential part of his nature. They gave her a sense of security in a very uncertain world. Antonio was never an easy man, prone as he grew older to sudden rages, but she remained sensitive all her life to his good looks and the enthusiasm that had captivated many young women in Florentine society.

CHAPTER NINE

Only man is mad

All through the 1930s, while Iris was coming and going between Italy and England and the United States, Fascist rule and Fascist customs were spreading to every corner of Italian life. In order to force a country and a people still very half-hearted about their masters to live up to Fascist ideals of duty and discipline – most of which ran counter to the Italian temperament – the Fascist leadership imposed what they considered to be models of efficiency, productivity and decisiveness. Other European countries were held to suffer from extreme decadence; Italy, under the rule of Mussolini's 'collective significance' of life, was to be a very different place. (Filippo Tommaso Marinetti, a close supporter of Mussolini, took a different view: he blamed what he saw as his compatriots' lethargy on too much spaghetti. 'By eating it,' he wrote, 'they develop that typical ironical and sentimental scepticism which all too often dampens their enthusiasm.' The British, by contrast, did well on their cod and roast beef, and the Germans flourished on a diet of sauerkraut, smoked lard and sausages.)

Towards the end of the 1930s the Fascist Party numbered just over two million members. The Party secretary, Achille Starace – his name was later used to refer to the period, '*era* Starace' – was given the task of reshaping Italians into Mussolini's mould. People were forbidden to shake hands and instructed to use the cleaner, more ceremonious Roman salute instead. They were told to gesticulate less. Mussolini – and Starace opposed him in this – decided that the traditionally polite form of address using the second person plural *lei* was to be abandoned, and the more familiar *voi* used in conversation. Women's clothes were no longer to be 'straight and angular' but to have 'womanly curves'. The '*stile fascista*' dictated that Italian national sports teams were to wear only black. Good Fascists were to walk as much as possible, and avoid fashionable restaurants. What became known as the *passo romano* was modelled on the German goose-step. In the hideous new marble Forum erected by Mussolini in Rome, elderly party leaders who had been ordered to take exercise could be seen from time to time, scrambling up its slippery walls. Mussolini had no interest in art, once boasting that he had never set foot in a gallery before he accompanied Hitler to the Pitti Palace and the Uffizi during the Führer's visit to Florence. He told Count Galeazzo Ciano, his son-in-law and Foreign Minister, that he would have liked museums to have fewer pictures and statues and more enemy flags captured in battle. Italians, he added, were not to be influenced by the writings of such men as Robert Graves, Axel Munthe and Machiavelli, who were 'unsuitable to the Fascist spirit'.

The Fascists loved their uniforms. Part of the pride of being a high-ranking Party member or serving in the army lay in the superb outfits they were allowed to wear. The Commander of the Fascist Militia, for example, wore a black Fascist fez with a silk fringe along one side, a gold belt with a silver dagger strapped round his waist, and boots with spurs; in foul weather, a grey-green cape fell becomingly to his heels. Fascist women, like dully-plumaged female birds, wore a plain dark uniform with a wide-brimmed hat.

In order that Rome should 'appear wonderful to the whole world, immense, orderly and powerful, as she was in the days of the first Empire of Augustus', extensive archaeological works were started, to clear the ruins of everything 'that has grown up round them during the centuries of decadence'.

And, in the early days at least, many Italians loved Mussolini. They loved his speeches and his determination, and they willingly hung his photograph on their sitting room walls, and talked of him as an idol.

Some of the new measures, of course, were so absurd as to seem quite unthreatening. But they were all part of a system that was becoming day by day more repressive. People began to find the steadily increasing interference in their daily lives irksome, while discovering that Mussolini's promises of a better, more prosperous life were hollow: the government had singularly failed to deliver improvements, though skilful Fascist propaganda convinced many that it had. The conditions of agricultural workers in particular were especially miserable: their working hours had been lengthened and their right to insurance denied. The good things Mussolini had so loudly proclaimed to be the right of the landless, the poor, and the returning soldiers of the Great War had gone instead to the agricultural Consorzi and large private landowners. Year by year, the number of farm workers had declined and many marginal owners had lost their land altogether. Much had been made by Mussolini of the reclamation of the Pontine Marshes, and they had indeed been drained and were now under cultivation, but at the expense of investment in other areas. In his determination that Italy should achieve self-sufficiency through a planned economy by the end of the 1930s, Mussolini had embarked on vast schemes, not only on the mainland but in Sicily, Sardinia, Abyssinia and the Italian colonies in Africa. Between 1922 and 1942 the Ministry of Public Works spent 33 million lire on these ventures.

In addition, the 'complete Fascistization' of Italy saw the suppression one by one of the free newspapers: both the *Corriere della Sera* and *La Stampa* were put into Fascist hands. There were to be no more free elections, for the Grand Council of Fascism, with Mussolini as its President, watched over every aspect of Italian life. There were new laws about freemasons. There was much chanting of 'Giovinezza' and Fascist slogans.

What Mussolini had promised in the Chamber early in 1925, a speech often regarded as a milestone for Fascism, he had more or less carried out. 'Italy wants peace and quiet,' he had declared, 'work and calm. I will give these things with love if possible and with force if necessary.'

Since the Great War Italy had enjoyed no military victory, and Mussolini saw a victorious colonial war as a way of making the Italians forget the growing economic depression at home. Abyssinia, the last remaining uncolonised nation in Africa, seemed to offer the best prospects, despite the twenty-year treaty of friendship he had signed with its ruler, the Negus, in 1928. To send an army to war in Africa, however, needed some kind of European endorsement: this he did not quite secure, but Europe and the League of Nations initially showed little zest for blocking his ambitions, and on 5 October 1935 Italy invaded Abyssinia. This blatant aggression prompted the League of Nations to impose sanctions, and the Hoare-Laval proposals to cede him the most fertile part of the country provoked widespread public condemnation in Britain and France – but not the will to oppose him with force. On 9 May 1936, Abyssinia was formally annexed by Italy. It had taken Mussolini's army six months to reach Addis Ababa, by which time it was widely known that they had resorted to using poison gas, despite Italy's ratification of the 1925 Convention prohibiting it, and the fact that it caused horrific injuries. Photographs of grotesquely burnt and misshapen Abyssinian soldiers – and civilians – were soon circulating.

His annexation of Abyssinia caused Mussolini, who throughout had argued, and had managed to convince many Italians, that it was a defensive war fought against an attacking army, a number of immediate difficulties. It isolated Italy, broke the Anglo-Italian Entente and later brought about the alliance with Hitler, 'an axis around which', explained Mussolini, 'may revolve all those European states with a will to collaboration and peace'. It also fatally wounded the League of Nations. Inside Italy, however, it shored up, if only briefly, the myth that the country possessed an unbeatable military force.

All this time Mussolini had been turning against the bourgeoisie, whom he attacked as pacifist, pro-League, and pro-England. More and more he began to talk about strengthening the race, declaring with bravado that not nearly enough Abyssinians had been killed in the war.

The question of race took some time to catch on in Italy. Throughout the early 1930s, Mussolini himself had been contemptuous of 'anti-Semitism' as a German vice. The idea of a 'master race' was, he declared, 'arrant nonsense, stupid and idiotic', as he told Emil Ludwig, the German writer to whom he granted a number of interviews. At that time there were said to be some 30,000 to 50,000 Jews in Italy, their numbers swelling as many left Germany. Judaism was widely perceived as essentially religious rather than racial, and most Italian Jews had felt themselves very much a part of the struggle for Italian unity. As Dan Segre wrote in *Memoirs of a Fortunate Jew*: 'From the days of the Risorgimento many Jews felt like Pilgrim Fathers . . . In a way, they could feel more Italian than the Italian, particularly as Italy itself is a country of provinces, dialects and regions, one enormously different from the other.' It was generally understood that it was right to oppose the persecution of the Jews, not because they were Jews, but because those who persecuted them were Germans.

In July 1938, this casual, tolerant attitude changed, at least officially. Mussolini published a Race Manifesto, designed to test the reactions of Italians to a possible campaign against their Jewish neighbours, though it seems he had no intention of going as far as the Nuremberg Race laws of 1935 which had deprived German Jews of their citizenship and persecuted them because of their so-called 'racial identity'. Discrimination against Jews was, he believed, a cheap way of pleasing Hitler, but anti-Semitism never became an integral part of Italian Fascist doctrine. Persecution began quietly: Jews were ordered to stop sending their children to state schools; Italians were forbidden to use textbooks written by Jews; Jews were banned from marrying non-Jews; a hundred Jewish professors in the universities lost their jobs. 'I lived', wrote Segre, 'in the belly of the monster.' In theory, Jewish members of the Fascist party, and those who served in the army, were partially exempt. Fey Pirzio-Biroli, daughter of Ulrich von Hassell, who was the German ambassador to Rome from 1932, insists it is essential to remember that in those early days, when it came to anti-Semitism, Mussolini and Hitler could not be compared. 'Mussolini', she says, 'was an Italian – and you cannot compare sending people to the *confine* . . . to [sending them to] concentration camps.' Though later in the war Italian Jews were arrested and sent to German camps, where many died, at no time was their persecution as virulent or as meticulously planned as in Germany.

What little opposition there was to Mussolini had largely been suppressed by the end of the 1930s. The murder of Giacomo Matteotti in 1924 had briefly stirred reaction against Fascism, but had also demonstrated how very weak that opposition was. In 1926 a special police force was set up to prosecute anti-Fascists; cases were held *in camera*, without appeal. Opponents such as writers foolish enough to try to tell people what was really happening were for the most part sent to the *confine*, though if they were particularly irksome they might be beaten up first, or forced to drink castor oil. Others, after brutal experiences at the hands of the police, fled abroad. The anti-Fascist intelligentsia, small as it was, lay scattered around Italy, in Switzerland, France and the United States, and it was possible to travel from one to another, from Croce in Turin to the Venturi in Padua, the Papafavas in Rome, to the circles in Paris. In Italy a broad anti-Fascist coalition was founded, spanning the political spectrum from Togliatti and the Communists to Salvemini and the Liberal socialists, and while it did not last it served to throw up a number of brave figures on the right as well as the left, all equally intent on defeating Fascism. Among them was the young poet and playwright Lauro de Bosis, who believed clandestine propaganda was the way to awaken public opinion in Italy and cause an uprising against Mussolini. Founder of the Alleanza Nazionale, a grouping of the right, he held that anti-Fascist action should not be left to the Communists alone. In the summer of 1931 de Bosis staged a stunt in which he flew over Rome dropping 400,000 leaflets which called on Italian mothers not to let their children be enrolled in the Balilla 'in order to be turned into cannon fodder'. Having completed its drop, de Bosis's plane veered westwards, and was never seen again. It simply disappeared: possibly, said other pilots, because he had run out of fuel, or because he was still an inexperienced pilot.

Then there was Gaetano Salvemini, the socialist historian and friend of Berenson, who had lost his family in the Palermo earthquake. After Matteotti's murder Salvemini became the leader of anti-Fascist opposition in Florence, advising his friends to break off all contact with those they knew to be Fascists. A close friend of Umberto Morra, Salvemini was imprisoned in the 1920s and then given 'provisional liberty', during which he escaped to France. Eventually he made his way to the United States, where he was torn between his métier as an historian and the need he felt to maintain anti-Fascist action even from his exile. Before leaving Paris Salvemini had co-founded *Giustizia e Libertà* (Justice and Liberty), not so much a party as a grouping of people intent on overthrowing Mussolini and Fascism. During her many trips to America in the 1930s Iris invariably went to see Salvemini, who in 1934 was appointed Lauro de Bosis lecturer in the History of Italian Civilisation at Harvard. An affectionate man, somewhat corpulent, he would sink back into his chair and ask: 'And my friends? Tell me about my friends.'

Most tragic, perhaps, was the story of the journalist Carlo Rosselli. One of the most remarkable and outspoken of all the opponents of Fascism, Rosselli, who had founded the clandestine paper *Non-Mollare* (Don't Weaken) in Italy in the 1920s, had been arrested and imprisoned on Lipari, then escaped to Paris where he edited the best of the anti-Fascist papers, *Justice and Liberty*. Later he fought against Franco in

Spain. When he returned to Paris he was murdered, together with his brother Nello, by Mussolini's men.

Throughout the 1930s Antonio had been meaning to go to Tripolitania and Cyrenaica – Libya – to see what Italian settlers had made of the land confiscated from the Beduin and given them by Mussolini. In April 1939 he and Iris sailed from Syracuse for Tripoli on the *Città di Ban*, a small, ungainly ship smelling nauseatingly of rubber, her stern decks full of young men returning from leave in Italy. At dinner the Captain railed against the American President's recent appeal to Hitler and Mussolini for peace, and his meddling in Europe's affairs, which he put down to Roosevelt being Jewish; when Iris protested quietly that he was not, no one took any notice.

Tripoli was gleaming, with palm-shaded avenues and glistening white minarets. As they drove out of the city they passed magnificent vineyards and olive groves sheltered by hedges of tamarisk. In Leptis Magna they found the entire European population of nine crouched over a radio in the hotel, listening to another violent attack on Roosevelt, declared by the speaker to be 'one of the most crafty and dangerous politicians that has ever appeared in that fox's den of politicians, America'. President Woodrow Wilson, the speaker went on, champion of the League of Nations of which Italy had fallen foul over her seizure of Abyssinia, was in comparison merely 'a mad visionary whose Utopia never touched reality'.

The further they drove from Tripoli, the less prosperity they found. The settlements nearest the coast had wheat, olives, and rudimentary gardens with a few geraniums planted around the houses. But as they went on, they came to the most recent settlements, shabby and desolate, white houses losing the battle against the sand; inside, extreme poverty, little to eat, and very few possessions. One woman with thirteen children told Iris how wonderful everything seemed when they landed: they had been shown the fertile plains around Tripoli, and allowed to believe that their own land would be like this. It was only when they reached the new settlement that they realised that their lives were likely to be even worse than they had been in Italy.

Yet Iris was impressed. 'I am not defending the methods by which it was acquired,' she wrote of the settlement policy. 'But the Arabs have kept their full rights, the Italians are creating farms where previously there had only been sand and scrub.' As an experiment in land reclamation it had parallels with what they had been trying todo at La Foce. Most of all, however, she was cheered to find a great deal of spirit in the settlers they spoke to, 'not combative, but of courage, self sacrifice and endurance, directed towards a *constructive*, peaceful end'. One sometimes wonders whether her own courage and powers of endurance did not blind her to the vulnerabilities of others, and indeed she herself, re-reading her diary of the Libyan trip many years later, felt a profound sense of unease. What, she wondered, had become of all the settlers? Through one of Italy's social services organisations, she discovered the truth: after Gaddafi came to power at the end of the 1960s the settlers were evicted from Libya. The Italians took them back and homes were found for a number in the Agro Pontino, which none had ever visited before and with which they had no connection. Many were miserably lonely. Very few found work.

The Italian people were still absolutely unprepared for war, so news of the Italian invasion of Albania on 7 April 1939 came 'to the public here as a bombshell', wrote Iris in her diary. A radio bulletin described it as a measure 'necessary to safeguard the peace'. On 11 April she noted how struck she had been by the lack of objection among her friends to the fact that the attack had taken place on Good Friday; but the 'disinclination' for war, she added, was growing all the time. Protest swelled all over Italy as the first men were called up, but as some were sent home again 'the general public', she noted, 'has decided that there won't be a war after all'. Should one now come, she went on, public opinion had been shaped so cleverly that most Italians were prepared to believe they had been forced into it in self-defence.

While Antonio, due to be called up as a retired officer, was busy preparing himself, Iris tried to get a new kindergarten running, to free women to help in the fields. The anti-English feeling can hardly be overstated – its bitterness,' she wrote to Irene, 'except of course here in the country, where the peasant preserves his usual indifference.' Mussolini meanwhile had astutely brought in new legislation concerning the agricultural development of Sicily. In her diary Iris was among those to greet this as a sign of the 'Duce's wish for peace', welcoming any move tending to develop more of Italy's own resources: 'whatever his motive, and however imperfect, the execution is a good one,' and, she added, 'there is no going back . . . steps which provide development or *human* awareness are irrevocable; no adult can become a *child* again'.

Mussolini's relationship with the aristocratic families of Italy had throughout his years in power been somewhat like Sulla's, who, railing on the Roman aristocracy to save him, promised to protect them. He offered them important jobs in the Fascist administration, or in banks, and they took them. The Duce felt that the aristocratic backing this symbolised added to the power and dignity of the nation; and many continued to support him more or less unreservedly. Those who did not do so he tended to leave alone, providing they kept absolutely quiet about their views. It is important to remember that Italy in 1939 was a country still deeply divided between rich and poor in which little had changed since before the First World War; and such changes as the Fascists had initiated had been extremely helpful to more enlightened aristocratic landlords like Antonio. To make the most of them he, like others, had had to deal with prominent Fascists in the government, and on several occasions with Mussolini himself; he was seen by them as a useful figure, known to have contacts abroad. These cross-currents muddied the waters and helped to create an impression that Antonio was an active member of the Fascist party, and a dedicated supporter.

The years before Italy entered the war were ones on which Iris later looked back with distress and distaste. 'Even the most confirmed sleep-walker then', she wrote, 'could hardly fail to wake up.'

At La Foce, listening to the radio, Iris found it increasingly hard to reconcile propaganda and truth. 'Those harsh words', she wrote, 'became for me the true echo of our times'. In theory the air waves were jammed, to exclude all but Nazi or Fascist stations, and war bulletins were supposed to be listened to standing up; but in practice other stations, including the BBC, could be received, though often in confused and overlapping waves. 'This cacophony', Iris noted in her diary, 'represents my personal nightmare of the war years, and of those that preceded them.'

Even now, most Italians still believed that there would be no general war in Europe. As Iris made short trips around the country, everywhere she went people were discussing what might happen. In Assisi she heard Hitler and Mussolini described as 'those two murderers'; in Bologna she found widespread and violent disagreement, and much anti-German feeling. New recruits were being called up, and at every little station the platforms were crowded with bewildered country boys, their possessions tied up in bundles or carried in little fibre-board suitcases. By the middle of August half a million men had received their papers, and still it was believed that the Duce would stop the war at the last moment. 'Compare their calm', a young officer said to Iris, 'with the feverish tension in France and England!' 'But it isn't exactly calm,' she wrote in her diary. 'It's a mixture of passive fatalism, and a genuine faith in their leader – the fruits of fifteen years of being taught not to think. It is certainly not a readiness for war, but merely a blind belief that "somehow" it won't happen.'

One day Iris took the train to Rome from Chianciano. On board were a thousand *squadristi*, the 'fascists of the first hour', on their way to the capital to celebrate the twentieth anniversary of the Fascia. She saw them later, looking like any other group of young men on an outing, sitting in the cafés, strolling along the Corso or throwing lira pieces into the Trevi Fountain for luck; except, of course, for their black shirts. She reflected how impossible it was not to like them, not to feel that Fascism had been, in its very beginnings at least, a genuine revolutionary movement of the people; and how vulnerable such people were to incitement to hatred of countries portrayed by their rulers as 'obese, capitalistic and decadent', which was how Mussolini had taken to describing the British.

In Rome she discovered society life going on virtually unchanged. Count Galeazzo Ciano, who in 1930 had married Edda, Mussolini's eldest daughter, and was now Foreign Minister, continued to accept invitations to diplomatic receptions and to reassure his fellow aristocratic families as to the impossibility of war. Ciano was the acceptable Fascist, friend to many of Italy's older titled families. He was vain, self-indulgent and pretentious, and spent much of his time not in the office but on the golf course, but his good looks and charm endeared him to many of the foreign residents. The German Ambassador von Hassell, however, complained that he was trivial, and pinched the bottom of every pretty woman: 'My father', Fey Pirzio-Biroli remembers, 'called him a badly behaved superficial boy.' Everywhere she went in Rome, Iris was struck by the gaiety and prosperity of the city.

In Florence, where she went several times, she found the Maggio Musicale, Florence's music festival, crowded, but there were not many foreigners around. The Florentines were still eating their caviar, *foie-gras* and chocolate at Doneys, drifting to the café at about midday, and their doughnuts at the Casa dei Bombonini (famous for its method of sending the cooked doughnuts down a herring-bone chute to remove excess oil before dunking them in a pan of sugar on the floor). Though the walls of many of the streets were plastered with anti-British posters, no one took them seriously, except perhaps Signor Carlo, who now prudently changed the name of his shop on the Via Tornabuoni from 'Old England' to 'Giovane Italia'. As in Rome, there was no trace, and little talk, of war.

Because of its distinguished history – it was the oldest such organisation in Europe – and its political leanings, the British Institute had continued to enjoy semi-official recognition, even in the heyday of Fascist nationalism, and its lectures continued throughout the autumn of 1939. Harold Goad, openly pro-Fascist, had been replaced by a man not much less sympathetic to Mussolini, Francis Troye, who was given to understand that the acceptance of Jews as members would not be taken well. It was round the British Institute and its large and famous library, started by Lina Waterfield in the First World War, that milled what Troye called 'stranded paupers', mainly women getting on in years, who had almost no money of their own and nowhere to go in the event of war, and were dependent on the British Relief Fund. The Florence they had so enjoyed in the past, with its cheap flats and food and nice friends with whom to walk along the Via Tornabuoni in the afternoons, was rapidly vanishing as all the expatriates who could caught a train for London. These elderly Englishwomen who had regarded Florence as their home for so many years felt confused and upset by the anti-British campaign, and by the hostility which seemed to render all but their best friends 'poisonously polite'. Even Iris's old friend Nesta de Robeck had decided to leave for England. Before she did so, she gave Iris the names and addresses of some of the very oldest ladies, too frail now to move, in case of their later desperate need. Up at the Ombrellino, George and Alice Keppel had now become the leaders of what was left of the once flourishing foreign community.

The German consul, Dr Gerhardt Wolff, whose sympathies towards the British were much what Troye's were towards the Fascists, had become a friend of Iris in the 1930s. He was a remarkable man. Decorated with an Iron Cross in the Great War, he then joined the Foreign Office, and continued despite warnings to give useful tips of forthcoming Gestapo arrests when appointed to Paris in 1937. Wolff soon became disheartened by the mood in Germany. Though obliged to become a Nazi Party member in 1939, he declared that he would follow Plato's advice that 'it is natural that a man should seek to escape from evil and tragic circumstances, and to survive them'. He managed to get himself posted as Consul to Florence, with his wife and small daughter, to the four white-washed rooms between the German

Evangelical Mission and the Lutheran pastorate that served as the Consul's offices. He removed the Führer's portrait from its position of prominence and hung a lithograph of Goethe in its place. Gerhardt Wolff was to play a significant part in Iris's war.

By the late 1930s, the Bracci family at Montepulciano were very good friends of both Iris and Antonio. Margherita and her twelve brothers and sisters belonged to the Papafava, an old Veneto family of long-standing Liberal traditions: her grandfather and father had both taken part in the Risorgimento. Among those to be found at Montepulciano in the 1920s and 1930s there ran a strong current of anti-Fascism, directed not so much towards positive action as to keeping alive the spirit of democracy. Salvemini was a visitor before he went into exile, as were the Rosselli brothers. For them, as for other writers and journalists of the opposition, it was somewhere safe and pleasant, where they could meet and talk. When not at Montepulciano the Braccis were in Rome, where they lived in a flat in the same palazzo as Umberto Morra and on Wednesday and Thursday afternoons received visitors. These might include Morra himself, never a public figure, but a man much loved by his friends and, because he was seen to be particularly honest, much consulted by those on the left who hoped to steer Italy in a different direction. He had a house, called Metelliano, near Cortona, where the anti-Fascists met, and later hid. Early in 1939, Morra held a meeting there which brought together various members of the Movimento Liberalsocialista from all over Italy with a view to planning how to keep alive some kind of underground opposition to the Fascists.

Present at the Braccis' might also be Giuliana Benzoni, an exceptional and brave woman belonging to an aristocratic Milanese family, who in the Great War had smuggled documents to a young Czech patriot, Milau Stefanik, whose plane crashed twenty days before they were due to marry. Giuliana believed that the best way to continue Stefanik's work was to fight Fascism. Her equally remarkable mother had a home in Sorrento which became a safe house for many anti-Fascists; Berenson later described it, using Turgenev's phrase, as a 'house of *galantuomini*.' (She was also a wise woman; to Giuliana's protests against 'coming out' in formal Italian society, she replied: 'You will attend dances. I know that you won't like them, but you must convince the world that you are neither a martyr, nor a heroine, nor even a saint, but that you have chosen the life that you prefer.') In the mid 1930s Giuliana was responsible for drawing Principessa Maria Jose, wife of Crown Prince Umberto and President of the Italian Red Cross, into the group of anti-Fascist intelligentsia; the Princess was later despatched to a remote part of Piedmont for intriguing on their behalf. A fighter by nature, Giuliana, like Iris, had her doubts about the strength and resolution of some of the anti-Fascists: 'Have we the strength to *act* or are we merely intellectuals,' she wrote, 'impotent in the face of action, but cerebrally obsessed by the thought of it? This is the first doubt which tortures me . . .'

Between 1918 and 1924 Lucangelo Bracci, Margherita's husband, had been responsible for an outspoken broadsheet against Fascism; it was seized several times, and the day came when he had no alternatives but to lie low or face arrest, not least because the Fascists had effectively closed all political and journalistic doors to him. In Montepulciano he opened a carpentry works, giving employment to a number of people, and did nothing further to attract the attention of the *squadristi*.

It was the Braccis and their friends who taught Iris what was really going on in Italy, and among them that she first felt a sense of shame at having known so little. Increasingly, whether in Rome or at Montepulciano, she found their house the one place where she could speak out. Yet she remained unsure how much these informed and conscientious people counted in the world of real politics: at Montepulciano, in particular, the form their anti-Fascism took was discreet and prudent; for the most part, they seemed simply to despair of the present and to believe in the ultimate triumph of reason. Denied an outlet in the newspapers or in politics, constantly in danger from spies, they lived, Iris felt, 'in a closed, semi-conspiratorial circle', meeting only others who shared their hopes, 'often embittered and factious', she wrote in her diary, 'sometimes not entirely free from persecution mania, but firmly clinging to their principles and determined to come to no compromise with any aspect of the regime they hated and despised'. She would come away from a day in their company feeling, like Giuliana, that for all their passion and conviction it was not among them that a constructive anti-Fascist front would arise to challenge Mussolini: 'These are enlightened, high-principled, courageous people, but they are not, as yet, of any importance.' Later, looking back on the long discussions, Iris felt she had been wrong after all, for the Braccis and their friends were a token that all over Italy there were still men and women 'whom . . . Fascism had not numbed into conformity'. With their clandestine anti-Fascist press and their contacts abroad, they had fostered the spirit that eventually paved the way for the fall of Fascism.

Throughout that August of 1939 Italians went on thinking that war would not come. But on the 29th, Iris noted, the atmosphere began to change. Restrictions on petrol and food, no more tea or coffee, made an impression where the radio and the newspapers had entirely failed to do so. Arriving back at

La Foce on a still late-summer's day with the grapes ripening and the oxen ploughing, Iris wrote: 'Only man is mad.' Many of the peasant farmers had been called up, and seemed more angry than upset, with no realisation that this threatened war promised to be far worse than anything seen in Abyssinia or Spain. 'Ora basta,' the men on the farm said to her, 'we've had enough of this. We want to be left alone.' At the Braccis' there was little but sadness and anxiety, as her friends foresaw the fulfilment of their gloomiest prophecies.

Iris had time for one more meeting with English friends. Somewhat to everyone's surprise, Colin MacKenzie had married Pin Meade, still barely in her twenties. They were on their way to America for their honeymoon, and when their ship stopped at Genoa Iris went to meet them. Later she recorded her great pleasure at finding Pin 'her real, gay, loving self'. Pin MacKenzie remembers the occasion rather differently. Iris arrived in their stateroom looking extremely elegant in a leopard-skin coat; 'She then started talking to Colin – and I suddenly saw, by the way they talked and the things they remembered, what I had never seen before: that they had once been lovers.' For a long time, the knowledge made her very unhappy.

But since Colin there had been Leo Myers, and now Iris was back at La Foce with Antonio. In the summer of 1939 she wrote three letters to Irene which at last explained her apparently sudden decision to return to her Italian life. 'I wonder whether perhaps, you guessed', she wrote in the first, 'that my leaving England last time was not quite like other times – that it was the beginning of a longer, more complete separation. We had both known for a long time (though *fighting against* the knowledge) that things could not go on quite as they were and as I still could not bring myself to a complete break with Antonio . . . we at last reached the decision. I want you to know that it was reached *together* – that was the only thing that made it bearable. And perhaps the pain will not be *quite* so bad, and we shall meet as friends again . . . I did not know until I got back here what A. would feel. We are trying to begin again – and to do better. And the dark daily cloud of guilt and remorse – that has lifted.'

Two weeks later, she wrote again: '. . . it wasn't because of any change between L. and me that this decision was taken. Indeed I do not think that we ever had a time of such complete harmony and happiness as in these last months . . . Something had reached its maturity – and so is indestructible for us, for ever.' Once again she had tried to leave Antonio and La Foce, and once again she had failed. She did not try to do so again. These letters to Irene say much about the love she had felt for Leo Myers which does not really come across in her earlier letters, but also much about the strength of her attachment to Antonio. 'I have done *wrong*, very *wrong*, for years,' she wrote in her third letter to Irene. 'But now I can't go back. Nor, it sometimes seems, forward. Perhaps there are times when one must just *hold* on, and wait, and try and stick anyway to the truth.'

At the end of August 1939 Iris and Antonio were in Lucerne, to hear a series of concerts conducted by Bruno Walter and Toscanini, who had been exiled from Italy for refusing to play 'Giovinezza' at La Scala. The concert hall and the hotels were full of foreigners, and the Italians in particular could be heard loudly discussing cheap restaurants, for it was considered unpatriotic to take much money abroad. Some worried lest the numbers of their car plates were being taken down by the secret police. In the interval people discussed a tragedy that had cast its shadow over the concert season: Walter's daughter, married to a young Bavarian Nazi, had been shot dead by her husband, who had then shot himself. She had refused to accompany him back from Switzerland to Germany, on the grounds that her sister was in a concentration camp. 'The family, for a woman, must come first', Iris heard one woman say. 'But the Jews have no principles.' Toscanini took Walter's place. The last performance he conducted was the *Götterdämmerung*.

In the hotel that night the Origos heard on the radio that the USSR had ratified the Non-Aggression Pact between Germany and Russia; next morning, the foreigners began to hurry home. Iris phoned England, for what she feared might be the last time. At the Italian-Swiss frontier they watched as a car with Italian number plates was turned back into Italy. After the Origos had gone through, Iris wrote in her autobiography, 'The pole of the barrier swung slowly back behind us. I realised that I had made my choice'. It must have been a strange moment for her, turning her back on England and a world she had come to love and believe was hers, to go back to what in the last analysis remained for her a foreign country, and to a husband from whom she had been separated for much of the last five years. Nor can it have been made any easier by the anti-English slogans that had been painted on many walls. She was not to leave Italy for six years.

Early in the morning of 1 September, Germany invaded Poland in the wake of a fabricated border incident which Germany characterised as a 'fresh act of provocation'; the Italian papers were quick to adopt a pro-German tone, referring to Poland's 'mad gesture'. The Führer, they declared, had by his 'reasonable and logical proposals' – that Poland should cede Danzig to Germany – done all he could to save the peace of Europe. 'Italy', noted Iris in her diary, 'is given Germany's thanks for her "comprehension", but no word is said about her as an ally. Germany, Hitler says, will settle her own problems alone . . . Total silence from Rome.' The question now on everyone's mind was whether or not Italy would remain neutral. After trying all day to get a French or English wireless station, for more accurate news, Iris heard the full report of Chamberlain's speech on the BBC. Almost all her days, whether she was at La Foce or with the Braccis, were now spent listening to the radio, trying to find a French station, or the BBC, for more accurate news, following the final steps.

Then came Chamberlain's speech. 'September 3rd', reads her diary: 'We know, and it is war.'

Two days later Mussolini issued a statement in which he presented himself as the 'single just man' who made a last attempt 'to save the peace of Europe'. Antonio, called up as an officer in the reserve, set out to join his regiment, which had been in Albania and was to be re-formed in Florence.

CHAPTER TEN

Thunder in the air

For Iris, daily life was now filled with rumours, uncertainty, and anxiety. All through the autumn of 1939 and the spring of 1940 she recorded in her diary the growing Italian mistrust of the British, fanned by a shrewd Italian exercise in propaganda. It affected her personally very little – her Italian was excellent, she was often taken for an American, and she spent most of her time at La Foce – but she worried about the stranded elderly ladies in Florence, who found the hatred of the British and the many posters enumerating their crimes extremely painful. In her unpublished diary Iris carefully recorded the day-to-day political balance, the information she culled from the radio and the newspapers, and the attitude of ordinary Italians to the possibility of war. It is like a piece of good journalism, clear, thoughtful and evocative: few people have drawn a clearer picture of Italy's slow steps towards war. But it is curiously dispassionate, with none of the warmth of the earlier ones, or of the later diary which became so famous when it was published as *War in Val d'Orcia*. Perhaps the best explanation, not only of the tone of this diary but also of her decision not to publish it, is to be found in something Iris herself wrote: 'Just as I do not believe that one is likely to write a good biography unless one feels some sympathy with one's subject, so I doubt whether much is to be gained by dwelling on those periods of one's life of which the dominant flavour is distaste. Periods of grief, hardship or danger may be fruitful, but not a reluctant acceptance of what one cannot change.'

On 9 September 1939 Iris recorded a note of 'complacent calm' in the tone of the *Corriere della Sera:* 'Since the bulletin of the Council of Ministers has expressed in unequivocal terms Italy's decision to take no military initiative, the life of the nation has returned to its normal rhythm.' Neutrality, then, at least for the moment, even though the Pact of Steel, signed in May, obliged Italy to fight alongside Germany in the event of war. The *Corriere della Sera* was an influential paper, and in any case Italians longed for reassurance that they would not be involved in Germany's war. As a young Fascist woman put it to Iris: 'A good Italian's duty is now to have *no* opinions.'

On 16 September news from Turin suggested the importance of keeping calm. The Prefect there had been dismissed on the grounds that he had 'aroused the fears of the civil population'; Starace, the Party Secretary, hurried to Turin, summoned the *gerarchi* – the Fascist leaders – of the district, and told them that normal life was the first duty of every citizen. On 24 September came a long-awaited speech from Mussolini. Many had assumed he would end the state of uncertainty, but the speech contained little more than directives about keeping calm and not interfering. The duty of Italians, Mussolini went on, was to prepare for any event, and 'to work and wait in silence'.

William Phillips was the American ambassador to Rome, and Iris's godfather; through him she learnt more precise details of the course of events in Europe. Phillips described how he had visited King Victor-Emmanuel to take him President Roosevelt's 'peace message'. The King was in his fishing lodge near Turin,

273

and Ciano did his best to discourage the visit. Phillips got lost, and arrived rather late; it was drizzling. A guard let him in. In the middle of the drive stood 'a very small man in a brown overcoat . . . quite alone'. Phillips expressed his pleasure at this chance of meeting the King away from the Palace in Rome. 'The King's weary, sad, little monkey face' (Iris cut out this sentence in a second, corrected version of the unpublished diaries, suggesting that at some point she may have been thinking of using these diaries as well) 'expanded in a sudden school-boyish grin. "I hate palaces!"' Phillips then read him Roosevelt's message. The King listened, absolutely without expression. Then, rising: "You must remember, Ambassador . . . I'm a constitutional monarch . . . I must refer everything to my government."' He then told Phillips about all the fish he had caught. 'But of the affairs of Europe, he said no single word.'

It seemed to Iris by the end of September that anti-British feeling was on the increase. 'I am so *affligée* by the tone of the radio and the press', an acquaintance once wholeheartedly pro-Fascist wrote to her, 'that it is making me ill. What I have long dreaded is happening: no distinctions are made any longer: the laying of a mine-field is exactly the same as invading a crushed country. It is slavish, an echoing of all that horrible doctrine, so at variance with the real Italian spirit.' But even she could not help adding: 'I do feel that England has heavy responsibility . . . Will England *never* arrive in time and save a small country before talking about it?'

Iris also noted a particularly unpleasant recurrence of the bullying tactics of the militia and the *squadristi*. On a brief visit to Florence she saw posters on the walls warning that the *squadristi* intended to be just as ruthless and vigilant as in the past: 'The truncheon', declared one, 'has not been put away for good. Let those who have a bad conscience remember this!' Every shop window was plastered with little notices, hung up there at night when the shop closed: '*Il Duce ha sempre ragione*' (the Duce is always right) . . . '*Il Duce sa tutto, vede tutto – e ricorda tutto*' (the Duce knows everything, sees everything – and remembers everything).

On 10 November, unable any longer to stand by uselessly, Iris travelled to Rome to see whether she might find some work to do connected with Polish relief, through either the International Red Cross or the Vatican. Both turned her away (the strength of pro-German influence on the Vatican was common knowledge). She was again staying with her godfather at the American embassy, and one night two young people recently escaped from Poland came to dinner. They described scenes of unimaginable brutality and horror, and Iris, who had known little of the details of Poland's downfall, was appalled. She was haunted by a story they told of a Polish prisoner tied to the front of a German tank to prevent Polish resistance fighters from firing on it. Senator Walcott, who had served with Hoover on the same sort of mission to Eastern Europe after the First World War, passed through Rome on his way to Poland with an American Relief Mission: Iris begged her godfather to ask the senator whether she might go with him – as secretary, typist, anything. There was nothing for her.

When she was in Rome again early in 1940, a friend described to Iris a recent showing of a German propaganda film about Poland, staged by the Government for the edification of Fascist leaders, the German colony, and pro-German members of the Italian aristocracy. Its reception, Iris was surprised to learn, had been poor. The first part, showing an intransigent Poland preparing for war against a conciliatory Germany, was greeted with bored scepticism. The second, portraying effete and decrepit English government ministers, was considered to be vulgar. (The smart, cosmopolitan section of Roman society was on the whole anti-German, but their reason for preferring the English, Iris decided, had little to do with loyalty or politics – it really came down to a taste for English country life and English tweeds, guns and riding boots – and these people increasingly infuriated Mussolini, rousing him 'to his most violent outbursts of rage'.) But the last part, which dealt with Germany's ruthless destruction of the Polish people, had provoked real revulsion. 'A low murmur of disgust spread through the hall', recorded Iris, 'and the guests walked out in a grim, unhappy silence'.

In May, still able to get letters to England via Portugal, Iris wrote to Aileen Meade. 'Don't think that I do not feel optimistic about the ultimate issue . . . But the price – the sheer weight of human suffering . . . oh darling, *wish* I was there with you all . . .' She was planning to spend most of her time at La Foce, and it was here, from the library where the radio had now been set up, that she listened to Mussolini's prevarications.

On 8 May 1940 she noted that there now fresh rumours every day. At La Foce, everyone kept asking what she thought. She recounted meeting an old friend, now a high-ranking military figure, who told her that not long before he had asked Mussolini about Italy's future. '*Stai tranquillo,*' Mussolini had replied, '*eriditemo ancora*' (don't worry, we'll inherit some more). 'Inherit what?' wrote Iris. 'From whom? One can only inherit from the dead – in the sense that Austria and Czechoslovakia are now dead.' Her diary reveals her increasing despondency. 'After Norway – what? Every country in Europe is waiting, and Italy not amongst the least curious. If the Norwegian campaign has not increased the Italians' liking for Germany, it has certainly increased their respect and fear. The cult of violence flourishes on success. Meanwhile – what next? Switzerland? Holland? Belgium? Sweden? Romania? The Caucasus? Every day brings fresh rumours, and with them the conviction that Italy too will be in before the end of the month.'

Throughout May people were scanning the newspapers and listening to the radio in at attempt to pick up clues to what exactly was being planned. An anti-British, anti-French campaign was in full swing, promoted by the *Corriere della Sera*, which spoke of Britain as a country with 'an insupportable tyranny and a fundamental enmity [to Italy]'. In Rome there were organised demonstrations against the Allied embassies. England was branded as cowardly.

On 10 May came one brief entry in Iris's diary: 'It has come. Belgium and Holland are invaded this morning.'

The feeling was growing, encouraged by well-placed propaganda, that it was impossible for any country to stand up to Germany, given the sheer quantity and quality of its war material, and that there might soon be no choice but to join her; the better informed, however, were increasingly anxious about the lack of preparedness of the Italian army. Such was the tension, Iris felt, that many Italians were actually longing for the certainty of war. Anxiety, a mood of fear, hung over La Foce's ceremonies for the anniversary of Italy's entry into the Great War, although Iris was slightly reassured when a local dignitary in his black shirt unwound sufficiently to say to her, '*Eppure i tedeschi . . . quanto sono antipatici.*' (And yet the Germans, how odious they are!) Nor was the opening of the first men's club at La Foce as festive as it might have been: 'too many officials, thunder in the air and anxiety'.

The newspapers of 29 May compared the German advance to Napoleon's campaign, the 'martial virtues' and moral 'superiority' of Hitler to those of Napoleon himself. As Germany triumphed in France, the papers gave themselves over entirely to anti-British tirades, describing her as a blind and grasping imperial country.

At some point, Irene evidently asked Iris about Antonio's views. Having been called up as soon as war was declared, Antonio, she replied, felt 'quite grim about it'. 'Briefly,' she went on, '[he also feels] that the Anschluss was bound to happen; that the majority of Austrians do want it, that it is not for us to comment on the method of it; that Hitler does mean to 'respect' the Brenner; that the Jews are a filthy race . . . that Chamberlain has got some sense, [and] had he shown it earlier, some of the worst might have been avoided.' For all her somewhat flippant tone, it cannot have been easy or pleasant at this stage to be about to find herself emotionally on the other side of a war from her husband. Nor was she much cheered by a letter she received from Charlie Meade: 'I am sorry for [Antonio], no one here will ever bring himself to speak to him again . . . Your in-laws would not be flattered to know their advent is viewed with no apprehension at all.' A joke perhaps, but not well chosen. Iris felt under attack from all sides. 'While once the resentment against British morality and condescension was accompanied by respect,' she wrote a little sourly, 'that respect is now turning to contempt.'

Iris herself continued to believe, to hope, that one of the strongest cards against Italy entering the war was Mussolini's widely-known reluctance to commit himself. What she did not perhaps appreciate was that one reason for this was Mussolini's awareness of how ill-prepared his army was; though he talked so swaggeringly about war, he had little idea about how to prepare for it. For all the black shirts and the Balillas, Italy was not very military minded, and Mussolini later confessed that she had been better prepared for war in 1915 than she was in 1939. 'And indeed,' Iris wrote, 'to the best of my belief, the truth *is* that Mussolini does not want war . . . He does not want war now because he believes that he can achieve his aims' – to appear heroic at home, and to win more colonial territory – 'without it. It remains to be seen whether he is right.'

He was not. On 7 June, Iris's diary records, 'the first outward signs of war reach our valley. In the early morning thirty-five bombing planes, heading south, fly over us; and in the afternoon about fifty military lorries, bound for the aviation camp at Castiglion del Lago, drive up the road from Rome. The peasants look up as they hear the rumble, say resignedly "*ci siamo*", and get back, when they can, to their hay.' Is it possible, she wondered, to move a 'country to war against its normal instincts and characters of the majority of its inhabitants, and very possibly against its own interests?' and concluded sadly: 'Apparently it is.'

On 10 June 1940 the Fascio of Chianciano rang to tell the Origos to gather all their farm workers and their families together at five that evening to hear a speech by the Duce from the Palazzo Venezia. Antonio carried the radio out into the loggia while gradually La Foce's inhabitants filed onto the lawn. Ugolino and Flavia della Gherardesca were staying with the Origos. The *fattore* was there, and the teachers and the cook. At five, the radio announced an hour's delay. 'The tense faces relax, the crowd breaks up into little groups. The older men stand under the ilex tree, talking in low voices . . . one group sits in a semicircle on the gravel playing cards . . . Antonio and the keepers discuss the young partridges and the twin calves born that morning . . . It is all curiously unreal and also *boring*. At 6 o'clock, the radio stops playing Giovinezza, and there are deafening cheers, presumably as the Duce appears on the balcony. "Fighting men of the land, the sea and the air," Mussolini could be heard shouting out, "Blackshirts of the Revolution and of the Legions, men and women of Italy, of the Empire, and of the Kingdom of Albania, hearken! . . . We will conquer. And we will give finally a long period of peace with justice to Italy, to Europe, and to the world. People of Italy, to arms! Show your courage, your tenacity and your worth!'"

Italy was at last at war.

As both the war news and their health grew worse, Sybil and Percy had returned to the Villa Medici. Percy had entirely lost the sight in one eye but had had a successful operation for a cataract in the other; Sybil had undergone an operation to straighten her 'contracted' legs, having been told that unless she did so she would never walk again. According to Percy, in a letter to a friend, this muscular contraction was due 'to the long blood poisoning of last year', but it was a feature of Sybil's ill-health that only rarely could the root cause of any complaint be diagnosed: it is possible that depression may have played a part. As it was, she had taken to her bed for a year after the operation. Many who mocked Sybil were also very fond of her, acknowledging that, when she was well, there was no one who had more understanding, vitality and charm. She had been known, for example, to paddle her canoe round and round the bay in front of Gli Scafari, standing up. But she was now seldom well, and those who met her for the first time in these days tended to echo the words of one sharp-tongued Italian acquaintance to Nesta de Robeck: 'Sybil is very like Iris, except that Iris is human.' In Florence, stories about her did the rounds of the now shrunken foreign community; a favourite concerned the day Sybil, having a headache and famous in any case for her hatred of all noise, got Percy to ring up the Admiral at the naval base at La Spezia with a request that his warships should cease their gunnery practice while she was having her siesta.

Iris was worried about what would happen to her mother and Percy in the event of Italy entering the war. Visits to the American and British consulates yielded differing advice as to whether they should stay or go, and if go, then when. Late in May 1940 came a warning from the British Embassy that they should delay no longer. Through well placed contacts and a lot of trouble, Iris had managed not only to get special visas for them in Switzerland – the Swiss were becoming extremely tough about those they let in, demanding evidence of a great deal of money, genuine medical need, or a ticket onto another country – and also beds in a Red Cross Ambulance coach attached to a north-bound train. At midnight on 5 June, just five days, as it turned out, before Italy's declaration of hostilities, the Lubbocks set off. They were destined for Montreux, where Iris had found them rooms in a hotel. Sybil protested that she didn't like 'dark lakes', but Percy, more politely, claimed to rather enjoy the 'honest wholeheartedness of the Swiss'. They were accompanied on the train by three servants, and at every station there were whispers about *la principessa musulmana* – the Muslim princess – who was most delicate and needed to keep her blinds down.

Sybil was soon 'very ill' again. She hated the cold weather and the company of the other rich and elderly refugee expatriates who filled Switzerland's lakeside luxury hotels. She felt cut off and longed for news. The next few years in Switzerland would follow a pattern: Montreux for the cold winter months, a rented villa above Vevey for the summer, less lonely and more enjoyable because people came to visit, except that Sybil did not like the sound of the servants having their meals in the next room. 'The climate gives Sybil no chances,' wrote Percy gloomily to a friend, the weather being 'much what you would expect at Aberdeen in February, varied by an occasional day in a tropical jungle' (in August this became 'Greenland by night and Aden by day'). He took to referring to Switzerland as 'this fubsy little land'. Homesickness, he said, 'becomes almost frenzied at times – but we try to keep our heads', adding that he was growing very stout and shabby in appearance. To Berenson, Sybil wrote reproachfully that he had not sent her a single letter since she had been in her 'bookless, letterless, friendless station in this little island universe'. Like others before and since, she became irritated by the oppressive cleanliness of the country, and longed for the clutter and randomness that marked life in Italy. Berenson had decided to stay at I Tatti with his books and his pictures. In the event of trouble, Ciano had promised him 'special care'.

Switzerland was not all terrible for the Lubbocks. One letter of Percy's describes a good patch, 'better than I thought Switzerland to be capable of – sunlight sifts through silver rime even as I write'. When the autumn remained warm they would linger on in their villa above Vevey, walking as much as Sybil could manage in the beech woods and the 'tinkling pastures (tinkling even to excess, in a scale from muffin-bells to cathedral towers, but always ringed round by dense silence)'. Sybil loved flowers, and from the gardens at the Villa Medici, which she had sometimes worked on with Pinsent, she knew a certain amount about how they grew. She, too, loved the walks in the mountains, writing on one occasion to Lina Waterfield: 'There is a golden Adonis in flower here that is incredibly beautiful – as luminous as a celandine and much larger – but it grows in the Valais, not on these hills, where so far we have gathered only wood anemones and oxlips, primroses and an enchanting pale blue scilla.'

In the spring of 1940, Iris had realised that she was pregnant. She was thirty-eight and it was sixteen years since Gianni's birth. 'It's such a strange feeling,' she wrote to Irene, 'the same kind of planning (new nanny, nurseries, baby-clothes etc etc) . . .' She was feeling extremely well, 'not sick, but tired, older . . . I think that slight op. in the spring [of 1939] must have done the trick. Antonio is incredibly happy – an entirely different human being.' The years of wandering were over.

She had been listening to Hitler on the radio – 'very nightmarish, but *not* impressive' – and was again haunted by not being able to do anything in the way of war work, finding herself as a result 'retreating more and more into the living world of one's everyday life'. The news of the baby was greeted 'with sombre congratulations' by the people at La Foce, and to her relief Antonio told her he did not mind whether it was a boy or a girl. To Berenson she wrote of the 'small creature who has chosen this bleak moment to enter the world. Only fortunately it will not seem bleak to him – and indeed, if I am to be honest, it already seems a strangely changed place to me. Perhaps hope is, after all, the most persistent of all one's feelings – indestructible in spite of all the plagues and torments that lay above it in Pandora's chest . . . !'

Iris had made contact with an obstetrician in Switzerland, where she wanted to have the baby. But exit from Italy was regarded as a serious issue, and Mussolini, to whom her request finally made its way, refused her permission, on the grounds that he wanted Italian babies to be born in Italy; she was, however, allowed to go there to interview Swiss nannies at the Grand Hotel in Geneva. It was now that Fate produced a stroke of luck: there were ten candidates, among them Marie Blaser, affectionate and highly efficient. 'Iris spoke adequate German,' remembers 'Schwester Marie', now Marie Uetz. 'I was thirty and had worked for a long time in children's hospitals. I was longing to see the world.' When Iris offered her the job, Marie took it.

Notwithstanding Mussolini's declaration of war, there were many in Italy who continued to believe in the real possibility of a swift peace. On 22 June France concluded an armistice with Germany, and on the 24th terms were concluded between Vichy France and Italy. The radio and newspapers now redoubled their attacks on Britain, characterised as a treacherous and greedy nation. Most ordinary Italians had but the vaguest idea of what their country's old friend and ally, now their enemy, was actually like. They saw the Englishman, wrote Iris, as a 'prosperous elderly gentleman in a top hat. This old gentleman – vaguely and fabulously rich and eating five meals a day – combines a firm determination to hold on to his riches with a sanctimonious justification of his right to them . . .' The return of seven hundred members of the Italian community in England aboard the troop ship *Monarch of Bermuda*, together with the Italian ambassador Giuseppe Bastianini and Iris's specialist Dr Castellani, gave rise to a fresh outburst against 'revolting instances of British brutality': most of the Italians, before they left England, had suffered, even to the extent of violence, from being branded as a 'fifth column'; the ship was filthy, the travellers were kept below decks in Glasgow for forty-eight hours with all the portholes sealed shut, they were given very little water and terrible food, and everyone was rude to them. By contrast, British diplomats travelling in the opposite direction reported 'most considerate and courteous treatment'. Even Dr Castellani, a man of pronounced pro-British views who had spent a great deal of time in London, confirmed that their treatment had been unnecessarily unpleasant.

Through the first ten days of July there was a lull. The long-expected German invasion of Britain did not take place, and people began again to talk of peace. Not that this prevented the hostess of one party saying to Iris, as she rose from the table, 'There's no doubt: England is done for.'

Iris spent the last few weeks of her pregnancy staying with her godfather in the American Embassy in Rome. One night there were air raids, and she and William Phillips 'sat talking pleasantly in the dark for about an hour'. When they were able to go back to bed, Iris wrote to Aileen: 'The four air raids were chiefly upsetting to the lions in the zoo, who appear to have very delicate nerves and went on roaring all night.'

Then on 11 July came a BBC broadcast announcing that 'the German bombardment has begun in real earnest'. Sitting in the Embassy, Iris wrote: 'It is a clear, breathless night: I look out of my window and see the young moon rising over the ilexes and domes of Rome. What will it see before it wanes?' Her entries have a dispirited note. Every night she listened to the BBC and thought about the Battle of Britain and what it was doing to her friends in London. 'What is happening? What can be happening?' One night two Italians, a Belgian and three Americans came to dinner at the Embassy. 'Do you think the door to peace is still open?' asked one Italian. 'Shut and barred,' replied the other.

The baby was late; the Ambassador's wife and diplomatic staff had long since departed and eventually Phillips could no longer defer his recall to Washington: Iris was left alone in the embassy with a skeleton domestic staff. On 1 August, after a quick labour of two hours, a girl was born, 'very pink and ugly and touching'. Antonio was delighted with his daughter, whom they called Benedetta, and to Iris's relief there was indeed no hurtful talk of boys. Schwester Marie, who had been awaiting the birth with Iris in Rome, remembers that they were given three rooms in the nursing home – one for Iris, one for herself and Benedetta, and one for the wet-nurse, found for them by the Red Cross (there were to be six different wet-nurses over the next six months). Iris, always secretly haunted by the fear that she might have given Gianni the tuberculosis that eventually contributed to his death, refused to feed Benedetta herself – in the face of disapproval from Antonio, who believed so strongly in the importance of giving babies their mother's milk that he left crossly for La Foce. Marie Uetz remembers that once they were back at the villa 'it was terribly hard for Iris. She couldn't bear to see the child on the wet-nurse's breast. She didn't spend all that much time with us. She had Benedetta early in the morning on her bed, then for an hour in the afternoon.' Iris returned to her garden, but not to her diary, which she gave up and did not resume until January 1943.

It was still just possible to get letters to England, and Iris now wrote to Aileen: 'A. is still at home and quite potty about Benedetta – who is rather an engaging baby, and very alive . . . The rest of the daily life much happiness – so long as we avoid any discussion of the events of the world (alas, but I suppose inevitably). A.'s views are *hardening*. And perhaps in the opposite direction mine too.'

By the autumn of 1940, Iris found once again that she could bear her inactivity no longer. With a war going on, she no longer felt that running La Foce – which anyway, as far as she was concerned, ran itself – was enough. Not only did she feel useless, but there was too much time in which to worry about her friends in England, to whom she wrote anxiously of how much she thought about them, and longed to be with them. She went up to Rome, to see whether the Italian Red Cross might have work for her. It helped that she knew Count Umberto Morra, who had joined the Red Cross some months earlier and was now head of the section for Allied prisoners of war and the Italian representative on the International Committee of the Red Cross. To her pleasure and relief, she was given a job in the Prisoner of War Office, trying to locate missing prisoners and put them in touch, where possible, with their families. For two years, every weekend that she was free, she returned to La Foce to see Benedetta; on Mondays, at dawn, she caught the first train back to Rome.

It was now that Iris met a woman who was to become her closest friend for the next twenty years. Elsa Dallolio would not only provide her with the affection and intimacy on which she thrived but, like first Colin and then Leo, feed her hunger for knowledge and understanding. More spiritual than either of them, a believing though not a practising Catholic, her life was given to trying to help others; for herself, she preferred to 'live in the shadows'. Over the years to come she brought out an important side to Iris's nature: her desire to do good, to spread her own good fortune, to do more, always more, for those in need. Colin and Leo had brought her books, music and the company of people who amused and impressed her. Elsa brought her a greater curiosity about the world, and extreme humility in the face of it. Twelve years older than Iris, she also provided some of the almost maternal warmth her life had lacked.

Iris and Elsa first met in 1939 at the Braccis' house in the Via IV Novembre in Rome, where they had both been invited to watch from the balcony the procession of the newly elected Pope, Pius XII, who was paying his first formal visit to the Quirinal Palace. Because Elsa looked tired, Iris offered to drive her back to her flat in the Palazzo Taverna. 'The twenty minute drive', Iris noted many years later in a memoir of Elsa, 'was enough to sow the seeds of friendship.' The two women agreed to meet the following week in Switzerland, where Iris was going to see her mother, Elsa on Red Cross business. Later Iris remembered Robert Graves's words 'friendship at first sight'.

Elsa was a remarkable woman with a huge circle of friends who admired her selflessness, appreciated her irony, and consulted her about all their plans. She was a little like Mrs Tiggywinkle in appearance, sensibly dressed, and good-humoured but with a strong underlying melancholy. She was the elder daughter of a renowned Italian Great War general, Alfredo Dallolio, and a German mother. Both her father and her uncle, who was the mayor of Bologna, were committed to the ideal of service to their country, an idealism which, understandably, they felt was lacking in the Italian aristocracy. Elsa's education had been minimal, something she regretted all her life, but she was widely read and spoke French, German, and some English. By the age of twenty she was possessed, though she scarcely seemed aware of it, of an unusual sense of moral integrity. After serving as a nurse at the front in the Great War she became involved with a group of young intellectuals trying to do social work among the poor of southern Italy. For a while she believed, like her companions, that

Fascism might have the solution to such extremities of poverty; like them, she soon became disillusioned. She met both Salvemini and Umberto Zanotti Bianco, later head of the Italian Red Cross, and with them threw herself into a project to develop education in the south: with virtually no money, they nevertheless managed to set up fifteen travelling libraries. In the 1920s she started to do the kind of work she later did for Iris, reading manuscripts, editing, checking. By this point she claimed to have lost all interest in politics, and to be preoccupied only with 'fundamental human problems'. Her health, which had always been bad, with arthritis and heart trouble, was growing steadily worse.

Alone at the American embassy awaiting the birth of her child, Iris often met Elsa for lunch in a small trattoria in Piazza San Pietro. When Benedetta was born, Elsa was there. Iris asked her to act as the baby's godmother, but Elsa refused, on the grounds that she did not know Antonio well enough.

It was through Elsa that Iris secured her job with the Italian Red Cross, despite her Anglo-American origins and her known non-Fascist views. She started as a typist, but before long was helping Elsa sort through the lists of missing, wounded and dead Italian prisoners of war, her English helpful in deciphering notes jotted down by British officers with no knowledge of Italian. She also took over the job of translating the chaplains' letters that accompanied the packages of personal effects, photographs of weddings and children, notes written just before the end, which were returned to his family when a prisoner of war died. Before sending them off Iris would add a note of sympathy of her own to try to soften the pain of the news. She never got used to the haunting image of mothers and wives as they opened the parcels and learnt what had happened.

Nevertheless, Iris could be daunting, and young Roman

society women applying for Red Cross jobs sometimes found her particularly intimidating. Twenty-year-old Orietta Doria Pamphili could not understand why Iris gave her such a hard grilling (her father, Prince Filippo Doria Pamphili, was one of the very few members of the Italian aristocracy to be gaoled by Mussolini, arrested by the Fascist militia while attending mass and exiled to southern Italy), and went away from the interview dismayed. Her mother too was English, yet not only had Iris insisted they speak Italian, but she had firmly used the Fascist *voi*. Orietta Doria Pamphili never forgot this, nor Iris's somewhat imperious manner. Perhaps Iris's old awkwardness with strangers was complicated by the fact that in working for the Italian Red Cross she felt herself to be in a slightly anomalous position, constrained to be ultra-Italian.

Iris worked very long hours. There was a brief pause at two o'clock, when she and Elsa had lunch, then she returned to her files until late at night. When Elsa went down with diphtheria and Iris could not see her, she realised how much she had come to depend on her new friend. She was intensely relieved to be working: it helped to take her mind off all those of whom she had had no news for many months. 'Separation of all kinds – from family, friends, books, talk, everything except ideas,' she wrote to Berenson in January 1941, '– does seem to me one of the worst of the many bad things that this time has brought us, and in this separation one realises more clearly *how* much one's old friends meant to one . . .' She added, in words that betray how many parents with her background regarded their children in those days, 'I find it a great comfort to have a definite occupation – since Benedetta, engaging as she is, occupies as yet only the heart and not the mind.' To Sybil in Vevey, Iris wrote that Benedetta had cut her first tooth and 'looks like the infant

Hercules, as indeed her portraits show'. There was no time now, however, for the family album charting every step of the baby's development, such as she had kept for Gianni.

Elsa was with her when she miscarried not long afterwards. Then, in the autumn of 1942, she found herself pregnant once again. In Rome in the early summer of 1943, as she awaited the birth of her baby, air raid warnings marked the beginning of the Allied advance into Sicily in the south: when the sirens went she joined princesses wearing their family jewels and women from the slums in the shelter of the old dungeons of the Palazzo Taverna, where Lucrezia Borgia had been imprisoned. As the days passed and the baby failed to come, she thought of going back to La Foce but, reasoning that the 'bombing of Rome is problematical, the baby's arrival certain', she stayed on. The weather was wonderful and she wandered about the city, admiring the flower stalls piled high, despite the war, with roses, irises and Madonna lilies. On 9 June 1943 she gave birth to a second daughter, and while she was in labour listened to a young airman whose leg had been amputated, groaning for morphine. It was all very different from her first two confinements, surrounded by luxury and excitement. She called her new daughter Donata, but had wept when told that it was 'another girl': not for herself, as she explained, but 'for Antonio, who longed for a son'. If he did, he seems not to have shown it: when he arrived on leave, 'he took Donata in his arms, and I too forgot my disappointment'.

This time, Iris fed the baby herself, and Elsa agreed to be a godmother. She wrote to Iris: 'I always think: will this be a *good* person? Everything depends on that: there is nothing one needs more.' The christening was held in the parish church at the Castellucio, after a mass celebrated in Gianni's chapel in the morning. Elsa wrote to their mutual friend, Nannina Fossi: 'Antonio is basically delighted: it will be La Foce that will be the most disappointed – where they were longing for a boy . . . The baby weighs 3.670, is more delicate, more "Nordic" than Benedetta, with huge eyes and hair that will be very blonde, long and thin like Gianni, with a lively expression and beautiful colouring.'

As friends, often in distant places, heard the news, letters began to arrive. 'And don't write and ask me why you should bring a child into such a foul world,' wrote Colin, from America, 'because though I don't believe in much of Nietzsche any more, I do still believe in his life-force, in his "yes" to life – and I do believe that, however nasty, life is worth anyone's while having a look at. Dearest, dearest Iris, I am so glad for you.'

Soon after the christening Iris seems to have written to Elsa in a downcast mood; the reply is interesting, and shrewd: 'I was very touched by your letter. I feel for you in your longing for Gianni and in your sense of loss; I know that your two dear girls are a consolation, but can't replace him. I ask myself, however, whether even another little boy, another Gianni, could have filled the emptiness. You have to remember that it is in this very emptiness that he lives on in you. Memories that solidify and settle are like the stones in a cemetery.'

After her miscarriage and Donata's birth, Antonio and her specialist in Switzerland convinced Iris that she should have no more children. She gave up her Red Cross work and returned to La Foce. She was about to embark on quite another kind of work, no less committed and demanding than that of the Prisoners of War Office.

CHAPTER ELEVEN

La progettista

The first refugee children arrived at La Foce at the end of January 1943. The eldest was six, the smallest just one. They came from families made homeless by the Allied bombing raids on Genoa. Iris had long been talking about helping refugee children, but had been constantly thwarted by official policy which insisted on finding shelter for bombed-out mothers and children together. It says something about the clarity of her ideas and her growing firmness of manner that she wasted no time on considering an approach that she was certain was wrong. No surprise, then, that friends now affectionately referred to her as '*la progettista*' (the planner). The streak of determination and even ruthlessness in carrying out plans and ideas she had convinced herself were in everyone's best interests, noticed by Pinsent when Iris was eighteen, had become more marked.

Having wasted three months waiting for an answer to her request, she approached the Principessa di Piemonte, head of the Red Cross, and twelve children, all 'urgent' cases, arrived within two weeks. The children were dazed and apprehensive. After being bombed out of their homes they had survived in recent months living in tunnels and underground passages, many having lost a parent or a brother or sister; they were grubby, ill-dressed and very thin. In the bright light of the nursery school, the children 'stood blinking', Iris noted in the first entry of a new diary, 'like small bewildered owls'. On 10 February a second batch of children arrived, this time six little girls from Turin, aged between eight and twelve, more self-possessed than the younger ones, but they were 'nervy and easily become hysterical'. The kindergarten had been rebuilt shortly before the war with a large classroom with big windows and lots of light, waxed floors and the walls painted different shades of blue, with little rectangular tables that could be moved around to make the most of the light. Iris now gave over the building to the refugees. Next she brought in a remarkable young teacher called Vera Berrettini, soon known to the children as La Tata, to run it, while the school nurse came up to inspect for nits. The children were given a detailed medical examination, which Iris sent off to their mothers, together with a photograph and a letter saying how they were getting on. The number of children rose to twenty three when parents, delighted with the safety of one child, begged her to take a brother or sister. Iris planned to run her refugee home on Montessori principles, with herself as 'director' of the psychological, physical and social development of the children.

One of the girls from Turin was ten-year-old Liberata Nardi, whom Iris quickly identified as 'by far the most intelligent and sensitive . . . a born school teacher'. Liberata describes arriving at La Foce in the dark, after a long, bewildering day, while the city children, unused to the woods at night, wailed loudly. In the converted school they found dormitories with neat rows of beds, food and warmth. Iris was not well, but Antonio was there to settle them in; they found him frighteningly tall, but very friendly. Some of the children talked of going home to their mothers at once, but they were soon seduced by the food, the comfort, and toys the like of which they had never seen before. When Iris appeared, as she did every day, Liberata found her a bit cool and distant at first, but this vanished as Iris recognised her ability and started to give her private lessons.

The Origos did what they could to make the children content. In the course of the summer, their mothers were invited to come to visit them. They went away impressed, if more than a little daunted by the grandeur of La Foce. The food the children were given was good, and olive oil was added to the diets of the more malnourished. Fannina Fe is now in her late seventies. She was a helper working at the school – her entire family worked for the Origos – when the refugees arrived. She remembers the way Iris appeared every day, tasted their food and brought across new toys. On Sundays, the older children went with the Origos through the garden and the woods and down the little path to the cemetery to mass.

At Christmas there was a party, with Antonio dressed up as Father Christmas, and Fannina helped Iris pack up presents for all the children. 'I once asked her', Fannina remembers, 'why she did all this for us.' She replied that 'if you have too much, you never really want the things that life gives you', something that Fannina only came to understand many years later. Liberata remembers the Origos inventing games for the children in the garden, with little prizes, and Antonio taking them blackberrying with no shoes on, saying that it was better for their feet. They were taught songs in Italian, English and German. Many of the children, says Liberata, had never known such luxury and such fun.

In April 1943 daylight raids by Allied bombers killed six thousand people at Cagliari in Sardinia. In Grosseto on the coast south of Pisa on Easter Monday, when people were strolling up and down the Corso in their best clothes, Allied Liberators flew in low and bombed the city. The war, which had so far touched La Foce little, was growing closer all the time. All over Italy Allied prisoners of war taken in the fighting in North Africa were being held in camps, or sent out as agricultural workers to fill the places left by die men who were now fighting. There was no question of choice: the prisoners were simply allocated to estates where it was thought they were most needed, and, at first at least, they were often treated by the farmers' families with considerable hostility and wariness. So when fifty British prisoners of war arrived at La Foce from the Laterina Camp in Arezzo no one was very pleased to see them, though both Antonio and Iris made efforts to convince everyone that they were desperately needed on the farms and would prove useful. Antonio went to meet them at Chianciano with an ox-cart for their kit, and took them to the Castelluccio where they had been billeted. They were led by a corporal called Trott, who in peacetime was gardener to the Earl of Durham. They liked their quarters at the Castelluccio and did not find their Italian lieutenant and ten Sicilian guards too irksome. Iris made a conscious decision to distance herself from the prisoners, suspecting that the day might come when she might be of some use to them, and therefore not wishing to be seen to be close to them now. She sent over books and packs of cards.

In Rome, the underground opposition were trying to find some common ground; they were a disparate lot, made up of Communists, monarchists, old Liberals, parish priests, and the ladies of Principessa di Piemonte's entourage. They met secretly in cafés and safe houses. British propaganda urging Italians to overthrow Mussolini was increasing all the time, with leaflets dropped from airplanes saying that if they acted fast this would earn them 'a respected place among the free peoples of Europe'.

In the north, which was still occupied by the Germans, there was a widespread feeling of terror, with arbitrary arrests and executions; but there was still enough food. In the south, now partly occupied by the Allies, the population was free and safe, but hungry because the Allies could not spare the ships to bring food. Everywhere you went in the south you saw starving children surrounding the troops and begging for food.

In Rome, too, food was becoming extremely scarce, with almost no fruit or vegetables, while incessant air raid warnings kept the Romans scurrying for shelter. At night, people with nowhere to go would seek safety in the shadow of St Peter. Even at the height of the war, the Origos managed to keep in touch with most of their friends, through their many varied and useful contacts. The La Foce estate itself was in the fortunate position of producing almost all the food it needed, ham, beef, flour, vegetables, but calls on supplies, from refugees and later partisans, were increasing all the time.

On 26 July 1943, while Elsa was visiting La Foce, the news came that Mussolini had resigned and the King had appointed Pietro Badoglio, the Italian general who had entered Addis Ababa and concluded the war in Abyssinia, as Prime Minister. Iris and Elsa thought Badoglio's new Cabinet disappointing and feeble. He announced that Italy would continue the war on the side of the Germans. Having listened to the accounts of the Allies' progress on the radio, the two women took the children blackberrying.

On 8 September, while on a trip to Siena to do some essential shopping, with Donata, whom she was still feeding, Iris heard that Badoglio, after forty-five days in office, had signed an armistice with the Allies. Bit by bit, in the days that followed, opposition members and partisans began to emerge from hiding. The arrests of Fascists began. But the news that reached La Foce was extremely confused – was Rome occupied? What would now happen? It became clear that all the Allied prisoners of war were now technically free. Iris hurried up to the Castelluccio to tell Trott and his men that they were no longer prisoners, and that if they wanted to leave there was nothing to stop them.

On the night of 8 September Allied forces landed at Salerno, south of Naples. The Italian armed forces had been expecting a landing nearer Rome and, although they outnumbered the Germans around the capital, panic set in and the High Command advised the King and Badoglio to leave for the south and Allied protection. Early on 9 September they escaped via Pescara to Brindisi, the Italian defence of Rome crumbled, and on 10 September the Germans occupied the city. Fearing what would come next – Chiusi, only fifteen kilometres away, was occupied by German soldiers – the Origos and their *fattore* started hiding stores of food and petrol, and taking the wheels off the cars. A whole new stage of war at La Foce was about to begin.

There were some 80,000 Allied prisoners in captivity on the day of the armistice, scattered across seventy-two camps throughout Italy – English, Welsh and Scots, Ukrainians and Cossacks, Indians and Burmese, Gurkhas and Canadians, Free French and units of Senegalese, Algerians and Moroccans, soldiers from General Anders's Polish corps, men of the Royal Hellenic Greeks, and a Palestinian Jewish brigade. Many could not communicate with each other, and only a very few spoke Italian. Half of them, due to the generosity and courage of the Italians, survived the rest of the war as free men, whether by escaping south through the lines and rejoining their regiments, or by going north and crossing the border into Switzerland, or by lying low in the houses of peasants in the countryside and of anti-Fascists in the cities.

The day the armistice was announced, the more sympathetic and liberal Italian camp commandants opened their camp gates and helped the prisoners of war to escape; and, fearing the arrival of Fascists and Germans, they urged them to go as quickly as possible. A few Fascist commandants simply kept their gates locked, in order to wait and see what would happen next; their prisoners, about 30,000 men, were deported to Germany when the German occupying forces arrived.

After Badoglio and the King fled south, the Germans turned to brutally attacking the Italians. Many were taken by surprise and surrendered. The former Italian army ceased to exist, though many Italian soldiers joined the Allies. By September, four-fifths of Italy was occupied by German troops, and fifty-six Italian divisions had been disarmed. Almost three-quarters of a million soldiers were taken prisoner. No one had really anticipated the savagery of the German response. The Wehrmacht sent in large numbers of troops and SS formations. There was already, because of Italian Fascist incompetence, very little food; the Germans now requisitioned whatever they could find, reducing entire towns to near starvation, and soldiers foraged about the countryside, killing chickens and herding away pigs and cows. At one point a litre of olive oil was said to fetch a gram of gold on the black market. One of the more peculiar sights was that of German tourists, whether officers on leave or civilians from Germany, come to see the sights of Tuscany.

By the time Field Marshal Kesselring, Commander of the German army in Italy, announced that the whole of Italy behind the German front line was a war zone subject to martial law, and that any Italian soldier caught fighting against the Germans would be shot as a traitor, not only were there about 50,000 Allied former prisoners of war loose and on the run, said to be the greatest mass escape in history, but also large numbers of ordinary Italian soldiers who had decided to take off their uniforms and make a run for home. Together with the different groups of anti-Fascists now about to jostle for power – some six parties making up the Central Committee of National Liberation – there were also the partisans coming down from the mountains. In Tuscany, which lay within German-occupied territory, the woods and undergrowth were full of lost, hungry, dirty, ill-dressed men, of every nationality. Over the radio came German orders that the men, whether Allied soldiers or Italian deserters, should give themselves up, or be subject to the severity of martial law. What was more, those sheltering them faced the same penalties. 'The treachery of the Italians', announced Hitler, 'would not pass unpunished and the measures against them would be very hard.' It says an enormous amount for the Italians that so many, in the days after the proclamation, set out to help the men on the run, and did so until the end of the war, at great risk to themselves and their families.

Meanwhile, from the South, advancing up the Italian peninsula as rapidly as they could, came the Allied forces, also a very disparate group, made up of Americans and every ethnic group within the Empire; while against them were the Germans and what Fascist military supporters there remained. This would be the beginning of the hardest part of the Origos' war. As the resistance movement in Tuscany with its partisan bands intensified its activities, joined by a number of the escaping Allies and disaffected Italian soldiers, so did the Fascists and the Germans intensify theirs. Attacks, counter-attacks, reprisals, and hostage taking became the nature of the war as the partisans, reinforced by escaping prisoners of war, harried the Germans trying to hold the line against the advancing Allies.

March 1943, three months into Iris's new diary, would later be called the 'month of blood'.

La Foce's mountainous scrub, woods and what was left of the *crete senesi* were ideal for men in hiding. Some of the prisoners had been told by the underground of a system for identifying a safe peasant house: if it had five haystacks it was too rich and the farmer was possibly a Fascist; one haystack suggested extreme poverty; but two to three were about right, 'not rich enough to have too much to lose, and friendly'. By the late autumn of 1943, the Germans had ordered death as the penalty for anyone harbouring English or Allied agents and prisoners of war. Soon the Origos began to notice that everywhere around the estate they went they were aware of people in the undergrowth, and as their reputation for generosity and helpfulness spread, so they were approached by the men for food, medical help and maps. Iris was most often the one who talked to them – many of the prisoners of war could speak nothing but English – and she was often summoned by a partisan after dark to see someone in trouble or to help with a translation. It seldom occurred to her to be nervous.

Her first duty, however, she felt to be towards her own fifty British prisoners of war in the Castelluccio; her first thought, when she heard that the prisoners of war had been liberated, was to take a cask of wine up to the men to celebrate. There was the obvious risk that if the Origos simply let them go, she and Antonio would become suspect in the eyes of local Fascists and Germans. A deft plan was drawn up by the men who, having been well treated at La Foce, agreed that they should not leave their hosts in trouble. They could all work as usual in the fields below the house. When the German patrol sent to take them to a camp to await deportation to Germany appeared, someone on watch would give a signal and they would very conspicuously drop their tools and make off as fast as they could to the woods and to the cache of food and maps that had been left for them. All went as planned. The Germans arrived, the signal was given and Trott and his fellow prisoners of war vanished into the undergrowth. The Germans made a faint effort to chase them but soon, unnerved by what they might encounter in the woods, fell back. Though they complained bitterly to the Origos about what had happened, no blame could be attached to Iris or Antonio.

A sense of chaos and lawlessness spread as winter approached. Iris hid from the Germans the remaining supplies of oil, ham and cheese. The Origos went to great lengths to remain on good terms with the partisans, who were increasing in number all the time, with their headquarters on Monte Amiata. The partisans, made up of a mixture of young Italians with a few deserters, Russians, Poles, Indians, Canadians and others, many of them lawyers and accountants and teachers in civilian life, were not all either very friendly or very polite, and some descended arrogantly on La Foce to demand food when their resources ran low. Iris now decided to pack up all linen, blankets and silver, and to wall them up. The Germans had been told by the Fascists in Chianciano that the Castelluccio, where the prisoners of war had been housed, would make an excellent billet. The Origos had friendly spies everywhere: the day the Germans came to inspect it, the building was entirely full of refugees, hastily moved up there from La Foce. Sometimes, as Iris was talking to partisans or escaped prisoners of war in the garden, giving them maps and food, Antonio would be tying up a German patrol in conversation at the front of the house. Iris would never forget one elderly man, in his eighties, with a young grandson, who came to ask her for warm clothes. The man had a heart condition but was determined to join what remained of his family in Naples. Iris gave them what she could, and watched as they stumbled off across the mountain, the old man leaning heavily on his grandson.

Berenson had refused to leave Italy, saying only that he believed absolutely in an Allied victory. Earlier in the war he had written to a friend, 'the world grows no better, now that the dark of night grows near. I fear that I shall not live long enough to see the dawning of better days, even though I am utterly convinced that they will return.' By this time most of the English and American residents had left Florence, and those who had failed to get away in time were being rounded up by the Germans and their Fascist supporters to be sent either to Germany or to small remote mountain villages. Harold Acton's parents, who had insisted on staying in Florence as long as possible, now managed to get away across the border. The Berensons and Nicky Mariano, to whom the Swiss Consul, Carlo Steinhausen, had promised visas, refused to follow them on the grounds that, as Berenson put it, he 'could not face deserting them [the Italians] in a moment like this'.

Life at I Tatti had grown quieter and quieter, as rumours began to circulate among the Fascists in Florence that Berenson was a spy. Ciano had kept his promise, however, and ordered the *questore* in Florence to leave the Berenson household in peace to continue its normal life. But as the situation worsened after the fall of Mussolini, and with Tuscany occupied by the Germans, he now accepted an invitation from Marchese Serlupi, the Ambassador of San Marino to the Holy See, to move to his house on the brow of Monte Vecchio. Sheltered from the wind by the mountainside, it was not unlike the Riviera in winter, with grassy terraces, and oak, pine, mimosa and ilex. The hills around were later full of partisans, many of them Italian soldiers who refused to fight for the Fascists of Saló; they were taken in and fed by the peasants, as at La Foce, despite the intensive manhunts mounted by the Germans.

Mary did not go with them. When the moment came for the move in September 1943, she was too ill to travel. No one realised how long it would be before Berenson and Nicky could return – almost a year – and a somewhat forlorn Mary wrote to Nicky: The truth is I am dying, only I cannot die . . . I suffer so much that the gate is already open on the long road we have to travel alone, but I cannot start.' Her misery had been made far worse by the news that her daughter Ray had died after an operation. Before leaving I Tatti, Berenson oversaw the walling-up of some of his more valuable books; the best paintings travelled with him to Monte Vecchio, and the pro-British German consul Gerhardt Wolff, who had befriended those who were left of the expatriate community, promised to do all that he could to safeguard what had to be left behind.

Early in October 1943 Antonio went into Florence to collect Iris's winter furs from store. He found that, as in Rome, the furriers had long since been looted. During Badoglio's forty-five days Florence had become cold and its citizens hungry. The Germans were now in full occupation, having set up their headquarters on Piazza San Marco. Dr Wolff, often at some risk to himself, was engaged in a frantic battle to save the bridges, the buildings, the treasures and the people of his adopted city. He was also doing all he could, in the face of opposition from the new and fanatically pro-Nazi Republican Fascist Prefect, to rescue the aged ladies, widows of First World War veterans, and members of the Italian Red Cross. After one fierce disagreement, he managed to prevent the Germans from cutting down the ancient cypresses of the Villa

Medici. The Germans argued that they were entitled to cut down the trees, since they belonged to an English woman. Dr Wolff argued that they belonged to the State and were subject to State protection. He won.

As international pressure increased for the countries at war to declare Florence an open city, and entreaties were made to Hitler, who vacillated, so a particularly vicious German official called Dr Poppe, with heavy jowls and a mouth like a frog, arrived in a requisitioned ambulance to round up Florentine academics. In his wake special SS and Gestapo anti-Jewish commandos descended on the city to find the Jews and deport them to Germany. But such was the determination to save them that many were quickly hidden in the woods. In all, 248 out of Florence's Jewish population of about a thousand could not be saved, and died as a result of shootings and deportation. Italy – with four governments, Allied, German, Fascist and Badoglio – was in a state of extreme confusion. There were first of all the partisans, growing in number all the time; then there were those who were shocked by what they saw as Badoglio's betrayal, and still uncertain of their position; then there were the anti-Fascists, and the fleeing prisoners of war and Italian soldiers; there were also all the ordinary Italians, exhausted, cynical, and worrying about how they would get enough food to survive the coming winter. The Germans looted supplies constantly. Everyone was longing for the arrival of the Allies. 'A grim, long winter lies before us,' wrote Iris in her diary, 'at the end of which none of us can tell whether our homes will still be standing, or our children safe; and we must meet it with what we can muster of patience, courage and hope.' There was no situation Iris ever felt wholly defeated by, and she greeted this one with the courage and spirit which had increasingly become a mark of her character.

As the bombing drew nearer, and bombs were now falling on Grosseto and Perugia, the Origos were overwhelmed by requests for help. Some came from starving refugees, making their way north or south to escape the bombing; some from the band of partisans who had made the woods of La Foce their base and with whom the Origos were determined to remain on good terms, though they feared repercussions as the partisans grew bolder and the Germans more desperate. So often did escaped British prisoners now find their way to La Foce that Antonio and Iris began to suspect that their name was being passed up and down the line as a place of safety. Later, they discovered this was indeed the case.

One soldier who escaped from a train carrying deportees to Germany when it was bombed on a bridge not far away was Richard Morris, a platoon sergeant in the American infantry. 'There were roughly a thousand of us on the train,' Morris remembers. 'Most of the prisoners ran west; a friend and I ran north. The fog came down. As we crossed into the Val d'Orcia we met some Eighth Army Brits who told us that there was a very helpful Englishwoman in the house on the hill. We asked one of her farmers to go and tell her we were there. She strode out of the woods, dressed in tweeds. She advised us not to go north, because a German staff officer had warned her that once the Allies took Rome they would retreat up central Italy. She told us to go back to the peasant family who had taken us in first. We did what she suggested. Later, when it got warmer we built a small shanty in the woods where she brought us food and news.' Morris survived the war by sheltering with the peasants until the front reached La Foce. Before he left, Iris tried to teach him some basic words of Italian. During his weeks on the estate he heard nothing but praise for what she was doing.

He survived the war, and kept in touch with Iris until her death.

Another prisoner who escaped from the same train was Bill Blewitt, who died in his eighties in 1998. Blewitt remembered wandering with a friend through the woods for several days, not knowing where they were and increasingly hungry; they had stopped in a clearing when suddenly a tall Englishwoman silently appeared and asked them in English if they needed help. 'It was terrible weather, pouring with rain. We told her we had had nothing to eat for four days. Just as silently she disappeared among the trees, and reappeared a little later, bringing a servant with her carrying in a basket bread, milk and hard boiled eggs. She told us to tell no one that she had given us food, and showed us the direction we should travel in.' Eventually, Blewitt joined up with the partisans on Monte Amiata. The fact that so many people now knew of their activities alarmed the Origos, who did their best to keep their visitors off the land immediately surrounding La Foce. By the end of 1943 there were said to be about a thousand partisans, former soldiers and Allied prisoners of war in the area, sometimes receiving drops of food and supplies, but in between the drops increasingly hungry. And the refugees kept on coming, many of them, like one destitute grandmother with four small grandchildren, who had struggled all the way up from Chianciano on foot, searching for clothes and food.

It was a bitterly cold winter, and the snow had come early to the Monte Amiata; many of the people who now came to the door begged for warm clothes. Iris, Schwester Marie and La Foce's women knitted as fast as they could, using every scrap of wool that could be taken from curtains, old clothes and the sheep they had left. They made nappies from old sheets. 'As the circle in which our life moves grows smaller and smaller,' wrote Iris, 'and the immediate menace more threatening, all mental language shrinks to that of the peasants.' Mussolini's 'ruralization programmes' had effectively meant that Italy was still basically a rural country, crowded with peasant families essentially governed by ancestral traditions of generosity towards travellers. In the evening, after the children had eaten, they were now taken over to the main house to sleep in dormitories hastily made out of mattresses on the floor and blankets. As Fannina Fé crossed with her crocodile of children below the cypresses to where one of the servants was meeting her to take them in, she often heard the sound of men's voices and saw the light from their cigarettes as they waited to see Iris and receive food.

Back from a trip to Rome, Antonio reported that the city was also full of escaped prisoners and soldiers living hidden in the heart of Rome, supplied with false identity papers and ration cards by a special underground office. Those most in danger, hidden in lofts or secret rooms and never going out, were called the *sepolti vivi*, the buried-alive: Jews, Italian army officers, members of the Badoglio government. Ciano's small group of society friends and the smart women members of the court, known to have been actively anti-Fascist, also lived at some risk. Others were being hidden in convents, in the catacombs, even in the domes of churches. Women from the underground Resistance acted as messengers; if caught, they faced deportation to the German concentration camps. Women from the Resistance were also hard at work printing false passports and papers in the Palazzo Taverna, which had been declared a safe area under the 'Protection of the Holy See'. One of them was a friend of Iris's, Julienne Bunsen, who when she went out wore as disguise a Red Cross outfit. Later, Julienne learnt how to use a radio transmitter, hiding one in a church, its pieces concealed behind the altar and in the Cardinal's *prie-dieu*. Iris later remembered how Julienne would turn up with an enormous bag of money, and lists of partisans and escaped prisoners of war and where they were to be found; she and her friends begged her not to take such risks, neither on her behalf, nor on behalf of the men in hiding. Of Rome's Jewish population of seven thousand before the war, over a thousand had already been taken to Germany; the rest were in hiding. There were said to be over a million refugees from the bombed cities elsewhere in Italy now in Rome, living on the starvation rations handed out at public kitchens.

In the middle of November the Origos heard that the Villa Medici had been requisitioned, and Iris went to Florence to see what was happening. One of the stranger aspects of their war was that both of them, as ordinary Italian civilians in an occupied country, were able to travel around the countryside; the fact that both spoke German, Antonio particularly well, obviously helped. In Fiesole the Germans were just installing themselves in the Villa Medici; they treated her politely, and she was given permission to seal off the *sala degli uccelli*, and to pack up the good glass and silver. 'I have a strong presentiment', she wrote, 'that this is the end of something: of this house, of a whole way of living. It will never be the same again.' On the surface, Florence appeared strangely normal, except that in the streets you met gangs of teenaged boys who, modelling themselves on the German SS, were busy arresting anyone they could identify, however vaguely, as guilty of some minor infringement of the martial laws. Most recently they had rounded up all people accused of helping British prisoners of war, the long-term residents of Florence, 'kindly, naive people, with English connections or friends, who wanted to "help the boys".' Dr Wolff could do little for them, and several were deported to Germany, in the many trains now carrying people north to prisons or labour camps. The Florentines were close to starvation.

Of Mussolini there was little news. It was rumoured that, asked whether he would like to broadcast, he had replied: 'What can a dead man say to a nation of corpses?' On 11 January 1944, after what Iris called a 'grotesque and brutal trial', Ciano was one of five former Mussolini ministers, members of the Fascist Grand Council, sentenced to death and shot.

In January, severe snow cut off La Foce: there was no light, no post, and no radio. The German troops patrolling the area had increased, and they frequently stopped at La Foce to demand food and livestock. Hearing that German paratroopers recuperating from Cassino were in Chianciano, Iris decided that the moment had come to pack up her good furniture, books and mattresses and send them off to distant farms on the ox-cart. In February, hearing of a ten-day-old baby born in Montepulciano Hospital whose mother was dying of septicaemia, Iris offered to take him in: 'a miserable little scrap,' she wrote, 'with sores on his legs and in his mouth from salivation, and I only hope that we may be able to save him'. There was an outbreak of a virulent form of the Spanish 'flu, which frequently resulted in pneumonia, and one of the youngest partisans on the La Foce estate, little more than a boy, died of it in April. He was buried in a ceremony in the church and the partisans could be seen on the surrounding hills, watching the proceedings as it grew dark. Later, when night fell, they came down silently and put flowers on the new grave.

Then came a warning from a friendly Carabinieri officer in Pienza that an order to keep the Origos under surveillance had gone out, after it was reported that they were helping their peasants to avoid military call-up, as well as funding the local partisans. The Fascist militia, who summoned Antonio, told him that there were drawers full of denunciations against them. 'Nothing has been uglier,' wrote Iris, 'in the story of these tragic last months, than the avalanche of denunciations . . . All these now end up in reports to the Fascist police, and cause the suspected person to be handed over to prison, to questioning by torture, or to a firing squad. No one feels safe.' There is a story, which may very well be apocryphal, that in the winter of 1943, while Iris had been away, Antonio had called a meeting of the men on the estate and suggested to them that they should enrol in the Fascist Republican army, on the grounds that the Allies were being held up at Cassino, and that with extra men, the war would come to a victorious end sooner. What was never made clear was whether this was just a clever bluff to confuse spies and stop people searching La Foce too closely, which seems the most likely explanation. In any case, none of Iris's work for the Allied prisoners or for the partisans could have been done without Antonio's approval and help. That the Origos should have had enemies was perhaps not surprising, and they came in for much of the same opprobrium that was levelled after the war at all the landowning families – of which the Origos are widely reckoned to be one of the few who really helped the partisans and escaping prisoners. Many years later, the historian Nardi claimed that life at La Foce during the war remained a 'universe of good manners, interwoven out of friendships with Italians, English and Germans, in which the old values of courtesy, culture and mutual respect were painfully and punctiliously kept up'. It is clearly intended as a sneer, but his comment was not far from the truth, for attention to civility and manners were things that mattered to Iris.

Iris herself was now summoned to Montepulciano and shown an article about herself printed in Siena's official Fascist paper. It referred to her as 'an Anglo-American woman, rolling in wealth' on whose 'lovely property . . . rebel bands are committing deeds of violence of every kind', and added that 'alone of the whole of this province' the 'lonely property' had not featured in the 'official reports of robbery and violence'. Another article said that the English prisoners of war called her their 'loving sister' and the refugees 'our generous mother', and it went on to remind people that enemies everywhere, whatever their standing or rank, 'must be isolated and watched'. After an unpleasant conversation, Iris decided to go to Florence, to talk to Dr Wolff. He advised her to produce a long written report, clearly denying all accusations. While in Florence she met Ludwig Heydenreich, the German archaeologist and art historian responsible for art treasures, who was hoping to reach a 'gentleman's agreement' about Florence with both the German command and the Allies. 'A queer, comforting conversation,' she noted with some relief, 'a reminder of eternal values, which may outlast the present madness.' She was touched on her return to La Foce to find that Beppe, leader of the local partisans, hearing of the accusations against the Origos, had come to see whether Iris and Antonio would like to join them underground in hiding in the woods. He told her that a special room had been cleaned and prepared for her. It was another gesture of the sort of kindness she most valued; but she had twenty-five children to look after, and the newborn baby, who was thriving, fed on milk gathered from lactating mothers on the farm, so they declined. But she did decide to keep some clothes packed ready, by her bed. 'So, at last,' Iris wrote in her autobiography many years later, 'the old barriers of tradition and class were broken down, and we were held together by the same difficulties, fears, expectations and hopes.'

The war was coming nearer. Every day Iris found refugee

families sitting in her courtyard, driven there by hunger, begging for food to take back to Rome. Even La Foce's supplies were running low, now that she was feeding her own household, twenty-three refugee children and two hundred partisans in the woods. The Spanish 'flu that had come to the area meant that there were at least eighty cases that needed nursing.

From Rome came the news of the Fosse Ardeatine massacre of 320 hostages in reprisal for a bomb that had killed thirty-two Germans. Every day brought more confusion and more violence. The Allied planes were bombing all around, while the Germans and Republican Fascists shot at the partisans. There were repeated instances of local families being hit, whether in their pony carts or walking along the road. Conflicting leaflets showered down from the sky, the German ones saying that anyone found harbouring a rebel would be shot, the British advising Italian soldiers on the run to 'at all costs refrain from giving yourselves up'. Iris was constantly asked by the farmers what they should do.

The Origos were now very conscious that there were spies everywhere, who came to visit them pretending they wanted to join the partisans. Two in particular hung around La Foce for a while, then joined a band in the mountains. The partisans also lived in fear of being given away. A family called Bianchi, a father and three sons all belonging to the band on Monte Amiata, were picked up by the Germans and held for sixty-two days, tortured and endlessly questioned about what weapons were concealed at La Foce and the Castelluccio. The father and two of the boys were eventually released; the third son, Lepanto, spent the rest of the war in Buchenwald.

On 22 May Iris noted: 'Our personal crisis is just beginning.' On 5 June, the day the Allies entered Rome, the Germans arrived to takeover the Castelluccio and the school. The Origos moved the children into the house. Then German Red Cross lorries began to arrive. From them, Iris learnt that the Carabinieri had all gone over to the partisans, who were now being urged by General Alexander to rise up, with the words 'Your hour has come.' 'Fascism', noted Iris, 'is not so much being destroyed as crumbling before our eyes.' Antonio, more than ever necessary as middleman because of his excellent German, was approached by the partisans and invited to become mayor of the commune of Chianciano the moment the Germans left, which says much for the respect in which he was held locally. He was an obvious choice. A natural leader and tall, he stood very erect and spoke with assurance. People who met him then remembered his stature and courage. In taking the position of *podestà*, Antonio must also have felt considerable relief that all suggestion of his past sympathy for the Fascists would be dispelled. Personally revolted by many aspects of Fascism, not least the pomposity and self-satisfied rhetoric, he had long felt ashamed that Italy should be represented by such men. However, belonging to an earlier generation who had fought in the First World War, he was also deeply patriotic, which explained some of his irritation and resentment when friends and acquaintances ridiculed a country he felt they did not understand. For him, the early days of Fascism had really meant one thing: help to create La Foce and the Bonifica of the Val d'Orcia, thereby improving the lives of the people there.

More Germans were now arriving all the time, many of them looting as they came, and with partisan activity increasing the escaped Allied prisoners of war were again on the move, as their presence became too dangerous for the farmers who were sheltering them. Germans with machine-guns, tipped off by spies and informers, now surrounded local villages, dragging out partisans and shooting them. For nearly a month La Foce was in the front line of the German retreat, surrounded by a parachute division.

Iris was in the garden one afternoon with some of the children, singing, when a fully-armed German patrol surrounded them. She feared terrible trouble. Instead the soldiers crouched down and asked them to sing 'Tannenbaum' and 'Stille Nacht', which the children had learnt at Christmas.

By 17 June the Allies had reached Radicofani, the mountain village about fifteen kilometres away to which the Origos had taken so many of their guests. Then a new group of Germans drove up, commandeered the house, took possession of everything and, in the great summer heat, bathed naked in the laundry fountain. The area was full of stray parties of German soldiers and the peasant farmers begged Iris for help, saying that the Germans were ransacking their houses and raping their daughters.

With the new patrol came a German artillery major who advised Iris to move the children into the cellar; here they spent ten days, in boiling summer heat, among the barrels of wine, with as many of La Foce's inhabitants as could fit. The Germans had left them the use of the kitchen, and from time to time Iris went over to the house to collect something for everyone to eat. It began to rain hard. In what was now mud, the stout artillery major started positioning batteries all round the house. As Iris was wondering what to do, the major reappeared, told her that they needed the cellar, and advised her to get the children away from the fighting. Shells began to fall on the house. There was little else to do but to leave, with the twenty-five refugee children, the three-month-old baby they had taken in, and dozens of old men, women and children from the farms, all of whom Iris had to feed. There was even a very frail elderly grandmother, and several new babies whimpering from hunger. A local boy, who had left to join the partisans and fallen ill, was dying of TB. They could only leave him in the surgery.

The Origos were now surrounded by clamouring and terrified people, wanting to know what to do. Antonio proposed that they all set off together at once, and that when they reached the crossroads, those who had friends in either Montepulciano or Chianciano should split up and go there. He and Iris planned to make for the Braccis' house in Montepulciano, some ten kilometres away, in the hopes of finding safety there.

Iris, Schwester Marie and La Tata now prepared the children to leave. They took a pram full of clothes and nappies for the babies and a basket of their food. What Iris herself took is revealing not only of the times but of her. She had long since packed a small case, containing a change of underwear for herself and Antonio, a pair of shoes, some soap, eau-de-Cologne and face powder, a clock, and a photograph of Gianni. Her dog, which she loved dearly, was forgotten.

It was a very hot, still day. By the time the long, straggling line of children clutching at the adults set out, the sun was already high in the sky. Soon, they were all begging for water. Benedetta, then aged four, remembers her mother telling her: 'You are the eldest. You must carry your coat and you must walk on your own.' Iris's idea was to give each child a small task, to keep up morale and concentration. Each child, like Benedetta, carried its own coat and jersey. At the head of the file walked Antonio, with Donata, aged one, on his shoulders. Liberata Nardi, who was on what later became known to everyone as 'the walk', remembers the way that he made everyone sing.

There were corpses on the road, which had been mined. A

passing German patrol advised them to walk carefully in the middle, and to spread out if they heard Allied planes. From time to time one of the smaller children whimpered to be carried, but was urged on. On the hill before Chianciano, where the roads divide, those who had friends in Montepulciano split away to the left. The Origos' group now consisted of sixty adults, twenty-eight children and four babies.

After a while, they reached the open cornfields. Shelling began again, and every time they heard planes come over, they flung themselves down in the corn. Another German patrol they met told them that the road ahead was safe (half an hour later they heard it being shelled), and the exhausted, straggling, footsore procession of elderly people and small children struggled on. Four long, unhappy hours passed, the Origos keeping everyone going, giving short lifts to the weakest children, urging the others on, helping the women with babies. When they reached the Montepulciano hill, the town standing high above the surrounding flat countryside, they sat down for a while to get their breath back and to give the children the energy for the last struggle to the top. As they sat there, a somewhat forlorn party, people from Montepulciano, having seen them from the ramparts, suddenly appeared, running towards them across the fields.

'Never', wrote Iris in her diary, 'was there a more touching welcome.'

Hoisting the smaller children on to their shoulders, taking the older ones by the hands, the welcoming party escorted them up the hill, and 'in a triumphant procession, cheered by so much kindness, we climbed up the village street'.

To the immense relief of the Origos, the Braccis were in their house, and they soon settled the children on cushions on the terrace and fed them on bread and cheese. They unwalled their supply of mattresses and blankets and made up beds for them. The smaller children fell instantly asleep. The Braccis made room for the Origos and all the children; the rest of the party were taken in by willing Montepulciano families.

The village itself was in a state of fear and uncertainty. The shops were shut and barred, there was no water or light, and food was growing scarce. Schwester Marie put a notice on the door saying 'Kinderheim La Foce' (La Foce's Children's Home), with a Red Cross above it, in the hope of deterring looters. A young partisan, accused of killing a German in Chiusi, was hanged publicly by the Germans from a lamp-post in the main street, and ordered to be left there for twenty-four hours. His swinging body haunted everyone.

There was firing from all directions, as the front moved backwards and forwards around them. And every day', noted Iris on 27 June, 'the pall of fear – reasonable and unreasonable – hangs heavily over this little town.' The Germans had blown up some of the houses on the outskirts and set their guns on the fourteenth-century arcades attached to the hospital. Antonio intervened and the arcades were reprieved.

The next night firing started at around eleven o'clock; it was still going at four in the morning. The children sat trembling, fully dressed, in the cellars. At four-thirty an incredible noise was heard: the entire house shook violently. It turned out that the bridge below had been blown up.

On 29 June the Allies reached the wheat fields below Montepulciano, and a partisan came to ask Antonio to go down and talk to some men from the Scots Guards, who wanted to know the number of Germans left and where their gun emplacements were. The regiment arrived in force that afternoon. As the shelling began again, Antonio got a lift in

318

a military car to La Foce, where he was longing to see the state that the house and property were in. Iris and the children spent one more stuffy, crowded and uncomfortable night in the Braccis' cellars. It was as well that they did so: the Germans scored a direct hit on the house, and one of the bedrooms was damaged. Before they went to bed that night, a couple of British officers appeared at the house. The Braccis offered them wine and they opened some biscuits they had brought with them. Iris wished she had a 'clean frock'. It is 'like a party in a dream', she wrote. 'Our long nightmare is over at last.'

Though the fighting would continue throughout Italy for another ten months, until 25 April 1945, the front had now definitively moved north. For the Origos, the war was over. The wooded countryside around La Foce emptied of its hidden visitors as the prisoners of war came out of hiding and prepared to rejoin the army, though some preferred to sit out the rest of the war as agricultural workers on their hosts' farms, and the partisans went north in the wake of the Allies as they swept by.

It so happened that Ulick Verney, the cousin Iris had played with as a child and who had wanted to marry her, was with the Allied GHQ: He appeared in Montepulciano with a staff car and offered to take Iris, Schwester Marie and the two Origo children back to La Foce. It was an unnerving moment for her: returning to a house she had left not many days before and not knowing whether she might find it flattened and the whole farm destroyed. Things were not as bad as she had feared. The damage was mendable. The house itself had received one direct shell hit in the facade giving on to the garden; the clinic had been partly destroyed; there were shell-holes in the *fattoria* and on the roof. More immediately distressing was what the departing Germans had done to the inside of the house. What they had not been able to carry away they had done their best to destroy. They had ripped the stuffing from the furniture and strewn it, together with photographs and letters found in the desks, around the garden; they had taken the mattresses from the beds and ripped them up; they had emptied and broken up the desks and chairs. Downstairs the house was full of smashed glass and broken furniture. There was no water and no light. The courtyard at the back was one vast refuse heap of broken objects, torn books and broken glass. The lavatories were blocked, filled to the brim and overflowing. Everywhere were remnants of food, thickly covered in flies. The smell was appalling.

And there had been deaths: Gigi, the gardener whose colour sense – orange and purple mixed flowers – she had once deplored but of whom both they were very fond, had been hit by a shell and was lying dead in a ditch; two children from one of the farms were dead, as was one of the peasant farmers. The young partisan in the clinic had died. Because of the danger from the mines, liberally strewn about the woods, the dead were buried just where they were found. The young partisan had already been buried by the Germans, under the cypresses, with a rough cross labelled, in German, 'Unknown Italian'.

Fifteen of the farmhouses had been destroyed, and many had been looted. The peasant farmers and their wives now turned gratefully to Iris for help and advice: about how to fill in forms, how to get information about missing sons and husbands. It was the war and what she had been able to do to help them that finally broke down the barriers between Iris and the families of La Foce. From now on she would be accepted and loved in a way she had never believed possible. More strongly than ever before, she knew now where she belonged. Her decision to return to Italy for the war had been the right one.

Glass and tiles were essential for repairs before winter set in, but it was not clear where they might come from. Iris, once again, had a great deal to do and to arrange: all the cooking pans from La Foce and the farmhouses had been taken and must be urgently replaced. She wanted wool with which to make warm winter clothes for the children who now had no clothes left; and she wanted all the dead animals buried as quickly as possible: there was paratyphoid in the area and she was desperate to stop it reaching the refugee children. As soon as she could find transport, she went to fetch the twenty-three children from the Braccis', and tried to settle them again in their daily routine, while Antonio supervised the bringing-in of the harvest. It was exactly what she once said that she thrived on. She had a very proper knowledge of her own efficiency, and if this could make her somewhat bossy, it would achieve a great deal in the days to come. Elsa's teasing and affectionate nickname of *la progettista* had proved to fit her well. Restoring order to chaos was something she relished. Better still, looking around the half-ruined estate she saw reason for hope. 'For the future,' she wrote at the close of her war diary, which was to become a bestseller when it was published in England in 1946, 'I am hopeful . . . it is here that the deepest qualities of the Italian people will have a chance to show themselves . . . it is they who will bring the land to life again.'

CHAPTER TWELVE

Voices whispering welcome

'When letters begin again,' wrote Iris in the spring of 1944, 'how many other such pieces of news shall we all receive? Which of our close friends and relations are already dead, or will be before we meet them again? And, even among those who survive, what barriers of constraint and unfamiliarity will have arisen in these years – not only of physical separation, but of experience unshared, of differing feelings and opinions? What ties will survive the strain?'

The first news of a death had already reached her: that of her mother. Sometime during the winter of 1942 Sybil had picked up yet another undiagnosed illness. (An unkind Florentine wit remarked: 'Another bug? Might it be the humbug?') Once again she lost a lot of weight and spent most of her days lying down, fretting over the lack of news from Italy and the way the foreign newspapers arrived so late in the day at Montreux. In September 1943 she suddenly began to grow weaker, her arms and body becoming 'as thin as an Indian famine baby's'. Percy and her doctor thought she would rally, as she had so often before. But from November she never left her bed, and, perhaps exhausted by years of cures and medicines, virtually stopped eating. Towards the end, which came on the afternoon of 26 December 1943, she fell unconscious, heavily drugged by morphine. She had starved slowly to death. Percy sent a telegram to Iris in Italian, hoping it would get through: '*Dopo apparve incredilmente giovane, come una piccola fanciulla sottile e stanca*' (Afterwards she looked incredibly young, like a slender and tired young girl). The telegram never reached Iris. But a message smuggled out by a partisan across the Alps arrived at La Foce in January. Later, in a letter that got through, Percy told Iris that they had had two last happy evenings together, talking about Gli Scafari. She had been cremated, as she had wanted, in Vevey with a short service and a reading of St Paul's 'Behold I show you a mystery'. From this day on, Percy kept her ashes on top of his bookcase.

Sybil had once told Berenson how much she wanted and needed to be loved. There is little doubt that Percy, having perhaps married her for respectability and financial security, came to love her and look after her, even though Iris sometimes wondered whether the malnutrition which certainly speeded up her death could have been avoided had he been firmer with her in her early days of hypochondria. But they had been happy, as Percy was to say again and again. 'After more than three months without her,' he wrote bleakly to Iris, 'I begin to realise what life without her really is . . . I am finding it very strange and difficult to have to get back into my own life again, after living for so many years entirely in hers.' Finally, Iris was able to get a letter to Switzerland. (Into it, the censor had put a slip of paper asking for more *deutlich*, legible, writing, to which Percy, in a reply, added 'and my eyesight seconds the plea'.) It was not only Percy who found Iris's handwriting increasingly illegible. Cheap wartime pens with broad and smudging nibs were by now making her famously idiosyncratic handwriting even harder to read. It would never recover.

Later Percy talked of living with a 'dream Sybil' and began work on a memoir of her which he called 'Evening in Italy: a Soliloquy'. Purple, flowery, full of whimsy, it celebrated Sybil at the Villa Medici as a 'lightly informal familiar princess . . . casual minded and most unguarded, so quick that every edge of her seemed lost and blurred in speed, in the urgency of her eagerness' – a somewhat peculiar analogy, given that during their marriage Sybil spent most of her time in bed or reclining on the sofa. After Percy's death in 1963, when Iris and some of his Lubbock relations found the memoir in his bedroom, it was thought far too sentimental to publish. 'Evening in Italy' became known as 'Percy's terrible book about Sybil'.

Percy longed to get back to Gli Scafari, but it was some time before the people who had been occupying it during the war years could be persuaded to move. So he stayed on at Montreux, writing forlornly to an old friend of how strange it was 'after so many years of knowing always the meaning of one's life, whatever it happened to be . . .'

News of another sad death was brought to Iris by Pinsent when he arrived in Florence as an officer with the Monuments, Fine Arts and Archive Commission: Leo Myers had committed suicide on the night of 7 April 1944 by means of an overdose of veronal. Just before taking his life he had written to Charlie Meade: 'By the time you get this letter I shall be dead, so you may as well read it over cursorily before ringing Elsie . . . or taking any other action . . . I have loved and do love both Elsie and Iris, and they both know it and understand. They understand that I have always felt suicide to be legitimate, although often *foolish* . . . But at last I am old enough to be justified [he was sixty-three]: I have accomplished my little job in life; and there is nothing of work or of experience to stand between me and what I so profoundly desire.'

No one in England was much surprised by Myers's suicide. For months, even years, he had been preparing Elsie for his death, writing her long and affectionate letters explaining why he no longer wished to live. When it happened, she seems simply to have accepted it. His last years were marked by a growing sense of isolation. He had turned against all the groups to which he had once belonged, Eton, the Foreign Office, Bloomsbury, and become obsessed with the idea that his increasing depression came from a corrupt social order which was distorting human beings. He felt that even Russia, which he once considered a model society, had betrayed him.

What was more, like Sybil, Myers had always been prey to neurotic ill-health. He was convinced that he had cancer, and no amount of reassurance from doctors could persuade him that his aches were nothing more sinister than age and unfitness. In September 1943 he had written to Elsie: 'I am sixty-two and old, physically and mentally, for my age'. He decided he could not bear the pain and mental anguish of a proposed prostate operation, 'only to die in the end'. He was going to die, he repeated several times, and contradicting much of what he had said before, solely for 'Elsie's sake'. 'This world is not only grey but terrible to me,' he wrote to her on another occasion. 'I am crushed by the world's miseries. And I am a useless thing.' The last letter, addressed to his two daughters, asking them to look after their mother, was dated after his death.

When Pinsent told Iris about Myers she wrote immediately to Elsie, hoping that her letter would get through. 'I can hardly take it in . . . there is such an unbelievable sense of loss. I have had a sort of premonition that I would not see him again.' Myers had left a letter for her, which Elsie sent on to her but which has not been preserved. To judge from Iris's reply to Elsie, however, it must have contained many of the same assurances that Myers had written to his wife: that he was too ill and frightened to carry on, and that his complete block about writing another new book was oppressing him. 'For all of us', wrote Iris, 'the world is poorer. You know, Elsie, even during those five years there was no time when I did not know that he really belonged to you, and we both knew that the time would come for him to return to it, and me to mine . . . Life goes on, but fortunately one goes on loving – and separation or death makes no difference.' Iris asked whether she might have back a little Chinese toad she had given him, and a picture given to her by Edgar Davies that she had lent him. In return she sent Elsie a copy of her memoir of Gianni.

The *Tribune* gave Myers a fine send-off, describing him as 'perhaps the greatest contemporary figure' in English literature, on a par with Thomas Hardy and Joseph Conrad.

No other news which reached Iris at this time was more painful to her than that of these two deaths.

Mary Berenson was also failing. Iris had never been very close to her, but remembered the children's tea parties that meant escape from the dull routine of her schoolroom, and Mary saying that if one behaved as though one were happy, one became so: 'Perhaps', she now wrote to Berenson, 'she was right.'

When Berenson and Nicky Mariano returned to I Tatti from Vallombrosa in September 1944, not having seen Mary for almost a year, they found her weak, lonely and wretched; she now had only a few months to live. The worst of the not very substantial damage to the villa – broken windows and skylights – had already been repaired, and the pictures and books retrieved from their various hiding places. People now began to drop in on I Tatti, most of them American or British, to enquire about Berenson's welfare and check that he had survived the war, though some of course were really no more than tourists, aware of Berenson as an interesting and important figure. Since there was no electricity the bell did not work, and it was hard to prevent people strolling in unannounced. It was not all bad: army lorries were diverted to the Val d'Arno to buy peat for fires at I Tatti, and one officer arranged for a private to call every other day to recharge the battery for Berenson's bedside light. When he was writing his autobiography *Self-Portrait* (he called it 'self dipping'), Iris wrote to him again, a long letter setting out what she owed him. She realised, she said, as she had on other occasions, 'more clearly *what it* is that I owe you . . . that "joyous offering" which you have made, to a greater or lesser degree, to all who knew you who had "eyes to see and ears to hear" must, I suppose, have taken different forms for each of us. For me it is as if you had given me, every time that I was with you, something of your own gift of vision . . . Most people . . . have great areas of their mind, which, in maturity, become stale and, mirror coated with dust, no longer capable of reflection . . . But you "have exhausted nothing that the human spirit has created". And this unfailing freshness and acuteness of vision is *contagious*, while we are with you we think we share it; when we have left you, our eyes are forever a little sharper, our ears a little better attuned . . .'

Not everyone revered Berenson: there were those who found his autocracy unnerving and his conversation too erudite. Iris herself was not always so fulsome in her praise of him. But there were aspects of him that she genuinely admired, and if he was not quite the mentor her grandfather and Monti, her classics teacher, had been, she felt that when it came to looking at pictures and taking in the world around her, there was no one from whom she had learnt more. Berenson wrote most of *Self-Portrait* during his year at Vallombrosa, noting that he had been 'born to talk and not to write and, worse still, to converse rather than to talk and then only with stimulating interlocutors . . . Pity', he wrote, 'that talk is not self-registering. Hundreds and hundreds, thousands and thousands of yards of paper would preserve my bright sayings, my provoking epithets, my wit, my wisdom and my learning, in short the outpourings of my heart and mind and spirit.' It must have been a relief for him to return from almost solitary exile in the mountains to an audience once again, even if there was no immediate prospect of electricity and Florence was running out of candles.

Iris suffered one more loss in the immediate post-war years, though this time a departure rather than a death. Cecil Pinsent, mentioned in despatches for his excellent work with the Monuments Commission, was demobbed in September 1945, but stayed on in Italy only for a while. He felt there was no longer a life for him in Florence, writing a little sadly to Berenson that 'though dead tired of Italy' he was yet strongly drawn to it, 'if only to one or two focal points, yourself and Iris chiefly, for I Tatti and La Foce were the scenes of my most poignant experiences . . .' As a person with whom she had spent so much time, and gone through so much, Iris missed him acutely. He went to Exeter, to share a house with his sister-in-law, Kitty, but returned every year to Italy, to tinker with the garden she had made before the war, or undertake some small new commission. The last was a memorial, in the form of a classical temple, on the edge of the woods above the village of Bolgheri. It was made for Flavia della Gherardesca when her husband, Antonio's old friend Ugolino, was killed in a car crash; he had once said to her that underground crypts always seemed damp to him, and he would prefer to be in the open air. Pinsent's original plan was for a simple circle of tombs, with a single cross; but the local bishop protested that such a design was only suitable for a battlefield, so he changed it to a small temple with an altar, and square columns at the corners. Berenson, to whom he showed the model, did not like it; but Flavia did.

There was always something of the journalist in Iris. She was intrigued by events she witnessed, and even more by the people taking part in them, and their ambitions and failings. If her travel diaries of the 1920s and 1930s were uncharacteristically flat and lifeless, her writing during the war years was altogether more lively, her eye more alert to all that was interesting and strange. The friendship of Elsa, with her passionate concern for social problems, combined with Iris's own experiences of war, had made her far more alive to the gulf that separated the world she had known from that of ordinary people, and brought a certain humility of outlook. Although biography and social history were what she liked to write, her diaries of the war years, both published and unpublished, contain some of her best writing.

On 2 July 1944 her cousin Ulick took Iris to breakfast with General Sir Oliver Leese, commander of the Eighth Army. In an unpublished part of her diary she describes the luxurious caravans the officers lived in, with their gleaming metalwork, and the breakfast of eggs and bacon 'served on nice china, at a table on the lawn'. Everyone was extremely civil, and altogether it reminded her of the Fourth of June at Eton. After breakfast the General and his senior officers put on straw hats as protection from the summer sun and began to discuss mutual acquaintances. In tones somewhat reminiscent of the traveller and Arabist Freya Stark when describing a pleasant military gathering, she noted that Sir Oliver, 'talks a little, with a quiet, unstressed optimism, about the next stages of the campaign'. Iris had spoken very little English for four years, and had certainly not gossiped with top-ranking military officers about London affairs. In her new, critical voice she expressed some of the strangeness she felt, those very 'barriers of constraint and unfamiliarity' she had pondered at the beginning of the year: 'Is it that I have been away from England too long or is there really something a little sinister, as well as irritating, in so bland a detachment? I think of the women and children I have seen, crouching in ditches under shellfire, like terrified animals . . . and then I look at these well fed, humorous, cultured and oh so comfortable soldiers . . . with their family jokes and their assumption of "privilege" – and their blank Olympian detachment . . . and a deep wave of depression sweeps over me.' Unlike Freya Stark, who revelled in them, Iris quickly grew impatient with the niceties of British diplomacy and social small talk, and had no taste for uniforms, medals and braid. It was some time before any feeling of belonging to the Anglo-Saxon world returned to her – and in some senses it never did.

Ulick asked Iris whether she would like to go to Rome with him. It was the sort of outing she longed for. Leaving the children with Schwester Marie, she and Ulick set off in the General's car to join the long line of jeeps on the road to Viterbo, the more direct route along the Via Cassia having been blown up. She marvelled at the sheer numbers of the British forces. Orvieto had not been bombed, but Viterbo was in ruins. On the Via Cassia she saw 'large negroes (both African and American) working on the roads'. They reached Rome at three o'clock to find every hotel commandeered by Allied officers, but finally persuaded the Grand Hotel to give them rooms. Strolling round the city, Iris was appalled to find the Borghese Gardens full of tents, trailers, car parks, and a 'seething mass of troops'. Most of the Allied troops who first occupied Rome were Americans, and scores of GIs were to be seen lying in the shade of the plane trees, sleeping off heavy drinking. Their attitude towards the Italians – a country that had changed sides when it looked to be losing – was one of disdain, which extended to the monuments that distinguished Rome.

In the three days Iris spent seeing old friends she noticed how thin and worn they were. Rome had suffered from food shortages for months, and the Americans had decided to segregate the starving refugees outside the city and reduce rations within: Romans were now living on vegetables and a little rationed bread. The children looked shrunken and hungry. Deploring the muddle and the misguided policies, Iris noted that the new Italian government was really only interested in *epurazione* (purification), the elimination from every sector of the population of anyone in any way connected with the Fascists. In their haste to do so they were carelessly losing some of the cleverest and most necessary: doctors, lawyers, teachers and scientists. Everywhere she went she heard details of the looting, arrests, torture and executions carried out by the Germans. From old friends among the Allied forces she learnt with great relief that her American grandmother was alive and well, and that there had been no losses among her close New York friends. Rome had become a city of black marketeers, and she could not afford to replace, as she had hoped, the cups, plates and pans taken by the Germans from every farmhouse at La Foce.

Back at La Foce, the harvest was being taken in. A team of oxen was killed by a mine and the driver's legs smashed; just outside Chianciano, a woman was killed by a half-buried mine.

331

Her British Army connections were unable to help her with mine-clearers, or even a mine-detector: the British were moving north and had no men or equipment to spare from making the way ahead safe for the troops. The postmaster of Chianciano unexpectedly announced some experience of explosives, and soon he and several volunteers could be heard pacing the woods, to the occasional sound of explosions. 'How strange it is', Iris wrote to Irene, 'to be able to *look forward* again – to see the horizon widening, instead of narrowing . . . Most of the garden is beans and cauliflower, but there is still jasmine on the walls and there are still fireflies in the corn.'

Most of all Iris wanted to go to Florence. She had no idea how the Villa Medici had withstood the war, and there were many old friends of whom she had had no news. By 21 July 1944 the Allies were within twenty kilometres of the city. As the Germans retreated, so they looted, burnt or destroyed all they could not take with them, and shot civilians in reprisal for any German deaths. The two main telegraph exchanges had been smashed; the city's flour mill and pasta factories were blown up; ambulances and hearses were requisitioned for transport. A colonel who had been there told her the Germans were planning to blow up the bridges. 'Looks as if there won't be much left,' he ended, laughing loudly. To Italian ears, Iris noted sharply, 'it is less funny'.

Tuscany was being fought for inch by inch, as the German resistance proved tougher than had been expected. When the Allies finally reached the southern end of Florence, on 4 August, they found the Germans had indeed blown up all the bridges, including the magnificent Ponte Trinitá, sending its statues into the Arno; they had however spared the Ponte Vecchio, as some small gesture to Hitler's half-hearted agreement that Florence, like Rome, should be an open city. But the streets leading up to it had all been destroyed in order to slow the Allied advance, their inhabitants driven from the their houses and flats into the Boboli Gardens. Iris found her capacity for optimism and understanding was beginning to fade; hearing of the Allied landings in the south of France on 14 August she noted 'negative relief at the end of the war – yes, infinite. But positive faith in the future? I don't know. I think we are all tired, deeply tired mentally as well as physically – and have almost lost the capacity to look ahead.'

Still the battle for Florence was not over. While the Germans continued to shell the northern part of the city, the Allies advanced slowly through the southern outskirts. From the Monte Vecchio, Berenson later said, he had been able to hear the sound of the guns even as the Germans dynamited viaducts, bridges and roads: 'Cannonading continues under a sky as crystalline, as pure as has ever been seen . . . from dark to well on in the morning, a continuous roar and rattle of traffic . . . Living like moles in the dark is depressing, stupefying and hypnotic,' he wrote later in *Rumour and Reflections*; 'the mind gets lazier, emptier and almost ceases to function, leaving one in a state of hallucination.' Young Florentine women wore Red Cross armbands when they needed to leave their houses, since it was said that the Germans would not molest nurses.

On 1 September Iris heard that Fiesole had been liberated. When she was at last allowed to go there, she found the Villa Medici damaged and full of booby traps, and the Villino in flames. Florence had been reduced almost to nothing: no transport, light, gas, water; no meat, vegetables, fruit or milk. All the windows had been shattered. 'The people', wrote Iris, 'look *really* hungry.' She was at last able to get news of friends such as Nannina Fossi, who had been her postbox for Elsa and was now occupying herself with helping in the hospital. Everyone had terrible stories to tell, not only of their own tragedies, but of the squalor and remorselessness of the Germans, who before they left relieved themselves everywhere – on carpets, mattresses, chairs. Others described boisterous young Fascist officers so gun-happy that they carried their machine-guns in one hand and put their grenades on the tables when they ate. Susanna Agnelli, later a minister in the Italian government, was in Florence during the war, and in her memoirs, *We Always Wore Sailor Suits*, wrote that they 'looked rather like a ballet troupe preparing a performance about war'. Others told Iris how two hundred Fascist and German sharpshooters had settled in the top floors of houses leading into the city and shot at whoever moved; and how, at dusk, a friar pushed a cart around the town, picking up the corpses, which he piled one on top of the other, their heads hanging down over the sides, and took them to the cemetery, where coffins that had been left unburied were exploding in the heat. She had news too, of her friend the German Consul, Dr Gerhardt Wolff, who had managed to do so much to help the most persecuted Florentines during the German occupation. He had survived the fighting.

By the next day, the Germans were virtually gone, the last groups of wounded men limping slowly out of the city, clinging to one another, as the Florentines stood in silence and stared. Because of the shortage of petrol, each lorry that passed was towing another vehicle. When the last had disappeared up the road the church bells rang out, as the Allies in their open jeeps came bumping over the rubble. They smelt, as Susanna Agnelli put it, 'of different, other armies, of soap and strong tea'.

The partisans had declared a wish to go through the town first, without Allied support. A British officer, The Hon. Hubert

Howard, a friend of Iris's serving with the Psychological Warfare Branch, was one of a small number of Allied officers who followed closely in their steps. The streets of the medieval city were deserted and shadowy. There was no one about. Then Howard noticed that the bottom halves of the shuttered windows lining the streets were all slightly open, and that hundreds of pairs of eyes were staring at him. 'Then', as he recalled later, 'there reached our ears a strange and wonderful sound which we shall surely never hear again. Behind the shutters we were made aware of the gentle muffled applause of hundreds of hands and the sound of voices whispering welcome.'

It soon became plain to Iris that, quite apart from hundreds of homeless refugees, Florence was full of children, lost, orphaned or who had followed the soldiers northwards and now been abandoned. There was little she could do for them, but on her return to La Foce she heard that a group of starving refugees headed south was expected to pass by the house. She hastily prepared all the food she had left, peaches and bread, and was promised milk and sugar by the Allied forces, for the children travelling with them. 'But nothing arrived: only two large lorries packed with angry men, weeping women and hungry and screaming children.'

Iris had not seen Elsa for two years. From time to time, when he visited Florence, Antonio had been able to leave letters with Nannina Fossi, who found ways of getting them to Bologna, north of the Germans' Gothic Line, where Elsa was looking after her elderly father in their family home. From the few letters Elsa herself managed to get through, it was clear that, though devoted to her father, she felt trapped and lonely away from the friends she was so close to. 'I feel as if I had been crippled,' she wrote to Iris. 'Tell me about yourself, send me news of everything . . . and above all, tell me about you, you, you. How are you? What are you thinking about? What are you doing? Where are you going?' Her feelings of being isolated and forgotten grew stronger, and Elsa complained that at Nono, her family home, she now felt like a visitor, 'ever more prey to melancholy, which comes in waves,' so that she took to her bed. She longed for Iris to be there. She believed it very unlikely that she would survive the heavy Allied bombing of Bologna and wrote a farewell letter to Iris: 'I had hoped, I hope still to see you all again . . . I shall not die content; I accept the will of God and I ask for his mercy . . . but I can't even pray . . . Thank you for all the good you have done me, all that was bright and clean.'

As the war moved slowly northwards, Iris was asked by the Italian Red Cross to accompany them in the wake of the Allies. Passing close to Nono but unable to leave her group, she agonised that she could get no news of the Dallolios. After the Allied advance in north Italy in April 1945 Bologna descended into anarchy as the partisans set about exacting revenge on those suspected of having helped the Fascists. Secret courts whose only verdict was death were held in basements and cellars.

Iris was asked to visit the British officers in charge of the city to see if they could not do something about these summary executions. They told her that there was nothing they could do, as they were about to pull out, but they thought the reprisals would probably cease soon. It has been estimated that by the end of the last phase of the war 10,000 Italian Fascists or suspected Fascists had been killed. Umberto Zanotti Bianco, the head of the Red Cross, sent Iris to Reggio-Emilia to locate the head nurse of the Red Cross, Sister Paola Menada, who together with all the other anti-Fascist nurses had gone into hiding after refusing to swear an oath of loyalty to Mussolini and the Saló Republic, and escort them back so that they could help in Bologna.

It was now that Iris learnt that Nono had been destroyed, but that Elsa and her father were safe. They found each other in Bologna, and together went to see the ruins of the house. Everything had gone, first bombed and then reduced to rubble by a British military bulldozer after the Allies were informed that the General was a well-known Fascist. Not one brick remained on another, and even the chapel had been totally flattened. What very few possessions had escaped the bombs and the bulldozer had been looted. In the garden, only one climbing rose remained alive: the two women dug it up to plant on Elsa's terrace in Rome.

Elsa had grown fond of Antonio. She admired him and liked his straightforward and genial ways. In 1948, when Zanotti Bianco announced his retirement from the presidency of the Italian Red Cross on the grounds of his ill-health, Elsa discussed the possibility of appointing Antonio with their old friend Umberto Morra, who had spent the war working for the Red Cross. In a letter to Morra she set out Antonio's strengths and weaknesses:

> The disadvantages: not many acquaintances or friends in the political world, little experience of office work, administrative skills, or running an organisation. The advantages: political and financial independence of thought, perfect knowledge of four languages, as well as of international life, particularly Anglo-Saxon and American, great deal of respect and liking for foreigners . . . Very cordial, yet firm and well able to stand up to opponents . . . Developed sense of social needs . . . Clear in discussions, would talk very well, if somewhat timid . . . Absolutely without personal vanity

or ambition . . . Would make a fine representative of the
Italian Red Cross abroad at any time . . . Antonio is *good*,
and given what the Red Cross stands for in the world, it
would be no bad thing to have for President a man who
is compassionate simply because he is good.

Antonio was not appointed, and nothing was mentioned to Iris.
But it says a great deal about how Antonio was perceived not
only by the post-war political order, but by the anti-Fascists –
Zanotti Bianco, Umberto Morra and Elsa had all been passionate
anti-Fascists – that they were ready to appoint him to such a
position.

The end of the war came slowly. Unknown to Mussolini,
the Germans had been trying to negotiate with the Allies for
the surrender of the German armies in Italy for some time.
Throughout 1944 and 1945 the partisans were growing ever
more numerous and organised – people later spoke of some
10,000 men, swollen by escaped prisoners of war and Italian
soldiers who had deserted – and the Allies had been dropping
them supplies. The Committee of National Liberation for
Northern Italy, a coalition of five groups, gave orders for a
general uprising against Mussolini's remaining government
on 25 April 1945. Mussolini continued to turn down all
suggestions of unconditional surrender, and on 19 April moved
into the Prefecture in Milan.

Bologna was finally taken by the Allies on 21 April; British
and American soldiers advanced along the Po valley; Modena,
Reggio, then Parma fell to them. The partisans occupied Genoa,
and the Germans quickened their withdrawal. Mussolini, urged
to escape while there was still time, at first refused, saying that

while he knew perfectly well he himself was finished, he could not believe Fascism was. On 28 April he was captured by partisans, shot, and hanged upside down in Milan's Piazzale Loreto.

The terms of the proposed Armistice with Italy had laid down that post-war treatment would depend on how much armed help Italy gave. For the young Italian men and boys who had grown up knowing of no political rule except for Fascism, and had watched the confusion of Italy's war, it was sometimes hard to know what to feel. But as the weeks passed, and the atrocities committed by the retreating Germans intensified, so they became more and more hostile towards their former ally. For the British and Americans their main value as partisans lay in tying up large numbers of German troops. Unfortunately the partisan movement itself was split by squabbles between the Communists (Garibaldi) and the non-Communists (Green Flames), and partisan leaders irresponsibly wasted time attacking German posts, instead of concentrating on the sabotage they had agreed to carry out. Since such attacks invariably led to savage German reprisals, the partisans were not popular everywhere. Not very far from La Foce, at a small town in the foothills of the Apennines, when some retreating Germans were apparently killed by partisan sniper fire, General Max Simon, the German in charge, decided to follow the spirit of Kesselring's order of June 1944 regarding severe measures against partisans and those who harboured them. In one of the most notoriously vicious incidents of the war, SS troops and Fascists machine-gunned the entire congregation of the church, then rounded up all the inhabitants left in their houses and drove them to the cemetery where they too were massacred. Altogether 1830 people were killed. In their efforts to deal with the partisans, the Germans committed atrocity after atrocity. Though the orders issued by the High Command stipulated that there should be proper trials and courts, the soldiers continued to shoot and hang unarmed civilians, loot their belongings and burn down their houses.

As the end of the war drew near an estimated sixty partisan brigades consisting of every sort of person and profession, deserters, Poles, Canadians, elderly professors, lawyers, young boys, controlled long stretches of the mountains, from where they descended to torment the retreating Germans. The Allies feared civil war would develop as the Germans finally pulled out of Italy, leaving the Garibaldi and the Green Flames vying for power. Six anti-Fascist parties emerged in Rome to form the Central Committee of National Liberation. They bickered among themselves. Churchill dismissed them as 'political ghosts'. But it was to prove even more complicated in the months to come. The Central Committee also bickered and disagreed with the five-party National Liberation Committee of Northern Italy, the very success of whose guerrilla activities in the spring of 1945 later provided fertile soil for political divisions between north and south.

The general climate of confusion and mistrust led also to a wave of arrests, both by the Allies as they moved north and by the partisans, of those suspected of fomenting trouble. Count Umberto Morra, accused by the Allies of holding meetings of Communists at Metelliano, was picked up with a group of friends and put into prison. Iris hurried to her British military friends, and he was released. 'What wonderful news!' she wrote to Margherita Bracci. 'I really do believe that it was my intervention for Umberto that secured his release . . . and I'm so happy. But I believe that it will be harder to get the others released.' In Morra's case, the hardships of gaol were somewhat mitigated by the fact that his manservant brought him in meals of spaghetti and chicken.

The Jews fared less badly under the Italians than perhaps anywhere else in German-occupied Europe. There was no particular history of anti-Semitism among Italians, and as the Germans began their deportations, so all sides dragged their heels in helping them. Despite the damaging effect of Mussolini's anti-Semitic laws of 1938, in practice even many Fascists helped Jewish friends, and in Saló Mussolini himself took steps to hinder the Germans in their pursuit. All over Italy, wherever Italians retained any power, they simply refused to hand Jews over to the Germans. In Rome, where some 12,000 Jews lived, mainly in the ghetto, Pope Pius XII, who had done nothing to protest against the slaughter of Jews in Occupied Europe, did eventually open convents and monasteries to Jews on the run and instructed priests to help them. In Florence, quite apart from Dr Wolff, who as ever did what he could, the mayor himself quietly got rid of any evidence of the 'racial' origins of the town's citizens, telling the Germans it had been destroyed in a fire; in Umbria, a number of Jews were dressed up as novices and hidden in convents.

Kesselring, as Commander of the German Army in Italy, was determined to push through as many deportations as possible. He was helped in this from January 1944 by the appointment to the Ministry for Jewish Affairs of an Italian called Giovanni Preziosi, who had orders to propose new laws similar to the Nuremberg Laws of 1935. Once again, other ministers dragged their feet. Naturally not every Italian helped the Jews, and deportations and shootings did go on. At the end of the war, it was estimated that of the 32,000 Italian and 12,500 foreign Jews in Rome, 7682 had perished. One of the 979 out of 8369 deportees who survived the camps to come home was a baby, born in Belsen.

The very end of the campaign came quickly. On the night of 9 April 1945 the final Allied offensive began. Allied soldiers entered Bologna on 21 April; on the 29 April, the day after Mussolini's execution, the German Command in Italy signed an act of unconditional surrender at Caserta. Hitler had ordered a scorched earth policy; his senior generals, seeing the end coming, cancelled his orders. Now began the widespread execution of Fascists and suspected Fascist sympathisers; sometimes they took the form of massacres. These were the reprisals that Iris had tried and failed to stop on her journey north with the Red Cross. It was now a question of political stability and the rebuilding of a country in which nearly half the hospitals were out of commission, 8,000 bridges had been destroyed, and sixty per cent of roads were impassable. Nearly half a million homeless people were adrift and wandering up and down the country in search of their lost families, food, and somewhere to live.

Thousands of Italians had sheltered people on the run, at great risk to themselves, with remarkable generosity. For the most part, the rich landowners had not been among them. Very few indeed of the aristocratic families are remembered for their help towards escaping prisoners, partisans or deserters. In this the Origos can be counted as almost unique. They had helped all who came to them in need without enquiring who they were, giving them food and shelter, until they had used up most of their supplies, with little heed for their own safety. For two dangerous years they had turned no one away. Across the whole of the Val d'Orcia, and beyond, the name of Origo became known to the escaping prisoners of war, so that men in desperate need found their way to La Foce's door. A band of about two hundred partisans eventually made the estate their base, and they were fed largely by La Foce's kitchens. When the day came that the Origos' own prisoners of war were able to go free, the Origos had hurried to the Castelluccio to plan their escape from the Germans. Even when they were reported to the local Fascist officials and appeared to be in some danger themselves, they had preferred to stay at La Foce where they were needed.

Yet after the war was over, when claims were made on the Allies for financial restitution of all that had been paid out, and the Allies were extraordinarily ungenerous and petty, the Origos were not among those who came forward. The British recommended 443 awards; the Americans 17. But only the American awards were ever actually conferred. The British ones were withheld, 'mainly for political reasons'; and then simply forgotten. Were it not for the testimonials of those who had sheltered at La Foce for two dangerous years, and for the book of war diaries that Iris was now about to put together, it is possible that all they had done might long since have been forgotten. On the wall of the Castelluccio the Origos put up a tablet in memory of all those who had died, whether soldier, civilian, partisan, friend or enemy: '*Tu che passi e guardi / La pace di questa valle / Sosta e ricorda / I nostri morti*' (You who pass by and feel the peace of this valley, pause and remember our dead).'

Inspecting the damage to La Foce, Iris calculated that 98 cattle had been either killed or stolen, together with 600 sheep, 150 pigs, and all the hens and geese. She worried about how to feed the children or build up supplies once again in a country that was now destitute and hungry. It was a green and lush spring. She sat in the garden reading the papers, the new Italian ones, starting up one after the other, and the English ones when she could get hold of them, but she felt increasingly alienated from the post-war world that everyone was now writing about. 'In all of them, or nearly all,' she wrote in her unpublished diary for 1945, 'there is a conviction – implicit, even where not stated –

343

that under certain forms of government the "good life" is not possible. With every year of my life, I disagree more profoundly with that view. I believe, of course, that under certain forms of government – "totalitarianism", whether Fascist or Communist – the free development of the individual, the full blooming of the human spirit is more *difficult* than in others. But I believe that in all countries, under all governments, the "good life" is *possible*. It is, like Heaven, not a place but a state.'

With England at war with Italy, Iris had at first felt herself at a loss. Where did her loyalties lie? With her grandfather and his intense commitment to Britain and its values? With Antonio and her two half-Italian daughters? And what of America and the father she still remembered with such affection? Fearing to spend too long pondering her opposing allegiances, she had resolved that her only possible position was to keep as 'steady' as she could, 'to close my ears to alarming rumours and my heart to nostalgia and dismay'. Even so, she would say that nothing was more painful to her during the years that Italy was cut off from news than not knowing what had happened to those she loved.

It was then that she decided to keep a diary. The work in the Roman office of the Red Cross had left her very little time for herself. The few fragments that she managed to get down between 1939 and 1943 have never been published; nor have those written later between 1944 and 1945. It was only when she returned to La Foce after the German occupation that the diary began to take shape, Iris having determined to 'put down each day as it occurred, and whenever possible only first hand knowledge'. She would add and touch up nothing later. She kept to her plan. The diary opens on 30 January 1943, with the arrival of her first group of bombed-out refugee children; it ends on 5 July 1944, after the departure of the Germans.

In the diary – consciously, thinking of publication? or because it reflected her feelings about herself? – Iris consistently made light of her own experiences at La Foce, comparing her relatively easy life with the hardships endured elsewhere; saying that it was not a question of weighing between courage and cowardice, but between 'equally urgent conflicting duties and responsibilities'. How did one decide between giving shelter to an escaped Allied prisoner of war and putting in danger the peasant family you asked to hide him? At the end of each day, she noted, she would ask herself, 'Have I done too much? Have I done enough?' The very writing of the diary made her reflect that she was becoming wary of generalisations about countries; and that what she really believed in was individuals and their relationships.

At first the diary was hidden casually among the children's books in the nursery. Later, as the Germans drew nearer, she buried most of it, apart from the current pages, in a tin box in the garden, together with propaganda leaflets and her jewellery. Some of the entries were written at night, after the household was in bed; a few while Germans were actually in the house.

It is not clear who had the idea of turning the diary into a book – perhaps it was Iris herself. In any case, Jonathan Cape, who had in the past published both Sybil and Percy Lubbock, brought it out early in 1947. *War in Val d'Orcia* contains some of the best of Iris's personal writing: at times almost dispassionate, at others quietly outraged, at others again, philosophical and reflective. It is also among the best books written about wartime Italy. In its very lack of artifice and its simplicity, it stands apart. The people she describes are real, and she writes about them not only with sympathy but with a redeeming wryness and humour.

War in Val d'Orcia was an immediate success. The reviews, as for her *Leopardi* and *Allegra*, were excellent. Many reviewers took the opportunity to air their own ideas about the nature of Fascism, but not one failed to praise Iris's style, and her evocative writing. It was an age of generous reviewing. 'One could discourse at length on the literary quality of *War in Val d'Orcia*,' wrote L. P. Hartley in the *Sketch*, highlighting her humour, charity, intelligence and selflessness. In the *Tatler*, Elizabeth Bowen remarked upon her true and sane sense of proportion, and described some of the scenes as 'Biblical'. Even Berenson, to whom she sent a copy, found in it 'una musica'.

In Italy, where *Leopardi* and *Allegra* had been all but ignored, the diary's success was greeted with astonishment. In the wake of praise from Piero Calamandrei, one of Italy's most prominent literary figures (his long article later became the preface for the Italian edition), reporters were sent to La Foce to interview the unknown English writer living in their midst. Their tone was one of surprise, hardly flattering to someone with several highly praised books to her credit. She was described as 'tall, serious, big boned, measured and elegant, even if of great simplicity'. The incredulity sometimes bordered on rudeness. 'Why wasn't Iris part of the literary scene?' asked one. Why did she never attend literary gatherings? Was she afraid of being attacked? Was she solitary by nature? Iris declined to be drawn, merely reminding him that she was English, and her literary friends and influences were English; that she had been a friend of Virginia Woolf; and that, 'as is customary among the English', she had spent much of her life in the country. 'I hope', she added, 'that you can see that it's nothing to do with feeling superior or arrogant: it's to do with how one organises one's life.' Organisation, control, plans – it was in these that safety lay.

After that she gave an interesting answer. Asked what plans she had for the future, she replied that her most pressing concern was an 'essay on compassion, in its original meaning of "to suffer with", from the Crucifixion to Simone Weil'. After that, she would write her memoirs: 'If you think about it, all women who reach a certain age feel an irresistible urge to go back over their own lives.' Her memoirs had not been mentioned before, at least not to her publishers, or in any of her letters that exist. Had *War in Val d'Orcia* given her a taste for more personal writing?

In England, as in Italy, among those who were able to read them, the publication of Iris's diaries had one particular unexpected and significant result. Elizabeth Bowen was the first to wonder, in her *Tatler* review of the book, whether this was 'the first record of the war in Italy from the civilian angle?' The *Times Literary Supplement* also saw more in the diary than just a 'commentary on the Italian campaign in particular . . .': it allowed 'the war to be seen historically instead of nationally'. The *TLS* writer also commented on Dr Gerhardt Wolff as a 'civilised man' who had probably done more than any Italian to protect Italian houses and works of art.

The Allies had in fact been extremely slow and reluctant to give the Italians any due for the part they played after 1943. War correspondents had always tended to ignore the dedication of the loyal Italian soldiers who joined forces with the Allies, and had even given little praise to the partisans. Despite the collaboration of the Italian army in the liberation, Italy was treated in the peace negotiations as an enemy power. The terms laid down by the Allies were harsh: a limit to their naval forces, and an agreement that Fascism would henceforth be banned. In fact, the traditional good will and friendship between Italy and England, dating back to the Risorgimento, had been badly dented by the attack on Abyssinia in 1935. What Iris's book had drawn attention to was the fact that ordinary Italians, whether in towns or villages or on farms, had given exceptional help to escaping Allied prisoners of war, without which many more of them would have died. And they had done so at profound risk to themselves and their families, particularly after the German announcement that anyone found sheltering a prisoner of war would be shot. For those many thousands of brave Italians, *War in Val d'Orcia* was a rightful recognition of what they had done.

It sparked off an enormous number of letters. Former soldiers who had spent eighteen months on the run, helped by one family after another, wrote to Iris in their dozens, to describe their adventures. A few had even passed through La Foce. Many others came from people who liked and admired the Italians, and felt that a terrible injustice had been done to them. Daniel Marlow from South Wales wrote to say that he had been one of the men on the train bombed not far from La Foce, 'the boys trapped like rats in those rail tracks', and had made his way south with the help of Italian families. One woman wrote to tell Iris that *War in Val d'Orcia* had helped her and her husband overcome their reluctance to let their daughter marry an Italian; another claimed it had enabled her to shed the suspicion and revulsion she admitted to having felt towards Italy since the war. Lionel Fielden, who had worked for the BBC and spent many years in Italy, spoke for many who had read the book in writing to Iris: 'Personally I feel very keen that more interest should be whipped up and help given [to break the wall of indifference about Italy] . . . I hate to see Anglo-Italian friendship withering away . . . I have a vague and misty idea that it's a crucial time for people who want Anglo-Italian friendship to get together and do something about it: and you obviously should be the *fons et origo*. What a nasty pun and I wasn't thinking about it.' As it had always been one of Iris's intentions to show the British just how generous and selfless the ordinary Italians had been, she must have been delighted by Fielden's words. The diary not only made her far better-known as a writer: it also contributed to the slow process of revising the image of the Italians at war. In *La Stampa*, Alessandro Passerin d'Entreves, Professor of Italian Studies at Oxford, wrote that here at last was a book which did not play on old stereotypes and present Italy as an *opera buffa*. 'For myself', he wrote, 'I wouldn't hesitate to say that *War in Val d'Orcia* has done us more good than a battle won by our side.' In a speech given many years later, Iris herself said: 'What is absolutely clear is that the Italian peasants of this area, as of many others, could not have done more . . . They saw in these people men in need of help. In these terrible hours, they turned back to age-old traditions of hospitality.'

The final paragraph of *War in Val d'Orcia* is characteristic of Iris at her most optimistic. 'The day will come', she wrote, 'when at last the boys will return to their ploughs, and the dusty clay-hills of the Val d'Orcia will again "blossom like the rose". Destruction and death have visited us, but now – there is hope in the air.'

One of Iris's most hopeful enterprises concerned La Foce's children. Remembering only too clearly the lost children she had seen wandering around Florence, she now began to look for orphans, and children whose parents had been deported to the camps. Once most of the child evacuees from the bombing of Genoa and Turin had gone home to their parents, she decided to turn the Casa dei Bambini into a home, as little as possible like an institution, limited to twenty children between the ages of four and twelve.

International Social Service was an organisation based in Geneva with the job of resettling refugees or helping them to find their families. Elsa had been one of the founders and was the director of the Roman office; money, to start with at least, came from the International Committee of the Red Cross. It was in talking to Elsa that the idea came to Iris that she should take in children referred to her by the ISS, and then help them to find their families; if they could not be found the children would stay at the Casa dei Bambini either until they moved on to some trade or were adopted, for the most part in America.

The first twenty children arrived in La Foce to surroundings made as soothing and homelike as possible after the trauma of the war. The model was a large family, with the Origos as grandparents, and the children were looked after and taught by La Tata. Like the earlier refugees, they were to inhabit a world 'in which reigned order and stability'. In a letter written much later, Iris remarked that she had come to believe that 'every child (in fact every one of God's creatures) should be taken as he is. We can help, but only rarely can we transform.' As with many of Iris's remarks, the sharp and interesting part came in its tail.

Soon, the authorities from Florence and elsewhere were making the long journey to La Foce to try to persuade Iris to take in more children. Though she refused ever to have more than twenty at anyone time in the Casa dei Bambini, she did throw herself into setting up adoptions, mostly in the United States. Requests for children poured in; they were processed by the ISS and vetted by Iris. Once a child had left to be adopted by an American family, a social worker and the local Italian Consul would keep an eye on them. Not all children, particularly those too traumatised by the war or abused by their parents, were suitable for adoption. These stayed at La Foce until they were old enough to leave for training or further education. Later, when Iris became President of the Italian branch of the ISS, she continued to run her Casa dei Bambini, and to welcome adoptive parents for interviews and vetting. She was not always entirely easy to deal with. If irritated, she could be imperious; her views on the upbringing of children became, with the years, more fixed. Would-be parents who demurred were rebuked. Yet what everyone who visited La Casa dei Bambini remarked on was how affectionate and tender she was with the children, and how good at soothing the disturbed ones. Hopeful parents went away either overcome by admiration or intimidated, their interviews not helped either by Iris's somewhat haughty manner, or the speed with which she talked. 'She could be like an Empress,' remembers one woman who worked for her. 'A request for a meeting could sound like a royal summons.' And by this time she had worked in this field for so long that she genuinely believed she knew best what was good for La Foce's children, and she had little patience with those who ventured to disagree. 'She could be like a match and flare up if you made a mistake; but she had great self-control.' When spending her own money, and she spent a very great deal on her projects, she was really interested in the most needy. 'She wanted to know exactly how it had been spent'.

It was after the war that Iris really began to reveal her innate generosity and charitable spirit. Many of her friends have to this day only the dimmest idea of her many commitments. Yet in the villages around La Foce, as in Florentine hospitals – she set up one for children with tuberculosis – and American towns, there are many young men and women whose lives have been completely altered by what she did for them. Seldom was it just a question of money: it was her interest and encouragement that counted. Not far from La Foce, at Chianciano Scala, lives Professor Roberto Baiocchi, who at the age of nine had to leave his studies to help his destitute parents. But he was an ambitious boy, and a teacher who knew Iris sent him to see her. She paid for his schooling, then his training. 'Above all,' he says, 'she gave me moral support. I would never have got through without it.' He is now a plastic surgeon. There is Liberata Nardi, one of the refugee children who arrived at La Foce early in 1943. Iris recognised Liberata's aptitude at once – 'she is a born teacher,' she noted in her diary for 10 February – and after the war paid for her training. Liberata says today that teaching has given her the greatest pleasure in her life; as a new graduate, her first thought was to go back to help at La Foce. Iris's papers are full of letters of thanks typed, handwritten, in pencil. They come from all over Italy, the United States, and England, where her adoption plans eventually spread. They thank for a course, a mortgage, an operation; for financial help for the refugees of the Hungarian revolution; for help after a flood, an epidemic, an earthquake. Influenced by Elsa, Umberto Morra and Umberto Zanotti Bianco, as well as by the years of war and the miseries she witnessed, these various charitable activities soon came to occupy as much as half Iris's time; and in the end they came to be as important to her as her books. But she told no one about what she was doing.

CHAPTER THIRTEEN

Shadows and doubts

After the war, Iris had no wish to return to Florence to live. The Villa Medici, and the Villino where Gianni had died, held too many memories for her, and though it meant leaving good friends like Nannina Fossi behind, Rome offered a new life. Explaining her decision, she told Irene there were 'too many, and too sad, ghosts'. There was also the question of an education for the girls. Close to her daughters, she was very strict about their manners, and the way they were to be brought up. They were to be taught music from an early age. At meals, they were to speak both English and Italian. Mrs MacKenzie, a Scottish nanny, replaced Schwester Marie, who had returned to Switzerland to look after her mother; she took Benedetta to school every day in a chauffeur-driven car. Like everyone employed by Iris, she felt notably well and kindly treated, never forgotten or left out.

Like many Italian cities after the war, Rome was in ruins. In time the Origos were fortunate enough to find a big flat in the Palazzo Orsini, built directly into the Teatro Marcello, which they rented from three Tuscan sisters. When the sisters finally put it up for sale, the Origos bought it. As she described it to friends in England, it was a 'lovely seicento palace in a most attractive little piazza – in the heart of Rome, but yet with an *agreeable* provincial feel to it'.

A civil engineer, Enrico Gentiloni Silverj, carried out alterations to make what eventually became top-floor flats for the two girls and, beneath, a magnificent flat for Iris and Antonio, with a frescoed library opening directly onto a large internal courtyard which they turned into a formal garden, with orange and tangerine trees, and box hedges. An immense gallery or ballroom that ran down one side of the courtyard was later rented out to a bank.

One of the first ventures Iris became involved in was the setting-up of Il Ritrovo, a sort of club in which Allies and Italians could meet. Umberto Morra was behind the idea and several liberals and anti-Fascists were eager to join in, offering their elegant houses and apartments for regular gatherings which it was hoped might revive some of the pre-war friendship between the various countries which had been at war with Italy. Whether what proved somewhat artificial and awkward tea parties actually achieved any renewal of warmth in what had become decidedly frosty relations is not clear; Il Ritrovo gradually faded away.

Roman society in the years after the war was as smart and rich as it had ever been. Those who belonged to Italy's aristocratic families all knew one another, and a great deal of entertaining went on. Conversation revolved mostly around gossip, new shows, travel, money and alliances; but no one talked about the convulsions Italy had recently been through, or had the bad taste ever to mention Mussolini, or Ciano, or the years of Fascism. It was as if none of it had ever happened. Apart from there being so much to repair, and the fact that the rhetoric of anti-Fascism now replaced that of Fascism, these Italians seemed almost totally unaffected by a regime that had endured for more than twenty years.

Such wilful forgetting did not appeal to Iris, who had never cared for large parties, preferring always the intimacy of a *tête-à-tête* or the company of a few good friends. Luckily, Rome also contained another group of people much more to her taste. Many of them English or American, highly literate and cultivated, ready both to understand the past and to talk about books and art, they were now trickling back to their old positions, or arriving to take up new ones in Rome's various colleges and institutes. For Iris, it was a wonderful breath of all she had missed in six years of isolation.

Among the first to come were Laurance Roberts, director of the American Academy during the late 1940s and 1950s, and his wife Isabel. Soon, Iris was a regular visitor to their house. 'On our first meeting,' remembers Isabel Roberts, 'I thought Iris one of the most elegant women I had ever met, mentally and physically. She was totally in order. She was trilingual, and she wanted to talk about books like someone who has been starved for too long. I asked her one day why no one we met ever talked about the Fascists? "Italians", she replied, "live in the continuous present. The war is over. Mussolini is dead. They have put it all behind them."' The American Academy soon became a convivial meeting place for writers and artists, both those who lived in Italy and passers-by from England and America. 'The feeling of liberation', says Isabel Roberts, 'was palpable. Iris was really only interested in writers – not in painters; she had no strong visual sense. But she loved to talk. We talked a lot about biography – and her list of dos and don'ts: don't make things up, don't guess.' One of the first things the two women became involved in together was bringing over from America Iris's friend of pre-war days, Ruth Draper, the American actress who gave one-woman shows, in order to raise money for the orphans living in the Colosseum: there were still thousands of refugees living packed in the Roman ruins, with nowhere to go and not much to eat. There were to be two performances, and Iris and Isabel had imagined rich Romans would flock to buy tickets. 'Can you imagine Romans paying money to hear a single woman talk?' asks Isabel Roberts. 'Italy has no tradition of charity outside the Church.' The first night was a disaster: almost no one turned up. But word got round of Ruth Draper's magnetic performance, the show acquired an overnight *cachet*, and the next night it was booked out. The two women enjoyed the whole thing, and laughed at the absurdity of it all. Did Isabel Roberts become close to Iris? 'No. We were friends, good friends, but it all remained very private, almost formal in some funny way. She never spoke about Gianni. She was not a happy woman. Gianni's death had shattered her. And the war had brought up terrible stresses between her country, England, and her friends.'

Another friend who resurfaced in her life was George Santayana, who had decided to spend his last years in Rome, which he told her was the 'one anthropological centre where nature and art were most beautiful, and mankind least distorted from their complete character'. He had settled in a room in a convent, where Iris visited him. 'I desired solitude and independence,' he wrote, 'rather after the fashion of ancient philosophers, often in exile, but always in sight of the market place and the theatre.'

A new friend was Isaiah Berlin, to whom she wrote not long after the war, praising his work. Berlin thanked her, and expressed his appreciation of her writing: 'I have for years admired your books exceedingly; not only because [of] the knowledge and civilised sensibility and depth of understanding which they possess, but because, as surely you must often have been told, you are such a very very good writer; and consequently what you say will 'stand up' during the years far more securely than the quite decent, perfectly civilised critical works, of Messrs Nicolson, Quennell etc., and even they shine in the gathering darkness.' These people, and many others, remember Iris with respect, with gratitude for her various kindnesses, or interest in her views, but not always with real affection. She was, they say, an intensely private person, and liked you all the more if you respected her privacy; she lived in a refined, old-fashioned world in which servants drew the curtains and the linen was embroidered, and she liked everything to be just right, like the proportion of gin to vermouth in a dry martini. But she was not often warm. She had, as one person put it, a 'built-in-distance'; and those who were intimidated by her shied away from a manner they called cold and imperious. Not everyone, of course, felt this way: the American writer Bill Weaver, for instance, says of her that she was 'shy, yes, reserved, yes, but not cold'. She had, as some of her post-war friends soon recognised, a hierarchy of friendships, reserving certain confidences for one person, others for another. Some resented being put into a compartment, conscious that there was just so much friendship she would give them, and no more. Women speak of her occasional easy chat about 'homey' things or mundane, everyday arrangements. But the sense of humour, the overflowing laughter, the gaiety seen and enjoyed with the Meades do not seem to have surfaced in post-war Rome.

Iris had first met Hubert Howard when he was a schoolboy in Washington, son of the renowned British Ambassador, Sir Esme Howard, later Baron Howard of Penrith; on Saturdays he and his brother would occasionally accompany her to her grandmother's box at the Metropolitan Opera. Despite the difference in their ages, some five years, a great separation in childhood, they became lifelong friends. It was only natural, then, that when Iris arrived in Rome after the war she should get in touch with him again; he was now married to Lelia, the daughter of Marguerite and Roffredo Caetani, duca di Sermoneta.

Marguerite was from New England, a keen gardener now carrying on with the work started at a ruined thirteenth-century village south of Rome by her mother-in-law Ada, who was a great figure in turn-of-the-century Rome. It was Ada who, going to a picnic by the lake at a place called Ninfa on Caetani land, came across the ruins, concealed for seven hundred years under moss and creepers, abandoned by its inhabitants after a feud with another village in the Middle Ages. Ada was a passionate gardener. She saw what could be done with this romantic place through which flowed a fast-moving stream, totally secluded in the lee of the mountains. With her son Gelasio, who cleared the marshes for Mussolini (only to have 250,000 hectares of reclaimed Caetani land confiscated later), she began the process of turning Ninfa into a garden in the wilderness, leaving the ruins of thirteen churches, a ducal palace and some houses untouched, partially covered in creeper among wild flowers and trees, to give the impression that all had been created by nature. Trees were Ada's speciality, and the planting of both rare and familiar trees in great numbers was her main contribution to Ninfa; she died in 1935, by which time the garden was, as they put it, *pensato*, thought out.

Marguerite was once described by Alice B. Toklas as a 'bundle of complexities'. She was beautiful, with a smile everyone remarked on, but as she grew older she became firmer in her views, and more dictatorial. She was funny, clever, and a marvellous, natural hostess. It was Marguerite who introduced climbing roses and clematis to soften the ruins of Ninfa, and planted orchards of Japanese fruit trees, magnolias and mimosa, delphiniums and peonies. In the spring the reservoir pool became a sea of calla lilies. She particularly loved cherry trees, and an explosion of nature in the spring months. Before she moved to Italy, however, Marguerite had had little interest in gardens: when Roffredo unexpectedly inherited the ducal tide she was running a literary magazine, *Commerce*, from her house in Versailles.

Commerce had published new French and English writers in their original language, and had been wound up before the war. Feeling that Italy was emerging from one of the worst moments in her history, and that a literary magazine would provide inspiring contributions, Marguerite decided after the war to start a new one in Rome. *Botteghe Oscure*, named after the street in which Palazzo Caetani stood, was a mixture of poetry, short stories, fragments and letters, again all in the original language except for Polish, Dutch, Korean, Latin and Greek, which were translated. Marguerite saw it as a direct descendant of *Commerce*, but of its time and place, and purposely chose writers who were *oscure*, young and not well-known. *Botteghe Oscure* never went in for experimental literature, nor for reviews, but looked for writing that was trying to express something simple and direct.

The thirteenth-century municipal building at Ninfa was restored as a small country house, with beams and tiles, an open fireplace and Liszt's piano, Roffredo having been his pupil. From the beginning Ninfa was an enchanted place, where good friends, all lifelong committed anti-Fascists and in some way involved in literature, came to talk, and plan future editions. The only banned topic, in this household where everything was said, was the death of the Caetanis' only son and heir, Camillo, on the Albanian front, ostensibly of untreated wounds. Marguerite had been summoned by the authorities when Italy entered the war and told that, as the only son of one of Rome's most distinguished families, Camillo could look for a desk job instead of fighting; Marguerite replied that she would never accept a favour from a Fascist. The Caetanis had long been outspoken in their feelings about Mussolini, and once the war started willingly took Communists and partisans into hiding at Ninfa. It is believed, though it has never been proved, that Camillo was shot on Mussolini's orders, in revenge for their criticisms of him, a story later corroborated to some extent when the OSS files were opened. Marguerite was so devastated by Camillo's loss that she never mentioned his name in public again.

On fine Sundays in spring and summer Marguerite's friends descended on Ninfa, many bringing their children. There you might find a foreign ambassador or a rising young politician, but above all Marguerite's particular circle of friends, T. S. Eliot, Stephen Spender, Umberto Morra, Eleanor Croce and Ignazio Silone; and Marguerite kept a large kitchen garden to feed them all. It is hard to convey the beauty of Ninfa: a lake, a fast-flowing stream, weeping willows, white wisteria, wild grasses, a hundred plants and shrubs few of the guests had ever seen before but which fitted naturally into this planned wilderness; and in spring daffodils, growing under the avenue of cypresses planted by Ada so long ago. After lunch, eaten at a round table under a pergola by the stream, to the sound of birds in the spring and cicadas in the summer, the guests pushed back their chairs and talked. They discussed who should be invited to contribute to *Botteghe Oscure*, who fitted their mould of young and talented writer. They picked over the most recent number; they talked, long into the afternoon, about Italy and the war, and friendship, and they recited poetry to one another. 'Our friends show us what we can do,' they told each other, echoing Goethe, 'our enemies teach us what we must do.' Sometimes they said nothing, Marguerite maintaining that silence was good for inspiration, and for writing. And when it grew cooler they walked around the garden and marvelled at its sense of peace and, after it grew dark, at the number of its nightingales.

Iris, a friend of Marguerite as she was of her daughter Lelia and Hubert, was a frequent visitor to Ninfa. In many ways Marguerite and Iris were alike: both hated the smart life of Rome, both were passionate about literature, and about gardens. Here she found, as at the Roberts's, her natural milieu, a small group of congenial friends all of whom shared a horror of Fascism and an obsession with literature. As with the Robertses, she felt at ease, exhilarated, in a way she never did at grand Roman gatherings. And the gardens were part of Iris's pleasure in visiting Ninfa: she wanted to learn more, and both Marguerite and Lelia were happy to advise her on plants that did particularly well, on botanical discoveries and failures, and to suggest flowers for her borders and wild patches of grass at La Foce. Sundays spent at Ninfa were some of her happiest times.

Botteghe Oscure, in the thirteen years of its existence, became something of a cult among literary people. The opening chapter of Lampedusa's *The Leopard* was first published in its pages, as was a first draught of Dylan Thomas's *Under Milk Wood*. Giorgio Bassani, who was closely involved with the magazine, later said that everything that went into *The Garden of the Finzi-Contini* had been born in the gardens of Ninfa: 'It was the strange atmosphere, as of death, that drew me . . . Like the Jews in my novel, they too were rich and self-sufficient, but at the margins of society. Like the Finzi-Contini, the Caetani had taken refuge in a world of their own: cultured and refined, which protected them and at the same time excluded the rest of the world.' In the Ninfa archives are many hundreds of letters, tributes and messages from many of the best writers of the day whom Marguerite published and befriended. There are letters from Moravia, Elsa Morante, Carson McCullers, Truman Capote and many others. Surprisingly, Iris never contributed to *Botteghe Oscure*. Was she perhaps too English? Too established? Or was it, as people say, that *Botteghe Oscure* was Marguerite's magazine, and that she did not want to share any part of it with a friend, a woman in so many ways like herself? Like Iris, she could be altruistic; but she was far more single-minded. She was enthusiastic and extremely energetic, but she could also show the persistence and unreasonableness of a wilful child.

The funds to keep the magazine afloat came almost entirely from Marguerite herself, and no one questioned that it was a bottomless fortune, particularly as she was very generous to impoverished authors, and would forward advances when they wrote her desperate letters. Among her archives is a letter from Dylan Thomas begging for the second £50 of a forthcoming fee of £100: he spent his time, he wrote, trying to earn money from 'exhibitionist broadcasts . . . and journalistic snippets . . . I can never spare the time to begin, work through, and complete a poem *regardless* of time; because my room is littered with beginnings, each staring me accusingly in the face.' One can confidently assume that Marguerite sent the £50, though another author's glimpse of her account books revealed that she had had to sell two cows to pay someone's fee. Archibald MacLeish and Kathleen Raine both wrote poems commemorating Ninfa, and there was much sadness when the magazine was wound up. Its twenty-five issues had published work by 650 writers of thirty nationalities, half of them writing in English. The end was triggered by the death, in a car crash, of Marguerite's friend Luigi di Luca, who had printed the magazine so beautifully since its beginning. When it was closing, Robert Lowell wrote to

Marguerite to tell her she should be proud of *Botteghe Oscure*: it had been 'part of Europe's recovery from the madness and desolation of war'. In any case, Marguerite herself was not well, suffering from artero-sclerosis of the brain, and though for a while the Sunday lunches went on, and she was carefully dressed and made up, she became increasingly forgetful and confused; she died in 1963. Towards the end of his life Roffredo took to wearing a long cape like Liszt's, looking, said one visitor, a little like a vampire. As Alzheimer's disease gradually clouded his mind until he could remember little of the past, he played the piano as if nothing were wrong. 'This is a beautiful place,' Iris wrote to a friend, 'but a sad house; and the sadness has infected me.'

Lelia, by nature silent and reticent, was also a talented and devoted gardener, and spent most of her life at Ninfa until her own death from cancer in 1977. Unlike her grandmother, who had planted trees, or her mother, who put in flowers and shrubs, she loved the light and shape and colour of trees and flowers blending with each other, so that Ninfa reflected the painter she was. Lelia was much loved by all who worked at Ninfa. 'She was', says Lauro Marchetti, director of the Ninfa Foundation, 'the best, the sweetest woman I ever knew. Everything she touched blossomed.'

In some ways Lelia, less competitive and forthright than Marguerite, was a better friend to Iris, who now came to Ninfa not to talk about literature but to enjoy the garden and to find inspiration. Among experts La Foce was considered an agreeable garden with many fine points and superb views, but not one with great depth. Iris, says Marchetti, came to Ninfa, saw plants, talked to Lelia, and then ordered things for La Foce. 'But she never quite kept it up. She was too busy, had too much to do. A garden dies unless it is kept up all the time.'

Given the beauty of La Foce at its peak in the 1930s and 1940s, Marchetti's words seem a little harsh.

With Lelia's death, the Caetani family died out. Ninfa has survived, run by the Foundation, as enchanted and beautiful as ever, the garden tended and loved as in the days of Ada, Marguerite and Lelia. But there are no more long summer lunches under the wisteria, to the sound of the fast-running stream.

It was perhaps through someone in the Italian Red Cross that Iris was introduced to William Hughes, Chief of Staff to the General Commanding the Allied forces. He was fun, and a wonderful talker; and would later become a distinguished judge. His job in Rome was to help with the distribution of food and medicines, and to put the city back on its feet. Though their lives had settled into a more domestic pattern, neither had become immune to romantic adventures, and Iris now found a brief liaison hard to resist.

Iris and Billy had much in common. Like her, he had lost his father when he was a child; like her, he had at one point been wrongly diagnosed as having TB. They talked about books, discovering the same tastes and a knowledge of much the same works. Billy also had a touch of Antonio about him: he was charming, with excellent manners, a good shot and fisherman; and, as one person put it, had a certain 'grace'. Everyone liked him. For a while he and Iris were very close, and he spent a weekend at Lerici with her, ostensibly to work on a book. He had been called as prosecution witness in one of the many Fascist trials, and was troubled by knowing that on his evidence alone the prisoner would be shot. Everywhere in these years there were trials of Fascists, and many ended in execution.

Friends both in Italy and England soon heard of this new

relationship, though Iris did her best to put Aileen off the scent: 'Darling, about B, you are barking up the wrong tree. He is devoted to me – and to all of us – and considers us as his family in Italy and I hope always will . . . You imagination is too active . . . I have now, darling, reached the age of being the "confidante". Very nice too! Also my life is a very full one.' It wasn't long after this that she and Billy went to Scotland and stayed in a pub in a village where Virginia Charteris, a long-standing family friend, was also staying. One day Iris said to her, 'I'm far too old to be doing this sort of thing, darling.'

Iris's relationship with Billy drifted on for a few years, with meetings in London and Paris once he had left the army. He provided her with literary talk and briefly he made her feel that he was someone she could love and be loved by. But this romantic involvement was no threat to her marriage, and she would never have left Antonio for him. Long after it was over, they continued to keep in touch by letter.

Writing to an English friend after the war, Iris described how she now spent much of her time with Elsa Dallolio, who was ill with heart trouble. 'I have never told you about her – but she has made more difference in my life than anyone in the last six years.' Elsa and Iris were the closest, the greatest of friends in Rome after the war years; Elsa became more important to Iris even than the Meades. They were so close that Iris's daughters and Elsa's sister sometimes felt jealous of their intimacy. In the twenty years that remained of Elsa's life they became inseparable; when not actually together, they wrote and they telephoned. There was no subject, no aspect of either woman's life that the other did not know of or comment on. For Iris, says Elsa's niece Maria Teresa Tamassia, Elsa, ten years older, was the mother she never had; for Elsa, Iris was the daughter. This intimacy, in which nothing was held back, changed Iris's life and provided her with the unconditional affection she craved. It was in many ways safer and happier than any of the close relationships she had had before. If Iris seemed cold to others, Elsa brought out in her a warmth like her own. Did she, asks Maria Teresa, 'find in Elsa the only person to whom she could express love without doubt or fear?' 'Our times together', Iris wrote in October 1945, 'have been one of the best things in my life: maybe the only relationship (apart from my children) completely without shadows . . .'

After the destruction of Nono, Elsa and her father moved into two communicating flats in the Palazzo Taverna in central Rome. As Elsa's health worsened, with bad asthma as well as heart trouble and arthritis of the spine, so she took to spending much of her time in an armchair in her sitting room, with a rug Iris had given her over her knees. In winter her chair was placed near the stove; in summer, by the little balcony Iris had had built for her, where lived the rose that had survived the bombing of Nona. Every day that she was in Rome, Iris spent the afternoon with Elsa. She brought her flowers, nice things to eat, small presents: Elsa, once rich, had distributed her money to nephews and nieces, and left herself with too little. And whenever Iris went to the Palazzo Taverna she never failed to drop in on the old General, which gave him much pleasure.

From the first, Iris's and Elsa's friendship was expressed, in their letters, in somewhat extravagant language. Though Elsa was the more circumspect of the two, both used terms that, as between women, sound excessive to modern ears. Elsa came to feel that through Iris she regained some interest and pleasure in life, and she was grateful for her generosity and closeness; Iris, that Elsa taught her to be peaceful, not to struggle so hard to control the world about her. Both rated their mutual love and affection most highly. Elsa had grown increasingly fond of Antonio, and it was she who really guided Iris into appreciating him once more. 'You have brought me close to Antonio again,' Iris wrote one day. 'You pushed me into writing my books, you helped me with the girls. Your judgment – always clear, always humane, and when necessary, severe – saved me.'

In 1940, soon after they met, Iris and Elsa decided they would write to one another late every Christmas Eve, so that each would know she was being thought of at that very moment. On Iris's side, many of the letters are as loving as those to Colin so many years before.

Christmas, 1941, La Foce: Thinking about our year of friendship, thinking about you and what you are, I am overwhelmed by a wave of tenderness . . .

Christmas, 1950, Rome: Elsina cara, cara. Here we are, yet again, and again I send you the only true feeling that exists in the world: that most fragile feeling that we so often long for, which is stronger than ourselves and yet we speak of almost only with shame: love . . . I sense you to be profoundly sad, and I no longer delude myself, as I once did, that simply by loving someone you can make them less sad – or perhaps it is that my love for you is not enough to help you . . .

At some point Iris acquired the nickname 'Yoshi'.

Christmas, 1952, La Foce: I have a great need to feel your hands in mine – to tell you that you can lean your head on my shoulder . . . Happy Christmas, my dear, dear Elsa – the dearest and sweetest and most secure thing in my life for these last twelve years . . . I hug you tenderly. Yoshi.

Many of Elsa's letters reflect her particular sense of melancholy, not the general malcontent of the Romantic poets but a sadder, harsher, appraisal of a world she saw as unjust and pitiless; she never really got over her horror and hatred of the war. Iris's answers reveal a growing and sad acceptance that she could do very little to comfort Elsa's dark broodings, and indeed that she could in the end do little for anyone.

And so they went on, these loving letters, the friendship of two intelligent women whose lives had contained sadness and tragedy and who now found in one another a comfort and a closeness that neither had dreamt they would ever have again. Elsa grew very attached to Benedetta and Donata, and many of Iris's letters are full of descriptions of what the girls were doing and saying.

What both women, no longer young when they first met, seem to have felt is that rare experience of total closeness and commitment, of a degree and intensity very few people are lucky enough to feel at some moment of their lives. Complete trust was certainly part of it, but it also contained much amusement and laughter. The fact that both were women had nothing to do with it, beyond the very particular kind of friendship women enjoy and excel at. But they could as easily have been two men, or a man and a woman. Friendship seems an inadequate word to convey the sense of belonging each felt, and the pleasure each took in the other's company, but that was what it was: friendship carried to a remarkable and enviable level of mutual understanding and devotion. 'There is, or can be,' Iris wrote later, in a revealing remark about her attitude towards the men and women she had known, 'between friends of the same sex, a great feeling of relaxation: less danger of emotional complications, nothing to suppress or conceal, but comfort, trust, security, and delight – and an exchange that makes no demands. One can afford to be – perhaps it is only in such company that one ever becomes – fully oneself.' For Iris, who needed to love and to be loved, this friendship filled the deep black hole in her nature, the hunger for closeness she experienced all her life; to Elsa, more cerebral, more spiritual, and afflicted by bouts of deep pessimism about the modern world, it gave not only a reason to live, but the possibility of anticipating pleasure. Elsa also reined in some of Iris's more impulsive gestures, urging on her reflection, and patience. Though of different nationality, age and upbringing they were granted, Iris wrote later, 'a friendship the key to which we could no longer trace, and which was perhaps best expressed in Montaigne's words: *"Parceque c'était lui, parceque c'était moi"*.'

Elsa had friends all over the world, many of them writers and thinkers, who kept in constant touch with her, and something of their philosophy of abnegation struck a chord with Iris. Iris recognised that she could do little to avert Elsa's many periods of depression. Writing one Christmas Eve she remarked: 'When we first knew each other, I hoped to be able to *change* your life – to bring you a bit more happiness. But I have known for some time that you can never change anything for anyone.' She did, however, fill Elsa's life with companionship and affection, and gave her another family to care for; and Elsa gave Iris not only love but greater calm and serenity. Iris came to believe that over the years each had 'softened' the life of the other: 'If I have done something good, in these last twenty-five years – intellectually or morally,' she wrote to Elsa, 'then it is due to you.' And as the years passed and Iris became increasingly conscious of the solitude in which most people live, so she became more aware of the trust and tenderness between them, growing ever more intense and deeply rooted with the passing of the years.

Antonio was even less keen on the Roman aristocracy than Iris. Nor did he get much pleasure from the literary gatherings at the Roberts's or the Sunday lunches at Ninfa. He was fond of individual people – Elsa, Isabel Roberts, the della Gherardescas – but like Iris felt uneasy in a crowd; and though his English was excellent, he felt he had little to say on the literary and historical topics she so much enjoyed. He also felt embarrassingly alien in these predominantly left wing circles, having remained strongly conservative and paternalistic. What was more, some members of the Roman aristocracy, themselves far more implicated in dealings with the Fascists than ever he had been, chose to let it be known that they felt there was something a little suspicious about the speed and success of La Foce's pre-war transformation from arid hills and plains to a model farm almost unique in the region. It all added to his discomfort.

Where Antonio himself wanted to be, now and always, was at La Foce, and it must have given him considerable satisfaction that he was held in such high regard locally. Not only had he been the partisans' immediate choice as mayor of Chianciano, but his appointment had been instantly ratified by the Allied Commander in the region. Soon after the war, a Major Riley wrote to him on behalf of the British, to thank him for the 'kindness and the assistance you gave me during those difficult days, when the area was first entered by the Allied troops . . . Chianciano was the first place in which I had worked where I found that the people thought and worked for themselves without having to be prompted, and this I know was largely due to the leadership of yourself.'

The war, however, brought considerable changes to the nature of farming in Tuscany, and especially to estates the size of La Foce, where it took a tractor an entire day to get from one end to the other. Before the war La Foce had been a hamlet, a community, revolving around the life of the *fattoria*, where Antonio, the *fattore*, the two under-*fattores* and the three gamekeepers met at around seven every evening to discuss the day's work. La Foce employed a resident builder, blacksmith and carpenter to look after the estate's needs, which included keeping the tenant farmers' houses in good running order. Whenever there was a problem of any kind a farmer had only to tell the *fattore*, who would send one of the craftsmen to deal with it. In the pre-war years La Foce was considered throughout Tuscany not just a good estate but a remarkable one, on which water flowed, the erosion of the *creti senesi* had been halted, the tenant farmers had houses they could be proud of, and the fields yielded a good return of corn, olives, wine, fruit and vegetables. Not long after Gianni's death, a cottage hospital such as Iris had discussed with Mussolini was opened in his name, and two new schools were started in other parts of the Val d'Orcia. Pietro Marchionni, who later became the *fattore*, arrived at La Foce late in the war as an orphan of eighteen, wearing ragged shorts and extremely hungry. 'Here you will eat as much as you want,' Antonio had told him, giving him a job in the *fattoria*.

After the war, however, in the late 1940s and early 1950s, the power of the Communists, greatly increased by their successes in the partisan movement, began to make itself felt throughout the country. In Rome and the main cities of the north there were real fears that they might take over the country; there was talk of a coup after the last of the Allies departed in 1948. Many of the richer Italians began to send their money abroad. The growth of Communism was extremely threatening for agriculture, particularly to large estates like La Foce which were still run entirely on the *mezzadria* system. Communist Party members from Siena talked directly to the tenant farmers about the iniquities of their position, being tied to the landowner's property, with no rights to land of their own. Some Italian historians believe that those who listened to these Communists, particularly in Tuscany, who were now in their fifties, were the men who had been involved when young in the famous battles for basic rights in the early 1920s, and as boys had heard their fathers talk of the struggles of 1902. The popularity of the Communist Party peaked in Tuscany in 1968, when they had forty-seven per cent of the vote.

At La Foce, faced by these demands, Antonio altered the division of profits to fifty-three per cent for the farmers and forty-seven per cent for the family; other local landowners immediately accused him of capitulating, and letting the side down. In time, in the few remaining years of the mezzadria system, these percentages gradually changed further in the peasant farmers' favour, until the day came when they stood at only thirty per cent to the Origos. Even so, there were disaffected younger farmers among those who had been at La Foce all their lives and whose way of life had been immeasurably transformed by the Origos, who had given them good homes, schools, visiting doctors, and many gestures of help with transport and medical expenses. They listened to the talk about cinemas and televisions and washing machines, and the wonderful life to be found in the cities, where there was work on a salaried basis, and where men owned their own homes and were accountable to no one. Groups of dissatisfied men gathered to talk while their anxious wives, more conscious of the benefits they had received and would go on receiving, hastened to Iris, begging her to tell Antonio to take no notice. The trouble was that while La Foce was accepted as a model farm, a byword for productivity and for the good conditions in which the *mezzadri* and their families lived, elsewhere *mezzadria* had acquired a bad name; particularly on those estates largely abandoned by their owners and left in the hands of the senior *fattore*, who often wielded dictatorial power when acting as intermediary between landowner and *mezzadri*. All this had an increasingly sour effect on what had once been the most easy-going relations between Antonio and the men who worked at La Foce; and the day came when the Origos were informed that they would have to collect their share of the produce from the farms themselves, rather than the farmers delivering it to the *fattoria*, as had always happened in the past.

As the *mezzadri* grew restless in the countryside and the threat of a Communist takeover began to terrify the cities, the rapid post-war rebuilding and industrialisation of Italy was beginning to call for huge increases in manpower. Lured by the promise of better wages the tenant farmers began to drift away from the countryside to work in industry, mostly in the north. By the middle of the 1950s between a third and a half of all *mezzadri* in Tuscany had gone to the cities, leaving behind them unpruned olive trees and overgrown vineyards. In ten years the agricultural population halved. At La Foce, the closeness of a community in which *mezzadri* and landowner had worked so hard in the 1920s and 1930s to create a working estate out of barren land – for the benefit of the peasant families as well as themselves – began to dissolve. The men gave in their notice and left; their model houses stood empty. A few *mezzadri* did stay, and they became ordinary day-workers, like the local men employed for the rest of the work. 'Not only was the spirit of the place absolutely different,' remembers Pietro Marchionni, 'but how do you suddenly stop all work on a farm at a given hour – when cattle need bringing in and not all the ripe crops have been gathered?' Antonio, who had given so much of his life to a vision, who felt that he and Iris had been pioneers in a great and valuable experiment and provided conditions for their *mezzadri* unequalled anywhere in Tuscany, felt very bitter.

In January 1947, taking Benedetta and Donata with them, the Origos went to the United States, as Iris wanted to see her grandmother. They went again in 1950 when Antonio, hurt and angry about the *mezzadri*, was thinking of buying a farm in Virginia and starting again. To Irene, Iris wrote: 'We are enjoying America very much, all of us . . . Of course the abundance of everything is breath-taking . . . not only the fleshpots, but books, music, pictures . . .' They left the girls at Westbrook and travelled around Virginia, but nowhere could Antonio find anything to rival La Foce.

Once he had resolved to stay in Tuscany, Antonio began work on restoring the land to its pre-war state. He had a passion for farm machinery: he ordered a thresher, a Ferguson, directly from America, and when it arrived, people came for miles on foot and by bicycle to look at it. Gradually the flock of 1,600 sheep was built up again; more of the famous Sienese *calanchi*, the ridges cutting through the hills, were filled in and cultivated (later the recovery of the *calanchi* for agriculture was widely condemned and they were declared protected landmarks of the area); the vineyards and olive groves were brought back to full production; and the fruit trees, corn fields and livestock were made productive once more. Antonio experimented with new breeding cattle, and was particularly proud of a bull weighing 1,500 kilograms, which he took to the agricultural shows. The labour troubles were far from being over – they persisted into the 1970s, if in a slightly different form – but in the 1950s La Foce began to enjoy a new period of prosperity. Later, at a time of greater agricultural unrest, Antonio signed contracts directly with the peasant farmers, a move that solved the problems at La Foce, but caused such anger among other landowners that he was expelled from their union. By 1970 only six of the farms were still in the hands of their original tenants and run as a *mezzadria*. Once again, Antonio was to be seen striding across his land from early morning until the evening, at what Pietro Marchionni remembers as an enormous pace, covering many miles each day. Was it now that he missed having a son? He loved Benedetta and Donata dearly, and told a friend he liked the fact that they were tomboys, and did not mind getting their hands dirty, but he never really considered girls to have a place on the farm. A revealing letter was written by Donata to Percy Lubbock when she was nine, thanking him for his Christmas present. Benedetta, she told him, had received a bicycle, while she had been given a toy stove. But, she went on, 'We still like to be boys.' The two girls often heard about Gianni, and how angelic and loveable he had been. He was, Iris told them, 'too good to live'. Benedetta remembers her mother reading to her from the privately printed memoir, but never being allowed to reach the end, or to see the photograph of Gianni dead. The result was that, even though she knew perfectly well he was dead, the thought of what those few last pages contained haunted her for years. When she grew much older, unlike Marguerite Caetani, who never mentioned her dead son Camillo, Iris talked incessantly about Gianni, even to virtual strangers.

As well as travelling back and forth between Rome and La Foce, Iris also resumed her visits to England, to see friends and to buy books from John Sandoe and Heywood Hill, in the early days biographies and histories, later thrillers as well. She never stayed very long. The London literary life that she had once so enjoyed was now conducted by correspondence, or through reading. As always, she hurried straight down to Wales to see the Meades, whose brief disapproval of Antonio over the war had long since been resolved. Nearly eight years of separation had done nothing to alter the ease and laughter of their friendship, although a niece recalls that Aileen Meade was very jealous of Iris's friendship with Elsa, whom she sensed had displaced her. When she was in London Iris found that from having been away for so many years she was no longer properly in touch with the friends and social acquaintances with whom she had once dined, gone to the theatre and danced. People like Frances Partridge remembered only ever seeing her again across a crowded room; their earlier friendship, through Colin, had somehow disappeared with the war. One rather touching letter Iris wrote to a friend shows how very remote and insecure the war had made her feel. 'We have lost the *habit* of both holidays and travel . . . What are people wearing? I mean, dining out in London, say at Savoy or Quaglino, or going to a play? . . . And it is ridiculous, but I can't even remember the *weather* in England at the end of September.'

Iris too loved La Foce, but she had never engaged herself in the running of the estate, preferring to keep her energies for the people who lived on it, and for her garden, which had never looked so good, with a last terrace created by Pinsent looking out over the Monte Amiata and magnificent herbaceous borders largely her own creation. It was not that country life did not suit her; but she found some of its rituals rather too rigorous. The della Gherardescas were great hunters, and not long after the war the Origos were invited to Bolgheri for a boar-hunt. They walked or climbed for hours in the mountains, through scrub and brush, following the dogs and the calls of the keepers, and returned home frozen and exhausted. To a friend, Iris complained bitterly of the extreme cold: the Castello was full of suits of armour and stuffed wolves, but there was only a single small fireplace: 'I feel myself a creature of an insufficiently *robust* race – physically and mentally.' Antonio had given up shooting, saying that after the war he never wanted to kill anything again.

At La Foce Iris began to entertain again, both new friends from Rome and old English friends who could once again get to Italy, as well as a number of Antonio's relations, who, she complained, needed constant looking after. Virginia Charteris remembers the wonderful food, the many servants and the comfort, after the years of wartime austerity at home. From Rome came Ignazio Silone, and Darina, his beautiful young Irish wife, who always felt slightly uneasy with Iris, conscious that Iris and Ignazio had much to talk about from which she was left out. Umberto Morra, dubbed '*il Conte Rosso*' for his contacts with the Communists, came over from his house in Cortona. Morra was growing old, and he and Iris would exchange memories of a disappeared society and time, like two witnesses of a forgotten world. 'It was rather like *The Leopard*,' says Alain Vidal Naquet, another friend of Morra. 'They had seen, understood and observed many things.' English newcomers to her life at this time were the Menuhins, whom she met in Rome and asked to La Foce, as they wished to be introduced to Berensori. 'I would like to have known her better,' said Diana Menuhin. 'Did anyone get to know her really well? She was a woman of great intellectual curiosity, very proud, very distinguished, and when she relaxed she had a charm all of her own. Even though I personally never felt close to her, I felt I could absolutely trust her.' Diana Menuhin had another particular memory of Iris: 'She wasn't very athletic. When we went for walks she would stagger down the slopes on her pins. She was really too elegantly turned out for rough country life.' Schwester Marie, on Iris's enthusiastic recommendation, went to look after the Menuhin children in London. Iris was always solicitous when other people suffered tragedy – they brought out the warmest in her. When the Menuhins' child died, she wrote to them: 'It seems such an incredible blow . . . After Gianni's death, that was what went on tormenting me – "why? why?" In the end I tried to bring myself no longer to try to understand, but (against every natural instinct) to accept . . . Tolstoy, when he lost one of his young children, wrote of him as "a little swallow, who had come too soon and flown back from a world still too frosty". . . I myself', she went on, 'have never had, as I think you know, an orthodox faith to cling to – but in some strange way I did *not* feel exactly *rebellious* about Gianni's death . . . But these are not experiences that one ever throws off entirely . . . They became part of the very texture of life.'

The Origos' life now settled into a pattern that they would keep to for the rest of their lives. Until they grew up and left home Iris spent the girls' school terms in Rome, returning to La Foce for holidays. Writing to Irene about Benedetta and Donata when they were twelve and nine Iris admitted, almost with surprise, 'I do begin to see what you mean about the cosiness of daughters.' Antonio went to Rome every weekend and on business, or when Iris, rarely, gave the sort of party at which she really needed him. Holidays were spent at La Foce, with skiing at Christmas and at least a month at Gli Scafari in the summer. When Sybil and Percy first settled there thirty years earlier, the coast was empty and deserted; now a few new villas lined the rocks all around the house beyond the garden. Percy was sanguine about it. 'I don't see it,' he told a friend, 'Iris doesn't notice, and the children don't mind.' Percy was now completely blind, drinking too much and longing to die, and Iris was occasionally provoked by his extravagance. Benedetta and Donata swam off the rocks, and made friends with neighbouring children. Gaia Servadio, whose parents rented its Villino three summers running, remembers Gli Scafari having a 'Henry James feel to it: very dark, with beautiful furniture and silk embroidered curtains and poor blind Percy, like a huge Buddha on the terrace'. It was always her impression that Iris did not much care for Percy, particularly as he allowed the house to fall apart and, towards the end of his life, imported the wife of a distant relation, a young woman said to be neurotic, untidy, a terrible cook and penniless, so that there were always doubts about the accounts. Inefficiency and slovenliness maddened Iris. John Fleming and Hugh Honour, for some years Percy's 'readers' at Gli Scafari – post and newspapers in the morning, history in the afternoon, classics in the evening – observed Iris's arrival one day to look over the bills: 'Then this icicle appeared and the whole house pulled itself together.'

Gaia Servadio recalls an evening when Mary McCarthy, who had taken a nearby house, asked Iris to dinner with the publisher Giulio Einaudi. Sonia Orwell came in for a drink.

It was the sort of evening that should have appealed to Iris, but Gaia Servadio found her very uneasy, unable to relax, and suspected it was due to the hideous bad taste of the house, which Mary McCarthy, who had rented it for many years, appeared oblivious of. 'Perhaps in her puritan way it offended her.' Gaia's reaction was revealing. Iris, as the story of her life makes plain, was certainly not a puritan, and she was far more interested in people than in decoration; nor was she incapable of warmth, love and laughter. But she had assumed a sort of protective mask of reserve with strangers, or whenever she felt uneasy, and as she grew older those who met her only briefly seldom saw past it.

For all the troubles with Percy, the summers at Lerici are remembered by all who went there with great affection. All her life Iris loved celebrations: birthdays, Christmas, christenings and anniversaries enchanted her, and she was extremely imaginative and generous in planning them. Her own birthday, 15 August, fell on Ferragosto, the Day of the Assumption, an Italian holiday. She made it an occasion for a party for the children. Every year she arranged a treasure hunt, in which every child present received a prize, being inventive when it came to thinking up clues which would suit everyone. After it was over, there was an enormous picnic tea under the pine trees.

CHAPTER FOURTEEN

Splendid to its bones

It was the enormous success of *War in Val d'Orcia*, and the fact that peace at last gave her time for her own work, that prompted Iris to settle down seriously to write. She had never had any doubts about wanting to be a writer but, at some level at least, she had been uncertain of the part it played, or should play, in her life. To a friend who wrote to her around this time about not feeling fulfilled in her own life, she had written back a revealing letter. 'And yet, when you speak of "fulfilment" – think of it in terms of *life*, of *being* – not of *achievement*. I have found a *refuge*, as you know (and a *pleasure* – that is another matter) in writing. But it is *not* there that I find "fulfilment" – or only part of me. Perhaps I should write better books if I did. Anyway, much as it has helped in the last two years, I put life – living, learning, becoming – first. I am putting this badly – but what I am trying to say is that I feel life itself, day by day, to be such a creative process – one's relations to other human beings, and to oneself, and to God – that any other achievement, any art, is only at best an expression of this.' Now, with her biography of Leopardi, her short memoir of Allegra and her book about Cola di Rienzo behind her, it was time for her to explore just exactly how important writing was to be in her life. She had accepted that Antonio had little interest in her work, and did not read her books; but occasionally she would hear him say, with some pride: 'My wife is a writer: *E tutta una poesia.*'

What the war had taught her was that she could write anywhere, at any time, despite noise, discomfort or uncertainty. Conditions for her to become a writer were now very good and there were nine more books to come, including a children's book and an autobiography. It was as if the war years and the late 1940s had been a period of gestation, for her desk at La Foce is full of notebooks, lesson books, and odd scraps of paper covered with notes: notes for what was to be a life of Saint Francis, the beginnings of the book about compassion she had discussed so often with friends, and an almost complete manuscript of a book to be called *Prelude for Living*, which Elsa Dallolio apparently judged not good enough to publish. In this, Iris follows the different stages in women's lives through history ('Drake travels to America; and the fashionable housewife must learn the art of cooking potatoes. Raleigh returns from the East Indies; and his wife must become accustomed to the smell of tobacco') The manuscript is full of fascinating details and casts light on Iris's feelings about women: not exactly feminist, but conscious always of the distinction between men's and women's lives. It is a pity that Elsa took so strongly against it.

All Iris's published books were well-received, with the exception perhaps of a children's book, *Giovanna and Jane*, the story of an Italian girl who goes to England and an English girl who goes to Italy, and of their encounters with former prisoners of war and partisans, drawn from Iris's wartime experiences at La Foce. The reviewers were clearly somewhat baffled by the book; they said it had 'piquancy', and was 'unusual'. Invited by *Time and Tide* to comment on it, Jennifer Jones, aged nine, wrote 'I did not think this book is very exciting.' Percy Lubbock, on the other hand, declared it to be 'a little triumph'.

Iris was evidently also thinking of writing a novel, to be called *Mr Jonathon and the Saint*, and there are references to 'The Heart's Affection', which later became *A Need to Testify*. There are files on religion, heresy, superstition, and a possible play about Carlyle. Her daughter Donata remembers that her study, when she was at work, had pieces of paper, old notebooks, letters and books scattered all over the floor and covered with her spindly, looping handwriting and many crossings-out. From what is left of her notes, it is clear that her method was to do a great deal of work on a subject – research, chapter headings, draft paragraphs – before deciding whether it was going to work as a book. Even if it did not, the material was seldom all wasted; some would invariably make its way into lectures or articles. Iris was a marvellously lucid writer, though this was only achieved after many versions and much editing. But her handwriting became more and more unreadable, even by her family; she was an indifferent typist and not always totally accurate in her research, which led to constant revisions and amendments.

She now had the great good fortune of finding a team of helpers who read her manuscripts, corrected her mistakes, suggested editorial changes, and typed up the books, often several times. Few authors are as lucky. There was Elsa, who from the time they met had been Iris's severest critic; Elsa was exceptionally well read, probably better read than Iris herself, for though both women worked easily in English, Italian, French and German, and knew enough Latin to translate what they needed, Elsa had a broader culture and a more academic, reflective and disciplined mind. There was Nina Ruffini, a clever, down-to-earth Piedmontese woman who wore flat, sensible shoes and proved a superb translator of Iris's books into Italian, though she never learnt to speak English; she wrote for *Il Mondo* on literary subjects. Another of Iris's translators was Paola Ojetti, herself a writer and journalist, who was sometimes exasperated by the way Iris would telephone her ten times a day to discuss work. Finally there was Jehanne Marchesi, half Dutch, who had been at school in England and who typed for Elsa; she took on Iris's typing too, did some research for her, and tried to keep her papers in order – though that task, she says, was virtually impossible. Jehanne Marchesi speaks of Iris as a perfectionist, recalling many hours spent cutting and pasting the changes in manuscripts and doing draft after draft of everything she wrote.

In the summer of 1947 John Murray, as Byron's publishers, got wind of a collection of unpublished letters between Byron and Countess Guiccioli, held in the archives of Count Gamba, a descendant of Teresa Guiccioli, where no one had thought to look for them. It appeared that an Italian woman, Maria Borghese, was some way through a biography of the Countess based on these letters, in which she intended to include a few others she had in her possession. Some had also been published in the *Rivista d'Italia*, presumably from the same source. Then Maria Borghese died suddenly. While a way was being sought to get hold of her manuscript, to have it completed and brought out in Italy, Sir John Murray heard that Iris was already interested in the material. He wrote to her in March 1948, Billy Hughes acting as intermediary. Jock Murray, Sir John's nephew, took over the correspondence and wrote to her. It was the start of a long personal and literary friendship.

Meanwhile Iris, 'with some trepidation', had gone to Florence to try to persuade Count Gamba to allow her to consult his great-aunt's papers. She was not very hopeful, since the elderly Count had already refused access to a number of people, including André Maurois. Count Gamba heard her out, thought a bit, and agreed. Later, Iris put this down to the fact that she did not look 'too foreign or unreliable'. The Count rang a bell and asked a manservant to bring down 'Contessa Guiccioli's chest'. It was an extraordinary moment, of the kind that biographers dream about. In the carved mahogany box she found bundles of letters tied up in ribbon, a locket containing Teresa's hair which Byron had been wearing when he died, and a locket of his own hair which he had given to Teresa when he sailed away to Greece. There was also a little collection of objects: a piece of the wall-hangings of the room in Palazzo Gamba where Byron had come to visit Teresa, a crumbling rose-leaf and an acorn from Newstead Abbey, and a fat little volume, bound in purple plush, of Madame de Stael's *Corinne*, much underlined, in the same ink in which Byron had written a love letter to Teresa on the fly-leaf. Count Gamba not only gave Iris permission to read the contents: he lent her the entire box. Best of all, when she got home and spread the contents out, she found that there were 149 of Byron's love letters, most of them in Italian, and some of Teresa's replies.

As she read the letters, Iris realised that she had come across a new facet of Byron's personality: they showed him in an Italian setting and how he had been changed by it, 'in a manner which is not only interesting, but sometimes disconcerting'. 'Now I have *lived* among the Italians,' she quotes Byron as saying, 'not Florenced and Romed and Galleried and Conversationised . . .' They also convinced her that Teresa 'had more guts – for all her sentimentality – more sense' than he did. After going through the contents carefully at La Foce she began research in the libraries and state archives of Venice, Bologna, Forli, Florence and Lucca. The resulting book was *The Last Attachment*. 'It had', she wrote much later, 'the fascination of a crossword puzzle, but it was also a little like walking in Madame Tussaud's Gallery of Mirrors, in a world in which everything . . . was slightly out of focus, every motive misinterpreted, every image magnified or dwindled.' Her task had been, she noted in retrospect, that of Virginia Woolf's ideal biographer: 'like the miner's canary, testing the atmosphere, detecting falsity, unreality and the presence of obsolete conventions'.

Iris completed the book and sent it to Jock Murray, who was proposing to bring it out jointly with Jonathan Cape, publishers of *War in Val d'Orcia*. From Gli Scafari she wrote sternly to Jock, who had been appointed her editor. It was his first encounter with her imperiousness over the publication of her books. She did not, she said, like the proposed blurb: 'So please either change it, or do not make use of it at all.' Iris was to spend the rest of her life in altercation with her publishers, for as had been the case with *Allegra* there was no detail she was prepared to leave to anyone else, and over the years to come her many alterations, additions and deletions drove her publishers to the very edge of despair. Very occasionally, the publishers fought back. At John Murray's there was a strong feeling that Iris's lavish use of dashes, sometimes with commas attached, amounted to what Jock Murray called an 'unholy union'. He wrote to Iris sternly, saying that they 'tend to bespatter a page, divert the eye and reduce the effect of the dash when it performs its strong and proper function'; he suggested that she also had too many 'ands' and 'buts'. Even so, Iris had the last word.

She meekly agreed that she used too many dashes, but rather ominously added, 'I really think that I should prefer to consider each case on its own merit.'

Reviews of *The Last Attachment* were, as ever, excellent. Harold Nicolson, in the *Observer*, wrote that he had not for many years 'read a book which interested me so deeply.' What all her reviewers remarked on was that Iris had a gift for making the scholarly readable. It was a time when a mixture of scholarship and readability was rare in serious non-fiction; long before many writers and publishers, Iris seems to have understood that it is not necessary to be an academic historian to produce accurate and enjoyable history. In the *Sketch* L. P. Hartley, who had become one of Iris's most consistent fans, in greeting her as a 'newcomer to the art of biography' noted that she had 'adopted a tone less personal than is usual in biography today', and had become someone to whom one 'would gladly entrust the portrait of one's favourite character in history'. Michael Foot, a great Byron enthusiast, says that *The Last Attachment* was one of the first books on Byron he ever read, and that it was partly responsible for his life-long interest in the poet. 'Iris Origo, like Byron, was soaked in Italy,' he says. 'She instinctively understood Teresa Guiccioli.' Though the large numbers of true Byron scholars never went so far as to believe that she was one of them, they accepted Iris as a sort of honorary member, despite their mostly unspoken feelings of jealousy that an outsider should have produced such a good and accurate book.

Iris was still toying with the ideas for two books for which she had been collecting material for many years. One was the volume about compassion, for which no notes exist; the other was to be about the social life of Tuscany between 1300 and 1600. Unable to see the shape of either, she put them to one side and began instead to read for a proposed collection of travellers' tales of Italy; having read fifty books, she then abandoned the idea on the grounds that there was no need to add to what was in them, and that it was in any case an impossible subject to anthologise; later her notes became a long essay for the *Times Literary Supplement*. She briefly considered whether they might also make a piece for the *Cornhill* about a northerner's knowledge of the Mediterranean; that in its turn was abandoned, for a life of San Bernardino, but this too she put to one side.

In 1953 a revised edition of *Leopardi* was issued. Iris wrote to Hamish Hamilton, the book's original publishers, that since the1930s she had found a good deal of new material and felt, as she put it, that 'I know Leopardi a little better'. It ran into the now-familiar problems of revisions and alterations up to and beyond the last date for the printers, Iris at one point writing to warn of yet another delay 'as the copy you saw is legible to no human eye, including mine'. In no time, firm and displeased letters were pouring into Hamish Hamilton's office: the illustrations were not full-page, as had been agreed; the numbers on the pages were too big, and should not be in brackets. A letter regarding the setting-out of the dedication gives some insight into what her publishers were up against: 'I should prefer the "for" to be in smaller letters, and not Cap. and the "Elsa" in Cap. but Roman, not ital.' It was an age when distinguished authors were humoured, but even the courteous and charming Roger Machell, an editor at Hamish Hamilton, complained mildly that 'Iris Origo is really rather maddening as well as illegible'. Shortly before publication a new batch of instructions arrived from La Foce, this time accompanied by a note of apology. Her eyesight, she wrote, had become so poor that she had misread 1853 for 1835 as the date when Leopardi went to the opera; and it was *Lucia di Lammermoor* and not *Il Trovatore* that he had heard. The galleys for the reprint of *Leopardi* were the most corrected in the entire history of Hamish Hamilton. Reviews, as ever, were admiring and respectful; but sales were poor.

As a biographer, Iris Origo enjoyed two great pieces of good fortune. The first was the cache of Teresa Guiccioli's letters; the second stemmed from a monograph she wrote about the use of slaves in Italy in the fourteenth and fifteenth centuries, after the decimation of Florence's population by the Black Death in 1348. While combing libraries for material for her monograph, Iris chanced upon the deed of sale to a merchant in Prato, Francesco di Marco Datini, of a ten-year-old Tartar slave girl. She followed it up, thinking that Datini's papers, lodged in an archive in Prato and said to consist of letters to his wife and to his agents at home and abroad, might provide her with a portrait of a family in the fourteenth century. When Iris arrived at Datini's house in Prato, where the archive was held, she found, to her surprise but not, at this stage, with any great excitement, that the Datini papers consisted not of a few boxes, as she had imagined, but of an entire room full of documents. There were 575 fat account books and 126,000 business and private letters, which had been stuffed into sacks and put under the stairs of Datini's house, where they had remained, unseen, for three hundred years. It was perhaps the richest collection of medieval documents ever found. Iris was not the first on the scene; in the nineteenth century various historians had consulted them, and currently a Professor Melis was planning to put on an exhibition about Datini. However, no one had yet examined the papers in great detail, nor been interested in what they might yield in the way of a social portrait of Datini's times. Iris approached a young archivist working in Florence, Gino Conti, and asked whether he could help her decipher the dialect and early Italian in which they were written, and from which they had never been translated.

For the next two years Conti travelled between Florence and Prato, painstakingly transcribing and translating page after page, having been briefed by Iris to look out for anything particularly unusual or personal, or that gave some idea of the everyday life of the Datini household. While he was doing this, she visited other archives. It was not long before she began to realise what she had fallen upon. As Conti handed over paper after paper, she started to understand that here was a truly remarkable collection which, taken as a whole, would provide a unique portrait of one of the main merchant families of Tuscany in the fourteenth century. It was not only a question of the accounts and ledgers which had interested previous researchers; by examining every page and every document, it would be possible to discover many details of the Datinis' own lives and of those of merchant families of the time and how they lived and worked.

While Conti was at work day after day in Prato, Professor Melis began to perceive what was emerging from the papers. Feeling that they were really his discovery, he made every effort to impede Conti's work, going so far as to lock him out of the archives, of which Melis had the only key. 'Every day,' says Conti, 'I came across marvellous things. The Marchesa Origo came to see me regularly to take away what I had found. Every day, we seemed to have some new discovery.' Conti loved the work, and remembers his two years working on the Datini archives as among the most exciting moments of his life.

The Merchant of Prato is one of Iris's best books. The picture she conjures up of fourteenth-century Prato is rich in every detail, including the characters of Datini and his family. However, perhaps reflecting the existing split between history and general readership, it was not immediately attractive to her usual publishers. Knopf sent it to the Byron scholar Leslie Marchand and asked him for a reader's report. Having read it he replied that he found it 'hard to think of who would be interested in it except for mediaeval and Renaissance specialists'. To Iris herself, Leslie Marchand's letter was discouraging. 'In any event,' he concluded, 'let me congratulate you on the courage of the undertaking.'

In the end, in 1957, though reluctantly, Knopf did publish it in America, as did Jonathan Cape in England and Bompiani in Italy, translated into Italian by Nina Ruffini, and containing an excellent preface by the publisher Luigi Einaudi, senator and former President of Italy; but not before Iris had yet again tested her publishers' tempers and nerves. First the galleys bore innumerable corrections; then she sent in 1,230 source notes, together with additional foot-notes and translations. Henry Carlisle at Knopf tried to take a firm hand, writing to Iris that the quality of her writing was excellent, but that they were 'disappointed by the manuscript in its more technical aspects'. He fared no better than any previous editor: Iris, at times obstinate, at others mildly apologetic, went on making changes as she always had. The day came when Kurt Wolff at Knopf was forced to write her a stern note, though couched in the kindest of terms: 'My main preoccupation, dear Iris, is to preserve your energies and time for your real work . . . I beg of you, as a friend, to trust your publishers to look after their jobs in connection with your book.'

What the publishers' letters that flowed from London and New York to La Foce make clear is that in the 1950s there was seldom a moment when Iris and her editors were not in contact over some aspect of her work. Iris's correspondence with her publishers over forty years runs to many thousands of pages. Some of the altercations, such as mild quibbles over advances or confusions over delivery dates, might not have occurred, or might at least have been softened, had she chosen to employ an agent, who could have dealt with her anxieties and acted as a go-between. But Iris grew increasingly close to her various editors – people like Helen Wolff in New York and Jock Murray in London – and did not want anyone to come between her and them. On their side, her editors' admiration and fondness for her grew over the years, only occasionally tempered by exasperation with her endless meddling and her habit of revising up to the last moment before publication. As Iris now lived most of the time in Italy, she and her editors seldom met, but their letters grew fonder and more personal as the years passed. Often they even acted as disinterested advisers regarding other publishers, and suggested to her what steps to take. She never took money for the books herself but earmarked all advances and profits to charities, which caused her to press all the harder for good sales.

Despite Leslie Marchand's forebodings, the reviews for *The Merchant of Prato* were excellent. In England, as in the United States, reviewers again praised her scholarship and readability; the *Merchant of Prato* was taken by the American History Book Club. In Italy, where it also had good reviews, Elsa's fine editing and Nina Ruffini's translation were especially praised, and the historian Salvemini, Iris's friend from the days of anti-Fascist discussions at I Tatti, wrote to tell her: 'You have the ability to bring even mountains to life.' Quentin Bell, who was a recent friend, wrote describing it as a 'masterpiece . . . of late I have been spinning it out, eking it out crumb by crumb in order to stave off the inevitable moment . . . when it was finished'. Iris replied: 'You know, with Tuscan letters of that period it was almost too easy. They only had to open their mouths and one heard a living voice.'

The only sour note came from Professor Melis, who wrote disagreeably to tell Iris that she had fundamentally misinterpreted the character of Datini, and that the book contained dozens of mistakes. The breach between the two caused a certain amount of debate in Italy and rumbled on unpleasantly for some years, until an agreed position was taken and the matter tacitly forgotten. It was acknowledged that while the book did contain mistakes, they were in part due to Melis's having made such difficulties over the archives; and that nothing detracted from the fact that it was an excellent book. The sales proved very good, except in Italy, where it took a long time to make its mark, and *The Merchant of Prato* has remained in print to this day, and is regarded as a classic of its kind. Iris later turned it into a radio play for the BBC. There was just one final, less than happy note: the bill for corrections to the American edition came to $1,367.89, a considerable sum at the time; and Knopf, who had earlier made Iris agree to pay all the cost of any excessive alterations, sent her the bill. She was not pleased, and wrote to say so. Knopf reduced it by $14.

Iris was now writing at great speed, producing one idea after another. 'The trouble is,' she wrote to Jock Murray, 'I have more ideas than time.' She told a journalist that her method was to 'write quickly, badly and much too much. Then I read it again, am horrified, cut out half of it, and try to reshape what is left. I rewrite endlessly.' The reporter came away impressed. At nearly sixty she was still handsome, he wrote, with 'more than a hint of the great beauty she must have been in her youth. Her figure remains trim and her eyes are startlingly blue.' He was wrong: she had never been a great beauty, but grew better-looking as she grew older, when her elegance and style gave her great distinction. What she did not tell the reporter was that she did an enormous amount of research for everything she wrote, reading extensively around every subject, and in the end used just a little of all the knowledge she had accumulated. Nor did she admit how much she hated speaking in public, though she once wrote to a friend about the 'effort, strain and anxiety (compared to *writing*, which comes naturally to me)'.

By the early 1960s Iris had produced five biographies, and the seriousness with which she took the biographer's task was reflected again and again in what she wrote. 'Just as, in a conversation, there is sometimes a secondary silent conversation going on in which the real exchange of feelings takes place, so in writing there should be a rich background of unstated knowledge, a tapestry which is never unrolled.' And again: 'Biography is, or should be, a completion of life, finding in the routine and triviality of daily experience, the universal pattern that gives them harmony and meaning' As in so much of her thinking, she returned again and again to the idea of humility, and to what she referred to as the most crucial task of all, listening to the subject without interruption. It was then, and only then, that a biographer might see 'as suddenly as, at the turn of a passage, one comes upon one's image in a mirror, a living face . . . In that fleeting moment, he may perhaps reach a faint apprehension – as near to the truth as we are ever likely to get – of what another man was like.' Few biographers have ever been as obsessively fascinated by the art of biography itself, over and above the subject of their books. Remarking on the fact that all she wrote fell roughly into two categories, studies of figures of fourteenth-and-fifteenth-century Italy, and of nineteenth-century Italy and England, she observed: 'I did not choose them because I felt especially drawn to poets, merchants or great ladies, to the disabled, or even to saints, but because of an avid interest in *people*.' Like Marc Bloch, she felt that the biographer's real business 'is simply this: to bring the dead to life' – '*L'historien ressemble à l'ogre de la fable. Là où il flaire la chair humaine, il sait que là est son gibier.*'

Still little-known in Italy, she was now well-established in England, where she contributed essays and reviews to the *New Statesman*, the *Cornhill* and the *Times Literary Supplement*. In 1953 she had become a Fellow of the Royal Society of Literature. In 1972 she was made a Dame of the British Empire for 'services to British Cultural interests in Italy and to Anglo-Saxon relations'. From Isaiah Berlin came a letter speculating that 'Surely no Marchesa has ever been a Dame before?' and seeing her DBE as 'an uncharacteristic swipe at the Philistines'. Freya Stark, who received her own DBE at the same time, from Prince Charles, observed that they were like 'two old birds sitting in a tree'.

The finished manuscript of a new work appeared almost as soon as the last one was published. Late in 1957 *A Measure of Love* was ready, its title taken from John Gower's 'There is no man/In all the world so wise, that can/Of love temper the measure'. It was a collection of biographical essays, some reprinted from magazines, revised and with fresh material, and it included her early short book about Allegra, perhaps the best and most enjoyable of the pieces. Among them were also accounts of the relationship between the Carlyles and Lady Ashburton, and of the Italian patriot Mazzini's time in London. She was particularly drawn to Carlyle, who possessed, she believed, the second of her requisites for the good biographer, that of enthusiasm. Indeed, Carlyle was for her its most 'celebrated possessor', and his enthusiasm, she thought, was based on his conviction of the value of human life, the actual process of living, which she strongly shared. She wrote of his passion for setting down the truth, and claimed to know of no other writer who had approached biography with such a mixture of persistent eagerness and despair, closely reflecting her own. Iris was not only a clear and good writer, but wrote as few others were able to about how people loved each other, and about the small tragedies of everyday life. Her style was understated and almost cool. Like Virginia Woolf, Iris wanted to free biography from dates and the lives of kings and queens; but while Virginia Woolf wanted to replace them with passion, humour and the unexpected, Iris was looking for order and precision. If too even in tone and pace to sparkle, her writing never fails to convey the intensely pleasurable certainty of being in good hands.

The remarkable and perceptive Helen Wolff, who had been at Knopf and who then, with her husband Kurt, started Pantheon Books, had long admired Iris. Introduced to her by Marjorie Villars at the Harvill Press in London, also by now a publishing and personal friend, Helen wrote to tell Iris that the biographical pieces were excellent; but really, as she told friends, she hoped to coax some more saleable book from her. She asked Iris to New York for the launch of *A Measure of Love*, and gave a party to which the literary editors of all the major American newspapers and magazines were invited. From now on Helen and Iris wrote constantly to one another, long letters that were about both work and themselves.

Among the usual respectful reviews and letters that reached Iris at La Foce after the publication of *A Measure of Love* were two more interesting letters, both from woman writers. The first was from someone Iris had never met, Ethel Mannin, who wrote to say that the book had convinced her of her 'loathing of that old bore and boor' Carlyle, and that the Byron chapter confirmed her dislike of that 'handsome selfish man'. She went on: 'I've no idea how old *you* are (though I think middle-aged because I don't think anyone under forty could write with such understanding of the human heart as you do) . . . I don't know if you can write fiction. With your sense of period, yr. [*sic*] intimate knowledge of the Italian background, and your understanding of the human heart, I feel you could write a fine novel . . . I tried to determine, reading yr. book, whether you are a Catholic or not. Sometimes I thought you were, and again not.' Ethel Mannin was perhaps more astute than she was aware: the question of religion was soon to arise in Iris's life, and like many writers of non-fiction she had wondered at various times about a novel. She told Benedetta that she feared she could never write dialogue.

The other letter was from the writer Martha Gellhorn, an old friend, to whom Iris had evidently sent a copy of the new book. 'You have a paragraph', wrote Martha Gellhorn, 'of what I think the great luck in writing (not luck, but you know what I mean) where you put your finger on a truth – that all of us, unbearably, have flashes of foresight and hindsight about ourselves, see suddenly and with horror that there is no accident, this is how we are, this is where we are going. That is a sickening set of emotions, and true, and as you point out, happens seldom because we could not bear it . . . I do not share what I think to be your feeling – if marriage is an endurance contest, there is final virtue in simply enduring . . . I see the Carlyles' life as a long series of wavy bumps, and the basic cause for all the bumps seems to me lack of honesty, decision and guts.' In the margin, Iris has written a firm 'no'. Iris had evidently asked Martha Gellhorn whether she thought the essay on the Carlyles might make a play. '. . . unless you have much more dope than there is in the piece,' Martha Gellhorn wrote, 'some central event to change people's shapes and way, or to crystalize them, I don't see a play . . . How could one ever get a drama, out of fourteen years of hanging about? I am ready to be convinced, but you see what my doubts are. Big ones . . . I cannot deny that fiddling with words is the real thing; the thing that drives one bats and at which one cannot succeed; but there it is, the *itch* is there . . . Do write (I beg you to do so on a typewriter).'

Iris could be immensely generous to new and younger writers, taking great pains to help them without putting them down, knowing herself how fragile writers felt. Nancy Pearson, who went out to Italy with an introduction to Iris from the Meades, remembers that when she started writing novels, Iris took considerable trouble to help her. One of Iris's letters is typical of her approach: 'My warmest congratulations,' she wrote, 'I like the book very much indeed . . . The only thing I think you should sometimes beware of is a tendency to overwrite . . .'

Antonio did not altogether like the way Iris now seemed so caught up in her writing. He was undoubtedly somewhat jealous, not about her success, since it was most apparent in England and the United States, and he did not read her reviews, but about the hours she spent at her desk as the piles of paper built up all around her desk and on the floor. Mindful of his irritation, she took to writing at odd moments, as she had during the war, when he was out of the house or even at night, when he was asleep. Antonio was a reader, but of military history and politics; these were far from Iris's interests, and reflected in some ways a basic difference between Anglo-Saxon and Italians. So she did what she had done all her life with Antonio: she said nothing, and wrote at times when it would not annoy him.

In June 1960 she wrote to the Wolffs to tell them that a new biography, a life of San Bernardino, had only two chapters to go. When they received the manuscript in August 1961 they were delighted, and told her that she had 'evoked a marvellous and moving human figure and the world he lived in'. In London, Jonathan Cape accepted it for publication. The invariable series of corrections and changes of mind sped between Italy and the States, this time centring on the lavishness of the jacket, and on the illustrations (there was nearly a falling-out when Iris instructed the printer in Germany, behind the Wolffs' backs, to insert the many illustrations singly rather than in groups, thereby raising the costs considerably). Then there was the question of whether the Virgin was to be referred to as She or she, and how to deal with a zealous American promotion director who insisted on selling the book as 'San Bernardino, the patron saint of public relations', and was looking essentially for a Catholic readership only; Iris was even more disconcerted when she learnt that the Vatican had also started to describe San Bernardino as the 'patron saint of advertisers'. The book, when it was finally published, fell, as she put it, 'flat'. Sales were very poor. Helen explained that she thought it was because 'you are facing anti-religious bias among American intellectuals . . .' There was one consolation, however, when the Pope, having greatly liked the book, invited her to a private audience.

Relations with her long-suffering publishers over San Bernardino had been difficult, but this was nothing to what happened with her next book, an anthology she had been working towards for 'the last fifty years', as she told Helen. Jock Murray tried very hard to put her off it, after several discouraging readers' reports, writing to suggest that it might be allowed to 'simmer' for a while, but he soon lost this battle as he had others. *The Vagabond Path*, as the anthology was called, is full of charming and little-known selections which reflect the enormous amount of reading she had done in her life, in several different languages, as well as her views on history, death, friendship, youth and love. The first problem, which no publisher had foreseen, was that she wanted the German, Italian, Ancient Greek and Latin entries published in the original language with a translation alongside; the French as it stood, with no translation; and the Chinese and modern Greek in translation only. Chatto, who had agreed to publish it in England and had never encountered Iris's determined streak, were appalled, having simply assumed everything would be in English. The book, Iris announced in a somewhat lordly way, was intended for the 'few highbrows who really care for poetry'.

What made matters considerably worse, given the enterprise they were embarking on, was Iris's handwriting, now little better than a scrawl of ant-like symbols. Secretaries in the office with no previous experience of her writing, given entries to type out, sometimes in foreign languages, were forced to leave long gaps. Talking to Iris over the phone helped very little: the line to La Foce was often bad, and she spoke very quietly and at great speed. There is a wonderful story about Jock Murray, who had spent many hours grappling with Iris's squiggles. Coming back one day to his office in Albemarle Street he found the entire staff trying to decipher the last sentence of one of her letters. He took it home with him and put it on the edge of a table; the trick was, he said, 'to have the page at eye level, so I had a bath and a snifter, as Osbert [Lancaster] used to call it, and crept past the table on all fours.' The words now became perfectly clear: 'Dearest Jock,' it said, 'I can't read what I have written. Please type it out and send a copy to me.'

When at last the text of *The Vagabond Path* had been agreed, with for once a few concessions on both sides, the question of permissions became a publisher's nightmare. Iris had no idea where some of the quotations came from, and the copyright owners, even where they could be identified, proved almost impossible to track down. Iris had agreed to cover some of the costs, and when the accounts were done she found that her share of the galleys came to £200, while the total for permissions was £1,919.50. By the end of the first year *The Vagabond Path* had sold barely a thousand copies. 'Every civilised person I know has read *The Vagabond Path*,' Norah Smallwood wrote to Iris, 'and loves it. The trouble is, I don't know enough cultured people.' Iris, commenting sadly that 'clearly our kind of civilisation is slowly dying away', remarked that she would have to put it down 'as a great extravagance – perhaps my last'.

Not long after Berenson's death in 1959, Iris was asked to write an article about him for the *Atlantic Monthly*. Rather than trace his entire life, she decided to portray only a single aspect, 'the way in which he would look at what lay before him' during his many travels, prompted by his determination, expressed at the age of twenty-four, 'to be forever learning – never to petrify – that is what I yearn for'. 'It was this richness of mind', wrote Iris, 'as revealed in such wholly personal and often unexpected associations and images – layer upon layer – like the fine pastry called *mille-feuilles* – that made him so enchanting a companion.' The article is very admiring in tone.

In 1963, when the Wolffs were bringing out the last volume of Berenson's diaries, *Sunset and Twilight*, covering his years from eighty-two to ninety-three, they asked Iris for an introduction. She wrote to say that she was 'touched by your belief that I can do this', not from any sense of false modesty so much as because she remained as uncertain about her writing as she had been when she set out to write *Allegra* in the 1930s. She read the first half of the manuscript and pronounced it a 'triumph of self-awareness'; not surprisingly, perhaps, since it was not so very long since she had written to Berenson from La Foce: 'I never do *any* piece of work without referring it to you in my mind. And without you, of course, I should never have done anything at all' – something she had said to him many times since the day he had convinced her mother to give her a classical education.

Having finished the diaries, however, she felt very differently. While applauding them as a 'remarkable human document' by a man of great intellectual curiosity, she now felt, she wrote to Helen, a 'considerable distaste' for Berenson, and she feared that however well she tried to disguise it, for 'anyone of sensibility' there would be no mistaking her tone. What she did not do was spell out exactly why she felt such distaste, and one can only assume that something about the vanity and self-regard of Berenson offended her own very real modesty. She proposed to Helen that she ask Freya Stark to write the introduction, but this suggestion was turned down by Nicky Mariano, on the grounds that Iris had far more 'subtlety'. Reluctantly, she agreed to try.

After many drafts, she sent her piece off to the Wolffs.

They were delighted, and the introduction was also taken and published by the *Atlantic Monthly*. However, in it Iris unwittingly caused pain to Isaiah Berlin, by picking up a sentence written by Berenson on 29 October 1953: 'How easy and pleasant the atmosphere between born Jews like Isaiah Berlin, Lewis Namier, Bela Horowitz and myself, when we drop the mask of being goim and return to Yiddish reminiscences, and Yiddish stories and witticisms!' From New York, where he had seen the introduction in the *Atlantic Monthly*, Isaiah Berlin wrote: 'How extraordinary that B. B. should recollect . . . exchanging jolly Jewish anecdotes with me . . . I do not believe that this ever occurred, since I have never "swapped" Jewish stories – in Yiddish or otherwise – with anyone . . . B. B. *did* talk to me about Jews: always tragically and portentously. I don't believe Namier was jolly with him either: but Namier and Horowitz are in the grave: I alone survive.' He found the whole episode, he told Iris, 'embarrassing and disagreeable', and asked whether it could at least be left out of the introduction to the volume of diaries. Iris wrote at once to Hamish Hamilton, who was publishing the diaries in England, but was too late to stop the passage from appearing. 'I suppose I mind too much,' Isaiah wrote again, thanking Iris for her efforts, 'but this is what philosophers call a "brute" fact, unaltered and, I expect, unalterable, by rational explanation – like toothache. Stoic sages, saints, yogis may rise above this: I, alas, cannot . . . I had no idea that he was *so* tortured about his Jewish blood or so filled with dislike of everything sweet and ideal – nor so sentimental, or so self-hating: a marvellously gifted, shrewd, epicurean, cynical, mocking, savage old Jew – more like Disraeli or Heine than a calm noble humanist, surely. Peace be to his uneasy soul.'

Iris's introduction is in fact one of her best passages, lucid, sensitive and beautifully written. No one but a close friend would have been aware of the rather cooler and more dispassionate tone, a little sharper than one might expect about someone she once revered, in this balanced portrait of a man around whom had been built such a myth of brilliance and ruthlessness. It cannot have been easy to write. We are left', Iris concluded, 'with the outline of a man of infinite vitality and sensitivity, endowed with talent and knowledge of the very first order in one strictly defined field, and of intuitions and perceptions covering a far wider range, but which he himself felt he had never succeeded in fully developing or expressing: a man haunted, like the rest of us, by a nagging sense of failure, by remorse, fear and loneliness, but upheld by one tender affection – a man who had outlived his time. A figure who, just because he knew all this and set it down, has gained in stature:

> For there's more enterprise
> In walking naked.

No book ever cost Iris so much to write, in terms of anxiety and uncertainty, as her autobiography. Yet it is possibly her finest book, a remarkable portrait of a way of life now long past, by a deeply moral woman who thought ceaselessly about the times she lived in, who took note of the distress and tragedies around her, who believed most of all in compassion, and whose endless questioning of herself and others made inevitably for unhappiness, broken by moments of pleasure. Iris had been thinking about the nature of both biography and autobiography all her adult life, and the same essay on the subject appears again and again, in slightly different form, in several of her books and in articles and talks she gave. Fierce on biographers and their responsibilities, she seemed more puzzled about the nature of autobiography: the degree of self-revelation needed, the ability to capture the true nature of oneself and translate it for the world, in a way that had meaning. 'We know little about other people,' she wrote, 'and it is gradually borne in on us how little more we know about ourselves.' And, she felt, of even that fraction in ourselves of which we are aware, only a minute part is ever communicated to other people. It is not surprising, then, to discover that she wrote and rewrote every part of her autobiography many times, abandoned it only to take it up again, and argued incessantly about what to include and what to leave out.

As early as 1959 Iris had written to Helen about the possibility of an autobiography. '"*Mettre le coeur a nu*" – it is not an easy process; and sometimes I wonder whether it is even a possible one, whether an element of insincerity or exhibitionism does not enter even the "frankest" confessions . . . And yet I think I *can* do it somehow – this book – at least I will try.' Two chapters, she added, were ready. Helen wrote back enthusiastically to say that, indeed, all Iris's friends felt 'that the moment has come when you should allow your own self to take over, your own voice to speak, instead of listening to other voices, brushing the dust from other people's lives'. At the end of the year Iris sent the Wolffs the first five chapters. They found them rather impersonal, but were agreed in doubting whether she would be capable of making them more candid. Kurt wrote back, congratulating her, but expressing his fears: 'Sometimes I wonder: will Iris Origo overcome the shadow of inhibitions, will she have the courage to make the big leap . . . It will be all or nothing, as far as your inner life is concerned – and "all" with you is very, very much, in many regions. If you can shed what holds you back nobody would experience a profounder happiness, a greater sense of liberation, than you.' But could she?

Over the next eight years the Wolffs and Jock Murray coaxed her along, Helen writing to her at one point: 'I have always loved Montaigne's approach to death and life – forgive me if I am inaccurate, but I am quoting from memory: "*Et que la mort me trouve, plantant mes choux nonchalant d'elle, ainsi que de mon jardin imparfait.*" Do let the garden be "imparfait", but plant your "choux". Otherwise there may be no book at all, and what a pity that would be.' Iris replied that the whole project 'frightened' her. She turned to other things. 'Please, please do not let yourself be tempted into other byways,' begged Helen the following year. 'I think this tendency is a subtle danger to your truly creative writing, an escape, or rather a veiling of your true face.'

At last, in 1967, came some more chapters, and revisions of the earlier ones. As expected, they were disappointing. It was simply not, the three publishers agreed, personal enough and too much had still been left out. Could she not, proposed Jock Murray, write about old age, 'not necessarily depressing', about Gianni, and about Elsa, 'the wielder of the green pen'? Something Jock said or wrote appears to have suddenly spurred her on, and the following year she was once more hard at work. It was now that she wrote Jock one of her most revealing letters, about some of the difficulties she faced in the book. They throw light on the question so often posed about Antonio, and never otherwise alluded to by her. From Rome, on 31 December 1968, she wrote: 'I don't want to hurt Antonio's feelings or those of any of his close friends, still living. Not that he was a wholly convinced Fascist, especially in the later years, but I doubt whether he realised how strong my views were the other way, and – having avoided political discussion for thirty years, in the family circle, I do not wish to embark on it now.' She added a postscript, saying that there were so many books about the Fascist period 'with the writer, all to often, either omniscient and/or self-justificatory, that it is not tempting to join their numbers. Whatever one says, moreover, will be read in the light of *today's* politics. It is, in short, exceedingly slippery ground, however honestly and firmly one tries to tread it.'

Iris's worries about revealing too much persisted as Jock Murray and Helen urged her on, and much of what they managed to persuade her to include had to be extracted from her sentence by sentence. But nothing could change her mind about Antonio, or make her write of any more personal matters than her father's death in Egypt, the buying and doing-up of La Foce, and her own struggles with learning to write. Possibly the most intimate parts of the book are those concerning her mother, the neurasthenic and demanding Sybil, about whom she felt a mixture of exasperation, affection and guilt. There are just five references to her daughters, a few more to Gianni, whose death is only mentioned in passing. Antonio is almost entirely absent. Neither Colin MacKenzie nor Leo Myers appears at all. Even her friendship with Elsa is dealt with in such a way as to give very little understanding of the remarkable closeness between them.

In the spring of 1970, when the manuscript at last went off to the printers, Jock Murray noted sadly in a letter to Marjorie Villars: 'If there is any fault in this book, it is one of excessive discretion on her part, and everything that might conceivably have been thought to be embarrassing was ironed out in the early drafts.' Iris herself felt rather guilty. 'At times', she wrote to Helen, 'I have a feeling that the essence did *not* get set down – and that what is left is "small beer" – but perhaps that is inevitable, and in any case it is too late now.'

There was very little trouble over corrections, but the question of a title exercised Iris and her publishers to the very end. At the back of one of her notebooks at La Foce is a page headed 'Possible titles for autobiography'. Under it she lists 'Fragments I have shored', from T. S. Eliot's 'The Waste Land' ('these fragments I have shored against my ruins'); 'Something I remember'; 'Pictures of the mind', from Yeats ('. . . while my mind remembers'); and 'The leaves, the blossoms and the fruit', from Montaigne ('I have seen the leaves, the blossom and the fruit, and now see their drooping and withering; happily, because naturally'). Whatever the title, there was to be a sub-title using the phrase 'a selective' or 'an elliptical autobiography'. However, the more she thought about it, the more she preferred 'Images and Shadows', from the 'passage about Plato's prisoners at the beginning, which is the real theme of the book' ('They see only their own shadows or the shadows of one another . . . To them, I said, truth would be literally nothing but the shadows or the images': *The Republic*, VII). Jock Murray, when he received the list of suggestions, protested that he did not like any of them, and said that if she insisted, she would have to have as a sub-title 'life in four worlds'. Many friends and editors were canvassed, but in the end, as usual, and after Kenneth Clark came in on her side, she got her way and *Images and Shadows* it became. It had no sub-title.

Iris's autobiography was published in England in October 1970, with a party given in her honour by Murray's in the Byron room at their offices in Albemarle Street. Among the guests were old friends like Frances Partridge, Gordon

Waterfield, Ulick Verney and David Cecil. *Images and Shadows* was a bestseller from the beginning, and named Book of the Year by four newspapers. The following spring it came out in the United States, where it went rapidly into a second printing. Everywhere the reviews were excellent, the anonymous writer in *The Listener* praising 'the absolute candour' which conveyed 'a sense of awe in the presence of truth'. An old friend, Louis Auchincloss, was rather more astute, telling her that she should have carried on beyond the war, for 'Up till then you have been very candid about yourself and your family. You have led the reader on so that he feels a door slammed on his intruding nose.' In the *Irish Times*, Terence de Vere White said that it had 'grace and authority', but that it was maddening in that Iris refused 'to lift even her veil'. To Iris, Storm Jameson wrote that she thought – with 'cold thinking, not in the warmth and pleasure of reading – that it is the finest modern autobiography of the many I have read . . . Just sometimes you must know what sort of book you have written, but sometimes, too, you will have a moment, moments of discouragement no doubt. Remember, do, that these last are utterly unreal. This book is real, and sounds splendid to its bones, its fine bones.' The letter, to someone as easily discouraged and constantly insecure about her writing, must have pleased her greatly.

Jock Murray's and the Wolffs' instincts were entirely right, however. Iris could, and did, write one of the most evocative and enjoyable of autobiographies. It is a wonderful book, readable and spare, creating a memorable picture not only of the Edwardian world she was born into but of an Italy few foreigners knew anything about. In *Images and Shadows*, more than in any other of her books, there comes across her particular voice, moral, sensitive to others, alert to the times she lived through. That she sounds so very truthful somehow obscures the fact that she has left so much out; but, after all, it is the book she chose to write, and it has been enjoyed by generations of readers.

But it is not really a true autobiography, in the sense that Bertrand Russell's three hugely enjoyable volumes of autobiography were not. It is a biography – the subject being herself – in which she faithfully obeys two out of the three essential requirements she laid down for a biographer: not to sit in judgment, and not to invent anything. The third, not to suppress material, she balks at. Were *Images and Shadows* not written with such detachment, were it more like autobiography than biography, she could hardly be faulted. But in suppressing so much, she also suppressed much of her own charm: her warmth, her ability to love, her humour. For someone who, like Johnson, believed so passionately that the unadorned truth 'keeps mankind from despair', she was untrue to herself. Doubts about all that she had not written continued indeed to preoccupy her; in March 1975, in a letter to Kenneth Clark, she wrote: '. . . It is of course no more true of me than of any of us that I can afford to "tell the truth", what is told is fairly true . . . but how much, too, is slurred over or left out – and how much more true (and more painful) that becomes with every year. One will end up like Pilate . . . Of course, in old age, one ought to be able to look back and just serenely remember . . . as (we are told) all sages have done in the past. But serenity – whither fled? And leisure?'

410

CHAPTER FIFTEEN

A vocation for friendship

'I thought so much about you last night and this morning,' Iris wrote to Elsa when they had been friends for ten years, 'and I tried to imagine what my life would be like without you. I couldn't . . . What is certain is that I love you . . . Dear Elsina, believe in the tenderness that we share . . . the safest thing in my life.'

Elsa's health was always bad, and year by year it seemed to be getting worse. She had increasing trouble breathing, and doctors worried about her heart. Constant illness added to her bleakness and despair and, though she seldom complained, they cast a sense of resignation and contemplation over the way she saw the world, which Iris, in many ways, came to share. The two women endlessly discussed Iris's lifelong idea about writing a book on compassion – they called it 'The ebb and flow of compassion' – and some notes left by Elsa read: 'To be compassionate not just in the book, but in oneself, and if possible hold on to that feeling for ever.'

By the early 1960s Elsa seldom left her flat in Rome any more, but she and Iris kept almost as closely in touch with daily telephone calls and letters. On Christmas Eve 1963, in the usual yearly exchange of greetings, Iris wrote: 'What a long way we have travelled since we became close . . . It is now more than twenty-three years since we started facing everything side by side, both happiness and pain – with the certainty of never having to explain anything, sharing the same thoughts in the same way. Does that seem unimportant to you? If we too had a Thanksgiving day, our friendship is one of the things I would give thanks for . . .' Elsa, like Iris, thought often about death, writing to her one day with what she felt to be comforting words: 'When you get old, you will see that old age puts many things in perspective . . . Everything gets sorted out in a game of life, which is also the game of death . . . There is a great deal of peace in understanding.'

In the late 1950s a well-known Florentine cardiologist who examined Elsa thoroughly told her that many of her health problems were due to anxiety. Early in November 1965 Elsa had an acute attack of asthma, which quickly turned into pneumonia. No one quite realised how serious it was, and it was three days before Iris went to Rome from La Foce to see her. Elsa had one slight stroke, then, ten days later, a second. One evening, when she seemed peaceful, Iris went to have dinner in a nearby restaurant, from where she was called to the telephone: Elsa was unconscious. When she reached the bedside, she said softly: 'It's Iris, Elsa, I'm here, I've come.' She watched, hoping for some sign of recognition, but saw none. On the 9th, towards dawn, Elsa died. Such was Iris's despair, remembers Elsa's niece Maria Teresa Tamassina, that she wept uncontrollably and they had to pull her away and out of the room. Later, she sat by Elsa all day, as friends came to talk and mourn. Elsa had always wanted to be buried at La Foce, but since official permission was needed to move her from Rome, she was buried first in Rome's cemetery at Verano. It was grey and cold, and the only people who attended, apart from Iris, Giuliana Benzoni and Umberto Morra, were a few close members of her family.

One of the things which most distressed Iris was the fact that, in those last moments, Elsa did not appear to recognise her. A few days after her death, however, she received a letter from Nina Ruffini, who had been in the room when Iris arrived. Nina had been watching Elsa closely and, she wrote, when she heard Iris's voice, 'on that dear face, on which one could no longer see anything but suffering, and difficulty in breathing, there passed the shadow of a smile. I don't tell you this to console you. Elsa was the last person in the world who would have wanted me to lie . . . You have done a lot of good in your life, Iris, but nothing, however important, is equal to what you did for Elsa. You allowed her to give to you that great wealth of feeling that she had shut up within herself.' Of Elsa Iris later wrote that she had given her, as she gave all those really close to her, a sense of peace: 'When you left her, you suddenly realised that all your anxieties and uncertainties had acquired a sense of proportion. We went there to comfort her; we left comforted.' For the moment, however, what Iris felt was guilt. Shortly after Elsa's death she wrote to Aileen, blaming herself for not having done more. 'I know of course that these are perhaps little things on the whole in twenty-five years of friendship – but I remember how I failed Gianni, too, by not looking after him well enough . . . and not realizing how ill he was. Then I had the excuse of youth and inexperience – not now. But I suppose the real truth is that at the end we *are* all alone – even perhaps should be. Part of us is already on the way . . . I wish I could pray. I could by her bedside, that she might not suffer any more, but I can't now. It is just plain emptiness and grief.'

It was indeed a terrible loss for Iris. For twenty-six years Elsa had been her closest friend, her confidante, and her editor.

She had, arguably, saved her marriage to Antonio, by her very real affection for him, and by helping Iris to reconcile herself to their relationship. She had been a devoted aunt figure to the children, even if it was sometimes impossible for them not to feel jealous of the closeness of their mother's friendship with her, and she had steered each of Iris's post-war books through to publication. Among the papers that Iris kept at La Foce is a small envelope marked 'last letters from Elsa'. There is one in pencil, on what looks like a sheet torn from a notebook, written in a shaky hand: 'Dear Iris. I want to thank you. Everything else you know already. God Bless you and the girls'; and to Antonio: 'For many years, I have been following your life in silence. I love you too.' Three days before she died, on another scrap of paper, she wrote the words: 'For Iris – look at my handwriting, what a mess it is. Look after Antonio . . . Look after them all.'

In March the coffin was unearthed and taken to La Foce. It was snowing and extremely cold. Iris, in poor health herself, insisted on following on foot down the long winding road to the little cemetery, where Gianni was buried. There was a terrible moment when the coffin slipped on one of the hills and fell into a ditch. But then it was laid to the right of Pinsent's chapel, in a grave lined with branches of cypress, as Gianni's coffin had been. Nearby Elsa's sister Gina planted a pomegranate tree, and Iris the rose from Elsa's balcony in Rome that had been the only thing to survive the bombing of Nono. 'There', Iris wrote later, 'I hope to join her.'

Since childhood Iris had shown little sign of belief in any of the organised religions. There is virtually nothing in any of her earlier writings to suggest more than an intellectual interest in faith and in the nature of good and evil and spirituality, together with a strong moral belief in goodness and compassion, subjects she returned to again and again. There are, sadly, no notes among her papers at La Foce about the book she and Elsa had so often discussed, 'The ebb and flow of compassion'.

Because Antonio was a Catholic, Gianni, Benedetta and Donata were all christened Catholics, and Iris attended mass with them when they were children. But Elsa and many of her friends, like Giuliana Benzoni and Nannina Fossi, were believing if not practising Catholics, and for them Catholicism took the form of a kind of peace and tranquillity in the face of the despair and tragedies of life. Elsa, whom Iris questioned repeatedly about faith, wrote to her one day: 'It is not that I want to conceal anything from you, but in all religious experiences there is an imponderable and inexplicable element that cannot be communicated . . . What I do know is this, and I knew it from the first moment we met . . . that it is only in God that you will find peace.' One day, going through the books in the library at La Foce, Elsa pulled out at random Dom John Chapman's *Spiritual Letters*, and found it heavily scored in Iris's hand. The book had fallen open, she later remarked to Iris, on the words: 'If you did not seek God, you would not feel this spiritual anguish and loss. Therefore the fact that you feel it should help you to find peace.'

The great move of renewal in the Catholic Church under Pope John XXIII made Rome, in the 1960s, a city in which there was constant debate about the nature of religion, and one where politics and religion met and emerged in parties and coalitions. For some of the former anti-Fascists, such as Iris's friends Ignazio Silone and Umberto Morra, left-wing Catholicism was a clear statement against Communism, and it seemed to bring them some of the peace of mind that Iris so longed for. It is not then surprising, perhaps, to find that sometime in the early

1960s she seems to have begun her own search for faith.

Iris was a friend of the head of the Indian Radio service in Rome, and through him she met a Jesuit priest, Father Jerome d'Souza, who had been a member of the Constituent Assembly in India. The Catholic intellectuals in Rome loved Father d'Souza. He was tall, good-looking, funny, and extremely clever. He knew a great deal of poetry, in several languages, and he and Iris were soon exchanging letters about different poets, Father d'Souza telling her that, of all the greatest English poets, 'Tennyson was the most influenced by Dante . . . I do not share in the denigration of Tennyson rather common these days'. An intellectual, immensely well-read and poetry-minded Jesuit priest was exactly what Iris was looking for.

Among Iris's papers is a brown envelope with 'Letters of Faith' written on the front. It contains a dozen or so letters from some of the priests, for the most part Jesuits, to whom Iris must have sent questions during the 1960s and early 1970s. All in some way address the question of faith, and how it is found. 'In this hall of mirrors in which we live', wrote a Father Devlin, 'we are haunted by immeasurable images of what might have been. But somewhere there is a door which opens to the wide air of heaven. And if we have the courage to gaze out of it occasionally into the blank unknown . . . then we get a little peace . . . I have long been convinced that absolute need is the only satisfactory basis of a relationship with God. It also seems to be the most practical proof – both logical and psychological – of the existence of God.'

Most interesting, however, are two of Father d'Souza's letters, once again clearly in answer to questions from Iris, who seems at this point – the summer of 1963 – to have reached some kind of peak of longing to find faith: '. . . it is not good to remain in a state of uncertainty and you should try to come to a decision one way or other . . . It is not good to leave the question unexamined and in a kind of haze in the hope that it might clear by itself. An active and positive pursuit of the enquiry is necessary . . . The only thing to remember is that the "grounds of faith" or the arguments for making the act will never be so clear as to compel the understanding; at the last stage . . . the *will* has to come in.' He suggested that she should tackle the Acts first, since the Epistles 'are difficult reading'. The second letter was written that October. Iris had clearly been talking to him about her feelings of depression and anxiety. Father d'Souza wrote that the 'significance of the "desolation" you experienced in a moment of suffering when spiritual consolation might have been expected . . . Even those who have the habit of faith may conceivably and do often pass through similar desolation and sense of emptiness. And what is more, even those who have less faith and love of God, at any rate less understanding and attraction for the Faith, may receive and do receive spiritual illuminations such as might have lit up your darkness . . . Remember Pascal's words: "you would not have sought me if you had not 'found me".' I believe that it is a great grace to have felt the humiliation of that darkness.' Writing to Silone in June 1965, Iris referred to herself as 'held by the invincible Protestantism of my ancestors, yet completely estranged from the Anglican Church'.

No one knows precisely when Iris was accepted into the Catholic Church. The only clue is a fragment of a letter, undated, with no name attached, on which she has written that she finally took the decision to convert on the day of the death of Pope John XXIII in 1963, as she stood with Donata among the vast crowds in St Peter's Square. 'I suddenly knew', she wrote, 'that it was here that I belonged.' How much time passed before she actually took the step no one knows, but several of her friends believe that it was not until after the death of Elsa in the autumn of 1965. Perhaps that moment in St Peter's Square, surrounded by kneeling people with apparently few doubts about their own faith, was the epiphany she had been waiting for. Conscious by now that her intellect would never allow her to accept certain Christian dogmas, what she was searching for was belief that went beyond the mind. This vision of the powerful draw of the Catholic Church may at that moment have seemed to her the answer to the question she kept posing Father d'Souza: How do I find faith? Witnessing the crowds, longing for the God who, Elsa had told her, would bring her peace, then later perhaps longing for something to help her bear Elsa's death, she may have believed that she too had at last glimpsed that beckoning light. 'It will come,' Father d'Souza had told her. 'Act as if it is there, and it will come.'

But did it? After her conversion, Iris spoke about religion as little as she had before. She gave generously to a number of Catholic causes, but like so many of her donations they were aimed at children, and the destitute and sick, not only in Italy but in Africa and Asia; and she gave as she carried out all her charitable work, in absolute silence and privacy. She did apparently grow close to Dom Corso Guicciardini, a saintly rather than intellectual priest. But did she ever find the light that Elsa had spoken of? Soon after Iris's conversion, Giuliana Benzoni wrote to her:

> You know how much Elsa longed for and believed that one day you would bring your religious feelings into the Catholic faith, *not* [the word has been underlined several times] in order to become better, but so that you might experience that sense of resignation and peace bestowed by faith on those who accept to carry the heaviest cross of all crosses: that of doubt, of rebellion . . .

And you, dear Iris, have received it. I had the proof of it at our last meeting when you gave me that sense of peace, of resignation that Elsa used to give us . . . I suddenly understood that you had the identical expression, the identical look of Elsa, at the moment when I was at my unhappiest and most exhausted. Do you remember it? The way that when you were with her, bit by bit, she gave one a mysterious sense of peace.

Had Iris really found that light, that sense of inner peace? For a while, say her friends, it is possible that she may have. But, bit by bit, it seems that she began to wonder whether she had not mistaken her very real feelings about human goodness and responsibility for faith. And it seems that at some point disillusion set in, and that, although she had so much wanted to trust Father d'Souza's assurance that the light of belief would follow, it never quite did. Towards the very end of her life, hoping that faith would help her through to death, which she feared, Iris felt religion to be as little comfort as anything else.

Benedetta was the first of Iris's daughters to marry. Her relationship with the two girls had not been altogether easy; friends remarked how intensely protective she was towards them, perhaps because of her memory of Gianni's death. Both Benedetta and Donata studied for a while in the United States, but neither was encouraged to go to university, or to take up a profession. At the same time, Iris's one great fear was that either should end up marrying a rich Roman aristocrat. Her views about life, as transmitted to her children, were strict. Donata remembers her mother saying to her once when she was upset: 'There are just two things you have to do when you are very unhappy, and you

419

must do one or the other. Get down to work, or do something for someone else.' It could almost stand as a motto for her own life. Donata also recalls, as a child, dreading her mother's lectures when she had done something wrong, for they always made her feel that she had not lived up to expectations.

But when Benedetta announced in 1960 – she was then twenty – that she intended to marry Alberto Lysy, a violinist, a pupil and protégé of Yehudi Menuhin, neither Iris nor Antonio was pleased, though some of their friends joked affectionately that it could hardly be considered a promising match for Alberto to marry a girl who could neither cook, wash up, clean, nor iron. Antonio in particular did not care for Alberto, yet the day came when, reluctantly, as Iris put it in a letter to Diana Menuhin, 'Antonio is beginning to become aware of his fundamental sweetness and goodness . . . so you see, a great thaw has begun.' The marriage took place at La Foce. Iris went on worrying about its suitability, however. To Iris's many complaints, Elsa wrote reprovingly: 'Iris, don't annoy them. Love for one's children consists of self sacrifice. And you're unhappy because you are worrying about things that cannot be changed. Alberto and Benedetta, living in their *own* much simpler house, done up as they want it, will be much happier than living in yours, which is done up as you want it.' It was the same pattern all over again. Iris, for all Elsa's coaching, never escaped the urge to manipulate those around her in order to make things work as she thought best, which was the only way she felt safe. It was *la progettista* all over again. When in the summer of 1962 Donata married Gian Giacomo Migone, son of the Italian ambassador to the Holy See, Iris was, by contrast, delighted, writing to Diana Menuhin that 'he is extremely intelligent, very amusing and extremely easy in family life'. This time the tendency to control worked in the opposite direction, infuriating Donata, who felt her mother was pushing them into marriage, regardless of her own feelings. Gian Giacomo Migone can recall a meeting in a café in Rome during which Iris never stopped urging them to hurry up and get married. Migone and Iris became friends, and long after his marriage to Donata broke up they continued to meet and exchange letters. Iris was always very generous to her children, pressing money on them if she felt they needed it, proposing in this case to give Migone and Donata money towards a flat.

Soon both Benedetta and Donata had children, and as these grew older Iris discovered a pleasure she had never anticipated: that of having small children around her once again to whom she could read and talk. In all she had seven grandchildren, three of Donata's, one an adopted Vietnamese girl, and four of Benedetta's. Katia, Benedetta's eldest daughter, and Bartolomeo, Donata's first son, became the two closest to Iris, and they remember their grandmother with real love and pleasure. For her part, as Iris wrote to a friend, 'Most of all, I value the warmth of their affection.'

For Katia, born in December 1961, the early closeness to her grandmother came about through reading together. 'She definitely hoped that I would become a writer,' she says, 'and I did try to write poems for her. Though she wasn't very physically affectionate, I felt very close to her, and she was always easy to talk to.' With Bartolomeo, Iris's affection took the shape of telling him stories about the war at La Foce, and also questioning him closely about his own life. She was very good to confide in, he says, but she definitely preferred to do so one-to-one. 'If ever she saw my mother approaching as we were talking, she would make a little flicking gesture with her hand to send her away. I had a feeling sometimes that I reminded her a bit of

Gianni and she used to tell me about things he had done. And perhaps when we were together, she remembered her own close relationship with her grandfather.' Bartolomeo too, as he grew older, observed Iris's tendency to try to organise things from behind the scenes and, though she was never confrontational, the way she somehow made them work as she wanted. Both Katia and Bartolomeo were a little in awe of Antonio.

What they and all the other grandchildren remember with delight is Iris's gift for celebrations and occasions. Christmas was always celebrated at La Foce, and was as nearly perfectly English an event as she could make it, with crackers and a Christmas pudding ordered from Fortnum & Mason – though before the turkey and chestnut stuffing came a *tagliatelle al ragù*. For these occasions Iris invariably wore a long Black Watch kilt and a cashmere sweater. What Migone remembers is Iris's immense pleasure in these gatherings, which grew larger and larger as the grandchildren became of an age to take part, and the way she would laugh and argue and not take herself too seriously. Presents, on the other hand, were taken very seriously: Iris began her lists and her shopping early in the autumn.

Summers were spent at Gli Scafari, where the children had the large garden full of trees and hidden places to play in, with the sea below. As more grandchildren came, so Gli Scafari became a sort of summer camp, to which the children looked forward all year. The only formality was at meals, for which they had to change into proper clothes.

Iris had always liked children, though she preferred them once they could read and talk. Livia Aldobrandini, whose father had known Antonio since before the First World War, as a child spent her holidays at either La Foce or Gli Scafari. What she remembers best, though she was somewhat in awe of her and the speed at which she spoke, is what a wonderful storyteller Iris was, best of all when she told ghost stories. Iris, determined that Donata and Benedetta should grow up well read and with a knowledge of the theatre, used to draw up lists of things the girls should do when she was away. Antonio, to whom she confided these lists, soon tore them up and put together programmes of his own. With these young friends he was both teasing and courteous, making them laugh with his sense of fun, even if they feared his sudden outbursts of temper. The many children and young people who met Iris during these holiday times do not all feel the same about her: some were enchanted by her conversation and the feeling that she was genuinely interested in what they had to say, while others were too much in awe to take her in. The fondest childhood memories of the Origos comes from Zamira, Yehudi Menuhin's daughter, who did not get on well with her stepmother; she was captivated by all the games and the books and, because she was not Iris's daughter, she avoided overprotection and smothering. She felt, she says, that 'Iris became a sort of mother figure to me'.

There always was a streak of sentimentality in Iris, when what was usually a very clear and intellectual appraisal suddenly became softer and less self-critical. Iris's grandchildren, perhaps more than anyone else, touched this particular chord, and two out of seven poems she had privately printed were addressed to Katia and Bartolomeo: 'Until this month, you knew no yesterday/and no tomorrow, only a today', she wrote, addressing the eighteen-month-old Katia, 'But now you can remember: every night /You claim the self same toy, the same delight.' A list in the same sentimental vein, entitled 'These things Have I Loved', was circulated to her friends: 'The *feel* of cool linen sheets, sleep-bringing, healing, of brown glossy chestnuts, of my dog's fur; the *taste* of sharp red currants, sugar-coated, of "summer pudding". . .' and so on.

All during the 1960s and early 1970s Iris continued to travel, both for pleasure with Antonio, to places like Cambodia and Thailand, and to see her relations and to lecture in the States. She had taken over a lease owned by the Meades of a flat in Onslow Square in London, where she invited friends for *tête-à-tête* lunches before taking a short siesta, and then perhaps going out for drinks and the theatre, much as she had done when she was young. Tall, upright, beautifully dressed, her hair impeccably tidy, there was something somehow foreign about her to English eyes, just as to the Italians she looked distinctly Anglo-Saxon.

Causes still drew from her the same immediacy and energy as they always had. When on the night of 3 November 1966, after ten days of incessant rain, the Arno broke its banks and flooded Florence, cutting off all electricity to hospitals and sweeping waves of water into houses, shops, museums and churches and drowning 300,000 books in the Biblioteca Nazionale, many of which were found floating about in the filthy water, she and Migone instantly launched an appeal. Their money was to go to the small craftsmen whose workrooms were generally in cellars, and who had lost not only their entire stock of leather, or jewellery, or whatever their speciality was, but even their tools. Florence was now a sea of water and mud. Iris left at once for the States, where she collected money from friends and gave talks, while Migone ran the Florence office.

Iris never gave up writing, or searching for new ideas. The two books that she did write and publish in the 1980s, when she was herself in her eighties, are far from being her best, but both reflected issues she held most dear. The first was a collection of portraits of four people she had known, each of whom had had an 'unswerving devotion to a common cause – the defeat of fascism'. They were Ignazio Silone, Gaetano Salvemini, Ruth Draper and Lauro de Bosis, each in some way connected to the others, and all of whom she had known. In the case of Silone, a slightly reproachful letter, written about his apparent unwillingness to become a closer friend, suggests she wished she had known him better. Silone was nevertheless very generous towards her, offering her all his notes on St Francis, whose life he had been considering writing, when she herself had the same idea. Each of her four characters, Iris wrote, had been 'pervaded by an irresistible, and a desperate need to tell – in so far as they were able – the truth that is at the crux of all human experience: the need to understand, and then tell us . . . This has been the motive underlying all sincere biography.' To these she wanted to add her earlier pieces on Berenson, and chapters on Strachey, Carrington and the Woolfs. She had decided the book should be called 'The Heart's Affections', from a quotation of Benjamin Bailey ('I am certain of nothing but the holiness of the Heart's affections and the truth of the imagination'). After many tactful letters, Jock Murray and Helen Wolff managed to persuade her to write just the four anti-Fascist essays, and to include her excellent and now somewhat amended essay on the art of biography. She agreed, though she noted anxiously that 'Evaluations are not immune to change. With the passing of the years, the muscles of moral indignation sometimes begin to sag, and the voice becomes less sharp.' She told Jock Murray that she now viewed biography somewhat differently, distinguishing between two essential types: 'the three volume notion of the "whole truth"', in which she included Boswell, and what she called 'the paper silhouette . . . a glimpse of the microcosm'. These four essays were paper silhouettes.

Three of the new pieces went relatively smoothly, though her publishers complained that her handwriting had by now become so illegible as to be incomprehensible, while she herself spoke sadly to a friend of her 'ceaseless struggle against a failing memory'. There were various hold-ups – Darina Silone, Ignazio's widow, asked for corrections, and Helen Wolff wanted the Salvemini chapter to be shorter: this was the chapter Iris herself liked best. But when she started work on the fourth, the story of her friend Ruth Draper, who once entertained audiences in Rome to raise money for refugees after the war, she discovered that someone else had been asked by the American publishers Scribner to edit Draper's papers, and had been given access to material Iris had not known about. Going through a bad patch of ill-health at the time, Iris became involved in what turned out to be an upsetting but unnecessary muddle over who had the right to the material. It took many months, hundreds of letters, and considerable agony on everyone's part to sort the matter out, with Dorothy Warren, the editor who had been appointed to produce a volume of letters, behaving generously over permissions and corrections. After this came the usual debate over titles. Iris now wanted 'What is man', from the Book of Job (What is man, that thou shouldst magnify him? and that thou should set thy heart upon him?').

They settled eventually on *A Need to Testify*, and the essays were published to somewhat muted reviews: perhaps because, as she had in *Images and Shadows*, she disobeyed one of her own fundamental rules. She certainly did not invent material, and she did not sit in judgement; but in the sense that she was protective towards her four subjects, holding back on certain aspects of their lives and personalities, she failed her own criterion regarding truth and the suppression of material. Such a position might not have mattered so much had she not continued to see Boswell and Carlyle as her mentors. Her voice had, indeed, become 'less sharp'.

Nor, though here it was a very different matter, was there much sharpness in the last book Iris wrote, an affectionate memoir of Elsa. In tone it is not unlike her unpublished short portrait of Gianni written almost half a century before, the sadness of loss conveyed with clarity and dignity. Elsa had in fact particularly asked that nothing of her own be published but, knowing how important this memoir would be to Iris, both Maria Teresa Tamassina and Nina Ruffini urged her to write it just the same, taking as much material as she thought right from the hundreds of letters in her possession, reassuring her that Elsa's doubts had referred only to the most personal matters. All three women, Elsa's closest friends, agreed that she had been too remarkable a figure to be too soon forgotten, and that by quoting her at some length it would be possible to give some idea of her 'personality, intelligence and profound goodness'. *Un'amica* was the only book Iris wrote in Italian; it has never been translated. In *La Repubblica*, Benedetta Craveri called Elsa 'a moral and intellectual influence on the liberal and anti-Fascist elite' from the 1920s right up until the end of the Second World War. To Quentin Bell, Iris wrote that just as 'some people are born with a vocation to be musicians, writers, painters, nurses etc, so some (very few) are born with a vocation for friendship'.

As Iris grew older, and less able to do the research she had once so enjoyed, she pressed her publishers to reprint some of her earlier works. But the publishing and reading world had become tougher, and tastes had changed, and books such as *Giovanna and Jane*, which she badly wanted reissued for her grandchildren, were judged too old-fashioned. Anthony Thwaite at *Encounter* turned down her poems, referring to her in writing to Catherine Porteous, who had helped edit *Images and Shadows*, as 'a distinguished old writer' whose poems were archaic and existed in 'some perhaps Edwardian world'. There is a touching note from Iris to Norah Smallwood, tentatively enquiring about the possibility of reviewing: 'I would promise to do the work very carefully and to return the reviews by first class post.' But she was kept going by talk of a possible film based on *War in Val d'Orcia* (asked by Robert Benton, the producer, whether she had any questions, she suggested her part might perhaps be taken by Meryl Streep), and a radio play written with Hallam Tennyson about *The Merchant of Prato*. And one by one some of her books were reprinted, bringing her readers of a new generation. Some idea of the softening of her tastes can be seen in an exchange of letters with Quentin Bell about favourite lines of poetry. Iris said hers were Walter de la Mare's 'Look thy last on all things lovely . . .' and Shakespeare's 'On such a night as this . . .'

Ideas for new books continued to come to her constantly – perhaps something on Mussolini? on St Francis ('getting down to the bare bones') – but she was increasingly frustrated by age. 'How nice it would be', she wrote to Jock Murray, 'to be ten years younger.' The very real affection felt for her by her various editors meant that they were happy to discuss new projects endlessly, despite her health, which had been increasingly poor for some time, and despite the knowledge that by now these were only dreams.

Both Antonio and Iris were severely ill during most of their last years. In 1976, when she was seventy-four, Iris was operated on for cancer of the colon. Among her papers is a most touching letter of farewell, addressed to Antonio, in the case of her death during the operation, which she wrote after reading an article in the *Corriere della Sera* by Virgilio Lilli. Lilli, who knew that he was about to die, wrote that his life 'had been a train'. Iris's letter to Antonio is written partly in English and partly in Italian.

Muflone mio. If you read this letter, it will mean that for us too the journey on the 'long train of our life' is about to end . . . But what a fine long journey we have travelled together! . . . our years together were *real* ones, with all their ups and downs, all the sadness and happiness. Our shared youthful dream, with all our dear helpers, to turn the Val d'Orcia green once again, and Gianni, Gianni, who should have had a whole lifetime together before him . . . and the births of Benedetta and Donata, and later of their children. We have had a wonderful life, Antonio, sometimes hard but rich and full. Now I am heartbroken to leave you alone.

At the very end, Iris switched to English:

What else can I say? That I wish I had always been gentler and kinder and more *present*, but not that I could love you more, for it wouldn't be possible . . . Goodbye my darling.

The operation was a success, but later came a second one, for breast cancer, and in her late seventies she fell in her study in Rome, while reaching for a dictionary, and dislocated her hip, so that she spent months on crutches. Later came cataract operations, which made her eyes water painfully in bright light, osteoporosis, arthritis, and bouts of cystitis and back-ache. In February 1923 she had written to Colin MacKenzie about courage: 'I wonder if I agree with you about courage as the crowning virtue . . . The kind which is essential "honesty to oneself or to others" I have got, but that is not so much courage as the dislike of living in a fog – but when it comes down to the only real thing which courage is needed for, physical pain . . . then I am the most hopeless, shameful coward – utterly despicable.' She had been wrong about herself. Faced with endless pain, she never complained. 'You must be very bored in hospital,' Donata wrote to her after one operation. 'I heard that although you are ill, you have a very busy life: business in the morning and forty [degrees Centigrade] of fever in the afternoon.' Iris could be just as sharp as ever. When a friend wrote to say she was thinking of throwing herself out of the window because of her worsening eyesight, Iris remarked that she was tempted to write back that it would be a mistake, since one 'does not want to end up a cripple, as well as blind . . .'

Antonio was no more fortunate. One day in 1969, while inspecting cattle with Pietro Marchionni on one of the farms, he suddenly found that he could no longer speak properly. 'He just made noises,' remembers Marchionni. 'He wanted to write something down but couldn't.' Iris hurried to La Foce from Rome, and took him back in an ambulance. It was the first of a series of minor strokes (known as cerebral spasms), each affecting a different part of Antonio's body, and though his speech returned, he grew increasingly frail and depressed, and dependent on Iris.

In old age, Antonio and Iris shared a secret complicity about their relationship, which seemed to have grown closer year by year. They called each other nicknames and laughed together. There was no mistaking, now, his pride in her achievements. After his stroke, he would sit in the garden at La Foce looking out over the valley he had transformed, or in the courtyard at Monte Savello in Rome, under the orange trees, whistling to the blackbirds. The countryside had been his great love and now that he could no longer walk around it he described it to his daughters, recounting to them again the successes and the failures in the long battle to turn La Foce into a model property.

'It is important sometimes to be idle,' he would say, adding that of course Iris was incapable of doing nothing. In the family there was often much laughter, and much shared pleasure between Iris and Antonio in their daughters, to whom both were close. Iris invariably wanted to be involved in everything that happened to them. When rebuffed, she would plan other tactics, from a different angle, once again showing how right Pinsent and Elsa had been in their nickname of *la progettista*.

Later, arteriosclerosis in his legs confined Antonio to a wheelchair. 'He now leads a dull, sedentary life,' Iris wrote to Kenneth Clark, whose wife Jane had also had a stroke, 'What is sad is the partial confusion of the mind, the inability to walk any distance, and the *isolation*, which of course he feels very much.' They were both, she and Kenneth Clark, living 'with similar webs of our own weaving'.

One by one, many of Iris's closest friends died. Percy Lubbock had died in the summer of 1965. Aileen Meade, in whose house she had been so happy in the 1920s and 1930s and with whom she had kept up a lifelong correspondence, changing from letter to tape after Aileen became blind, died in 1970. Charlie Meade wrote forlornly to Iris that she had been 'in my otherwise trivial life something apart and above all else in it'. Later he wrote again: 'Time is slipping from me . . . I taxi to the Geographical Society every day and walk back which curiously enough gives me the illusion that I'm alive.' He died soon after. Then Nesta de Robeck died and was buried at La Foce, near to Elsa. Colin MacKenzie and Gordon Waterfield followed soon after, and Silone in 1978. No death, perhaps, was sadder than that of Edoardo Ruffini. His eldest son had committed suicide in his rooms at Oxford; then his only grandson, a spastic, died at the age of ten, and his wife contracted such an unbearably painful illness that she committed suicide. Ruffini killed himself at the same time. Iris wrote sadly that while the number of her acquaintances seemed to grow, that of 'real friends . . . people with whom one speaks the same language, do not . . .'

On 4 March 1974, Iris and Antonio celebrated their golden wedding anniversary. Benedetta and Donata and all their children were there, as were numbers of friends and relations and many of the families who had once worked at La Foce. In *La Nazione* there was a short tribute to the Origos' work for the Val d'Orcia. Sometime before, Iris and Antonio had put together a speech for him to read out; in the event he did not feel up to it, and Iris spoke instead, not only about their work and the pleasure they had had in creating La Foce, but about themselves, about the fifty years of their married life, and the happiness it had brought them. 'After half a century,' she read, describing the work that had gone into La Foce, 'I can say that we never regretted any of it.' Her last words were for Antonio: 'When I look back on everything you taught me and gave me, on your support and love, only one word comes to mind: thank you, thank you for a whole lifetime.'

The words were, in some fundamental way, true. There had been other people in their lives, but the train of life, of which she had so recently written, had brought them to the same end. And it was an Italian end, for after the Second World War Iris had turned her mind firmly in the direction of Italy. The Origos had made their lives around the adventure of creating a green and prosperous world in an arid, forbidding corner of Tuscany, and if their marriage had had its problems, it had also contained genuine love and respect.

AFTERWORD

Just as no one has written better than Iris Origo about the art of biography, so few have painted a more painful and honest portrait of old age and solitude. Iris never did write the book on compassion that she had discussed so often with Elsa, but something of its spirit entered almost everything she wrote. She was more humorous in life than on the page, but she had a rare gift for listening to and understanding the meaning behind people's words and, in her clear, even cool style, writing it down. The rawness and loneliness of old age brought out her great sympathy for others and her own dread of what would happen to her. But she was never self-pitying. 'Old age is very merciless,' she wrote. 'How terrifyingly short life is, and also how unbearably long.'

On 27 June 1976 Antonio died of a cerebral haemorrhage, brought on possibly by going up to Chianciano to vote in the elections. Iris was to travel to La Foce from Rome later, as she was having stitches removed after her first cancer operation. She arrived to find him unconscious, so that, as she wrote to Kenneth Clark, 'we could not even say goodbye'. They had been married fifty-two years. 'I feel very rudderless and purposeless. I am sure you are right about writing being the best therapy – but at the moment I feel the spring is broken. I have nothing to say and no one to say it to. You see, unlike you, I am not really an "intellectual"; all my life has been bound up with my affections, and now there seems very little left.' Antonio, she told him, was buried in 'our graveyard beside Gianni, where I shall follow him. When I join them, I shall be close to all the people I have loved best.'

Iris lived another twelve years. She filled them with her seven grandchildren, her work and her garden, writing to Catherine Porteous from La Foce late one summer: 'It is beautiful here now: my garden is at its best, with the roses and Chinese paeonies in full bloom, the hills around with broom, and the whole valley golden with the wheat fields.' At night she looked out at the fireflies glimmering in the fields. But friends noted how lonely she seemed, and how many letters she wrote to stave off the emptiness of her life. To one, she quoted Santayana's phrase 'Those who do not remember the past, are condemned to constantly relive it', and commented, 'But it leaves out – or barely mentions – one insidious form of fear, particularly in old age – the fear of solitude.' She also worried constantly about what would happen to La Foce when she died, until friends and her daughters worked out the estate's future by selling some land, so that later Benedetta and Donata could continue to keep the house and farm. Looking back over her life, she said there had been two events of outstanding significance in it, the deaths of her father and of Gianni, and that though she never ceased to miss them, she felt that she had never actually lost them: 'They have been to me, at all times, as real as the people I see every day.'

Iris's father Bayard had felt strongly that the best gift a child can be given is that of belonging to no one country, in order to avoid the nationalism he so deplored. Iris, neither English nor

American nor Italian, had followed his wishes, and settled for a combination of all three. The lack of any one loyalty is a refrain that cropped up constantly in her early writing, and during the Second World War gave her great pain. But did it make her life more anxious, more rootless, did it cause and later feed her need to be needed, and to try to shape the world around her to keep the fears at bay?

As she grew older Iris remained close to Dom Corso Guicciardini, a priest she had come to know at the time of her conversion, but it was his goodness that continued to attract her, for the light that Elsa and Father d'Souza had described to her never seemed to shine bright enough. She had been drawn to Catholicism intellectually: the epiphany that she longed for did not seem to come. 'Surely', she wrote to Helen Wolff, 'we are meant gradually to detach ourselves, to let go – like a leaf falling from a tree or a candle blown by the wind. Not *our* will. An acceptance.' Her belief was clear, but it had little to do with religion.

For the last year of her life Iris talked very little, beyond the occasional dry remark, as if she had lost the desire to speak or was afraid that she could not talk as well as she once had. But she remained as elegant as always, her skin tight over her high cheekbones, her clothes and hair impeccable, her dignity intact. She ate very little, like her mother so long before her, as if she too were starving herself to death.

On 28 June 1988, at the age of eighty-six, Iris died, very suddenly, of heart failure. There was not even time to call a doctor.

In Italy, as in England and the United States, newspapers were full of tributes. '*Addio Iris della Val d'Orcia*', said *Il Resto del Carlino*. To *The Times*'s somewhat dry obituary, which remarked that 'she was not an easily accessible person, but her

435

small group of friends were devoted to her', Billy Hughes added a warmer memory. Though private and diffident, her 'friends were legion, worldwide and in every walk of life'. During an after-dinner game many years before, he wrote, Iris had selected her own epitaph:

> My heart I cannot still it,
> Nest that had songbirds in it.

It was a quotation no one at the table had been able to trace.

Many years earlier Iris had written to Kenneth Clark a revealing and poignant letter: 'I think that, in different ways, both you and I have come to be dependent on the very ties against which we sometimes rebel, the *need* to be needed, more than anything we may give up to meet that need. Of course it is not true all the time – and there are moments when one just longs for freedom and gaiety and (above all) the absence of anxiety. But the other need is deeper . . . "One's face" (as Teilhard de Chardin said of old age in general) "is to the wall".'

Not long before he died in Rome in 1952, Iris had visited Santayana. She asked him whether, looking back, there were many things that he would like to change? 'No', he 'gently replied', she wrote later: 'I have much the same things to say, but I wish to say them in a different voice.' Berenson at eighty-eight, answering the same question, said of life: 'I want another and another . . . there is so much I still want to do and could write, so much in nature and art and people I could still enjoy . . . more time, more time.' For Iris, it was all rather simpler. She wanted the past back: '*time in the past*, time in which to comfort, to complete and to repair – time wasted before I knew how quickly it would slip by.'

* * *

In the spring of 1980 I went to La Foce to write a profile of Iris Origo for *The Times*. She spoke quietly, and very fast, with the slight lisp to the 'r' that was so distinctive. She was, as everyone had described her to me, elegant and beautifully dressed, her features more delicate now in old age. Because slightly ill-at-ease, she was also rather formidable. She looked tired. I did not stay long. She said, as I left: 'Why don't you walk down through the woods to the cemetery? You will see Gianni's grave, and Antonio's, and the plot where I shall soon join them.'

The wisteria was in full flower along one wall of the house and over the pergola leading towards the cemetery. There were irises in the flower beds, and the box hedges had that particular warm, dry, musty smell. The early roses were just coming out, and with them the first scents of summer. The path led down, at first between banks of lavender and rosemary, gradually fading out into a wood of scrub oak and pine, and the occasional maple and birch. At the bottom of the hill stood the travertine chapel built by Cecil Pinsent. To the right lay the graves of Elsa Dallolio and Nesta de Robeck; to the left two graves, those of Antonio and Gianni, with an empty plot next to them.

ACKNOWLEDGEMENTS

I could not have written this book without the considerable help and kindness of Iris Origo's two daughters, Benedetta and Donata, who let me consult their mother's papers, and spent many hours answering my questions. My particular thanks go to them, and to Bartolomeo Migone and Katia Lysy, Iris Origo's two eldest grandchildren.

Most of the material in this book is based on Iris Origo's many letters to her family and friends, on her unpublished diaries, on her notebooks and scrapbooks, and drafts for books and articles that were never completed or published. I should like to thank Clodeagh MacKenzie for allowing me to read a long correspondence between Colin MacKenzie and Iris Origo; Maria Teresa Tamassina, for showing me the exchange of letters between her aunt, Elsa Dallolio, and Iris Origo; Virginia Charteris for drawing my attention to a lifelong exchange of letters between Iris Origo and her family; and Antony Beevor for letting me read an invaluable collection of unpublished letters and papers about Janet Ross.

I am also extremely grateful to the Society of Authors, for their grant. I would like to thank the archivists and librarians of the following institutions for their assistance: the Beinecke Rare Books and Manuscripts Library at Yale University; the

Public Record Office; the Tate Gallery and Archive; the Reading University collection of publishers' archives; the Brynmor Jones Library at the University of Hull; Smith College, Northampton, Massachussetts; the Hannah Whitall Smith papers in the Lilly Library; the Harry Ransom Humanities Research Centre at the University of Texas in Austin; the British Library; the London Library; The Bernhard Berenson archive at I Tatti.

I would also like to thank the following people for taking the time to tell me their memories of Iris Origo and letting me consult letters in their possession: Alfiero Mazzuoli, Professor Roberto Baiocchi, Helen Bastedo, Olivier Bell, Zamira Benthall, Jane Boulanger, Patric Bowe, Arabella Boxer, the late Henry Brewster, Lady Chaplin, Ann Charlton, Ethne Clarke, Lady Cobbold, Gino Corti, Luciana Corvini, Caroline Cranbrook, Lewis Creed, the late Quentin Crewe, Hayward Cutting, Elma Dangerfield, Cristina Dazzi, Vanya Dazzi, Dr Fram Dinshaw, James Dolan, Lady Ebbisham, Principessa Orietta Doria Pamfili, Fannina Fe, Franco Fe, John Fleming, Ann Flint, Heidi Flores, Luigi Fiorani, Milton Gendel, Enrico Gentiloni Silverj, Flavia della Gherardesca, Deenagh Goold Adams, Jennifer Greenleaves, Florence Hammond, Henry Hardy, Sybille Haynes, Derek Hill, Penelope Hobhouse, Anthony Hobson, Hugh Honour, Edmond Howard, Esme Howard, Jenny Hughes, Marchesa Clarice Incisa, Kim Isolani, Walter Kaiser, Keith Kilby, the late Richard Lamb, Irving Lavin, Meg Licht, Roger Lubbock, Adrian Lyttelton, Elspeth MacFarlane, H. D. McKechnie, Jehanne Marchesi, Lauro Marchetti, Pietro Marchionni, Lapo Mazzei, Simon Meade, Lady Menuhin, Gabriel Menuhin, Gian Giacomo Migone, Richard Morris, William Mostyn-Owen, Liberata Nardi, Tim Nicholson, Frances Partridge, Desideria Pasolini, Lyndall Passerini, Nancy

Pearson, Livia Pediconi, Antonello Petromarchi, Basil Pinsent, Fey Pirzio-Biroli, Catherine Porteous, John Pym, Roland Pym, Charles Quest Rixon, Laurance and Isabel Roberts, Letizia Rucellai, John Sandoe, Virginia Scaretti, Gaia Servadio, Julian Shuckburgh, Darina Silone, Joanna Simon, John Saumarez Smith, Lady Stephenson, Denis Mack Smith, Hallam Tennyson, Marie Uetz, Harry Verney, Alain Vidal-Naquet, Dorothy Warren, Bill Weaver, Francesca White, Cathy Williams, Christopher Woods, David Yencken.

My thanks to my agent, Anthony Sheil, and my editors, John and Diana Murray; and I am very grateful to Stephen Cang, Anne Chisholm and Teddy Hodgkin, who read the manuscript and made many helpful corrections and suggestions.

SELECT BIBLIOGRAPHY

(London publication, unless otherwise indicated)

Roger Absalom, *A Strange Alliance: Aspects of Escape and Survival in Italy 1943–1945* (Florence: 1991)

Harold Acton, *Memoirs of an Aesthete* (1948)

– –. *More Memoirs of an Aesthete* (1970)

Susanna Agnelli, *We Always Wore Sailor Suits* (1975)

Louis Auchincloss, *The Man behind the Book* (New York: 1996)

G. H. Bantock, *L. H. Myers: A Critical Study* (1956)

Olivier Bell (ed.), *Virginia Woolf, Diaries 1931–1935* Vol. 4 (1982)

Kinta Beever, *A Tuscan Childhood* (1993)

Bernhard Berenson, *Sunset and Twilight: Diaries 1947–1958*, edited by Nicky Mariano, introduction by Iris Origo, (1964)

– –. *Sketch for a Self-portrait*, (1949)

Marella Caracciolo & G. Pietromarchi, *Il giardino di Ninfa*, (Turin, 1995)

Kenneth Clark, *Another Part of the Wood*, (1974)

Quentin Crewe, *Well I Forget the Rest*, (1991)

Mable Dodge Luhan, *European Experiences*, (New York, 1935)

Lina Duff Gordon, *Home Life in Italy*, (1908)

Richard M. Dunn, *Geoffrey Scott and the Berenson Circle*, (Lampeter, 1988)

Marcello Fantoni, Heidi Flores and John Pfordresher (eds), *Cecil Pinsent and his Gardens in Tuscany*, (Florence, 1996)

Susan Goodman, *Edith Wharton's Inner Circle*, (Austin, Texas, 1994)

Georgina Grahame, *In a Tuscan Garden*, (1902)

Peter Gunn, *Vernon Lee – Violet Paget, 1856–1935*, (Oxford, 1964)

Alastair Hamilton, *The Appeal of Fascism*, (1971)

Olive Hamilton, *Paradise of Exiles: Tuscany and the British*, (1974)

Christopher Hibbert, *Benito Mussolini: The Rise and Fall of II Duce*, (1952)

– –. *Florence*, (1993)

– –. *The Grand Tour*, (1987)

Henry James, *Portraits of Places*, (1883)

Richard Lamb, *War in Italy 1943–45*, (1994)

– –. *Mussolini and the British*, (1997)

Gordon Lett, *Rossano*, (1955)

Percy Lubbock, *Portrait of Edith Wharton*, (1947)

– –. Evening in Italy, a Soliloquy (unpublished)

Kirsty McLeod, *A Passion for Friendship: Sybil Colefax and Her Circle*, (1991)

Antonio Mammana, *Scuole e educazione in Val d'Orcia dal 1930 al 1945*, (Ph. D. thesis, Siena, 1989–9)

Nicky Mariano, *Forty Years with Berenson*, (1966)

John Miller, *Friends and Romans*, (1987)

Nigel Nicolson, *Portrait of a Marriage*, (1973)

Iris Origo, *Leopardi*, (1935)

– –. *Allegra*, (1935)

– –. *War in Val d'Orcia*, (1947)

– –. *The Last Attachment*, (1949)

– –. *Giovanna and Jane*, (1950)

– –. *The Merchant of Prato*, (1957)

– –. *A Measure of Love*, (1957)

– –. *The World of San Bernardino*, (1963)

– –. *Images and Shadows*, (1970)

– –. *The Vagabond Path*, (1972)

– –. *Un'amica. Ritratto di Elsa Dallolio*, (Rome, 1982)

– –. *A Need to Testify*, (1984)

Charles Quest-Ritson, *The English Garden Abroad*, (1997)

Sandra Rosini, *Iris Origo e la sua opera di assistenza all'infanzia*, (Ph. D. thesis, Perugia, 1995–6)

Janet Ross, *Leaves from a Tuscan Kitchen*, (1903)

– –. *The Fourth Generation*, (1912)

William Rothenstein, *Recollections of Men and Memories, 1900–1922*, (1932)

George Santayana, *Persons and Places: Fragments of Autobiography*, (MIT, 1986)

Geoffrey Scott, *The Architecture of Humanism*, (1914)

– –. *The Portrait of Zélide*, (1925)

Dan Segre, *Memoirs of a Fortunate Jew*, (1987)

Harriet, Duchess of Sermoneta, *Letters 1862–1905*, (1912)

Denis Mack Smith, *Modern Italy: A Political History*, (Yale, 1997)

Ethel Smyth, *Impressions that Remained*, (1919)

Sylvia Sprigge, *Berenson: A Biography*, (1960)

Diana Souhami, *Mrs Keppel and Her Daughters*, (1996)

Barbara Strachey and Jayne Samuels (eds), *Mary Berenson: A Self-Portrait from her Letters and Diaries* (1983)

Giuliana Artom Treves, *The Golden Ring: the Anglo-Florentines, 1847–1862*, (1956)

Gordon Waterfield, *Aunt Janet: Her friends and victims: The Biography of Janet Ross* (unpublished)

Lina Waterfield, *Castle in Italy*, (1961)

William Weaver, *A Legacy of Excellence: The Story of Villa I Tatti*, (New York, 1998)

Edith Wharton, *A Backward Glance*, (New York, 1934)

Edmund Wilson, *Europe without Baedeker*, (1967)

INDEX

International Social Service
(organisation), 350–1
Isham, Colonel R. H., 97–8
Italian Academy, 188
Italian Red Cross: IO works
for tracing service, 185; IO's
wartime work in Prisoner
of War Office, 287, 289–90;
Antonio proposed for
presidency, 337–8
Italy: in Great War, 68–70,
77–8, 88–9; post-Great
War disorder, 89–91;
under Mussolini's Fascism,
128–32, 179–81, 183–9;
agricultural and land
reforms, 180–1, 308;
educational policy, 189;
invades and annexes
Abyssinia, 247, 253–4, 258;
women give gold wedding
rings to state, 248–9; forms
axis with Germany, 254,
273; race question in,
254–6; settlers in Libya,
258–9; invades Albania
(1939), 259–60; military
mobilisation (1939), 261–2;
anti-British sentiments, 263,
272, 274, 278, 284–5; and
outbreak of Second World
War, 267–8, 271, 273; enters
war (June 1940), 280; pact

with Vichy France, 284;
Allied advance in, 295–6,
300, 314–5, 318–19;
bombed in war, 295–6, 306;
armistice with Allies (1943),
297; wartime underground
movement and partisans, 296,
300–2, 305, 308–9, 312–15,
319, 336–7, Allied prisoners
of war in, 298–300; Germans
occupy after armistice, 299–
304; post-war *epurazione*
(purification), 331; German
retreat in, 332–6, 338–9;
partisan revenge in, 336;
German atrocities in, 339;
partisan factions, 339–40;
German unconditional
surrender in, 342; treatment
of Jews in, 341; Allied peace
terms with, 347; British
recognition of, 347–9; post-
war economic development,
349; *see also* Fascism;
Mussolini, Benito

James, Henry, 45, 148–9
James, Olivia (*née* Cutting;
IO's aunt), 13, 32, 86, 111,
137
Jameson, Storm, 409
Jellicoe, Sir Geoffrey, 102
Jews: in Italy, 254–6, 270,

wedding, 432; keeps La Foce
house and farm, 434
Lysy, Katia (Benedetta's
daughter), 421–2, 423

MacCarthy, (Sir) Desmond,
238
McCarthy, Mary, 379–80
McCullers, Carson, 362
Machell, Roger, 388
Machiavelli, Niccolo, 251
MacKenzie, Colin:
background and character,
104; correspondence with
IO, 104–6, 110, 112–3,
15, 124–5, 128, 130, 133,
136–7, 142, 154, 158–62,
165–70, 172–6, 429; and
IO's engagement to Antonio,
110–11; and IO's attitude to
anti-Fascist British Embassy,
128; sends plants to IO, 140;
IO advises on marriage, 145;
keeps IO's letters, 154; visits
Meades at Pen-y-lan, 155;
love affair with IO, 155–67,
170, 172–5, 205, 227, 241,
268; attracted to Frances
Marshall (Partridge), 158,
238; works in Colombia,
159; self-doubts, 162; IO
ends relations with, 175–7,
227; IO expresses dislike of

Leopardi to, 229; influence
on IO, 230, 287; marries Pin
Meade, 268; writes on birth
of IO's second daughter,
292; omitted from IO's
autobiography, 407; death,
431
MacKenzie, Mrs (nanny),
353
MacKenzie, Pin (née Meade):
and family visits with IO,
153, 155, 199, 205; marries
Colin, 268
MacLeish, Archibald, 362
Mafia, 146
Mann, Sir Horace, 36
Mannin, Ethel, 397
Mansfield, Katherine: Journal,
111
Marchand, Leslie, 391–2
Marchesi, Jehanne, 384
Marchetti, Lauro, 363–4
Marchionni, Pietro, 371,
374–5, 430
Marcucci (school inspector),
190
Maria Jose, Principessa, 266
Mariano, Nicky: on Vernon
Lee, 45; on social life at I
Tatti, 48, 97; Mary Berenson
urges Scott to marry, 76;
on Sybil's character, 79;
captivates Kenneth Clark,

Sanctis, Gaetano de, 187

Sandoe, John (London bookseller), 375

Sanseverino, Ottavia, 137

Santayana, George, 14, 32, 93, 226, 356, 434–6

Scafari, Gli (Lerice), 200, 244, 280, 324, 364, 378–80, 386, 422

Scott, Charles Prestwich, 51

Scott, Geoffrey: works in Florence, 51– 8, 69–71, 74; amours, 76; works at British Embassy in Rome, 76; engagement and marriage to Sybil, 78–80, 93; boils, 80; on IO's appearance, 82; marriage relations, 94–7, 99, 133; grows fat, 97; relations with Mary Berenson, 97–9; affair with Vita Sackville-West, 98–9, 113, 132; considers book on history of taste, 99–100; partnership with Pinsent ends, 100; maintains friendship with Pinsent, 102; motoring, 103; encourages IO's marriage to Antonio, 110–11; divorce from Sybil, 133; appearance, 133; death and funeral, 134, 152; edits Boswell letters in USA, 133, 161; at London

luncheon party with IO, 147; disdains Wharton's 'Inner Circle', 149; *The Architecture of Humanism*, 74, 79, 102, 134; *A Box of Paints*, 99; *Portrait of Zélide*, 68, 98, 133

Scott, Lady Sybil *see* Cutting, Lady Sybil

Scott Moncrieffe, C. K., 93

Scribner (Charles Scribner's Sons, US publishers), 426

Segovia, Andres, 160

Segre, Dan: *Memoirs of a Fortunate Jew*, 183

Senni, Mary, 196

Serlupi, Marchese, 30

Sermoneta, duca di *see* Caetani, Roffredo

Serpieri, Professore, 180–1

Servadio, Gaia, 379–80

Settignano, Tuscany, 42–3, 46 52, 62, 88

Shakespeare, William, 428

Sicily, 142, 145–6, 260, 291; *see also* Messina

Sickert, Walter, 147

Signorini, Signora (Italian teacher), 67

Silone, Darina, 377, 393

Silone, Ignazio: dismisses Fascism, 183; at Ninfa, 360; visits La Foce with wife, 377;

471

FREYA STARK

Born in Paris in 1893, by the time she was five Freya could speak three languages and the wandering life of her childhood left her 'precocious and pretty tough'. Self-disciplined, courageous, with a high regard for tradition and empire, yet also flamboyant and unorthodox, Freya Stark has remained fearlessly independent.

As an explorer she was unconventional, always travelling alone, without money or support. Her expeditions in Persia and the Hadhramaut during the thirties established her reputation not only as a great traveller and writer, but also as a geographer, historian and archaeologist. Yet her success has been tempered by a constant struggle against ill health, the disappointment of a failed marriage and loneliness.

Throughout her extraordinary and eventful life, travel remained her greatest love and solace. For her, 'the beckoning counts and not the clicking latch behind you: and all through life, the actual moment of emancipation still holds that delight, of the whole world coming to meet you like a wave.'